TECHNOLOGY AND SOCIAL JUSTICE

TECHNOLOGY AND SOCIAL JUSTICE

An International Symposium on the
Social and Economic Teaching of the
World Council of Churches from
Geneva 1966 to Uppsala 1968

EDITED BY

RONALD H. PRESTON

JUDSON PRESS
VALLEY FORGE

Sponsored by the
International Humanum Foundation,
Lugano, Switzerland

Library of Congress Catalog Card No. 78-152584
ISBN 0-8170-0536-6

© SCM Press Ltd 1971

First American edition 1971
published by Judson Press
Valley Forge, Pennsylvania 19481

To
The Reverend Doctor
Willem Adolf Visser 't Hooft

First General Secretary of the
World Council of Churches 1948–1966

who reached his seventieth birthday
on September 20, 1970

in gratitude, respect and affection
for all he has meant and still means
to the Ecumenical Movement

Theology has also to come to grips with the meaning and goal of peoples all over the world who have awakened to a new sense of the human. Indeed the interaction between technology and social justice is a crucial issue of our time.

Paragraph 46 of the Report of Section III of the Fourth Assembly of the World Council of Churches, Uppsala, 1968

CONTENTS

Part Seven

THE ROLE OF THE CHRISTIAN AND THE CHURCHES

FOREWORD

It is a pleasure to us to commend this second symposium sponsored by the International Humanum Foundation. The immediate inspiration of the Humanum Foundation was the concern expressed for the safeguarding of the dignity and worth of the human person in the modern world which underlies the Pastoral Constitution of the second Vatican Council, commonly known as *Gaudium et Spes*. Cardinal Bea, the first President of the Vatican Secretariat for Christian Unity, was a leader at the Council and the first Patron of the Foundation, even before it was officially founded, and gave it continued encouragement until his death.

The first symposium dealt with the economic sections of *Gaudium et Spes*. It is appropriate that this second one should deal with the economic teaching of the World Council of Churches from the Geneva Conference of 1966 to the Uppsala Assembly of 1968. Not only was this a very fruitful and intense period of two years in the social thought of the World Council, but it was a time when its thinking and that of the Vatican Council in this field came close together in many respects, and when there was a good deal of informal personal association between the two. It was therefore very appropriate that the Humanum Foundation should have financially supported the one official joint undertaking of the Roman Catholic Church and the World Council of Churches which has so far resulted, since it is concerned precisely with social ethics. We refer to the Joint Committee on Society, Development and Peace. This constructive action by the Foundation is a matter for gratitude.

This volume is a further fruit of the work of the Foundation. It is very valuable that an international group of social scientists and theologians from the main confessional traditions should have had the chance of more leisurely assessment of what was done in those two years. Some were closely connected with it, some were not. All have said exactly what they think. Neither the Foundation nor the Roman Catholic Church nor the World Council of Churches is committed

xiii

to what any of them say. Out of this free discussion may the churches become ever more alert to their responsibility to witness in word and deed to the worth of every man.

ACKNOWLEDGMENTS

My thanks are due, and gratefully given, to a number of people who have been a help to me in the preparation of this symposium. Mr K. H. Friedmann of the Humanum Foundation has given every encouragement. A number of the contributors also helped with advice on authors and content. So did others who are not contributors: Mlle Madeleine Barot, Professor Etienne Trocmé and Dr H. H. Walz. In the organization of the production of the symposium I would like to thank the Rev. John Bowden and the staff of the SCM Press, especially Miss Jean Cunningham and Miss Kathleen Downham; the Rev. Paul Abrecht, the Rev. David Gill and Herr Axel vom den Bussche of the staff of the Department on Church and Society of the World Council of Churches; Mrs Dorothy Johnson and Miss Gillian Shepherd in the Faculty of Theology Office of Manchester University; and Mrs Mary Scott of the Manchester Cathedral Office. Gratitude is due to Dr Peter Skrine of the Department of German in Manchester University and Mrs Celia Skrine for their translations from the German of the articles by Professor Hoffman, Dr Bührig, Dr Savramis and Professor Wolf; and to Mrs Margaret House for her translation from the French of the essays by Professor Dumas and Father Khodre. The translators kept admirably to the timetable laid down. I should also like to thank the contributors for their enthusiasm for the project and flexibility of mind in carrying it out. The Humanum Foundation as such is not committed in any way to the opinions expressed in this volume; they are solely the responsibility of the Editor and of the writer of each essay. To some extent the symposium is the legacy of a period of six months which I spent in Geneva in the first half of 1969 working with the Department on Church and Society and Sodepax (see p. 18); I should like it to be an expression of thanks to my temporary colleagues in both bodies for their friendship and co-operation.

Faculty of Theology   RONALD H. PRESTON
Manchester University
1 March 1970

THE CONTRIBUTORS

SAMUEL A. ALUKO Professor of Economics, The University of Ife, Nigeria

MARGA BÜHRIG Director of the Boldernhaus, Zurich, Switzerland, and author of *Die Frau in der Schweiz*

EDWARD DUFF Associate Professor of Political Science, College of the Holy Cross, Worcester, Massachusetts, USA, member of the Society of Jesus, and author of *The Social Thought of the World Council of Churches*, etc.

ANDRÉ DUMAS Professor of Philosophy and Ethics, Protestant Theological Faculty, Paris, and author of *Une Théologie de la Réalité: Dietrich Bonhoeffer*, etc.

ERICH HOFFMANN Professor of Agricultural Economics in the University of Halle, East Germany

DAVID E. JENKINS Director of the Humanum Studies of the World Council of Churches; formerly Fellow and Tutor of The Queen's College, Oxford; Canon Theologian of Leicester, Great Britain, and author of *The Glory of Man*, etc.

GEORGES KHODRE Greek Orthodox Metropolitan of Mount Lebanon

HENDRIK M. DE LANGE Director of the University Institute for Fundamental Training in Industry, Rotterdam, Holland

DAVID A. MARTIN Reader in Sociology at the London School of Economics, University of London, Great Britain

CANDIDO ANTONIO MENDES DE ALMEIDA Director of the Faculty of Political and Economic Sciences of the University of Rio de Janeiro, Brazil

ARNOLD S. NASH Professor of the Sociology of Religion, University of North Carolina, USA, and Faculty Member of the Carolina Population Centre

J. ROBERT NELSON Professor of Systematic Theology, the University of Boston, Massachusetts, USA, and Chairman of the Faith and Order Working Committee of the World Council of Churches

NIKOS A. NISSIOTIS Director of the Ecumenical Institute, Bossey, Switzerland, and Professor of the Philosophy of Religion in the University of Athens, Greece

SAMUEL L. PARMAR Reader in Economics in the University of Allahabad, India; Chairman of the Commission on Church and Society of the World Council of Churches

RONALD H. PRESTON Professor of Social and Pastoral Theology in the University of Manchester and Canon of Manchester Cathedral, Great Britain

DEMOSTHENES SAVRAMIS Dozent of the Sociology of Religion in the University of Cologne. Gastdozent of Sociology in the University of Bonn, West Germany and author of *Religionssoziologie: Eine Einführung*, etc.

ALEXANDER SCHMÉMANN Professor of Theology and Dean of St Vladimir's Orthodox Theological Seminary, Tuckahoe, New York, USA

T. PAUL VERGHESE Principal of the Orthodox Theological Seminary, Kottayam, Kerala, India

EGBERT DE VRIES Professor of International Development in the University of Pittsburgh, USA, and Vice-Chairman of the Board of the Council for the Study of Mankind; formerly Rector of the Institute of Social Studies, The Hague, Holland, and author of *Man in Rapid Social Change*, etc.

CHARLES C. WEST Professor of Christian Ethics, Princeton Theological Seminary, New Jersey, USA

HANS-HEINRICH WOLF Professor of Ecumenics, Ruhr University, Bochum, West Germany

NOTE ON THE DOCUMENTS

Published by the World Council of Churches, Geneva and New York

Christians in the Technical and Social Revolution of our Time, 1967: the Report of the World Conference on Church and Society held at Geneva, July 1966; cited as the Geneva Report

'Theological Issues of Church and Society', *Study Encounter*, vol. IV, no. 2, 1968, pp. 70–81; the Report of the Consultation between the Faith and Order Department and the Department of Church and Society of the World Council of Churches, held at Zagorsk, near Moscow, March 1968

World Development: The Challenge to the Churches, 1968: the Report of the Conference on World Cooperation for Development, jointly sponsored by the World Council of Churches and the Vatican Commission for Justice and Peace, held at Beirut, April 1968; cited as the Beirut Report

Uppsala Report: the Official Report of the Fourth Assembly of the World Council of Churches, ed. Norman Goodall, 1968; cited as *Uppsala Official Report*

Uppsala 68 Speaks: the Message and Section Reports of the Assembly, 1968; cited as *Uppsala Speaks*

The Report of Section III, Uppsala, on World Economic and Social Development, printed in full below, and cited as 'the Report of Uppsala, Section III' (or often, when the context makes it clear, 'the Uppsala Report' or simply 'the Report')

Roman Catholic Documents

Gaudium et Spes, the Pastoral Constitution on the Church in the Modern World, passed in December 1965 by the final session of the

Second Vatican Council, cited as *Gaudium et Spes* (or *GS*) from *The Documents of Vatican II*, ed. Walter M. Abbott, S.J., Association Press, New York, and Geoffrey Chapman, London, 1966, pp. 199–308

Populorum Progressio, Encyclical Letter 'On the Development of Peoples' issued by Pope Paul VI on 26 March 1967 (English translation, Catholic Truth Society, London, 1967), sometimes cited as *PP*

The Report of Section III on

World Economic and Social Development

as adopted by the Assembly

I THE CHRISTIAN CONCERN FOR DEVELOPMENT

1. We live in a new world of exciting prospects. For the first time in history we can see the oneness of mankind as a reality. For the first time we know that all men could share in the proper use of the world's resources. The new technological possibilities turn what were dreams into realities. Just as today we have the knowledge about the conditions of men throughout the earth, and the means, we are without excuse. It is one world and the gross inequalities between the peoples of different nations and different continents are as inexcusable as the gross inequalities within nations.

2. We also live in a world where men exploit other men. We know the reality of sin and the depth of its hold on human beings. The political and economic structures groan under the burden of grave injustice, but we do not despair, because we know that we are not in the grip of blind fate. In Christ God entered our world with all its structures and has already won the victory over all the 'principalities and powers'. His Kingdom is coming with his judgement and mercy.

3. The great majority of men and also of Christians are aware of their responsibility for members of their own national societies who are in need. But few have discovered that we now live in a world in which people in need in all parts of the world are our neighbours for whom we bear responsibility. Christians who know from their Scriptures that all men are created by God in his image and that Christ died for

all, should be in the forefront of the battle to overcome a provincial, narrow sense of solidarity and to create a sense of participation in a world-wide responsible society with justice for all.

4. Our hope is in him who makes all things new. He judges our structures of thought and action and renders them obsolete. If our false security in the old and our fear of revolutionary change tempt us to defend the *status quo* or to patch it up with half-hearted measures, we may all perish. The death of the old may cause pain to some, but failure to build up a new world community may bring death to all. In their faith in the coming Kingdom of God and in their search for his righteousness, Christians are urged to participate in the struggle of millions of people for greater social justice and for world development.

II   THE DYNAMICS OF DEVELOPMENT

5. We need not repeat in this statement the technical analysis of the world situation or the discussion of the specific measures to promote world economic and social development which have been provided in the Report of the World Conference on Church and Society (Geneva, 1966), *populorum progressio*, and the report of the Conference on World Cooperation for Development jointly sponsored by the Roman Catholic Church and the World Council of Churches (Beirut, April 1968). We recommend these reports to the churches for their study. In the light of these findings, we have sought to establish certain perspectives, to state certain moral imperatives, and to point to some basic directions for Christian social witness today.

6. Our world stands at a critical point in international economic relations. The first Development Decade, despite its achievements, has become a decade of disillusionment because events have falsified expectations.

7. The Charter of Algiers, drawn up by the 77 developing nations, was well received by developed nations and there is hope for positive negotiations in the future, and many developed nations are unhappy at the failure of the Second UN Conference on Trade and Development at New Delhi. However, this has not yet helped the developing nations in their struggle against underdevelopment.

8. The truth is that most of the developed nations are inclined to reduce their financial commitment to the developing nations and show a disinclination to make changes in patterns of trade, investment, technical assistance and aid commensurate with the demands of development in the 'two-third world'.

9. Neo-isolationism is gaining ground in many countries.

10. All this is happening at a time when we have the technical

ability to eradicate want and misery. Therefore, it would be unrealistic, even irresponsible, to talk about the Second Development Decade, about national and international policies to promote development, about the role of the churches in this area, without considering why the optimism of the early sixties has given way to recrimination and frustration.

11. Both developed and developing nations entered international economic co-operation with wrong pre-suppositions. They assumed that a mere transfer of capital and techniques would automatically generate self-sustained growth. But effective world development requires radical changes in institutions and structures at three levels: within developing countries, within developed countries, and in the international economy. Precisely because such structural changes have not been promoted, we find that as a community of nations we are unable to do the good we would and efforts for international co-operation tend to be paralysed.

12. At all three levels it is necessary to instil social and economic processes with a new dynamic of human solidarity and justice. In several developing nations ruling groups monopolize the produce of their economy and allow foreign resources to aid and abet them in such action. In the international economy, the amount received as aid is often neutralized by inequitable patterns of trade, excessive returns on private investment, and the burden of debt repayment.

13. For their part, developed nations must respond by a change in their pattern of production and investment, encourage acceptance of a new international division of labour so that debtor nations find growing markets for their new exports. Aid is dynamic if it is self-liquidating and leads to self-sustained growth. The transfer of capital and techniques from one nation to another thus sets in motion a process which can be positive and dynamic only if changes are made in both nations and in the pattern of their relationship. That is why our support of at least 1 per cent of the Gross National Product (GNP) of developed nations being made available as aid to the developing must be seen in the framework of equitable patterns of trade and investment.

III POLITICAL CONDITIONS OF WORLD DEVELOPMENT

14. Since the struggle against world poverty and promotion of development involve government policies and changes in economic, social and legal institutions of nations, the creation of the political instruments of development becomes important. Since mankind is politically organized in nation-states, these instruments have to be related to the politics of sovereign nations.

Developing Nations

15. To create the essential conditions of development, developing countries need to reshape their political structures in ways which will enable them to mobilize the mass of the people to participate in political and economic life, to utilize efficiently all aids for the implementation of a national plan for development and to enter as partners in the competitive conditions of the international market. The State should provide the legal and other framework of power within which national identity can be fostered, national community can be promoted, transcending tribal, caste and other narrow loyalties, and traditional society can be reshaped through suitable reforms of land-tenure, education and taxation. The State in a developing nation should be able to enthuse the people to make the sacrifices and to accept the measures necessary for development, by a programme of distributive justice. The building of political structures suitable to national development involves revolutionary changes in social structures. Revolution is not to be identified with violence, however. In countries where the ruling groups are oppressive or indifferent to the aspirations of the people, are often supported by foreign interests, and seek to resist all changes by the use of coercive or violent measures, including the 'law and order' which may itself be a form of violence, the revolutionary change may take a violent form. Such changes are morally ambiguous. The churches have a special contribution towards the development of effective non-violent strategies of revolution and social change. Nevertheless we are called to participate creatively in the building of political institutions to implement the social changes that are desperately needed.

16. In some countries, as a result of widespread illiteracy, lack of adequate social consciousness and strong resistance of established power-structures to change, decisions on development may have to be made by a relatively small centralized group before a full democratic structure can be achieved. Such strategy can only be justified as an interim stage and to the extent that it shows its ability to promote development and enlarge the participation of the people.

Developed Nations

17. Political structures and ideologies differ in developed countries, as do their policies regarding world development. Changes are needed in the existing political climate of all these developed countries to orientate national policies to world development as a moral and political priority of our times. The political structures of developed nations

must shed all tendencies to exploit economically or to dominate the poorer, and therefore weaker, economies of other nations. More positively, the developed nations must also structure their aid and trade policies so that these do not become instruments of their own political, ideological and security interests, narrowly conceived; in fact there is need to develop a political climate which can adopt development policies transcending purely ideological and political interests. The lifting of the economic blockade of Cuba would be an example of the kind of change in attitude we are describing.

International Political Structure

18. Collective international action to improve conditions conducive to development is called for; e.g., creation of supra-national structures to deal with regional and world economic planning involving the stabilization of the world market; an international taxation system to provide funds for development; increase of multilateral aid programmes and formation of regional associations of countries for economic cooperation, as steps toward a wider international community.

Public Opinion

19. Social structures and thinking often impede the evolution of an enlightened, positive attitude to development. The majority of people in developed and developing countries know little or nothing about the demands of development. Developing countries must assist the developed countries in generating awareness, genuine interest and commitment to development. Powerful political lobbies are essential to create the necessary conditions. Trade unions, political parties and other forces which have been instruments of political and economic changes in the past in many developed nations do not show adequate concern for development today. The students and the intelligentsia can play a crucial role in the shaping of public opinion. The Christian community in many countries could be an effective force.

IV SOME HUMAN ISSUES OF DEVELOPMENT

20. The central issue in development is the criteria of the human. We reject a definition of development which makes man the object of the operation of mechanical forces, but view it as a process with potential for promoting social and economic justice and world community and as an encounter between human beings. A high quality education suited to each culture is essential if development is to release millions of God's children from bondage.

21. Economic development has its ambiguities. Development has produced stresses and dislocations within societies. Projects which have not been well formulated have caused human suffering. Comprehensive schemes which have brought release from poverty for some have often further victimized and isolated other defenceless groups of people. Technology has made many cherished life patterns obsolete.

Discrimination

22. In the struggle of oppressed people for economic justice, white racism is often an aggressive force which impedes and distorts development. Feelings of superiority among white people – a critical area of spiritual sickness and underdevelopment – diminish their humanity, and make them unable to engage in meaningful encounter with persons of different colour. Racism, as it has become institutionalized in political, educational and economic systems, brutalizes and destroys those who suffer discrimination and prevents them from reaching their full potential as persons, citizens and participants in the economy. In many parts of the world, development has also increased the self-consciousness of religious, ethnic and tribal groups, leading to discrimination and conflicts. Discrimination against women is another pervasive impediment to personal and community development.

23. The Church must actively promote the redistribution of power, without discrimination of any kind, so that all men, women and young people may participate in the benefits of development.

Food and Population

24. New advances in agriculture hold the promise of freedom from hunger. But today world hunger must be a fundamental concern. The churches must insist that food is a resource which belongs to God and that all forces be mobilized to ensure that the earth produce adequate food for all. Agricultural policies should give primary emphasis to the alleviation of hunger.

25. The implications of the world's unprecedented population explosion are far-reaching with regard to long-range economic planning, the provision of food, employment, housing, education and health services. Many churches are agreed that we need to promote family planning and birth control as a matter of urgency. An evergrowing number of parents want to exercise their basic human right to plan their families. We recognize however that some churches may have moral objections to certain methods of population control.

Unemployment and Underemployment

26. The creation of job opportunities and the implementation of manpower programmes designed to provide training, retraining and employment should receive the fullest support. Efforts on behalf of migrant workers should be expanded by governmental and voluntary agencies, especially as regards discrimination, their need for pastoral care and their entitlement to social security benefits. The problem is not only the massive movement of people to centres of capital investment. Even more important is a more fluid deployment of development capital to areas where people already live.

27. As man begins to cope with the new control over his environment which technology brings, he needs to understand the changes in attitudes toward nature, work, leisure, human relations and community, and the social, legal and institutional patterns which are required if he is to live creatively.

28. Christians should promote social policies in which the technological revolution will redress the balance between the poor and the rich rather than merely make the rich richer.

V THE TASK OF CHRISTIANS, CHURCHES AND THE WORLD COUNCIL OF CHURCHES

The Challenge

29. The Church is called to work for a world-wide responsible society and to summon men and nations to repentance. To be complacent in the face of the world's need is to be guilty of practical heresy. As we try to meet this challenge, we recognize the importance of cooperating at every level with the Roman Catholic Church, with other non-member churches, with non-church organizations, adherents of other religions, men of no religion, indeed with men of good will everywhere.

30. We endorse the projected programme of the Joint Exploratory Committee on Society, Development and Peace and encourage the continuing cooperation of the member churches of the World Council of Churches and the Roman Catholic Church.

The Pastoral and Educational Task

31. Churches are called, in their preaching and teaching, including theological education, to set forth the biblical view of the God-given

oneness of mankind and to point out its concrete implications for the world-wide solidarity of man and the stewardship of the resources of the earth. A selfish concentration on welfare within one nation or region is a denial of that calling. More specifically, the churches should acquaint their members with the recommendations concerning development mentioned in the documents referred to in Paragraph 5 of this Report and the recommendations of this Assembly. Each church should determine and apply the concrete implications of these recommendations based on an analysis of its local, regional and national situation. The churches have the task of teaching people how to be politically effective.

The Service Task

32. The churches are already engaged in mission and service projects for economic and social development and some of these resources could be used strategically on a priority basis for pioneer or demonstration projects, as an important response to the most acute needs of specific peoples and areas. This would require a re-examination of the basic objectives of church programmes and budgets in the light of the urgent tasks of nation building in developing countries.

33. Every church should make available for development aid such proportion of its regular income as would entail sacrifice, this amount to be in addition to amounts spent on mission and other programmes.

34. The churches should use their resources for God's purpose of abundant life for all men. They should explore how international foundations could be set up through which endowments and other church funds may be responsibly invested for development.

The Prophetic and Critical Task

35. No structures – ecclesiastical, industrial, governmental or international – lie outside the scope of the churches' task as they seek to carry out their prophetic role in understanding the will of God for all men. The churches should constantly evaluate such structures, and foster a willingness to accept change and even to promote it.

36. They should especially consider how the present economic structures in which national sovereignty plays a decisive role can be transformed into a structure in which decisions affecting the welfare of all are taken at the international level.

37. One of the great needs of the churches is to develop more effective ways of discovering, recruiting and preparing leadership for development in church and society.

The Political Task

38. The churches should:

1. help to ensure that all political parties make development a priority in their programmes;

2. urge and influence the governments of industrialized countries: (*a*) to undertake international development measures which accord with the expressed interests of the developing countries (e.g. the Charter of Algiers); (*b*) as a first step, to increase annually the percentage of GNP (Gross National Product) officially transferred as financial resources to developing countries with a minimum net amount of 1 per cent to be reached by 1971; (*c*) to conclude agreements stabilizing and supporting at an acceptable level the prices of vulnerable primary products; and providing preferential access to developed markets for the manufactured products of the developing countries; (*d*) to accept the United Nations recommendations regarding the Second Development Decade;

3. participate in a responsible way in movements for radical structural changes necessary to establish more justice in the society;

4. urge governments to accept, as an alternative to compulsory military service, a term of volunteer service in development work in the volunteer's own country or in another.

39. Many of the foregoing tasks are especially appropriate for churches in developed countries. Churches in developing countries should:

1. integrate their social and educational services in a concerted effort to awaken the conscience of people to the realities of the existing situation, and reflect this concern in their normal worship activities;

2. make the cause of the disinherited their own, giving voice to the masses;

3. take an open and public position calling on their communities to realize the need for revolutionary change.

The Task of the World Council of Churches

40. The World Council of Churches must continue and increase its cooperation with United Nations agencies in the field of development.

41. In agreement with the recommendations of the World Conference on Church and Society and *populorum progressio*, the World Council of Churches and the Roman Catholic Church, acting together, should enlist the influence of all Christians and men of goodwill in the world to diminish expenditures on armaments and to transfer the resulting savings to development.

42. It is urged that in the restructuring of the World Council of Churches a concerted approach to economic and social development be made a priority consideration, drawing on the experience of missions, inter-church aid, social study and action in order to launch a new expanded development service.

The Individual Task

43. The individual Christian is called:

1. to know the facts about areas of poverty and Christian responsibility for economic justice;

2. to pray for the needs of men everywhere and to seek wisdom and courage to meet them;

3. to engage in constant dialogue with others and to join with them in forming groups pledged to launch a constructive effort of education and commitment;

4. to urge educational authorities to include information about development in their curricula;

5. to become involved in projects of community development;

6. to make the issue of development a major factor in his electoral choice and in other political commitments;

7. in developed countries, to make available for development aid, by means of a voluntary self-tax procedure, a percentage of his income related to the difference between what his government spends in development aid and what it should spend for this purpose;

8. to consider the challenge of world development in deciding on one's vocation and career;

9. to make a personal commitment of his resources, personal and material, to the struggle for human dignity, freedom and justice.

The New Theological Urgency

44. Running through this report is a sense of urgency – at times al-

most a note of desperation. This is created by two new factors: the revolution in technology and the demand of peoples for social justice.

45. Technology is a radically new way of exercising dominion over the earth. It is a discontinuity in our million years of history. So it is vital for theological thought to address itself to the constructive and destructive potentialities of this central source of change, as well as its visible consequences.

46. Theology has also to come to grips with the meaning and goal of peoples all over the world who have awakened to a new sense of the human. Indeed the interaction between technology and social justice is a crucial issue of our time.

47. Theological thought can only meet this challenge if those in administration, industry and technology join forces with the theologians in working out the response. They must give knowledge and receive vision.

48. We ask the World Council of Churches to press upon member churches the crying need for such studies within their own structures, to relate with basic studies of the Council – such as that on the Nature of Man.

PART ONE

The Context

Running through this report is a sense of urgency – at times almost a note of desperation. This is created by two new factors: the revolution in technology and the demand of peoples for social justice.

The Report of Uppsala, Section III, par. 44.

B

I

A Breakthrough in Ecumenical Social Ethics?

RONALD H. PRESTON

There is a widespread agreement that the years 1966–68 saw a break-through in ecumenical social ethics. That agreement is not universal. Schmémann's essay in this symposium takes another view, and Paul Ramsey regards the methods and results of this period as a serious decline from the Oxford Conference of 1937. I shall refer to his criticisms later. For the most part, however, it is held that a significant advance was made in these years.

1 *Geneva to Uppsala*

July 1966 saw the World Conference on Church and Society at Geneva which had been carefully prepared for from 1962. It followed logically upon the previous studies of rapid social change in Africa, Asia and Latin America by the Department on Church and Society of the World Council of Churches, but was on a much larger scale. Much of the preparatory work was embodied in four volumes of essays issued shortly before the conference.[1] In its last stages it had also been able to incorporate the work of two informal discussions on 'Theology and Social Ethics'[2] with Roman Catholics who had had some background part in the process which led to the Pastoral Constitution of the Second Vatican Council on 'The Church in the Modern World', generally known as *Gaudium et Spes*, which was passed at its final sessions in December 1965. In itself this was notable for its breadth, humanity and openness and for the fact that it was the first time a council of the church had ever addressed itself to such a theme.

There are at least five reasons for regarding the Geneva Conference as a breakthrough.

1. A conscious effort was made to ensure that it was as significant

as the great Oxford Conference of 1937 on Church, Community and State, which was a landmark in the development of the ecumenical movement in its formative stages, and in the field of social ethics in the dark days of mass unemployment, Nazism and Fascism.

2. It was the first ecumenical conference, both in a global and in a church sense, in which the 'third world' was so well represented that it could not be ignored. There were upwards of 400 present from over 70 countries, and among them black and brown skins were to be seen everywhere. There were not, unfortunately, enough yellow skins present, owing to the enforced lack of contact with China, but they were there from Japan and South-East Asia. It was impossible to carry on discussions of the 'Christian response to the technical and social revolutions of our time', which was the theme of the conference, in a Western context. Members from Western countries received many shocks and had rapidly to revise their perspectives. This was particularly true of those from the USA.

3. The Orthodox played a considerable part. The effect upon the World Council of Churches of the membership of leading Orthodox churches was evident. True, the Orthodox were at a disadvantage if they were not familiar with one of the Western European languages, for although Russian was one of the five official languages of the conference it was undeniably fifth in usefulness, and it was not easy for those whose language it was to intervene in the discussion with the freedom that most others enjoyed. But it was nevertheless impossible to carry on the discussion without a reminder of the weight of Orthodox Christian experience in the Communist world.

4. The Roman Catholic participant-observers, fresh from the work of the second Vatican Council with its decree on Ecumenism and its Pastoral Constitution, played a full part in the work of the conference, and were sufficiently numerous to give a new ecumenical dimension to the discussions.

5. There was a very strong lay element present. Clergy and ministers did not in fact predominate. The considerable amount of expert theoretical knowledge and practical expertise available ensured that the conference could not take refuge in theological abstractions. Great and successful efforts had been made to persuade churches to select as nominees well-qualified lay people and not just ecclesiastical dignitaries. In fact, it proved much harder to get laymen from the practical political field to come, or to stay the course, than it did from the world of economics and the social sciences, where the level of competence was very high. One can see why it was difficult when it is remembered that a British economic crisis broke out in the middle of it. This is clearly a permanent problem in ecumenical conferences.

No such ecumenical conference had ever been held before; and almost certainly no such radically-minded representative Christian conference had ever been held before. This is what the contemporary world does to those who face it as it is, and do not see it overwhelmingly through Western eyes. Furthermore the Christians present were brought face to face with things as they are now, not as they were some decades ago, or as we might prefer to think them to be.

If it had been an official church conference it would have been impossible to have had this composition; it would have been more Western and more clerical. It was possible for it to be as it was because the Central Committee of the World Council of Churches agreed to sponsor a conference which should be largely lay, expert, and representative of the 'third world', and which would speak *to* the Council, not *for* it. This distinction has been attacked by Paul Ramsey as an invitation to irresponsible utterance, and I shall return to this, and to other criticisms, later. It is certainly not part of any claim that it was a breakthrough that it was beyond criticism.

Some of the notes it struck were indeed startling. But the fact that it did speak to the problems of our time as men experience them was indicated both by the broad resemblances between what it said and what the second Vatican Council found it necessary to say in *Gaudium et Spes*,[3] and also by the fact that almost all the different departments of the World Council of Churches have begun to see their work in the perspective of the Geneva Conference. It is, for example, significant that the Faith and Order Department jointly sponsored a study conference with the Department on Church and Society to pursue further the theological issues lying behind the development of ecumenical social ethics. It saw that the unity of the church has to be seen in relation to the world in which the church is placed, a world in which the oneness of mankind is being forcibly brought home to us by rapid technological advances and the human consequences which follow from them. The consultation was held at Zagorsk, near Moscow, in 1968 and produced some important material, some of which is referred to by contributions to this symposium.[4] In particular the consultation looked at the meaning and theological status of the term *revolution* which has come to be on everyone's lips.

Meanwhile one of the pre-Geneva consultations with Roman Catholics had said it was 'firmly convinced that there is no sufficient reason why further work on this theme (Christian Social Ethics) should be carried on in isolation, but rather that there ought to be consultation (or, as far as their ways of working will allow, collaboration) between the World Council of Churches and the Roman Catholic Church'. It was therefore appropriate that one upshot of the Geneva

Conference and of the Second Vatican Council should be the setting up of an official joint Committee of the World Council of Churches and the Vatican Commission Justice and Peace; it covers the field of Society, Development and Peace and has in consequence come to be known as SODEPAX. It is so far the only official joint programme of the Roman Catholic Church and the World Council of Churches, and its potentialities are very great. Taking up the development issue it quickly sponsored an international expert consultation at Beirut in April 1968 'World Cooperation for Development', with the sub-title 'The Challenge to the Churches'. This and other work in the field of development and peace is now rapidly developing.[5]

Apart from this official follow-up of the Geneva Conference in the sphere of development, however, there was the question whether when it came to the Fourth Assembly of the World Council of Churches at Uppsala in July 1968 the official delegates of the Churches would accept the general lines of the Geneva Conference when they were confronted with what it said *to* them, or whether they would find it too radical and disturbing. The delegates had before them all the material I have mentioned, and the Report of the Department on Church and Society. In the event they broadly endorsed it.[6] All the sectional reports of Uppsala are permeated by it, but especially that of Section III on 'World Economic and Social Development' which is printed in this book.

II   *The Background and Structure of the Symposium*

One of the indirect results of *Gaudium et Spes* was the establishment of the private Humanum Foundation at Lugano in Switzerland to propagate its general point of view, which is to clarify and safeguard the dignity of the human person in the rapidly changing and growingly complex societies of our time. In particular the Foundation wants to relate this understanding to the whole realm of industry and commerce, and to help forward a *rapport* between that realm and the ongoing theological reflection of the church. Beginning as a purely Roman Catholic foundation it has now incorporated as Patrons, Trustees and Scientific Advisers those of other confessional traditions; and they now come not only from Western continental Europe but also from Britain and the USA.

In 1968 the Foundation sponsored an international symposium on the economic section of *Gaudium et Spes*, that is to say, paragraphs 63 to 72. This was in German, and its contributors were all Roman Catholics except for one Reformed and one Anglican.[7] It then wished to sponsor a second international symposium on a comparable text from the World Council of Churches, this time in English, with contributors who were predominantly not Roman Catholics, and with a special effort made to get Orthodox thinking represented. This book is the result.

The aims of this symposium are related to those of the previous one. This is why the text of Uppsala, Section III has been chosen. In some ways the report of Section I of the Geneva Conference, 'Economic Development in World Perspective', would have made a better basis. It is a much better document – superior in style, order and argument. But it is much longer to print. And in an important sense it is unofficial. If we are looking for a document coming from the World Council of Churches somewhat akin to a Council document of the Roman Catholic Church like *Gaudium et Spes*, then clearly a report generally endorsed by the Fourth Assembly of the World Council of Churches meets the case. There are, of course, important differences between the two, and these will be discussed later, but there is no other type of document coming from the World Council which can parallel a document of Vatican II.

There are two Roman Catholic contributors to this symposium. It seemed important to secure a reaction from that confessional tradition to World Council documents of the period 1966–68. Father Duff, who supplies it, was a Roman Catholic observer-participant at the Geneva Conference, and is the only contributor to write in both the symposia. In the first one he wrote on 'Economic Justice from an Ecumenical Point of View'. The second Roman Catholic contributor is, appropriately, from Latin America.

The reason for especially seeking Orthodox contributions is simply that, relatively speaking, contributions from that tradition have been lacking in this field. One of the reasons for this is that the political and social situation of the Orthodox Church in many countries and in many centuries – not least our own – has been such that it has not had the freedom to speak its mind or, indeed, the opportunity to think on the basis of investigation. It is also true that in countries where it has had the opportunity it has not shown much willingness to use it. The result is that there are treasures and perspectives preserved in Orthodox thought which the rest of Christendom is the poorer for not knowing, and on the other hand there are serious gaps in Orthodox social ethics. It was the hope that by asking several Orthodox to relate their thinking to a particular document there would be a gain for everyone; so they were asked to contribute to five of the seven sections. There was no particular reason for an Orthodox contribution to the first, and no obvious source of Orthodox enlightenment on the application of the concept of 'the human' to particular issues, the theme of the fifth section. In the event it will be seen that as in all other confessional traditions today, although the Orthodox have recognizably distinct traits they do not speak with one voice. Their differences of opinion within the field of this symposium are akin to differences of opinion that can be found in other confessions. In this respect Dr Savramis is mistaken in lumping 'Protestantism' and 'Protestant Churches' together as if they were characterized by a common attitude. (It is only an incidental point in his essay.) All confessions now show a wide range of opinion, the Roman Catholic included, as has been evident since Vatican II.

For the rest the symposium has two Lutheran and six Reformed contributors, and seven from Anglican, Methodist and other traditions together. It is also international in its authors. In terms of the amount of work done in theology and the social sciences in different areas of the world it is inevitable that the majority of the contributions come from Europe (eleven) and North America (five). But at least Africa, Asia and Latin America are represented, and among the Asians is one from the Middle East. It is also good that there is one writer from Eastern Europe, for the barriers to the cross-fertilization of ideas across the boundary between Eastern and Western Europe are still very considerable.

It was also intended that the symposium should contain a substantial number of contributions from social scientists and not only from theologians. It was thought that church documents in the social field ought to be scrutinized by those professionally concerned with it, just as they ought not to be produced in the first place without drawing on their knowledge and experience. As it turns out, of the twenty-one contributors, thirteen are primarily theologians and eight primarily social scientists. More important, perhaps, is that nearly all have some considerable competence in both, and some have been professionally trained in both. Certainly all the lay folk represented would qualify to my mind for the title of 'lay theologian', though they might be too modest to make the claim for themselves. So the contributors come from different confessions and intellectual disciplines, write from the background of different situations, and they all endeavour to stand back and make a relatively unhurried appraisal of a significant phase of work in Christian social ethics, 1966–68.

The structure of the symposium arises out of the Report of Uppsala, Section III, which, as will be seen, was divided into five sections:

1. The Christian Concern for Development
2. The Dynamics of Development
3. Political Conditions of World Development
4. Some Human Issues of Development

5. The Task of Christians, Churches, and the World Council of Churches

The aim, however, is not to produce a commentary on the text as such, but to consider it against its immediate background, and to develop its thought by taking up issues which arise from it. We look at the process by which the texts are produced and the problems and difficulties in doing so. How representative are they? What criticisms have been made of them? What sort of authority do they carry? We shall consider these questions in this essay. Then after Professor de Vries has dealt with the background of the texts in the immediate history of ecumenical social ethics, we go on to compare them with recent Roman Catholic texts. Next the question is raised, How do these documents, coming out of church processes and discussions, look to the layman who lives and works in the complexities of the *milieu* of which they treat? Are they of any use to him? We are often told that when we talk of the church and its responsibilities in society, its main contribution is through the life and activity of its members as they earn their living and fulfil their roles as workers and citizens. But that does not mean that corporate church statements are ruled out. Indeed they cannot be. Literally to rule them out and never say anything would mean an implicit and therefore thoughtless support of the *status quo*. When, however, the churches do say things in some corporate way they must be designed to influence the attitude in practical situations of those who hear and read them; so it is relevant to ask whether what is said is helpful to the layman who is supposed to use them. This is Dr de Lange's theme.

The second part tries to take further the deeper issues involved in Development, that being the theme of Uppsala, Section III. The reasons for the Christian concern for this are dealt with briefly in the first few paragraphs of the report, but can bear a good deal of expansion. Professor Hoffmann and Dr Parmar, both economists and lay theologians, indicate the theological issues as they see them in the light of their analysis of the global development situation as seen from their particular countries. Hoffman concludes with them. Parmar weaves them through his exposition. Professor Nissiotis, the theologian, suggests a theological framework for the whole enterprise and is particularly concerned to show that the horizontal and vertical dimension of Christian theology must be held together; the concern for this world must be seen in the light of the purposes of God who transcends it. He wants to make clear that the World Council of Churches has no intention of separating the two, and is in fact answering the protests of his fellow Orthodox Schmémann and Savramis without having seen what they wrote.

This leads naturally to a discussion of Christian hope. The vertical dimension of the Christian faith must mean that while the hope of Christians is grounded in what we believe God has accomplished for us in *this* world through Jesus Christ, it cannot be confined to this world. What is the nature of this transcendent hope, and how is it related to a Christian's terrestrial hope? What indeed is the Christian's hope for this world and how is it related to what Jesus Christ has done in it? How is it related to those who suffer from existentialist despair on the one hand, or on the other have hopes of release from crippling poverty and the advent of better things put before them by Marxist theory or the embryonic benefits brought by science and technology? What links are there between a Christian's hope for this world and his social tasks? It is to these questions that Professor Dumas from the Reformed and Father Verghese from the Orthodox standpoint address themselves.

The Geneva Report on this theme said:

Technology must be made to serve human purposes. This means that Christian theology must expound and defend the understanding of the 'human' as a criterion for judging economic and social change. . . . The Christian understanding of the human derives from the belief that Jesus Christ is the disclosure to us both of true God and true man.[8]

This thought has become more prominent since then, so much so that a whole series of studies in the World Council of Churches has come to focus on it, and Canon Jenkins, who writes on this theme in Part Four, has been appointed to co-ordinate it. 'The human' is referred to in the Report of Uppsala, Section III (par. 20), and the Geneva Report has an interesting footnote to the passage just quoted.

In stressing the criterion of the human we are well aware that there is no full theological agreement on the meaning of our humanity in Christ. Moreover, in the behavioural sciences the empirical understanding of the person is varied. The two need to be related. . . .

It is, therefore, very appropriate that Dr Martin should analyse the different understandings of the personal in the behavioural sciences (though he rightly does not like that term for them), and in his own way agrees with Jenkins that it is impossible to avoid some concept of the human which goes beyond what it is within the power of the natural or social sciences to establish. Such a concept involves a basic choice, made overtly or covertly, and for reasons which may be more or less cogent. Dean Schmémann's essay ranges widely, beyond this theme, but ends with a charge against the whole movement we are surveying, that it underplays distinctive Christian personalism.

The text of the Report of Uppsala, Section III, at this point, gives us the opportunity of moving from the necessary generalities of much of this discussion to take up three particular issues.[9] In fact a fourth issue is raised, unemployment and underemployment, but this is so varied a problem in different areas that to take it up would have unbalanced the volume. Indeed paragraph 27 is little more than a *catena* of varied points, most of which were dealt with in the Geneva report. Of the three, Racial Discrimination is taken up in Professor Nelson's essay. He had the advantage of being involved in the notable World Council Consultation on the subject in London in May 1969. The second, Food and Population, links two things which were put together by Uppsala though they are distinct, yet related, issues. Professor Nash shows the connection and provides much empirical evidence which has not yet been faced by the churches. The third comes in at the end of paragraph 22 of the Report, mainly about racism, where one sentence is added referring to discrimination against women. Knowing the way conference documents get compiled, one is inclined to surmise that an enthusiast for the question brought it up, stuck to it, encountered no strong feelings for or against, and ensured that it got into the final text. Whether this is so or not, it refers to an issue of great importance for the Christian faith, and the fact that it is there gives us a good reason for taking it up. In some ways it is unfortunate that this particular essay is the only one by a woman. All we can say, in defence, is that there was no plot to exclude women from the rest, and that the most competent people to deal with the subject are in fact women, Dr Bührig among them.

The sixth section provides an opportunity to take up issues of development and social change in the light of particular situations. Professors Aluko and Mendes de Almeida in fact give some substance to the miscellaneous list in paragraph 27 of Uppsala, Section III, in terms of Africa and Latin America. Professor West, in the course of a theoretical analysis, illuminates some more particular situations, notably that of China. His experience of having lived and worked there is valuable in helping towards an understanding of China and of those Marxists to whom Ernst Bloch points the way. Dr Savramis approaches the subject quite differently by concentrating on the proper relation between theology and dynamic social change. In spite of his many strictures on the theological failures from the time of the conversion of the Emperor Constantine to the present day, he is basically optimistic because in his view theology is potentially at last free from the secularization of Christianity which reached its zenith in the Middle Ages. This is a view which has to be related to the widespread discussions of the meaning of secularization, which are so confused as to have induced

Martin in another book to call for a moratorium on the use of the term.[10]

The last section of the symposium corresponds to the last section of the Uppsala, Section III Report. On this theme there is much more of a practical nature which could have been said had space permitted. Both Professor Wolf and Father Khodre concentrate on bringing out the basic dynamic and flexible attitude needed by the church in the world today. It is noteworthy how close they are, each from his own background deeply influenced by the ecumenical movement. No one is likely to be complacement about the church these days; one is more likely to be infuriated by it. Some have despaired of it. Here we are given reasons why we cannot do without it and why, when all her faults are admitted, and when we have pressed to the full the challenge to be a servant church, we still have to say that she is to be the centre and fulfilment of the world (Wolf), and an ikon of what humanity will become (Khodre). Church and world must not be set in contrast to each other. There has always in fact been, and there must be, a continuous co-relation between them. The task is to see that it is the right kind of co-relation.

There are many problems involved in an international symposium, not least that of time. Ideally there should be much more personal contact and exchanging of drafts and papers. One of our contributors suggested that topics should be allocated to groups of three or four people living near one another but of different backgrounds who could work on them co-operatively. This would indeed be a valuable way of working, but it would take a long time. There were in fact reasons for producing this symposium with reasonable speed. Firstly, the Humanum Foundation wished to have the second one available fairly soon after the first, thus covering both Roman Catholic and World Council of Churches work. Secondly, the second United Nations Development Decade began in 1970, and if background Christian reflections on the whole issue can be gathered together they can at least be indirectly helpful. Thirdly, the situation is changing so rapidly that it is wise not to take too long over a survey of the 1966–68 period in ecumenical Christian social ethics lest it get too out of date. So the symposium was planned and completed for publication in a year. The Editor managed to meet fourteen out of the twenty other contributors to discuss the project personally, but could not meet them all. They have not seen one another's essays.

It was inevitable with the hazards of so many contributors that not all could keep to the time-table envisaged. Editorial work has therefore chiefly consisted in helping those whose native language is not English to say what they mean and to suggest small changes of content. It was not assumed that the contributors agreed with any or all of the documents. They were all supplied with the texts of the Geneva, Zagorsk, Beirut and Uppsala Reports, and they were asked to treat them seriously as the fruit of a concerted ecumenical effort, and to write an appraisal of the issues as they saw them in the light of the broad scheme of the symposium. It is clear that some contributors have found it easier to stay closer to their brief than others. However in the case of those who seem at first to be more distant from the theme of the section of the book in which they are writing, this is itself illuminating as an indication of how particular theological traditions affect one's approach to particular themes, and serves as a means of insight into the variety within the ecumenical movement.

III   *The Production of Ecumenical Documents and their Authority*

It is worth while considering the method of production and status of ecumenical texts such as those of Geneva and Uppsala. These consultations, conferences and assemblies are part of a continuing movement with its own staff. The staff is chosen for its sensitivity and alertness to what is going on in the church and the world; and also to what is *not* going on in the church but very probably ought to be. They are servants of their committees, and make a particular point of keeping in touch with their chairman. The committees are made up of those chosen by official church bodies for ecumenical assemblies, or are approved by them for a less formal conference if a name has been put up to them asking for their approval. But a staff which is on the job all the time is naturally in a strong position *vis-à-vis* committee members who disappear to other preoccupations for most of the year. By their travels they also have wider contacts than most committee members. Out of the relationship between staff and committee proposals emerge which are usually in the first instance formulated by the staff. But they have to be agreed to by official committees, not least in order to secure the finance to implement them. Out of formal and informal discussions a good deal of refinement goes on. In the end if a conference or consultation is agreed to there will be a process of trial papers, comments, revisions as a result of verbal and written comments, perhaps consultative preparatory meetings, briefing of speakers and group leaders, and finally the event itself.

As we have just seen, the participants at the event may be chosen in various ways. They may be direct delegates of official church bodies appointed through legislative processes. This is, of course, especially the case with an Assembly of the World Council of Churches. Or they may be chosen in consultation with World Council staff because of special qualifications or qualities required. Or they may be directly nominated by the World Council. There are other possible categories. The upshot is that the quality of thought of any such conference is likely to be a good deal in advance of the average level in any of the constituent churches. Not merely is the membership carefully chosen and on the whole well informed, but it is subject to the correction of thought which comes from exposure to the reactions of those from other confessions and areas of the world.

Once a conference is assembled it is likely to be split into sections, and if large into sub-sections. The sub-sections may be told to produce a draft report of approximately a certain length in a certain time, perhaps three days. Problems of time are acute. There are those of the adequacy of the interpretations, even if competent simultaneous translation is available. It is not always easy to secure this; and there is a good deal of scope for misunderstanding because of the variety of theological idioms and the wide range of subject matter, which can be very demanding on translators. Members of widely different confessional and global backgrounds and with widely different assumptions have to reach some kind of understanding and mutual confidence. Draft documents have to be drawn up and translated, revised, and again translated. Sub-section reports have to be incorporated in main section reports. These need revision. Mimeographing is required at every stage. Finally the material has to go to the whole conference. Pressures on drafters, translators and stenographers gets heavier and heavier as the conference nears its end. The whole conference has a relatively brief and broad discussion. There is probably dispute over a few points. Finally a document is given general approval and commended for study and action by the churches.[11]

It is a rough and ready process. One of the contributors to this symposium has referred in a letter to 'confusions and compromises in documents drafted under intense pressure in all-too-brief, crowded and complex meetings, with representatives of different economic systems, cultures, ages, all articulate and insisting on voicing their conflicting points of view'. He adds that 'leisurely study and reflection on the direction and strength of, and gaps in, agreed statements is needed'. One of the sub-sections at the Geneva Conference spent almost all its time on hearing statements which its members who had come from different parts of the world were determined to give. There was little time for discussion. The rapporteur stayed up all night and, starting from these statements, produced a draft report of the sub-section which went through with acclaim and has survived practically unchanged in the final report. In another case a section had failed to provide in its discussions a theological framework for its report, and one member was asked to draft one. His free composition was accepted, with two improvements, and is in the Conference report, from which it is often quoted. Rough and ready, yes. But statements drawn up in this way do have broadly to commend themselves at every level of the conference. De Vries points out how often a consensus does emerge out of the initial divergences. Sometimes this is undoubtedly due to ambiguities in the wording of agreed statements, but this is only so in a small number of cases in the considerable body of texts of a conference like Geneva or the Assembly at Uppsala.

It is clear that much will depend on the selection of delegates, speakers and consultants. Here subjective factors are bound to have some influence in deciding which people and which points of view are significant. There is so much variety within the ecumenical movement that the biases of particular people and groups tend to cancel themselves out – but not entirely. No organization is infallible or immune from the sometimes ephemeral influences of the changing *Zeitgeist*, whether theological or in social thought. Those who are maintaining what may be an unfashionable position, or elaborating a new one, may feel that the whole enterprise is weighted against them. In any case where matters of expertise are concerned there is no *certain* way of distinguishing the pioneer or enthusiast from the crank.

For a long time the staff of the World Council of Churches was strongly influenced by the 'Biblical Theology' movement which came to the fore in the 1930s and of which Karl Barth was the major prophet. It has been taking some hard knocks in recent years and is now a shadow of what it was. One of its characteristics in its approach to ethical problems was its methodological arbitrariness. It certainly was not 'fundamentalist'. But the basis on which biblical texts were or were not used was never made clear. It had a fondness for moving from the Bible to some judgment about the modern world without any intervening steps in thought being made clear, or even without it being clear whether there were considered to be any intermediate steps. Many good things were said, and some not so good, but whether one agreed with them or not the basis on which they were arrived at remained obscure. One could not suppress the suspicion that the judgments were those of progressive twentieth-century Western European intellectuals and that suitable texts from the Bible were subsequently sought for as pegs on which to hang them. World Council documents on social ethics were full of this type of judgment. It seemed at times difficult for any other approach to get a look in. A similar experience has been the lot of those who wish to work within a 'natural law' ethic. It became a commonplace in ecumenical circles that the whole idea had been exploded, and it has been difficult to get it taken seriously. It has certainly been badly misused, and by those most attached to it, but it is hard to do without it in some form, as secular thinkers frequently discover, and it will have to be taken up again. Another example is the way in the last few years there has been general talk of a 'theology of hope' following upon the work of Moltmann and Pannenberg. There is no harm in this. New tendencies of thought often make their impact in an explosive fashion; but we must remember to scrutinize them with some care. The important thing is to keep open all channels of thought that are willing to associate with the ecumenical movement, and to seek to win over those which at present are not willing.

It is the temptation of 'Protestantism' to emphasize radical breaks with the past as it is of 'Catholicism' to emphasize continuity with it. Each has its dangers. The temptation of the World Council of Churches has been towards the former. It has not arisen where traditional confessional positions are in question; the Council is well schooled in seeing that all these get heard. It arises where theological tendencies and schools of thought are concerned which cut across confessional divisions; and there are more of them these days with the increasing pluralism within the confessions. There is no remedy except to be on guard against it, and to make a conscious effort to incorporate representatives of positions which those involved in planning World Council of Churches studies personally think to be mistaken.

When these qualifications are made, however, the ecumenical movement is astonishingly comprehensive. It seems to me, therefore, that documents coming out of its processes, rough and ready though they be, and receiving general approval, ought to possess a very high informal authority for the churches. This is brought out in the essay by Nelson. One can of course say that the only test is who rightly discerns a word of truth, and whether a document comes from one man, a small group, a large one, an unofficial one, or an official one is irrelevant to the question of its truth. In the last resort this must be so, but short of that it is too simple a view. The fact that a large body of diverse and representative people have agreed to something makes it *prima facie* more significant than if it is the consensus of a small and perhaps self-selected group. That is why it is important that the Uppsala Assembly did not repudiate the work of the Geneva Conference. That conference, too, had its own level of authority as against, for example, a private and local gathering, because of the nature of its membership and the care in its preparation. Even individual papers which come from one person in one place and are then re-written after comment and criticism by others in different places and of different traditions, begin to carry considerable weight. But in the case of the

Uppsala Assembly delegates formally appointed by the legislative processes of all the member churches in the World Council broadly endorsed the work of the Geneva Conference.

How else within the ecumenical movement can one secure an authoritative judgment on current questions of social ethics which have a world-wide reference? Where else in fact is it being secured? None of this work makes any claim to infallibility yet it surely shifts the onus on to those who disagree with it to justify their disagreement. If it has come through the fires of such a process and secured broad agreement it surely carries a certain presumption of cogency. The churches ought seriously to ask themselves whether they make enough use of it. There is evidence that the younger churches do, and that the 'established' churches of the 'West' do not. To them their domestic concerns loom larger, and ecumenical work tends to get what attention is left over after the former have had priority. Ecumenical work is usually in advance of where they have got to, and can conveniently be overlooked if it challenges cherished assumptions because they think themselves strong enough to do without it.

The situation slowly improves as the ecumenical movement grows. The churches are being led by the Spirit first to tolerate and then to approve a movement which has grown out of elements from within them and which acts as a goad and a spur to them. For centuries, ever since the breakdown of the medieval synthesis in fact, the tale has been of the churches trailing behind the changes in society or misunderstanding them. They have addressed themselves to problems of a past age without realizing it, or have failed to focus a problem correctly and therefore been ineffective because irrelevant. The history of church teaching on economic and social affairs is a good example of this. No tradition has come out well in its response to the Industrial Revolution. Now, for the first time for 500 years or more, the churches have been given a reasonably accurate and up-to-date picture of what is happening, what trends are at work, and the general direction in which Christian influence should be exercised. If they choose to hear they have the chance of acting relevantly. They cannot say that they have not had the chance to know.

IV *Comparison with Roman Catholic Documents*

The only comparable documents are Roman Catholic ones. Only one in the field of social ethics, *Gaudium et Spes*, has come from a council; the rest are Papal Encyclicals. A brief comparison between them and documents of the World Council of Churches from the point of view of their authority may be useful. As we have seen, the latter class of

documents commend themselves because of the global and inter-
confessional discussion which has gone into their composition, and
still more should the official delegates of the churches at an Assembly
see their cogency and support them. Papal Encyclicals appear to be
very different in authority as they are in composition and tone. They
are closely related to the understanding of the role of the *magisterium*
in the Roman Catholic Church and the place of the papacy in it. They
are prone to have a paternal and rotund style and to emphasize the
constancy and authority of their teaching and the duty of the faithful
to obey. Popes only quote their predecessors and classical Fathers
of the church. The process by which judgments are reached is not
usually known, nor what arguments led up to them. Sometimes the
name of their main drafter or inspirer is known (in the case of *Casti
Connubii* for instance) but by no means always. The background of
Humanae Vitae is exceptional in the amount that is known of what led
up to it, except for the final and crucial stages, the history of which is
not known. But the way in which it was issued is significant for our
present comparison. In the course of a long statement introducing the
Encyclical Monsignor Lambruschini said,

The faithful know that the Pope, the successor of St Peter and Vicar of
Christ, has a special assistance of the Holy Spirit which accompanies the
mission of confirming in the faith and in the ways of the Lord all the members
of the People of God, including the brothers in the episcopate. This assistance
does not restrict itself to infallible definitions. . . . The pronouncement has
come. It is not infallible but it does not leave the questions concerning birth
regulation in a condition of vague problematics. Assent of theological faith
is due only to the definitions properly so-called, but there is also loyal and
full assent, interior and not only exterior, to an authentic pronouncement
of the *magisterium*, in proportion to the level of authority from which it
emanates – which in this case is the supreme authority of the Supreme
Pontiff – and its object, which is most weighty since it is a matter of the
tormented question of the regulation of births.

In particular, it can and must be said that the authentic pronouncement
of the *Humanae Vitae* encyclical prevents the forming of a probable opinion,
that is to say an opinion acting on the moral plane in contrast with the
pronouncement itself, whatever the number and the hierarchical, scientific
and theological authority of those who considered in the past few years
that they could form it for themselves.

He went on to say that all those who had incautiously believed that
they could teach anything different from what is in the encyclical
must change their views and give full adhesion to its teachings.

As everyone knows, in spite of Monsignor Lambruschini's statement
there has been a widespread objection to the Encyclical from highly

responsible theologians in the Roman Catholic Church, both as to its contents and the way in which it was produced. Episcopal conferences in several countries, notably Germany, Holland, Belgium, France and Canada, issued statements which came close to denying its teaching. So the question of the authority of this type of teaching in the church, that is to say of encyclicals, has come to the fore, and the situation is not as clear between them and official documents of the World Council of Churches as at first appears. There seems to have been a tendency in the Roman Catholic Church, in reaction to what it disliked in the nineteenth century, increasingly to stress the personal authority of the Pope. The first Vatican Council reflected this, and the tendency continued well into this century. For practical purposes all papal statements came to be given an aura of infallibility, and much was made of the steady, unchanging and certain teaching of the Roman Catholic Church on any matter she dealt with. The Conciliar movement of the Second Vatican Council and its aftermath has checked this and brought a different emphasis to the fore, without denying all that was in the earlier one. The reception of *Humanae Vitae* is one instance of this. Very detailed and agonized analyses have been made of the precise nature and degree of assent which it is required to give to an encyclical according to the varying degrees of difficulty or disagreement one may have with it. It has been realized that the authority of the papacy has been over-called and the constancy of its teaching and the extent to which it has been followed have been exaggerated. We have had detailed analyses of how papal teaching has changed on particular issues in the past, and of instances in which it has been ignored.

This discussion is not a weakness in the Roman Catholic Church, it is a strength. The theory popular until recently was too rigid. In so far as it worked, which was never so far as was claimed for it, it could do so only in a static world. We are living in a pluralistic and rapidly changing one. There could be little likelihood of the papacy giving relevant advice or directions if the previous emphasis continued. That is why so many hope that as a result of the controversy occasioned by its appearance there will not be another *Humanae Vitae*. By contrast *Gaudium et Spes* was a much better document. And it was produced in a way much more like a document of the World Council of Churches. True, it was agreed to by a Council of all-male ecclesiastical persons, namely Bishops; but the delegates at a World Council Assembly are also almost all ecclesiastical persons, either ordained or 'ecclesiastically-minded laymen', and overwhelmingly male. Further, the second Vatican Council was able to call experts, again mostly in orders, as a World Council Assembly has its experts, though they are much less clerical and of a wider range, and youth is vociferously in the wings. Clearly the two are not the same, but their processes are not all that different in principle. It may be the case that the Roman Catholic Church is moving towards a way of producing church documents in the sphere of social ethics not unlike that of the World Council of Churches. It also has a possible theology of papal documents on the basis of which this could be done if it chose to use it. Perhaps the more it becomes associated with the one ecumenical movement the more this tendency will increase and papal authority come to be seen in a different way. Perhaps it will be seen more clearly that in the end the influence of papal documents depends upon their cogency being generally evident to the people of God, and the extent to which they draw upon the life of that people has a direct relation to that cogency being recognized. It certainly seems that the World Council of Churches is on the right lines in the process it adopts which finally leads to a document officially commended to the churches. There seems no other satisfactory way of setting about it.

v *Criticisms of Ecumenical Documents and Procedures*

This does not mean, however, that the execution of the process is beyond criticism. Some criticisms have already been noted, and there are others which deserve to be weighed. Some are mentioned elsewhere in this symposium. Savramis is by no means wholly critical, but he charges the World Council of Churches with being satisfied with empty formulas, compromises and clichés; and in particular with a desire to be 'with it' and conform to the latest 'pop theology' in vogue. Schmémann is entirely negative and his criticisms are similar. He charges the Council with an *a posteriori* theological method, which begins with a this-worldly outlook of a utopian and semi-Marxist character and then looks for odd biblical texts to justify it, theological criteria having had no controlling influence. In particular the talk of all things becoming new ignores God's newness. A correspondent, from a different confessional background, accuses the World Council's work of being 'based on a situation ethic combined with a mild and unsophisticated idea of human dignity and happiness'. These criticisms cannot be brushed aside. Every reader can judge for himself from the text of Uppsala, Section III, and these essays related to it how far they are justified. At any rate they point to obvious dangers against which it is necessary to be on the alert. Yet it would be odd if all the weighty delegates from so many different churches should have fallen so completely into these errors attributed to them. Several essays in this book suggest that their work can be seen in a much more favourable theological light. On this division of opinion two comments may be made. The first is that it is perfectly possible to start from the other end, from formally correct theological positions, from full credal orthodoxy, and still arrive at conclusions regarding this world which are irrelevant or even corrupt, because of failure adequately to grapple with empirical reality and, maybe, because of material vested interests in the *status quo* which lead to a quite unjustified support being given to it. Indeed this is precisely what has often happened in Christian history. To take one example, no one would accuse the church in Russia of heretical tendencies, and yet it explicitly or tacitly supported remediable evils for so long and to such an extent that it took the violence of the Bolshevik revolution with its equally one-sided stress and its many errors to induce the Russian people to tackle them.

The aim, of course, is not to begin either with formal theology or with the current empirical situation, but with both at once: it is to let one interact with the other, thereby allowing theology to use its categories to analyse the data of this world and our responsibilities in it; and the data of this world to call in question theological irrelevancies and abstractions. Ideally everyone would be equally competent to begin at either end. In fact some have one particular expertise, some another and some can move competently in more than one. There are many varying proportions of competence. That is why a co-operative effort is needed.

The second thing to be said is that there is often a great gulf between the way a trained theologian and an informed layman expresses himself when considering social and economic life in the light of the Christian faith. The layman often, indeed usually if he is sufficiently prominent in his church to be a delegate on ecumenical occasions, thinks in Christian categories but does not express them in a technical theological vocabulary. The theologian is at home in this but may not think about this world with any great precision or assurance. In conferences and consultations the two are intended to blend their contributions. But when this problem is added to those of differences of global and confessional background, and of language, it is possible to achieve this only to a partial extent in the time available. Many agreed documents do not necessarily express precisely the fullness of the theological insights which lie behind them, nor do they always achieve niceties of technical theological expression. It is important not to read them in too external a fashion. This is not, needless to say, an excuse for theological frivolity or an easy conformism to the *Zeitgeist*, against which alertness is always necessary.

The most weighty criticism, however, of the method of ecumenical social ethics has come from Paul Ramsey in his appraisal of the Geneva

Conference, *Who Speaks for the Church?*[12] He is by no means entirely
critical and, indeed, holds that much of its work is 'astonishingly
good', but he concentrates on the points on which he is critical. These
are concerned with what he was personally involved in himself, the
general meetings and his section and sub-section. Whether he would
have been as critical of the other sections and sub-sections one cannot
tell. It seems by implication that he is reasonably satisfied with Section I,
which corresponds to Uppsala, Section III, and which is the area
chiefly concerning this symposium. Some of his criticisms cover the
method of procedure in producing documents, which we have already
mentioned. Another relates to the unwisdom of a study conference
wanting to pass so many resolutions, many of them on detailed and
involved issues of policy. Here he has a strong case.[13] Again he alleges
that the conference was theologically slanted in terms of 'truncated
Barthianism', or what in the same paragraph he calls a 'contextual
revolutionary-christocentric eschatologism', as distinct from a theology
that follows the sequence of the creed – creation, law and ordinances,
then gospel – which had been well represented in ecumenical ethics
hitherto.[14] He has a point here, whether or not he has precisely succeeded in putting his finger on what seemed the most vocal theological
stance. Certainly a separate group on Christian Social Ethics (which
was given absurdly little time in which to work, in the spare intervals
of supposedly free afternoons) saw a quick Lutheran reaction on similar
lines, which there was no time adequately to discuss, and which was
simply printed as a separate statement.[15]

Ramsey's main criticism, however, is against a whole type of pronouncement on policy questions found in the work of the conference.
Instead of *basic* decisions and action-oriented *principles* of ethical and
political analysis, the conference continually went on to make particular
pronouncements on policy questions based on assertions on 'what
God is doing in the world', which could be highly disputable, and
without making clear the cost implications of the policies advocated.
The result was, Ramsey maintains, that ill-thought-out solutions to
particular problems which ought to be settled by prudence and worldly
wisdom were put forward on an allegedly Christian basis. Christians
who disagreed were implicitly put in the wrong and held to have a
faulty conscience.

Ramsey entirely agrees that purely general statements are not enough.
They give a spurious air of making a contribution to a problem when
in fact they have not enough content for anyone to have anything to
disagree with. They are like being 'against sin'.[16] On the other hand
to my mind the objection to particular policy conclusions being invested
with a Christian aura is that they are bound to depend upon an inter-

pretation of what are the facts, the weightage to be given to different facts, and the trends, and the likely consequences of possible lines of action in a particular empirical situation. About all of these there can in the nature of the case be no certainty, and therefore differences of opinion are likely. This does not mean that the church can *never* make an explicit policy recommendation; it is to say that it is not the typical thing for it to do. Ramsey agrees that in an exceptional situation, such as 'before the gates of Auschwitz', the church may have to take a stand on a precise point, though he adds that if the churches are more effective all the time things may not get to such a desperate pass.[17] But in general churches should aim to speak at a middle level half-way between general statements and political policies. This is the level at which the Oxford Conference of 1937 operated, the level which it called that of 'middle axioms', though the term – drawn by analogy from logic – may not be a particularly good one. Two quotations will give the flavour of Ramsey's argument:

Christians, meeting as such, should not allow themselves to advocate particular problems in the public forum without also specifying how we are to get from where we are.[18]

It is high time for it to be acknowledged on all sides that not every decision is a moral decision, and not every moral decision a Christian decision. The bearing of God's will and governance in relation to every aspect of life cannot possibly be construed in such a fashion that supposes that there is a Christian shape or style to every decision. Concerning a great many choices it has to be said that only a deliberately or inflexibly imprudent decision would be wrong, or an uncharitable exercise of prudence.[19]

Ramsey finds a good instance of what he advocates in a statement of the Archbishop of Canterbury at the time of the Rhodesian rebellion under Ian Smith against Britain. There was division in British opinion. The churches in exercising their public responsibility were right to find a word to say. Some people were pressing for military force to be used against Rhodesia to compel multi-racial guarantees before recognizing its independence. Speaking on behalf of the British Council of Churches the Archbishop said,

It is not for us as Christian Churches to give our Government military advice as to what is practicable or possible. . . . If [the Prime Minister] and his Government think it necessary to use force for the perpetuation of our existing obligations in Rhodesia, then a great body of Christian opinion in this country will support him in so doing.

That is to say, Christian support was given to certain ends; the question of means was not left out, but whether a particular one should be used was left to those in authority to determine.

There are still elements of disputable specificity in the Archbishop's statement, and Ramsey is prepared to admit that there is only a relative distinction between a statement in the realm of middle axioms or middle principles and a specific one. Nevertheless, the distinction is important. His aim is clear. He wants to avoid merely giving religious sanction to feelings and prejudice, and to achieve objectivity, prudence and rationality in judgment. To this end he wants to stay as far as possible within the middle principle of ethical decision and analysis arrived at by reflection upon the basic features of Christian faith and doctrine. Yet the admission that if these are to bear on a particular situation and not be purely theoretical *some* element of empirical analysis must enter in is crucial. There seems no reason in principle why these middle axioms (as referred to by J. H. Oldham at the Oxford Conference, and taken up in subsequent years)[20] should not go further than Ramsey's illustration does, *provided* general agreement to the empirical analysis can be secured. If church bodies get together groups of people on particular problems with the relevant background and experience and if a consensus develops as to the relevant facts and their weightage, and as to the likely consequences of possible courses of action, so that on the basis of Christian judgment they suggest the directions in which Christian efforts should be mobilized, there is no need to limit or prescribe the amount of detail in the recommendations they may come to, even though it is unlikely that it will get as far as detailed specific policies. If there is no agreement recommendations cannot be formulated. In any event they will need periodic checking as time goes by and the situation changes. This is what the ecumenical movement to a considerable extent has been doing, but it has not made this sufficiently clear since Amsterdam. In so far as it fails it may be due to too great a division of opinion (which cannot be helped); or that a not sufficiently representative cross-section of relevant opinion has been consulted, so that any agreement is in fact partial; or because of a sheer failure in procedure and technique in carrying out conferences and consultations. In particular it has not sufficiently made clear the implications and limitations of the 'what God is doing in the world' approach.

If conclusions are properly arrived at they do not unchurch those who disagree. What they do is to put the onus on them to produce cogent reasons for disagreeing with the consensus, rather than the onus being the other way round. They are extremely useful for at least six reasons.

    1. As a help to the individual Christian in his own decisions.

    2. As a link between those of different confessions.

    3. As a potential link between Christians and those of other faiths and none.

4. As a dissolver of the division between the parson and the layman, for the experience of both is needed to formulate them.

5. As a stimulus to creating a bad conscience when society, and perhaps the church as a whole, is complacent.

6. In helping the church to achieve some purchase over events and not lag behind them.

In making any such statements church studies need to think very clearly who is being asked to do what, at what cost, and why. If they do so, and succeed in producing relevant and responsible statements, they can make a valuable contribution to the political community by putting decision in a wider context, taking care to bring out facts which public opinion or governments or both may wish to avoid, and calling for the kind of justice which is the expression of love at the corporate level.[21]

Ramsey is formally correct in his exposition of middle axioms but has a too restricted view of their possible scope. His approach is clearly very close to a renewed Lutheran 'two realms' doctrine; indeed he may be said to have shown very usefully how it can be renewed. But just as it has generally been interpreted too negatively, so Ramsey is too negative in tone and temper. Maybe the fact that he did not like a good many of the particular conclusions of Geneva is the reason for this. If the onus is on those who dissent from a consensus to show why, he certainly goes into considerable detail to make the grounds of his disagreement plain on several issues. Not everything done at Geneva was well done. Subsequent reflection will show what has to be discarded.

Ramsey finds the root cause of what he considers ill-founded specific judgments in the tendency to jump to particular conclusions on the basis of what God is doing in the world. It was never made clear at Geneva what were the canons of judgment by which out of all the things happening in the world some were to be given the status of God's doing, and how such statements were to be delivered from a capricious situationism. Some seemed to think that he was solely making revolutions. Often the appeal was to 'prophetic religion', to the Old Testament prophets who for example would move directly from 'thus says the Lord' to a conclusion about foreign policy, perhaps a projected alliance. But in this and other respects it is a mistake to move too quickly from the Old Testament to the New, or we shall be like the English Reformers who saw in Henry VIII the equivalent of the godly prince David, and some of whose successors a century later justified the execution of Charles I by reference to the source in the book of Samuel which represents the desire of Israel for a king as disloyalty to Yahweh. Prophetic religion in the Old Testament was related to a state which was also a church, a people of God, a covenant community. In the New Testament that situation is split wide open. The people of God has now become a universal community; church and state are no longer one community, whether the church is established or not. St Augustine was quite clear that the fact that Christianity had become the adopted religion of the Roman state did not mean that there were no longer two cities but one. The city of God and the earthly city remained distinct. The injunction to discern the signs of the times remains an on-going task. Basic moral requirements of justice and the righteousness which is on the side of the needy and oppressed remain the same (would that the church had remembered this more effectively!). But the exercise of prophetic faith cannot be in precisely the Old Testament way. Basic Christian faith and contemporary insight are not on the same level. One cannot pass from what God is doing to a particular decision in the same breath. A basic Christian understanding of life has to be brought alongside an empirical situation. From the former broad criteria are available: the application involves the element of empirical analysis and the inevitable hazards we have been discussing.

Ramsey has a final criticism which is not well founded. He is altogether opposed to the method of churches sponsoring conferences whose members will not speak *for* them but *to* them, who are officially convened to speak unofficially. Geneva was an outstanding example of this. He says, 'One can scarcely imagine a situation that to a greater extent invites irresponsible utterance.'[22] In this he is surely mistaken. Official church bodies, largely made up of dignitaries of various kinds and ecclesiastically-minded laymen (all of them properly employed when carrying out their normal church duties), are not the best to investigate and reflect initially on the manifold empirical situation. Once other conferences and consultations have done their work the official bodies can weigh it and speak *for* the churches. That was precisely the relation of Geneva to Uppsala. It is true that less official bodies may be tempted to irresponsibility; the remedy is to guard against it, not to abolish them.

What other method is there? Ramsey proposes several sessions of the same council over a period of years. Only by this means, he thinks, will the theologians and the secular expert come to understand one another. He clearly has in mind the four sessions of seven weeks of the Fathers of the Second Vatican Council 1962–65, together with their attendant *periti*. But the suggestion is utterly impracticable. The Vatican Council was very costly. And it was composed almost entirely of Bishops. How could a conference with the number and quality of the laymen at Geneva meet for several weeks for several years? Problems of time as well as money are insuperable. As it was it was a hard task to assemble and keep them together for one fortnight.

The ecumenical movement is bound to work under severe limitations of time and money. Its processes are bound to be rough and ready and open to criticism. There is no reason for complacency. Criticisms must be attended to, weighed, and what is valid in them guarded against within the limits of practicability. When all is said, however, Geneva was a landmark which is likely to stand out in the church history of this century. Together with what followed in the two-year period 1966–68 at Zagorsk, Beirut and Uppsala, it marked an important advance in ecumenical social ethics. Time is rapidly sifting what was not well founded. We can thank God for all that remains.

NOTES

1. *Christian Social Ethics in a Changing World*, ed. J. C. Bennett; *Economic Growth in World Perspective*, ed. D. Munby; *Responsible Government in a Revolutionary Age*, ed. Z. K. Matthews; *Man in Community*, ed. E. de Vries (all published by Association Press, New York, and SCM Press, London, 1966). Many of the essays were issued in German in one volume, *Die Kirche als Faktor einer kommenden Weltgemeinschaft*, Kreuz-Verlag, Stuttgart, 1966.

2. Details in *Study Encounter* (WCC), vol. II, no. 2, 1966.

3. In 1967 Pope Paul's Encyclical *Populorum Progressio* followed the general lines of the Geneva Conference and just as radically.

4. Report in *Study Encounter*, vol. IV, no. 2, 1968.

5. A further expert conference on 'The Challenge of Development', which took the Beirut material further, was held at Montreal in May 1969, and one on 'Theological Issues of Development' in November 1969 in Switzerland.

6. It is proper to mention here the work of guiding that Department undertaken by the Reverend Paul Abrecht for over twenty years. To him more than any other single person is due the Geneva Conference and all that preceded and has followed it.

7. *Oeconomia Humana*, Bachem, Cologne, 1968.

8. Geneva Report, paragraphs 1 f.

9. We should not object to generalities and abstractions, provided they arise out of an attempt to grapple with real issues at a fundamental level and are not the pursuit of intellectual will-o'-the-wisps.

10. *The Religious and the Secular*, Routledge and Kegan Paul, London, 1969, ch. 1.

11. In a personal comment on the work of Section III at Uppsala, Chief Justice Cowan of Nova Scotia refers to pressures on sections and sub-sections to produce a draft report at an early stage of their work. He points out the importance of adequate time, especially for those not fluent in one of the major languages used to speak their minds, and pleads for 'more time for section members to read and digest the material placed before them and to discuss intelligently the issues raised' (*Uppsala Speaks*, p. 56).

12. Abingdon Press, USA, 1967, a Methodist publishing house; in 1969 it was published in Britain by the St Andrew Press, a Church of Scotland one. Ramsey presumably sees no need to modify it since 1967.

13. The British delegates, for instance, none of whom as far as I am aware were in favour of Ian Smith's régime, found themselves having to fight very hard in the full Assembly to modify an ill-informed resolution addressed to the British Government, to make it adequate. In the circumstances proper discussion was impossible. The passing of such resolutions was not the job of the Conference.

14. *Op. cit.*, p. 77.

15. Geneva Report, pp. 203 f.

16. A splendid example from an earlier epoch is one of the Archbishops' Peace Points in war-time Britain: 'The real needs and just demands of nations should be benevolently examined.'

17. But things may get to a desperate pass in countries where the church has had no power or opportunity to prevent it, and where the church (unless totally silenced) is driven to specific positions perforce. In short, a 'gates of Auschwitz' situation may arise more often than those living in relatively stable constitutional democracies think.

18. *Op. cit.*, p. 119.

19. *Op. cit.*, pp. 135 f.

20. See e.g. *The Church and its Function in Society*, ed. J. H. Oldham and W. A. Visser 't Hooft, Allen and Unwin, London, 1937 (for the Oxford Conference see p. 210); and *Man's Disorder and God's Design*, vol. 3: *The Church and the Disorder of Society*, SCM Press, London, 1948, Harper and Row, New York, 1949 (for the Amsterdam Assembly see note on p. 28).

21. The Christian as a citizen is, of course, required to go further in detailed political judgments if he lives in a state where there is scope for political participation, and sources of information. Ramsey is prone to make too wide a gulf between the 'magistrates' who have the duty of making political and public decisions and those in whose name and on whose behalf they do it. There have been enough blunders made by elected representatives and their expert advisers in the recent history of 'the West' (to look no further) to make unconvincing a sharp division between those who are competent to speak on policy matters and those who are not.

22. *The Just War*, Scribners, New York, 1968, p. 457; *Who Speaks for the Church?*, p. 140.

2

The Background of the Text in Ecumenical Ethics

EGBERT DE VRIES

The title of the essay, suggested by the editor, poses some intriguing questions. What is ecumenical ethics? Is it an existing or developing system of ethics, valid for 'the whole inhabited world', or at least for the churches in the ecumenical movement? Is there a coherent value system based upon revelation as interpreted by church tradition, and moulded by present-day world development?

As a preliminary remark, there is a tendency in reports of all large conferences, and Geneva 1966 and Uppsala 1968 certainly were large, to speak in such a degree of generality that very different convictions can be covered by words which have been used as a compromise. Therefore I shall at times call on other sources, and at times give a personal interpretation of the conference statements.

The Report of Uppsala, Section III starts with an exciting statement. 'For the first time in history we can see the oneness of mankind as a reality.' We are without the excuse of ignorance. 'The gross inequalities between the peoples of different nations and different continents are as inexcusable as the gross inequalities within nations' (par. 1).

Universal ethics

Are we then on the threshold of, or have we entered, the era of universal ethics?[1] A global reference was made in at least two different ways at Uppsala. (i) 'We must move from a welfare state to a welfare world' (Dr S. L. Parmar).[2] (ii) The Report states (par. 29): 'The Church is called to work for a world-wide responsible society.' It recognizes the importance of co-operating at every level with other churches and with non-church organizations, with adherents of other religions, and with men of goodwill everywhere.

These challenges indeed stretch beyond the 'ecumenical' in the traditional church-based sense, toward the *totality* of mankind. Obviously so, because who would consider him or herself or his group as not being of goodwill? Thus at points the report covers, or pretends to cover, in its ethical pronouncements all mankind and the individual, group and national problems common to all men.

This indeed is challenging, because one cannot, in all honesty, call for co-operation (except in a very superficial sense) with all 'men of goodwill everywhere' and feel compelled as a precondition to formulate first a convincing Christian, or even a World Council of Churches, '*theology* of world economic and social development'. (This remark, of course, is not meant to denigrate a 'theology of development'.) In my experience in World Council work and conferences since 1953, and long before in the national context, we have not achieved the formulation of a theology of development acceptable to people with a great diversity of social philosophies and living under different economic structures. Perhaps, even if Part Two in this symposium is extremely satisfactory, we might do somewhat better by searching for an *ethic* of development, a universal ethic in this crucial area of national and international life.

Acceptance of change in value systems

In the midst of overwhelming change in all aspects of human life and of society, ethics also changes. It is a necessity of ecumenical ethics that it *must* allow for this. In as far as ethical values are based upon an understanding of the human being and the structure of natural phenomena, they cannot be static. There is a distinction between law and ethics; 'A legalistic approach to ethics is traitorous; it is an effort to capture the creativity, diversity and movement of God's history, and cut it down to our own size where we can manipulate and control it.'[3] It is because of the danger of being manipulated and controlled by circumstances and events, against which these words are a warning, that ecumenical ethics – with very few exceptions – rejects 'situational ethics'.[4]

Values and ethical standards, rather, are the outcome of societal or group as well as individual confrontations with reality. Religious ones, although seen in the light of the revelation of God, are no exception.

There are undoubtedly in ecumenical circles within the World Council, and of course even more in wider groupings, considerable differences on the place and relative importance of church tradition.

But nobody starts wholly anew and nobody wants to be wholly static. There is resilience and plasticity in all values; there is hesitant as well as grateful acceptance of new insights. With all the differences on specific issues or evaluation of events, all views stem from an attempt to interpret the nature of the intrusion of the Kingdom of God in a secular world. Understandably the manner of the acceptance of change varies from suspicion and reluctance to joyful recognition and an almost messianic expectation.

The Report itself mentions (par. 44) the revolution in technology and the demand of peoples for social justice. It rightly in my view stresses urgency, and it calls the interaction between technology and social justice a crucial issue of our time (par. 41). It does not deal with the need as stated by Dr Parmar to 'imbue the revolutionary movements of our time with creativity and divest them of their anarchic content'. Yet here are important elements of the ethics of revolution. The insight that development (asked for by all) brings disorder (rejected by many) also enters into the ethical aspects of revolution.

There is no allusion in the Uppsala Report to the fact that development does not only bring about disorder and disintegration of values, standards and institutions, but that it also leads to re-integration, hopefully at a higher level, but at least at a different level. This, however, is implied in the search for a universal ethic.

The ethics of revolution

The concept 'revolution' can be translated into terms of change: drastic structural change, or even 'revolutionary' change. The Report gives no specific clues as to when such change is justified, needed or required in society and what are the modalities of change. Psychology and a variety of social sciences have probed these questions. The Report (par. 47) asks theologians to receive knowledge from and give vision to those in administration, industry, and technology.[5] Unfortunately most of these are by nature in favour of gradual change, or at the most rapid social adaptation to new technologies. They can hardly, as a group, be assumed to consider seriously as an alternative revolutionary change in structures and patterns of authority. As for the churches, they 'should constantly evaluate such structures, and foster a willingness to accept change and even to promote it' (par. 35). It seems to me that the secular forces of administration, industry and technology are far beyond this stage (called 'prophetic' in the Report, but better called pastoral in my view). It seems to me that ecumenical ethics has a long way to go to meet the challenge of creative, non-anarchic revolution. The Report asks for revolutionary changes in social structures in the developing countries, not to be identified with violence however (par. 15). Yet only 'changes' are asked of the developed nations (par. 17) in the orientation of national policies to world development. Yet the need for revolution is not confined to 'developing nations'.

Since the 1966 Geneva Conference the theme of revolution has become part of ecumenical ethics. The demand by young people everywhere, and by the representatives of the churches in Asia, Africa and Latin America for recognition by the churches of the existence of 'just' revolutions has reverberated throughout ecumenical circles. In 1955–56 the World Council of Churches could coin the phrase 'rapid social change' to refer to an important phenomenon in today's world. It was seen as a desirable process, though sometimes as a euphemism or even fraud, and as involving a clash between justifiable expectations and the resistence of hard core vested interests (nationally and internationally). Ten years later this does not satisfy these representatives. It has been stated that the industrialized countries also are in rapid social change. Thus there has been a change of gear in thought about the uphill struggle for social justice and a call for 'revolution'. This revolution is social and economic rather than political, although rapid political change is often a corollary of the 'revolution of rising expectations'. Perhaps this revolution is first of all against the established structural and authority patterns in society. Thus it is in part an expression of the generation gap, now often a chasm, rather than the traditional generation-tension. Secular literature devotes much attention to these problems, in relation to a host of phenomena. Vatican II, with the confrontations and tensions within the Roman Catholic Church over traditional patterns of authority, is considered to be one example. Ivan Illich is described as 'The Christian as Rebel'[6] in a liberal, secular American magazine. The churches therefore find this tension within their own structure.

The Zagorsk Consultation devoted a whole section to reflections on theology and revolution,[7] indicating the need for revolutionary change in some cases, and the almost unavoidable ambiguity of action in practice. Also it pointed to the tendency of revolutions to absolutize and harden themselves. Unfortunately the Uppsala Report contains little of the depth of thought on the ethical dilemmas of revolution which the Zagorsk Consultation so timely emphasized.

The Chairman of Section III at Uppsala, Professor Lochman, mentioned the agrarian revolution which, although not a solution, is often essential as a first step to a solution.[8] Dr Parmar referred to the way the technological revolution had been spoken of at Geneva 1966 and asked whether we had not been too optimistic in assuming that a revolution of aspirations can be met by such a revolution. To repeat what he said:

Development is disorder, it is revolution. . . . Our task is to imbue the revolutionary movements of our time with creativity and divest them of their anarchic content. For neither disorder nor revolution are ends in themselves. They are means to human betterment and establishment of a society based on justice.[9]

The ethics of violence, non-violence and involvement

The Uppsala document treats violence, the use of non-violent methods and the prevention of violence in more than one section. It accepts violence, in the form of revolution, and war as a method of last resort. In some reflections on Section Reports it is stated that some groups, for example, youth representatives from developing continents, would accept violence in the case of revolution rather than of war. Others obviously abhor revolution but accept the inevitability of war between sovereign states in certain circumstances. The report on international issues (Section IV: Towards Justice and Peace) sees a world-wide struggle for economic justice, and says that Christians have not always taken sides as Christ did.

We should work to vindicate the right of the poor and the oppressed and to establish economic justice among nations and within the state (par. 6). We are called at the same time to critical examination and to unhesitating involvement (par. 7).

Examine – take sides – become involved – adopt an activist attitude – start from the inequities in the world of today – these certainly are current attitudes in ecumenical ethics. At the same time Christians and churches should work for non-violent solutions, excepting that there is 'no clear cut or final solution for this tension' (Section IV, par. 25).

The psychologists working on tension and violence, the social scientists examining violence and revolution, and the political scientists examining issues of international tension and war, are in general agreement that violence breaks out on the surface suddenly and often for minute irritations, but has roots in tense group relations deep down in history and the interaction between peoples.

Insight into the explosive character of violence, including riot, revolution and war, as experienced day by day in recent history should have led the churches to a critical examination long before the tensions broke out in violence.

'The tension must be accepted and worked at constructively, but the churches should be ready to offer some criteria of human value by which to judge' (Section IV, par. 25). Here Uppsala, I feel, falls short of

c

'unhesitating involvement'. It seems to me that the world is not ready to apply and certainly not sufficiently assisted by 'some criteria of human value'. In the context of social, economic and political tension, injustice and violence, ecumenical ethics should call for a critical examination of root causes rather than a judgment of unpleasant events.

But what does 'unhesitating involvement' mean in the context of social ethics? The Uppsala Report does not spell this out in detail. Taking sides with the poor and oppressed certainly would call for many actions before violence is inescapable.

A vivid awareness of the situation, a thorough study of the root causes, calls for a prophetic attitude. Yet churches over the centuries have had their prophets, but have denounced them, or have let them be the lone voice, redemptive in retrospect rather than leading to timely preventive action. This is the lament over, or rather rebuke of, Jerusalem by Jesus for killing the prophets (Luke 13.34). It is a frequent complaint by delegates that it is near impossible to 'bring the message home to the home church'. But there certainly is a growing conviction that it is unethical to judge situations without deep knowledge and without careful analysis. On this point the Vatican Council and the World Council of Churches Conferences are in full accord. *A study department is an ethical requirement rather than a tactical support of action.*

When tensions mount, those who are aware of the dangers of violence have, in biblical terms, recourse not only to prophetic warning, but also to the ministry of reconciliation. This means deep involvement, including sacrifice, but even more it involves 'inclusive thinking' which encompasses both sides in their dilemma.

One may ask whether in the complexities of economic and social injustice and of international friction it is sufficient 'to take sides'. To do so is certainly involvement, often unhesitating. But it may make violence and repression even more unavoidable. Redemption and reconciliation must include both sides, or all sides, in the conflict.

In the study within the social sciences of labour mediation, of group conflicts, and in the psychology of marital problems it has been shown that the mediator must indeed stand in the middle, must suffer with both and may be denounced by both. Is not this 'bearing the cross' at the crossroads of the world?

The easy way out is a superficial judgment on the evils in both houses, but this is merely an intolerable intellectual exercise. Parties in the life and death conflict cannot stand the 'holier than thou' attitude. The Christian way (and many non-Christians share in it) is profound solidarity with both sides, and the search for a common element – for the redeeming ingredient in the situation.

Ethics of life and death

Ethical values concerned with life (including welfare and health) and death (including sickness and deprivation) are closely linked to theology, since they raise questions as to the meaning of life. Albert Schweitzer developed his ethics of respect for life in a century where human lives were sacrificed in wars and civil wars. Today genocide of untold millions is threatened, and at the same time medical science is devoting intellectual ingenuity and considerable economic resources on postponing death. Ecumenical ethics should be deeply involved in these problems. It is becoming so, but the various ecumenical conferences hardly mention the often heart-breaking dilemmas which arise.

Ecumenical ethics in our day is agreed on the value of life on earth itself, and does not see it mainly as a preparatory period for eternal life. It is '*diesseitig*' rather than '*jenseitig*'. Indeed the ethical impetus from expectations of 'heaven' or 'hell' is reduced to near zero. This of course has profound implications for individual and group decision-making, for education, for the judiciary and penal system and in fact for the whole of societal life.

Ethical behaviour must be a response to an inner motivation, rather than the reward for obedience to an impulse from outside. Certainly this is more difficult in many respects, but it is also more challenging. It is one of the more difficult aspects of ethics in a rapidly changing world.

Ecumenical ethics is united in its stress on the value of life and self-realization, within the boundaries of respect for the life and the values of others. There is no consensus however on whether there may be limitations to procreation, to the chances of not-yet-existing life, out of respect for the chances of a full life for those already living.

Influence through biological science and technology on the prevention of human life, or conception control, is accepted by nearly all churches. In the Roman Catholic Church the latest papal pronouncement draws a narrow line on the acceptability of influencing births (the safe period). The Orthodox churches are even more reluctant to tackle the issues. Other churches, together with Islam, accept the moral need to counteract the man-made population explosion. The Anglican and Protestant part of the ecumenical movement leaves the responsibility to parents and prospective parents, and uses the term 'responsible parenthood'.

It should be mentioned that the All-Islam Council in recent publications comes close to the same concept of responsible parenthood and even in certain socio-economic circumstances condemns unlimited procreation as the regrettable result of pride, greed and lust on the side of the father.

Most churches reject the destruction of pre-natal life, but all have accepted the efforts of medical science to postpone death. But there are serious doubts about the ethics of artificially prolonging agony. There is a tendency to look into the social consequences of violence and war rather than into the violation of the right to live by societal action. This means that death resulting from riots, revolutions and war is not called murder, in the sense of individual acts of killing. (The Mosaic law 'thou shalt not kill' was restricted in a similar fashion to kinship groups.) In our age many people sacrifice or endanger their lives as they did before. But they are considered victims rather than bearers of the cross, and society accepts the necessity of many victims. 'What is the value of a human life?' lies behind many technological questions.

Ecumenical and universal ethics still has some way to go in any effort to agree on these basic problems for the future of mankind.

The ethics of participation

Throughout the reports of ecumenical meetings one finds as a thread the demand for participation in the processes, the decision making and implementation. Those voices are, of course, clearest in the mouths of young people and of those from newly emerging countries. The term 'participatory democracy' is heard all around the world. It is felt to be unjust and unethical if those in power, or entrusted with administration, are not in communication with those who are affected by their processes. This is partly an expression of revolt against traditional authority patterns ('generation tension'). Partly also it is bewilderment in face of a maze of interconnected and only partially visible forces in small and large societies. As a result on both sides there is the accusation of a 'conspiracy'.

There is a great deal of lip-service in the organizational jungle, in international and national affairs, in parliaments and churches, in industry and labour movements, in non-governmental bodies, to consultation and participation, but there is a great resistance in the thousand and one governing bodies to allowing real participation. There is a great desire to 'grab power' through non-democratic 'democratic' processes. Yet there also is a need and expressed desire for *real participatory action*, which involves sharing of cost, of risk, of blame, and of responsibility.

The ethics of participation within small and large groups is part of social ethics. I did not find it spelled out in the reports. However, it is basic for ecumenical or universal ethics, unless one would want unity at the expense of freedom and diversity. But it is certainly at the roots of ecumenical contacts, discussion and action. It involves clear recognition of the right of the others to be different, clarity about one's own reason for differing from others, a joint goal, even if the ways to reach that goal are different, trust in the honesty and validity of the motivations of others and in the strength of one's own convictions.

It is easy to see how difficult the ethics of participation is and how 'realists' say that it is illusory, but the ecumenical movement refutes this scepticism. In my own experience the more complex in composition an ecumenical group or conference is, the more can ethics of participation be operative. Often people work together on a common report or resolution, coming from many theological and ecclesiastical traditions, multi-national and multi-racial, young and old, and with a variety of scientific backgrounds and job experiences. First of all everybody is critical of a pre-arranged draft. Then everybody listens with great interest, willing to learn more than to convince others. And in the end the group finds unity in diversity – a common concern. The result is more than a compromise[10] and it sometimes comes closer to a prophetic new insight. This work in an ecumenical group is, without any doubt, one of the most thrilling experiences. The ethics of participation thus becomes the ethics of ecumenism.

At the root of course is the allegiance to one common Lord, the desire to search for truth and new insights, and the desire to serve. There is also the effort to avoid the intellectual satisfaction of having reached a bland common formula. The recognition of the right of others to differ, even to err, or be old-fashioned or revolutionary (lessons which are difficult to learn) leads to rejection of proselytism. Basic rights of others to hold on to their faith, beliefs and traditions are at the root of religious freedom. The Orthodox churches have insisted, as an essential element in their participation, on a denunciation of 'proselytizing' within any member churches of the World Council of Churches.

Stewardship and management

Ecumenical ethics has moved fast in the direction of acceptance of technology and scientific progress – indeed, very fast. The Beirut Conference as well as the Uppsala Report almost rejoices in the enormous strides of science and technology. To some this may be the escape hatch from the dilemma of poverty, hunger and population pressure. To some it is the challenge to use the new possibilities. To me, it is somewhat surprising that there is not a more clear-cut support for the large majority of ethically worried scientists who see grave dangers in the abuse of technology. Many churches, it seems, have been conditioned to live with destructive weapons and the balance of terror.

Some of the possibilities of biological and chemical warfare are a
nightmare for those who know of them, but are almost unknown to
most churches and church audiences (and are kept secret by those
who are interested in their development).

The large-scale pollution of air, water and soil as a result of technology without public control is highly publicized nowadays, but has
hardly been identified as an ethical scandal, as distinct from being a
health hazard.

I have found no mention of either of these two in the Uppsala
Report. Yet it was known at the time that the United Nations is preparing a world conference on these issues in 1972. Ecumenical ethics
should highlight the moral issues involved in ruthless exploitation of
humans (because through the spoilage and waste of nature one *does*
exploit and harm others for one's own immediate profit).

Of course there is some awareness of these problems in ecumenical
circles. At an Ecumenical Study Conference at Arnoldsheim in 1956
it was especially the awesome prospects of mutual annihilation which
led to a call for giving a wide meaning to stewardship. But in recent
conferences the concept of stewardship has been underplayed.

It is strange that the ethical problems in the rapid development
of manipulation of living organisms, including humans, in medical and
psychological technology has not been stressed more explicitly.

Uppsala is somewhat more cautious than Beirut. The sentence
quoted from Beirut[11] is changed into 'For the first time we know that
all men could share in the proper use of the world's resources'. To me
this is in contrast to the world-wide concern about the depletion
and waste of natural resources, the pollution of air, of oceans, of water
and soil. It is in contrast to the grave concern of scientists in all branches
about the *goals* of research in science and technology, in atomic weapons,
in brain research (nerve gases, etc.). Perhaps economists and sociologists
were the main advisers at Beirut and Uppsala (although at least economists are deeply involved in resource-allocation for differing purposes).[12]
I heard in ecumenical circles that the word steward is not liked by a
younger generation, because in the parable the steward was set over
servants and other resources. The good steward is seen as a paternalistic
figure, and paternalism is a major vice nowadays.

Therefore ecumenical ethics might be served by using the more
modern term 'manager', a term accepted both in secular and in ecclesiastical affairs. Management opens the way to participation. Nationally,
economic and political power is based upon the mandate, given in one
way or another, to manage the human and material resources of others.
Secular insight, for instance, into 'the Managerial Revolution' has
made this manifestly clear long ago. But often this has been more

narrowly defined as managing the assets of a firm, or of the share-holders of a concern, or the wealth of a church, rather than a part of the resources of a nation or of mankind. Ecumenical ethics might make a contribution towards widening the scope of the 'management-principle' against the 'ownership-principle'.

The criterion of the human and the responsible society

The Geneva, Beirut and Uppsala Reports all mention the human as a common criterion in judging societal action and structures. This certainly could be the essence of a universal ethic.

The Geneva Report adds in parenthesis, 'This indeed is the purpose of the concept of "the responsible society".'[13] Uppsala (par. 20) repeats that 'the central issue in development is the criteria of the human', but it does not link this insight to the concept of the responsible society. Rather Uppsala takes this as an introduction to the definition of development 'as a process with potential for promoting social and economic justice and world-community and as an encounter between human beings'. It does so while rejecting a definition of development which makes man the object of the operation of mechanical forces. Accepting this last statement, development is seen as a human, societal process, with its ambiguities, oppression of the defenceless (par. 21), exploitation and domination of the poor (par. 17). This is the 'human' with its weakness, its sin, its controversies. But one thing is certain, the responsibility squarely lies with *man*. It is not with rational or irrational blind forces in nature or society. Yet man is a perpetrator of atrocities and men and women suffer from them. People, including churches and their members, are badly equipped to carry the burden. The majority of people in developed and developing countries know little or nothing about the demands of development (par. 19).

Here one would expect the Assembly to call the churches to a crusade. Instead it calls 'powerful political lobbies essential'. It condemns trade unions, political parties and other forces for 'lack of adequate concern', states that 'students and the intelligentsia can play a crucial role', and then adds, rather lamely, 'the Christian community in many countries could be an effective force' (par. 19). This weak statement is followed in later passages by an enumeration of the prophetic and critical tasks of the churches (pars. 35–39) and of the World Council of Churches (pars. 40–42). And the individual Christian, belonging to the majority which knows little or nothing, finds in paragraph 43 no less than nine tasks, many calling for dedication and sacrifice.

Indeed, when the Report continues, 'Running through this report is a sense of urgency – at times almost a note of desperation. This is created by two new factors; the revolution in technology and the demands of peoples for social justice' (par. 44), this writer must disagree. The demand for social justice is older than the prophet Amos. The new technology only made the demand audible and co-ordinated. It has revealed many injustices and sharpened others. What is new is the fact that mankind, thanks to mass communication, is seen to be one body, and the suffering of one part of mankind, anywhere in the world, resounds through all mankind. Thousands of public and private international organizations, the ecumenical movement being one sector of these relationships, are channels of communication. In terms of systems the *whole* of mankind acts and reacts as *one* super-system, with nations and churches as sub-systems. If one knows nothing or next to nothing, one cannot be held responsible. But people do know, unless they seal their eyes and ears, and churches and their leaders *should know and should speak.*

Churches and individual members, in fact all men, are *without excuse* in view of the channels of communication at their disposal. 'My people . . . have no understanding', says Jahweh through his prophet, because they do not *want* to hear (Jer. 4.22).

The Report (par. 11) states another important principle. 'Effective world development requires radical changes in institutions and structures at three levels: within developing countries, within developed countries, and in the international economy.' For universal ecumenical ethics this means that it is not sufficient to act responsibly within existing institutions and structures; radical change is required. New institutions and structures must be designed and put into efficient operation in order not to stultify the efforts of development. The examples given in paragraphs 12 and 13 do not exhaust the subject matter, and some of them are examples of bad performance of *existing* institutions and structures. But the principle has been stated: *ecumenical ethics must be structural and must aim at new institutions.*

Ecumenical or universal ethics considers change not only inevitable, but necessary. In a dynamic world society the values themselves must be dynamic. Ethical values are not *given* by nature (of man or society), they are *built* and *broken* in the process of change. Ethical values develop and deteriorate. Examples abound, and the document spells out some; but sometimes it stops short of the ecumenical in favour of the localized values; national identity and community is to be promoted, transcending tribal, caste and other narrow loyalties (par. 15). But are national, political, ideological and security interests, 'narrowly conceived' (par. 17) also to be transcended? The document (par. 14) states: 'Since mankind is politically organized in nation-states, these instruments have to be related to the politics of sovereign nations.' I am bound to ask, why not to the politics of interdependent nations? Anyhow, if there is sovereignty, is it not states, not nations or peoples, who profess sovereignty?

The accumulation and discretionary use of private wealth has been defended too often in the past on the basis of individual initiative and endeavour. Rather, ecumenical ethics demands that nations (and states, and international business, as well as the missionary endeavours of churches) recognize that they can only effectively operate within a concept of the oneness of mankind. Just as the great majority of men are aware of their responsibility for members of their own *national* societies who are in need (par. 3), so there is a call for collective international action for an international taxation system (par. 18). Thus some steps have been set on the thorny path of developing an ecumenical consensus on the call for a world-wide responsible society.

I have tried to rephrase the terminology of the Amsterdam Assembly of 1948 (where the term originated) regarding the 'responsible society' without losing its meaning. I could not avoid some lengthening of it (indicated by the italicized words), bringing in the dynamics of structural change, and some clarification of the words responsible and accountable. The proposed rephrasing is as follows:

A responsible society is one where freedom is the freedom of men who acknowledge *and help create the necessary new structures enabling them to carry* responsibility for justice *for all men, in all social, economic and political, national and international structures, where* public order *is the embodiment of constructive institutional change,* where those who hold *or aspire to* political authority or economic power or *managerial function, feel* responsible for its exercise to God and *are accountable* to the people, *the nations and mankind as a whole,* whose welfare is affected by (it), *through appropriate organs of society.*

The acceptance of responsibility: a redefinition of the 'responsible society'

Earlier conferences have asked for a thorough review of the call for responsible society, as formulated by the Amsterdam Assembly.[14]

One of the reassessments of the concept certainly is embedded in the realization of the world-wide scope of responsibility. In the absence of a world government there are people, groups, organizations, governments, inter-governmental groupings, which wield power and have a deep influence on other people and nations. But there is no formal accountability or specific responsibility entrusted to the powerful and mighty, there is only (*sic*!) moral responsibility.

In other aspects also the Amsterdam Assembly formulation, at least implicitly, does not suffice. 'Responsibility to justice and public order' is not very appealing to those who are caught in a life-and-death struggle *between* justice and public order. There was and is 'public order' in many historical settings without justice.

The representatives from developing countries and youth from all over the world question the ethical value of maintaining the present 'public order', and Uppsala declared (par. 15):

> In countries where the ruling groups are oppressive or indifferent to the aspirations of the people, are often supported by foreign interests, and seek to resist all changes by the use of coercive or violent measures, including the law and order which may itself be a form of violence, the revolutionary change may take a violent form. Such changes are morally ambiguous.[15] The churches have a special contribution towards the development of effective non-violent strategies of revolution and social change.

I put a question-mark to this last sentence. The 'morally ambiguous' changes seem to be only the ones which take a violent form. But ecumenical ethics cannot always choose order before justice if there is a clear clash. Obviously there is a clear preference for effective non-violent strategies. One has in mind Mahatma Gandhi and Martin Luther King. But these men made a contribution based on personal faith and vision rather than on church-made non-violent strategies. And one would want 'the churches' to become explicit in developing such effective non-violent strategies, if indeed at this point they have a special contribution, which it is my firm belief they have.

The texts of recent ecumenical conferences lead in this direction. Ecumenical ethics is being developed at the cross-roads of the world. Christians and churches are participating, together with many others. Revolutionary rapid social change is with humanity to stay, most likely for a long time. In this world, Christians accept responsibility and suffering, avoiding violence, 'suffering rather than resisting' in obedience to conscience and to the apostolic word that 'we must obey God rather than men' (Acts 5.29).

NOTES

1. Dr de Vries says that he is 'referring to an ethic which could only be developed within the concept of mankind as a communications social entity, just as ecumenical ethics is only thinkable in an "ecumenical pluralogue"; and mankind as such as a communicative entity is as recent as the "ecumene".' He would prefer the term Mankind Ethics. It is an awkward term because English usage so far is not accustomed to using 'mankind' as an adjective. It would also be interesting to examine wherein this differs from what a Natural Law ethic at bottom stands for, for that would claim to be a 'mankind ethic'; its roots, of course, far antedate the modern 'communicative entity'. (Editor)

2. *Uppsala Speaks*, p. 41.

3. Dr R. Dickinson – author of *Line and Plummet* (World Council of Churches, 1968), a basic document at Uppsala on social change – in his installation address as Professor of Christian Social Ethics, Christian Theological Seminary, Indianapolis (4 Dec. 1968).

4. This is not the sense in which advocates of 'situation ethics' think of it: it is their aim to be sufficiently flexible to be able to exercise purchase over events and not be controlled by them. For this reason there are more advocates of it within ecumenical discussions than Dr de Vries allows, but whether they succeed in avoiding the danger to which he draws attention is much debated. (Editor)

5. As written the sentence in the Report reads that the theologians have the opposite role, or else that the two groups should react reciprocally upon one another in both respects. It is probable, however, that the sentence is badly drafted and that Dr de Vries' interpretation of what was intended is correct. (Editor)

6. Peter Schrag on Ivan Illich, 'The Christian as Rebel', *Saturday Review*, 19 July 1969.

7. Reported in *Study Encounter*, vol. IV, no. 2, 1968.

8. *Uppsala Speaks*, p. 40.

9. *Ibid.*, pp. 42 f.

10. The compromises are more frequent in a large group, or plenary session, where delegates read a proposed text with an eye on their constituency; certainly a common 'parliamentary' procedure.

11. The Beirut Report says: 'For the first time in history we know that all men could enjoy the prosperity that has hitherto been enjoyed by a few' (par. 4).

12. After the completion of this essay in June 1969, the World Council of Churches organized an 'Exploratory Conference on the Future of Man and Society', which took place from 28 June to 4 July 1970 and which amply filled this gap. It promised ongoing deep ecumenical concern with the problem mentioned in this section of the essay.

13. Report of Section I, Economic Development in World Perspective, par. 2.

14. 'A responsible society is one where freedom is the freedom of men who acknowledge responsibility to justice and public order and where those who hold political authority or economic power are responsible for its exercise to God and the people whose welfare is affected by it.' *The First Assembly of the World Council of Churches; the Official Report*, ed. W. A. Visser 't Hooft, SCM Press, 1949, Report of Section III, The Church and the Disorder of Society, p. 77.

15. It should be noted that a proposal in the discussion to change 'morally ambiguous' into 'just' was not accepted by the Assembly.

3

The Common Christian Concern

A Roman Catholic Appraisal

EDWARD DUFF, S.J.

In his address at the Geneva headquarters of the World Council of Churches on 10 June 1969 Pope Paul VI noted 'the consciousness of our common responsibilities and the co-ordination of our efforts for social and economic development and for peace among the nations' as one of the examples of continuing co-operation between the Roman Catholic Church and the World Council, the permanent fellowship of 235 Protestant, Anglican and Orthodox churches. Indeed, functioning in the Ecumenical Centre the Pope was visiting is the office of the Committee on Society, Development and Peace, a project jointly sponsored by the World Council and the Roman Catholic Church with a Jesuit priest, George H. Dunne, S.J., as secretary. The Committee's first success was the Conference on World Co-operation for Development – its sub-title was 'The Common Christian Concern' – at Beirut, 20–27 April 1968, a consultation jointly planned, financed and organized which brought together forty specialists, half named by the Holy See, half by the World Council, to offer advice 'on economic and technical aspects of certain issues of grave interest to the churches and to the whole human family' as the Foreword of the *Official Report* explains. The Beirut Report, which did not presume to speak for the churches, but rather to them, was offered as an aid to theological reflection; it provided substantial and immediate preparatory material for the discussions of the World Council's Fourth Assembly at Uppsala, Sweden, 2–20 July 1968. Indeed, Section III of the Uppsala Assembly on 'World Social and Economic Development' explicitly invoked the findings of the Beirut Conference, as well as those of the Conference on Church and Society (Geneva, 1966), sponsored by the World Council, and the papal encyclical of 1967, *Populorum Progressio*, to establish 'certain perspectives, to state certain moral imperatives and to point out some basic directions for Christian social witness today'.

The Uppsala Assembly endorsed the continuance of the Roman Catholic/World Council Joint Committee on Society, Development and Peace, encouraging it to expand its common concerns to include human rights, race, strategies for peace and the theological perspectives in the separate traditions bearing on these problems. There exists, therefore, in SODEPAX an organized effort on the part of the Roman Catholic Church and the World Council constituency to examine the social evils that darken human existence. The programme, modest though it is, expresses the intention of the Third Assembly of the World Council of Churches (New Delhi, 1961) 'that we do separately only those things which we cannot do together', an injunction which goes back to the Lund Faith and Order Conference of 1952.

This development of continuing joint study and action had antecedents which, however tentative and temporary, should be listed. From the outset of the Second Vatican Council Cardinal Bea was determined that the non-Catholic delegate-observers would share as much as possible in the conciliar experience and effort. Drafts of all documents (refused to all journalists until their ultimate promulgation) at each stage of their elaboration were made available to them. Moreover, in weekly discussion sessions the comments and strictures of the delegate-observers were disclosed to the Secretariat for Unity and thus filtered into the editorial process. It may be assumed, then, that some of the thinking of the churches of the World Council was brought to bear on elaboration of the Pastoral Constitution on the Church in the Modern World, officially known by its Latin title *Gaudium et Spes* (*GS*). Nor should the Council's call for common action 'in social matters' be forgotten.[1] Initiatives from the side of the World Council would include two three-day consultations with Roman Catholic experts in preparation for the World Conference on Church and Society of 1966.[2] If a personal note is permissible, the present writer, an official observer of the Holy See at the Geneva Conference, was invited by the editor of this volume to supply suggested paragraphs for the draft of the Report of the Section on 'Economic and Social Development in a World Perspective'.

Clearly, then, there is a convergence in the social thinking, particularly on world economic justice, of the Roman Catholic Church and the World Council of Churches. An examination of that convergence can conveniently employ the positions and arguments of the Uppsala Assembly's Section III on 'World Economic and Social Development' (along with associated paragraphs from Section IV, 'Toward Justice and Peace in International Affairs') as the basis of comparison with recent Roman Catholic statements.

I

The encyclical of Pope Paul VI *Populorum Progressio* ('On the Development of Peoples') issued on 26 March 1967, after alluding to earlier encyclicals which proposed to shed 'the light of the gospel on the social questions of their times', stated sharply: 'Today the principal fact that we must all recognize is that the social question has become world-wide. . . . Today the peoples in hunger are making a dramatic appeal to the peoples blessed with abundance' (par. 3). The shift is significant: the social question is no longer, as in earlier, traditional Catholic social thought, primarily concerned with the class struggle in Western, industrial society, an emphasis which concentrated on considerations such as the living wage, the role of the state in the economy and the right of workers to participate in management. The economic inequalities, not of classes within industrialized nations, but those oppressing the pre-industrialized majority of mankind, the problems of the proper development of whole continents, this is the issue which is becoming central in contemporary Catholic social thinking. To be sure, Pope John's 1964 encyclical *Pacem in Terris* sketched the political conditions of a just international order, but prior to Vatican II Catholic social thought was associated with the ethical analysis of our Western economic environment; it was somewhat provincial, moreover, in that it did not take into account American experience; its leading experts were commonly seminary professors.[3]

The World Council of Churches had earlier addressed itself to the moral issues connected with the birth of new nations in Africa and Asia, the mass migration from rural areas to the cities, the effect of the population explosion and how all these changes influence the churches. In 1955 a six-year study was undertaken by the Council's secretariat on Church and Society, resulting in two books,[4] *Man in Rapid Social Change* by Professor Egbert de Vries, then Rector of the Institute of Social Studies at The Hague, and *The Churches and Rapid Social Change* by Paul Abrecht, chief of the Council's Church and Society work. In 1959 the World Council sponsored a World Christian Study Conference on Rapid Social Change at Thessalonica.[5] So Professor J. H. Lochman, as chairman, was expressing the World Council's major social preoccupation when in introducing the theme of Section III, 'World Economic and Social Development', at Uppsala, he observed:

This is issue number one which the world provides for our agenda. But it is ecumenical also in our Christian sense: the earnestness of our ecumenical conscience and the credibility of our ecumenical witness are tested by our willingness to engage ourselves in the overarching care of the world, its economic and social justice.

The Uppsala Report made its case for Christian involvement in the problems of development by invoking the oneness of mankind, a fact which makes 'the gross inequalities between the peoples of different nations and different continents as inexcusable as the gross inequalities within nations'; indeed, Christ's death for all men creates an essential solidarity transcending all national barriers; moreover, the hope of his coming kingdom defeats doubts that institutionalized inequalities are beyond human control and summons all Christians 'to participate in the struggle of millions of people for greater social justice and for world development'.

The comparable Catholic position in its most official (if diffuse) form is found in the Second Vatican Council's Pastoral Constitution on the Church in the Modern World, a document of nearly 25,000 words, elaborated and revised through several successive versions, debated and emended through three Council sessions before being promulgated on the last working day of Vatican II. In presenting one of its sections for public discussion in St Peter's Basilica, Bishop (now Cardinal) John Wright insisted that it made no pretence of being 'the last word' but could claim to be 'the first word' on the subjects broached. Representing a new orientation in conciliar utterance, the effort won this appraisal from Père M.-D. Chenu, O.P., one of the scores of consultants: 'This is the first time that the Church, in her solemn pronouncements, has stepped into history – not just for the sake of updating her apostolate but because of her very nature.' Broader in scope than what can be attempted in the less than three weeks' session of a World Council Assembly,[6] representing in fact a new orientation in conciliar utterance, the Constitution situates the Christian in the complexities of the times, indicating his expected ascetical outlook and then proposing his proper posture as he confronts multiple modern problems.[7] Duties toward developing nations were examined in the final chapter of the document, 'The Fostering of Peace and the Promotion of a Community of Nations'. Development was viewed, then, in the light of constructing a more coherent international legal order. The motivation for Christian effort against economic injustice on a continental scale, tellingly summarized in the opening paragraphs of the Report of Uppsala Section III, is expressed in several chapters of *Gaudium et Spes* and brought to bear on a whole gamut of temporal problems. Eighteen months after the close of the Council, however,

Pope Paul addressed himself explicitly and with greater urgency to the problem of underdevelopment, peremptorily pointing to its source in selfishness: 'The world is sick. The cause lies less in the lack of resources, or their monopolization by a small number of men, than in the lack of brotherhood among individuals and peoples.'[8]

II

In economic matters the delegates to the Uppsala Assembly disclaimed technical competence, announcing their reliance on the published analyses and recommendations of earlier consultations of experts. They did not essay an historical examination of the roots of economic inequality in international society. They could testify to a public fact: that the optimism accompanying the announcement of the Decade of Development 'has given way to recrimination and frustration'. This disillusionment was attributed to wrong suppositions, to the expectation 'that a mere transfer of capital and techniques would automatically generate self-sustaining growth'. What is really needed, they agreed, is something more complicated and more difficult: 'radical changes in institutions and structures' in both developed and developing countries and in the processes of international trade itself. Endorsed anew was the goal of 1 per cent of the Gross National Product to be made available each year by the developed countries in aid to developing countries, a figure considered a minimum at the 1966 Church and Society Conference, accepted as a target at the 1968 New Delhi meeting of the United Nations Conference on Trade, Aid and Development and listed by the Beirut Conference as a suitable sum for official transfers alone. But such a subsidy, Uppsala insisted, 'must be seen in the framework of equitable patterns of trade and investment'.

Vatican II was aware of the urgent need to transform present-day structures if justice is to obtain among nations.

It is now necessary for the family of nations to create for themselves an order which corresponds to modern obligations, particularly with reference to those numerous regions still laboring under intolerable need (*GS*, par. 84).

Moreover, the same document had earlier affirmed a principle whose implication condemns current trade practices and challenges all pretensions to absolute sovereignty:

God intended the earth and all that it contains for the use of every human being and people. Thus, as all men follow justice and unite in charity, created goods should abound for them on a reasonable basis. . . . Attention must always be paid to the universal purpose for which created goods are meant (*ibid.*, par. 69).

Nor does *Populorum Progressio* hesitate to identify the historical source of the economic inequalities in the world. It is colonialism and its consequence:

> It must certainly be recognized that colonizing powers have often furthered their own interests, power or glory and that their departure has sometimes left a precarious economy, bound up for instance with the production of one kind of crop whose market prices are subject to sudden and considerable variation (*PP*, par. 7).

Since World War II millions of people have achieved political independence, but their economic relationships with their former governors have not changed substantially. Their national boundaries, particularly in Africa, express the limits of the colonial power's ability to occupy territory, especially as it encountered the rival ambitions of other colonial powers. The occupied territory, the colony, supplied raw material – plantation crops of tea, sugar, coffee and later minerals, rubber and oil – for the maws of the workers and machines of what was jauntily termed 'the mother country', and absorbed in return the finished products from the factories of the country whose flag flew over distant lands and controlled the destinies of peoples of different civilizations and languages. It was a system which the late Père Lebret, O.P., one of those who collaborated in the drafting of *Populorum Progressio*, strikingly termed *l'économie de traite*. The milk-cow technique continues today in the relations of the affluent North of the globe in its dealings with the impoverished South – except that the milk-cow is becoming leaner and less docile. It is the technique which by tariff walls effectively forbids Brazil, for example, to manufacture instant coffee for sale in the United States, while the cost of an American-made tractor, compared with the market price of bulk coffee, mounts constantly. 'Manifestly inadequate' is *Populorum Progressio*'s description of our system of international trade.

> Left to itself it works rather to widen the differences in the world's levels of life, not to diminish them: rich peoples enjoy rapid growth whereas the poor develop slowly. The imbalance is on the increase: some produce a surplus of foodstuffs, others cruelly lack them and see their exports of what little they produce made uncertain (par. 8).

Clearly, the gap between the 'have' and the 'have not' nations is widening and this by the very working of the economic mechanism that has made one-third of mankind relatives of Dives, indifferent to the plight of billions of Lazaruses excluded from access to the means of decent human existence. If this trend is to be halted, radical changes of an institutional kind and on an international scale will have to be made. On this point the thinking of the World Council of Churches and the Roman Catholic Church is in full agreement.

III

The Uppsala Assembly had comment to offer on the political changes imperative in the developing countries, the developed countries and in international society to promote world development. A sense of national identity, it was suggested, must be achieved if the people are to be summoned successfully to the sacrifices involved in the multiple tasks of development. A sense of participation must be fostered if a national plan is to be implemented and reforms in land tenure, education and taxation introduced. Possibly in an allusion to military regimes in former colonial countries, and certainly a concession to those at the 1966 Geneva Conference who favoured single-party rule, the Report of Section III noted that in some countries and as an interim stage the nation-building process might have to be directed 'by a relatively small, centralized group', given the inflexibility of traditional society. Indeed, the social changes required for modernization imply a revolution and, while the churches have a special contribution to make in the form of non-violent strategies of change, the Report did not hesitate to observe:

In countries where the ruling groups are oppressive or indifferent to the aspirations of the people, are often supported by foreign interests, and seek to resist all changes by the use of coercive or violent measures, including the 'law and order' which may itself be a form of violence, the revolutionary change may take a violent form (par. 15).

Such changes, the Report declared, are 'morally ambiguous'.

This evocation of violence as the matrix of needed social change is of largely Latin American provenance. It is significant that at the 1966 Geneva Conference on Church and Society the Spanish term *violencia blanca* was employed to describe unjust and oppressive social systems. Dom Helder Camara, the Brazilian Catholic archbishop, uses the term freely in his public addresses abroad, speaking of the triple violence against the underdeveloped world as exercised by internal colonialism, by the developed world and by the established order 'which is legally installed violence which leads to subversion and more violence'.[9] Vatican II reserved its praise for non-violence (*GS*, n. 71). *Populorum Progressio*, however, was aware of the provocations:

There are certainly situations whose injustice cries to heaven. When whole populations destitute of necessities live in a state of subjection barring them from all initiative and responsibility and from all opportunity to advance culturally and to share in social and political life, men are easily led to have recourse to violence as a means to right those wrongs to human dignity (par. 30).

The encyclical was cautious, however, in its response – as if its author had meditated on the lessons of Professor Denis Brogan's book, *The Price of Revolution*:

It is clear, however, that a revolutionary uprising – save where there is a manifest, long-standing tyranny which would do great damage to fundamental personal rights and dangerous harm to the common good of the country – produces new injustices, throws more elements out of balance and brings on new disasters (*PP*, par. 31).

Of course it may be that both the encyclical and the Uppsala statements are heavy reflections on an intransigent, seemingly irremediable situation where the 'haves' are determined to yield none of their power to the oppressed masses; possibly the statements were intended to parallel the observation of President John F. Kennedy: 'Those who make peaceful revolution impossible make violent revolution inevitable.' Both statements manifest an appreciation of the gravity of the economic inequalities among nations and the growing clamour of the oppressed for justice. 'With us, despite us, or without us, the revolution is at hand. Woe to those who oppose it!' asserted Dom Helder Camara.

Vatican II's counsel to the developing nations was certainly unsentimental:

Let them be mindful that progress begins and develops primarily from the efforts of the people themselves. Hence, instead of depending wholly on outside help, they should rely chiefly on the unfolding of their own resources and the cultivation of their own qualities and tradition (*GS*, par. 86).

Populorum Progressio has no separate counsel for the developing nations. It appears to view them as passive victims of an unjust distribution of the world's wealth.

Uppsala's desire for the developed countries was a change of political climate so that national policies would be oriented 'to world development as a moral and political priority of our times', a move that would transcend all ideological, security or political interests. It is much to hope. Vatican II's observation that 'certain psychological and material adjustments will be needed among the advanced nations and should be brought about' (*GS*, par. 86) strikes the same note. *Populorum Progressio*, on the other hand, widens the argument by asserting claims of social justice in the trade relations between nations in the world economic system comparable to the claims between segments of the population within the national economy. The teaching of Leo XIII's 1890 encyclical *Rerum Novarum* – known in its English translation as 'On the

Condition of Workers' – on justice ruling the wage contract between the labourer and his employer is extended to an assertion of justice ruling trade between the developed and the developing nations:

What was true of the just wage for the individual is true of international contracts: an economy of exchange can no longer be based solely on free competition, a law which, in its turn, too often creates an economic dictatorship. Freedom of trade is fair only if it is subject to the demands of social justice (*PP*, par. 59).

In trade between developed and underdeveloped economies, conditions are too disparate and the degrees of genuine freedom too unequal. In order that international trade be human and moral, social justice requires that it restore to the participants a certain equality in buying and selling (par. 61).

The logic that produced the welfare state leads in identical terms to a welfare world. Evidence for this argument is at hand in, for example, a national policy of supporting 'agriculture at the price of sacrifices imposed on economically more favoured sectors' or again when national interests, narrowly conceived, are subordinated in a common market with national fiscal policies being stretched to assure comparable competitive opportunities to industries in other countries.

There is historical warrant, U Thant believes, for confidence that the same policies which levelled the gross inequalities in the national economies of the West can, if imitated and supplemented, narrow the present growing gap between the rich and the poor nations:

In the United Kingdom, for example, in the middle of the nineteenth century, after some fifty or sixty years of rapid economic growth, society was so divided between rich and poor, so diverse in opportunity and affluence, so alien in class and culture that it resembled not so much a unified community as two nations – separate in wealth, separate in understanding, indeed, almost as separate in contact and sympathy as are the two segments of the modern world – the rich 'North' and the still poverty-stricken 'South' below the Tropic of Cancer. The Victorian society bore a family resemblance to our deeply divided modern world economy.

Continuing his analysis, the UN Secretary General notes that the gap was growing more absolute between the income of the upper class and the misery of the workers to the point that a mood of hopelessness was endemic. Yet a century later, he reports, the situation in the developed countries has changed dramatically; middle-class comfort is now the accepted standard, not the impossible dream. 'It has taken time, but the chasm has been crossed. It can be crossed again.'[10]

None of the ecclesiastical documents under examination allude to the institutional mechanisms which over the past century helped to narrow the gap between the rich and the poor in the developed countries: the widening of the franchise, the growth of trade unionism, the progressive income tax. They are aware of the necessity of collective political action, strongly supported by public opinion, to create and/or strengthen supra-national structures empowered to supervise the world economy. Uppsala spoke of world and regional planning, an international taxation system, regional common markets and the increase of multilateral aid programmes. Roman Catholic thinking seems to expect more effective international economic co-operation as a function of (and in proportion to) a more co-operative political world order. Thus Vatican II viewed the whole development problem in the perspective of promoting peace through the construction of a more coherent international community of nations:

Today the bonds of mutual dependence become increasingly close between all citizens and all the peoples of the world. The universal common good needs to be intelligently pursued and more effectively achieved. Hence it is now necessary for the family of nations to create for themselves an order which corresponds to modern obligations, particularly with reference to those numerous regions still laboring under intolerable need (*GS*, par. 84).

The paragraphs which follow adumbrate the scope of the agencies envisioned. Nearly all of them exist under the UN aegis (except the aborted ITO, designed to monitor international trade); they are currently hobbled by the limitations imposed by jealous national sovereignties. In *Populorum Progressio* Pope Paul called for increased aid to the developing countries and for 'the rectification of inequitable trade relations between powerful and weak nations' (par. 44), but he capped his case with a plea for a set of institutions, clearly of a political character, capable of preparing, co-ordinating and directing international collaboration and resulting in 'an order of justice which is universally recognized'. He cited his own words before the UN Assembly in 1965: 'Who does not see the necessity of thus establishing progressively a world authority, capable of acting effectively in the juridical and political sectors?' (*PP*, par. 78).

IV

More specifically at the Geneva Conference, World Council statements have welcomed the advances of science and technology, seeing in the success of human creativity an expression of God's creative power; they approve as well increased economic productivity as freeing man from unnecessary want and material uncertainties, removing crippling squalor and offering greater potentialities of a more fully human existence. Adverting to the population expansion and growing human aspirations, Vatican II drew the conclusion:

Therefore technical progress must be fostered, along with a spirit of initiative, an eagerness to create and expand enterprises, the adaptation of methods of production, and the strenuous efforts of all who engage in production – in a word, all elements making for such development (*GS*, par. 64).

Yet genuine development is not to be measured by the multiplication of material goods. In the view of Uppsala 'the central issue in development is the criteria of the human' and therefore it must be seen 'as a process with potential for promoting social and economic justice and world community and as an encounter between human beings'. Economic growth must be accompanied by social and spiritual gains if it is to be authentic development. In the language of Vatican II:

The fundamental purpose of this productivity must not be the mere multiplication of products. It must not be profit or domination. Rather, it must be the service of man, and indeed of the whole man, viewed in terms of his material needs and the demands of his intellectual, moral, spiritual and religious life. And when we say man, we mean every man whatsoever, and every group of men of whatever race and from whatever part of the world (*GS*, par. 64).

An integral humanism of the type described by Jacques Maritain is the goal of development in *Populorum Progressio*. It is a process which respects man's total destiny and the true human values incorporated in other civilizations. Therefore, the encyclical insists:

Developing nations must know how to discriminate among those things that are held out to them; they must be able to assess critically, to eliminate those deceptive goods which would only bring about a lowering of the human ideal, and to accept those values that are sound and beneficial, in order to develop them alongside their own, in accordance with their own genius (par. 41).

The difficulties in even moving toward this goal of authentic development of whole peoples are multiple and manifest. As viewed at Uppsala they include the dislocations accompanying the introduction of modern technology, institutionalized racism and persistent discrimination on the basis of sex, or religion or ethnic inheritance, the pressure of population on the food supply and the stubborn human resistance to change. To this list from the Report of Section III must be added the comments from Section IV, 'Towards Justice and Peace in International Affairs', adverting explicitly to the question of justice in the world economy. Section IV examined the evil of racism in greater detail, noting that it is 'linked with economic and political exploitation'. While conceding that nationalism, especially in newly independent countries, often supplies a unifying force and a focus of loyalty, the Report remarks that 'in its negative sense, it has often been divisive and destructive, both within and among nations, magnifying their differences and aggravating their disputes'. National particularism is seen as an obstacle to regional integration and to the strengthening of those structures of international co-operation (structures subject always to the demands of emergent needs) imperative to the fostering of justice in the world economic system. As had previous World Council Assemblies, Uppsala endorsed the United Nations as at least symbolizing the future form of the 'structures of international co-operation'. Such, at least, is a legitimate conclusion from the Report's observation that the present inadequacies of the UN will be overcome 'chiefly to the extent that man will accord it the essential authority'.

No complaint can be made that Vatican II's listing of obstacles to genuine world development was not forthright:

If an economic order is to be created which is genuine and universal, there must be an abolition of excessive desire for profit, nationalistic pretensions, the lust for political domination, militaristic thinking, and intrigues designed to spread and impose ideologies (*GS*, par. 85).

But, as in its earlier discussion on the means of promoting peace, the Council relies on the emerging political mechanisms of international co-operation to foster greater equity in world economic relations; it refers to existing international agencies (presumably primarily those of the UN) as 'the first attempts to lay international foundations under the whole human community for the solving of the critical problems of our age, the promotion of global progress and the prevention of any kind of war' (*GS*, par. 84). As impediments to world development *Populorum Progressio* likewise indicts nationalism (par. 62), racism (par. 63) 'all public and private squandering of wealth, all expenditure prompted by motives of national or personal ostentation, every exhausting arms race' (par. 53). The encyclical had earlier condemned the abuses of liberal Capitalism,

the baseless theory . . . which considers material gain the key motive for economic progress, competition as the supreme law of economics, and the private ownership of the means of production as an absolute right that has no limit and carries no corresponding social obligation (par. 26).

At its close, however, *Populorum Progressio* calls for 'institutions that will prepare, co-ordinate and direct' international collaboration and for these to be eventually, as has been noted, under a progressively established 'world authority' (par. 78).

V

The next sentence in *Populorum Progressio* reads: 'Some would consider such hopes utopian.' Perhaps this is the place to inquire whether the expectations of the ecumenical documents under examination are realistic, whether they have ingenuously or disingenuously eschewed some of the more intractable features of the current international scene, economic and political.

One might begin by listening to some hard questions raised by S. L. Parmar, an Indian economist, in an introductory paper prepared for the deliberations of Section III of the Uppsala Assembly. At the outset Dr Parmar challenged the assumption underlying the global vision of the problem, one that saw the technological revolution which had taken place in the industrialized countries as corresponding to the new revolution of aspirations in the developing countries so that the skills of one could be used to meet the needs of the other and thus the limits (and lessons) of the welfare state could be broadened to become a welfare world. Parmar went on to argue that 'we do not have adequate political and economic structures to bring together possibilities and needs'.[11]

The technology of the industrial West, he points out, operates in function of planned obsolescence, a high consumption society being based on institutionalized waste – and this in the interest of efficiency and high effective demand. But such a technique, such an outlook, cannot be transferred to the developing countries where waste and the misuse of scarce resources must be rigorously eliminated. Again, the projection of the process of the growth of the welfare state to that of a welfare world neglects to take into account the pressures of agrarian movements and trade union protests, for example, that forced the possessing class to yield some of its privileges. The fact is becoming clearer that 'if the West and the East (socialist countries) come together, as they seem to be doing, they could maintain their economic prosperity, technological superiority, and military strength completely independently of the third world'. Whence the awkward question:

If the privileged group is unwilling to surrender any of its privileges without pressure, and if the ability to apply pressure in the international setting is negligible, how do we go about matching the possibilities of the technological revolution with the aspirations of the social revolution?

Moreover, in view of the poverty problem, particularly among blacks in the United States, and the plight of immigrant workers in some Western countries, can we really say that the welfare state has been achieved anywhere? Whence another question: 'Will the projection of this two-group welfare state to the whole world not lead to a projection of the elements of inequality and injustice it contains?' Finally, Parmar warns against the illusion that 'Development is the new name for peace', a phrase made familiar by Pope Paul; he points out that development, rightly understood, is disorder 'because it changes existing social and economic relationships, breaks up old institutions to create new, brings about radical alterations in the values and structures of society'.

Sometimes the impression emerges in reading ecumenical documents that the development process will enlarge the prosperity of the already industrialized countries. Any appeal to economic self-interest will get small hearing from the policy makers of the developed countries. An American economist has set down the realities of contemporary world economic life as manifested in United States policy. Professor James H. Weaver organized impressive statistical evidence to support three propositions: (1) The US supports free trade – when it works to our advantage – but frequently practises protectionism to the detriment of developing nations. (2) Foreign aid is designed to serve the political and economic needs of the United States rather than the development needs of the recipient nations. (3) Underdeveloped countries lose out on direct private investment from the US.[12] But surely the US needs the rest of the world to develop to serve as market? Not so, since the techniques of demand management in the hands of a government can enable a developed country to assure full employment. One of the points about the *General Theory* of which Keynes was most proud was that it made imperialism unnecessary and ended the need to have other countries buying a country's excess products. Nor does the United States, for one, depend on imports of raw materials, given its continental resources and capacity to produce synthetics. Then surely world development is to be desired for the sake of world peace? Professor Weaver here joins Dr Parmar in his caution: historically, he points out, developing countries have been, at least in the short run, 'belligerent and prone to expand'.

Barbara Ward, for one, insists that from the annual increase of the GNP of the developed countries funds are available for foreign aid despite expenditures for armaments. Available or not, such funds are not being appropriated.[13] The cost of the Vietnam war and the massive military machine of the United States has reduced the request to the Congress for foreign aid to the lowest sum ever, as well as cutting back on domestic welfare programmes. Aid from the communist bloc countries was down one-fourth, it was reported,[14] from the average annual figure of $1 billion during the earlier years of the decade, a drop undoubtedly influenced by the military expenditures resulting from the Soviet-China tension.

One might, then, expect in ecumenical documents dealing with world development a more vocal and persistent attack on the burden of armaments whose annual cost is variously estimated at between $150 and $180 billion. True, Vatican II condemned the arms race as 'one which injures the poor to an intolerable degree' (*GS*, par. 81) and in *Populorum Progressio* Pope Paul renewed the plea, first made at Bombay on 4 December 1964, 'for the establishment of a great world fund, to be made up in part of the money spent on arms, to relieve the most destitute of this world' (par. 51). Uppsala repeated the plea. Here, it seems to me, a stronger prophetic voice of the churches should be raised as the developed – and developing – countries multiply the resources assigned to military purposes. More criminal still (but excused as a help to achieving a balance of trade) is the active promotion of trade in arms, frequently obsolete, sometimes to both sides in a conflict. The height of hypocrisy is covering such sales as loans and terming them foreign aid.

Statements from ecumenical sources, both World Council and Catholic, have not been remiss in pointing to the injustice of the *latifundia* in the developing countries and in demanding that under-utilized land be made available to the impoverished peasants. *Populorum Progressio* indicted a further abuse:

Consequently, it is unacceptable that citizens with abundant incomes from the resources and activities of their country should transfer a considerable part of this income abroad purely for their own advantage without care for the manifest wrong they inflict on their country by doing this (par. 24).

There seems, however, a certain hesitation to assess the moral implication of 'the brain drain', a practice which deprives the developing countries of desperately needed trained personnel who opt for more rewarding, or at least more remunerative, employment in the developed nations. Not merely is their scientific and professional talent unavailable, but the cost of their early education adversely affects the trade balance of the developing country. As is the case in repaying many loans, by the brain drain the developing countries are subsidizing the developed ones.[15]

VI

Uppsala Section III was oriented toward action. Reviewing the draft of the Report at a plenary session of the Assembly, the chairman explained that the section, after examining the evidence of technical experts, had sought to respond to the question: 'What shall we do?'[16]

The reply constituted an extended and detailed series of assignments to the member churches, to church agencies, to the World Council and to individual Christians, and called for co-operation with all working for world development, notably with the Roman Catholic Church. The Assembly was clearly not moved by the remark of the Russian Orthodox Archimandrite German that 'the reference to the participation of the clergy in political and economic pressure groups could not apply to the Orthodox Church as canon law did not allow the clergy to take up political activities'.[17]

Pursuant to a request of the Council (*GS*, par. 90), a Commission on Justice and Peace, a permanent agency of the Holy See, was instituted by papal decree on 6 January 1967, charged with 'bringing to the whole of God's people the full knowledge of the part expected of them at the present time, so as to further the progress of poorer peoples, encourage social justice among nations and offer to less developed nations the means whereby they can further their own progress'. The Catholic hierarchies in different countries have, in several instances, organized national commissions with identical purposes. Even so, a reading of Catholic documents suggests that the task of world development is primarily that of the laity. Vatican II had declared:

Secular duties and activities belong properly although not exclusively to laymen. . . . Laymen should also know that it is generally the function of their well-formed Christian conscience to see that the divine law is inscribed in the life of the earthly city (*GS*, par. 43).

The clergy, it was said, could supply spiritual light and nourishment but should not be expected to supply solutions in areas where the layman has his distinctive role. The same conciliar Constitution, in its conclusion, concluded that its programme 'is but a general one in several of its parts', one 'which will have to be further pursued and amplified, since it often deals with matters in a constant state of development' (*GS*, par. 91). *Populorum Progressio* can be considered an amplification of the Council's discussion of world development, certainly heightening its sense of urgency: 'The time for action has now sounded. . . . It is time for all men and all peoples to face up to their responsibilities' (par. 80). And this responsibility falls first on the laity:

In countries undergoing development no less than in others, the laymen should take up as their own proper task the renewal of the temporal order. If the role of the hierarchy is to teach and to interpret authentically the norms of morality to be followed in this matter, it belongs to the laymen, without waiting passively for orders and directions, to take the initiative freely and to infuse a Christian spirit into the mentality, customs, laws and structures of the community in which they live (*PP*, par. 81).

VII

Whatever the modalities of action proposed for a concerted campaign for world development, it must be agreed that the World Council of Churches and the Roman Catholic Church have addressed themselves to the central issue of our times: the claims of justice for all people in a world made one, for peril or prosperity, by technological advances. In so doing they have examined the core of their teaching to discover that it is concerned with the life of every man on earth. In making their message meaningful for the needs of the poor they challenge the caustic comment that Christianity is concerned with religion, not with life. Perhaps this current focus of the World Council constituency and of Roman Catholicism will be an instrument of their renewal. In an address to the Uppsala Assembly, Dr W. A. Visser 't Hooft, for many years General Secretary of the World Council of Churches, declared that our troubles derive from the fact that 'at a time when history requires that humanity should live as a coherent responsible society, men still refuse to accept responsibility for their fellow-beings'. For this situation the churches are in part to blame, Dr Visser 't Hooft believed:

They are largely responsible for the false impression that Christians are advocates of the Church and leave the advocacy of humanity to the philosophers, the humanists, the Marxists.

The solution does not lie in resolution-making or in moralizing. We must

first recover in theology, in our teaching and in our preaching the clear biblical doctrine of the unity of mankind and so give our churches the strong foundation for a new approach to the whole question of world economic justice and to a better and more convincing motivation for development.[18]

Appropriately, the final recommendation of Uppsala's Section III was entitled 'The New Theological Urgency', and issued into a call for concentrated study on the theme of the Nature of Man. Thus Uppsala confirmed the summons to 'the deep thought and reflection of wise men in search of a new humanism which will enable modern man to find himself anew', a search which *Populorum Progressio* deemed more necessary than the work of more and more technicians (par. 20). That search is under way as a project of the Joint Committee on Society, Development and Peace. It had been foreshadowed at the Geneva World Conference on Church and Society when, in outlining recent developments in Catholic social thinking, Canon Charles Moeller suggested that efforts be co-ordinated. In his response to the paper Professor Roger Mehl exclaimed: 'Canon Moeller is right. The task which faces the Church today is that of rewriting the old treatise *De homine*. . . . It is a task that we can undertake together.' May this common study benefit the churches and through them all mankind. The Consultation on the Theological Issues of Church and Society, which met at St Sergius' Monastery, Zagorsk, USSR in March 1968 with representatives of the World Council constituency (including the Russian Orthodox Church) and Roman Catholicism expressed this hope in one of its memoranda: 'The nature of the Church and its unity can be understood afresh only if we begin to understand afresh this double relationship between Christ and the human and Christ and his people.'[19]

NOTES

1. The *Decree on Ecumenism* declares: 'Co-operation among all Christians vividly expresses that bond which already unites them and it sets in clearer relief the features of Christ the Servant. Such co-operation, which has already begun in many countries, should be ever increasingly developed, particularly in regions where social and technological evolution is taking place. It should contribute to a just appreciation of the dignity of the human person, the promotion of the blessings of peace, the application of gospel principles to social life and the advancement of the arts and sciences in a Christian spirit. Christians should also work together in the use of every possible means to relieve the afflictions of our times, such as famine and natural disasters, illiteracy and poverty, lack of housing and the unequal distribution of wealth. Through such co-operation, all believers in Christ are better able to learn easily how they can understand each other better and esteem each other more, and how the road to the unity of Christians may be made smooth' (par. 12). Later, speaking of the members of the non-Roman churches of the West, the Decree notes that their 'active faith [in Christ] has produced many organizations for the relief of spiritual and bodily distress, the education of youth, the advancement of humane social conditions and the promotion of peace throughout the world' (par. 23).

2. The first was held in Geneva, 28–31 March 1965, the second at Pinner, near London, 18–21 February 1966. A detailed and very useful account of them is in *Study Encounter*, vol. II, pp. 75–103.

3. Significantly, it was in commenting on a symposium on the revolutionary situation in Latin America in the 'Letters to the Editor' column of *America* that Father Georges Jarlot, S.J., for long a theoretician and historian of Catholic social thought at the Gregorian University, Rome, acknowledged that 'the Church's social doctrine, prior to the Council, inevitably was European and, even, like Pope John's two encyclicals, Italian' (*America*, vol. 119, 17 August 1968, p. 86). More brutal is the indictment of Professor Philipp Herder-Dorneich, Dean of Studies at the University of Cologne, of the earlier Catholic approach to social problems; he finds it fatally abstract, rigid and shaped by

a small group of men of limited experience. 'The corollaries and deductions, with all their subtleties, have been relegated to the archives of history. . . . The classical period of Catholic [social] doctrine abruptly ended with the death of Pius XII. The brains trust upon which he had depended and in which German Jesuits played an important role, was relegated to the background.' 'How Can the Church Provide Guidelines in Social Ethics?' *The Social Message of the Gospels* (being volume 35 of the *Concilium* series), 1968, pp. 82 f.

4. SCM Press, London, and Doubleday, New York, 1961.

5. Was it the greater participation of lay specialists in the Council's activities that turned its attention earlier to the problems of developing countries? Was it the Council's historic association with the missionary movement which broadened its concern? Was it a desire to be truly 'ecumenical', to extend its vision – and membership – to 'the whole inhabited world' that supplies the explanation? Not to be minimized is the influence of the General Secretary, Dr W. A. Visser 't Hooft. A speaker at the 1966 Geneva Conference remarked that even when, as a young man, Visser 't Hooft was Secretary of the World Student Christian Federation, his ready sympathy for any visitor of colour, especially one wearing a beard, was pronounced.

6. An indication of the inevitably hurried editorial task is found in the Hon. Gordon S. Cowan's 'Personal Comment on the Work of the Section on World Economic and Social Development': 'The subsection reports were considered in detail at several plenary sessions of the section and a section report was then prepared by a drafting committee composed of the officers of the section and the chairman of each sub-section or some person named by him. This section report was approved in principle by the section and again remitted to the officers of the section with instructions to shorten the report to meet the requirements of space and to include suggestions made at section meetings' (*Uppsala Speaks*, p. 56). At a subsequent plenary meeting the Assembly approved 'the substance of the Report of Section III', commending it to the churches for study and appropriate action (*Ibid.*, p. 44).

7. The structure of the Constitution indicates its scope. A sociological excursus on the situation of men in the modern world is followed by successive chapters analysing the nature of man, his social involvements and the proper role of the church in society. This primarily theological Part I serves as the basis for a Part II of equal length where 'a number of particularly urgent needs characterizing the present age' – marriage, culture, politics, economic affairs, peace, etc. – are assessed 'in the light of the gospel and of human experience'.

8. *Populorum Progressio* (*PP*), par. 66.

9. See his lecture 'Poverty is Violence: Exploitation of the Third World', delivered in London, 4 April 1969 and published in *New Blackfriars*, vol. 50, June, 1969, pp. 491–7.

10. *The United Nations Development Decade at Mid-point*, United Nations, A. 500/91, 1965, p. 9.

11. An abbreviated form of Dr Parmar's paper appears in *Uppsala Speaks*, pp. 41–43.

12. 'How to Stay the Richest Country in the World', *Commonweal*, XC, 4 April 1969, p. 67. Professor Weaver is chairman of the Department of Economics at The American University in Washington, D.C.

13. In Britain the Catholic Institute for International Relations recently arranged a public meeting in the House of Commons committee room, spon-

sored and attended by four prominent MPs, two Conservatives and two from the Labour Party, to discuss foreign aid and the means of increasing it. 'All four agreed that while the majority of MPs were well-disposed to overseas aid, the attainment of the target of 1 per cent of GNP was subject to the scale of political priorities which operates in the day-to-day running of a government' (*The Tablet*, 21 June 1969, p. 630). High among the priorities for England must be the maintenance of a balance of payments. The implications of the international monetary system might be fruitfully examined in ecumenical discussion on international trade.

14. *New York Times*, 3 June 1969, p. 8. Not to be discounted as a reason, of course, is a general disenchantment on the part of the donor nations as expressed by Robert McNamara, president of the World Bank, addressing the board of governors in September 1968: 'While the requirements for assistance were never higher, the will to provide it was never lower. And the disenchantment of the rich with the future of development aid was fed by performance deficiencies of many of the poorer nations. Blatant mismanagement of economies, diversion of scarce resources to wars of nationalism, perpetuation of discriminatory systems of social organization and income distribution have been all too common.'

15. Cf. *Notes et Etudes Documentaires* 9 juin 1969; also UN Doc.A/7406, Dec. 14/66.

16. *Uppsala Speaks*, p. 43.

17. *Ibid.*, p. 26.

18. *Uppsala Official Report*, p. 317.

19. *Study Encounter*, vol. IV, no. 2, 1968, p. 78.

4

Lay Reflections on Church Social Documents

HENDRIK M. DE LANGE

1 *Introduction and Criteria*

The object of this contribution is to describe how a layman, in this case a layman-economist, reacts to the contents of church documents on development. He is likely to have such questions in his mind as 'Can I gather anything from them that will deepen my own insight? Do the documents throw a new or a different light upon reality? Will their contents have an inspiring effect and will I therefore obtain some encouragement from them?' There will constantly pass through his mind not only the question as to the relevance of these documents, but also the question as to their necessity, and the further question how much more such documents will mean to him than those of secular institutions.

Before formulating replies to these and other questions I would like to state clearly what criteria I apply in this matter. I expect from church documents on socio-economic problems:

1. A balanced view of the nature and possibilities of man, i.e. a clear pronouncement concerning their anthropological foundations.

2. A good analysis of the problems.

3. A statement of the next steps to be taken towards betterment of the existing situation. Of course in the background there will then be a somewhat more distant goal, usually indicated in more general terms.

In my opinion these three criteria have everything to do with biblical thinking on mankind and society. This is, of course, expressed quite clearly in the first point. The Bible is practically always concerned with people, their relations with God and their relations with each other. Nevertheless, there is not agreement among Christians about human nature and the oneness of mankind. This is one of the reasons for the passing of the resolution in the Assembly at Uppsala to request the World Council to embark upon a study of 'the Humanum'.

Why do I so expressly make the demand (see 1) for well-balanced thinking on anthropological questions in the documents? What do I mean by 'balanced'? In theological manuals we find a vast variety of anthropological thinking, a variety which is so extensive that one sometimes begins to doubt, certainly in one's capacity as layman, whether it is all in keeping with biblical data. Biased attitudes and either pessimistic or optimistic thinking should be avoided, but what is so remarkable is that the whole range of thought, from extremely pessimistic to excessively optimistic, is to be found among Christians. We should at any rate think *hopefully* about man. (This implies that a certain latitude is allowed for creativeness.) Nevertheless those who are on the border-line of political decisions or who are responsible for preparing these decisions (both in the sense of public opinion and in the sense of policy-making) cannot afford to have too pessimistic or too optimistic a vision of man. Christians know very well (I quote some sentences from the Amsterdam 1948 Report) that 'changes of particular systems do not bring unqualified good, but fresh evils'; yet Christians ought also to know that their faith leaves no room for despair, 'being based on the fact that the Kingdom of God is firmly established in Christ and will come by God's act despite all human failure'.[1] Biblical thinking is also concerned with the criterion of clear analysis. Loving God with one's mind means searching for such a definition of reality that no elements of truth are obscured for any reason whatsoever. One may have some confidence in the power of clear analysis to remove the mask. The facts themselves may prove convincing, and the clear presentation of such facts as may remain concealed from others can be very helpful, at any rate in personal talks and in the development of opinion-forming in small groups. Social problems can only be solved through the channels of competency and study. Knowledge of facts is of course indispensable, but there are many cases where such knowledge still does not suffice to bring about a complete change in a person's attitude, or to call forth a change in the course of action so far pursued (for instance the course of action of a group or of a nation). Judgments are not always governed by facts, and taking cognizance of the facts through the channel of opinion-forming certainly does not always result at once in correct political action. Nevertheless, that which is not agreeable to us either as individuals or as a group, or as a nation, must not be omitted or intentionally presented in an incomplete manner. This is not an attempt to rescue the concept of objectivity,

D

since every analysis will to a certain extent be deficient and subjective. It will be so because of our inability to see everything, and our inability to see everything in its correct relationships. But by the use of the verb 'see' I wish to show that I do expect something worth while from church documents on political and socio-economic problems. Indeed biblical thinking – and this of course must always find its reflex in church documents! – is very concrete and offers no possibilities of escape into a nebulous, non-existent reality or to something that may be denoted by a pious term such as 'Heaven'. The essence of the Christian faith is that human relations are concerned with a God who calls us to account as to whether we have seen to this.

Biblical thinking always leads us into matters that lie *before* us. In other words: Where do we find situations in which peace and justice are an issue? What is going on? The answer to these questions brings us to our third point, for to indicate the next steps is always a matter of pointing to a specific reality, which is never a final reality. Therefore we should speak hopefully about man. If all is well, the formulation of the next steps will have something to do with what is being traced out as God's plans with the world. It is a bold venture, but we cannot escape it.

Formulating next steps is different from making a blue-print, a thing that the ecumenical movement has never been induced to undertake. Such a thing would be too much like a cut-and-dried plan. It would violate the plurality of situations in which we are placed. Or it would be too detailed and hence become too static. 'The *process* is more significant than a blue-print of exactly where we hope society will go.'[2]

This brief exposition of the criteria by which the documents and reports will be judged, may be summarized in the concise but, I think, still fruitful definition of *the responsible society* by the Amsterdam Assembly:

Freedom is the freedom of men who acknowledge responsibility to justice and public order, and in which those who hold public authority or economic power are responsible for its exercise to God and the people whose welfare is affected by it.

This means that we have in mind not a society which is an aim in itself, but a society which is so constituted that all men can experience the possibility of giving God and their fellow-men the answer that links up fully with their innermost being and destiny. To put it positively: we have in mind a society in which the whole and the parts feel responsible for the welfare of every member, a society in which all men can live as responsible beings and not be a mere object either of other men or of structures.

The criticism of this concept as 'a criterion by which we judge all existing social orders and at the same time a standard to guide us in the specific choices we have to make'[3] has never convinced me. I believe that the idea of the responsible society is still highly serviceable. It is obvious that the whole idea of *development* very closely links up with it. This pivotal concept, borrowed from international economic policy, has a great variety of aspects which cannot be enumerated here. Suffice it to make a few observations on its connection with a responsible society. Development aims at the acquisition of freedom, and particularly at the third freedom about which Franklin Delano Roosevelt spoke in his address to Congress on 6 January 1941. This third freedom is freedom from want. It is probable that the terms used by Roosevelt were influential in marking the present period – viewed from the standpoint of poorer countries – as the period of rising expectations. The proclamation of the Universal Declaration of Human Rights was also a contributory factor, as well as the launching of the idea of Development Decades. The Western countries have aroused expectations, but they have omitted to draw the political and economic consequences from the principles they enunciated. They have so far neglected to create the conditions for realization of the said freedom for the peoples of the third world. For millions of people the acquisition of this freedom is at the same time the condition for knowing that they are responsible for justice and public order. 'Development is an instrumental value, a means to the end of improving the quality of human life.'[4]

Vice versa, those who possess economic power, that is, the nations of the Northern hemisphere, owe responsibility to God and to the peoples of the third world for the use of this power. We are very far removed from a responsible world society and, as already stated, we shall have to investigate whether the church documents give sufficiently strong urgings towards this goal.

The realization of *international* social justice is now the primary task and responsibility of man. To speak of this responsibility as being the specific response to God's commands in the present epoch is only permissible if we acknowledge that man is fundamentally capable of responding to God. Moreover the organization of international society has to be such that every man and every nation is given the opportunity to respond to God, his fellow-men and other nations in a manner that is in complete harmony with his being and his destiny.

Before we proceed to respond in detail to the charge entrusted to us I will make a preliminary remark. It is of great importance to note that in church documents issued during the last few years on political and social matters the full stress is laid on the problem of the relation between rich and poor countries. If we ask ourselves where God is working we have indeed an ever-increasing measure of certainty that this is the case in those regions which (to use a somewhat peculiar Western terminology) are called the new nations and the new states; in brief the world of the poor. Here is revealed a new aspect of the freedom movement. The churches united in the World Council, along with the Roman Catholic Church, have acknowledged in their thinking on political and social problems that priority should be granted to the problems of the relations between rich and poor countries, as they have discovered that among the peoples of Asia, Africa and Latin America there is human suffering beyond all conception. If we ask ourselves what God's intention is, then we reply: that we should co-operate with him in putting an end to this suffering.

Since the cause and continuance of such suffering is due to a political and economic structure for the maintenance of which the people of the Northern hemisphere are responsible, it is their bounden duty to change this structure. So we shall have to investigate whether a sufficiently clear analysis of these international structures is put forward in the church documents, and whether these documents give a sufficiently concrete formulation of the steps that should be taken to alter these structures. Against the background of this preliminary remark I refer to the criticism that has been expressed of the term 'responsible society'. Objections have been made to this because for one thing the churches and the Christians of the rich countries have been too much inclined to adopt a waiting attitude. They have not sufficiently realized the urgency of the problems. What is wanted, say these critics, is a new strategy which brings a powerful pressure, maybe a violent pressure, to bear upon the social structures. Furthermore, the critics point out that in practice the fact of indicating the next steps will in many cases only lead to the adoption of a few minor changes in society. The solving of the problem of world poverty calls rather for radical changes.

(*a*) in the developing countries;

(*b*) in the international political and economic structures; and hence

(*c*) in the political and economic structure of the rich countries.

I can accept the major part of this criticism without having the feeling that I am thereby denying the concept of the responsible society. But the advocates of the idea of the responsible society have to reflect upon the *strategy* that will lead to the carrying out of the 'next steps' which they have planned. Therefore, it is not so much that their method is at fault, but that it is incomplete. It is impossible to maintain that, for instance, the World Conference on Church and Society (Geneva, 1966) confined itself to indicating a few minor changes in the structure of society. The trouble is that hardly any start has been made in carrying out these proposals. The failure of the World Conference on Trade, Aid and Development (New Delhi, 1968) is still weighing heavily upon us.

The fact of not having sufficiently realized the importance of strategy has resulted in an increasingly wide gap being created between the (top) management of the churches and the great multitude of Christians. This danger was, in my opinion, clearly discerned at the conferences at Beirut and Uppsala. I shall return to it later.

The advocates of a theology of drastic or even revolutionary change and those of the responsible society may differ as regards willingness to set the strategy of 'violence' against the existing violence of the present-day structure. Some may have their eyes insufficiently open to the menace of dehumanization in the conscious use of violence, others to the violence that is incorporated in the present structures. I cannot escape from this dilemma, though I would advocate that we should always adhere to the principle that Christians must under all circumstances stand surety for making humanity a reality. We must not think too lightly of the possibilities of making a revolution a just one. The acceptance, or even the starting of revolutionary processes fraught with violence, may be a phase in the idea of the responsible society, but in my opinion a perilous phase. History gives us no reason to view such phases through rose-coloured spectacles. We must try to prevent them by adopting other courses in good time. I admit that – at any rate in some parts of the world – it looks as if such phases cannot be avoided. In brief, my attitude amounts to the formulation that is to be found in the statement of the Zagorsk Consultation:

Violence remains a failure in the human capacity to manage evolution through word and persuasion, and is a source of destruction, cruelty and bitterness. Theology should help people to recognize the provisional character of violence even when it is considered necessary. Christian theology warns us against absolutizing either the *status quo* or the revolution.[5]

I think that the concept of the responsible society is a serviceable one even in discussions of the problems of rich and poor countries. We should of course – in accordance with the proposal of Dr Visser 't Hooft (in his speech during the Geneva Conference) – internationalize this concept. One might also say: we should introduce it into new contexts. I hope to be able to show in greater detail that the Geneva Conference has to a large extent succeeded in meeting this requirement. In the analysis of the church documents we shall therefore have to see whether this has been done in sufficient measure.

Lastly, I would observe that advocacy of revolution as a method is by no means an alternative to the idea of the responsible society, neither does it throw any new light upon the question of what it is to be a human being. In so far as they have expressed themselves upon the nature of the human the utterances of these advocates seem rather naïve to me. They are too apt to think that they can begin with a clean slate. The human being emerging from a revolution does not differ fundamentally from the human being that existed before the revolution.

II *Thinking about Man*

In *Gaudium et Spes* we find scattered throughout the text a large number of pronouncements about mankind. I will confine myself to a few outstanding passages, viz. paragraphs 10, 16, 17, 34, 35, and write a few words of comment on each.

10. The truth is that the imbalances under which the modern world labors are linked with that more basic imbalance rooted in the heart of man. For in man himself many elements wrestle with one another. [With a reference to Rom. 7.14 ff. it is stated:] Man often does what he would not and fails to do what he would. [At the close of this paragraph the Constitution poses some questions, culminating in the question:] What can man offer to society, what can he expect from it?

16. In the depths of his conscience, man detects a law which he does not impose upon himself, but which holds him to obedience. Always summoning him to love good and avoid evil, the voice of conscience can when necessary speak in his heart more specifically: do this, shun that. For man has in his heart a law written by God. To obey it is the very dignity of man: according to it he will be judged. Conscience is the most secret core and sanctuary of a man. There he is alone with God, whose voice echoes in his depths. In a wonderful manner conscience reveals that law which is fulfilled by love of God and neighbor. In fidelity to conscience Christians are joined with the rest of men in the search for truth, and for the genuine solution to the numerous problems which arise in the life of individuals and from social relationships. Hence the more that a correct conscience holds sway, the more persons and groups turn aside from blind choice and strive to be guided by objective norms of morality. Conscience frequently errs from invincible ignorance without losing its dignity. The same cannot be said of a man who cares but little for truth and goodness, or of a conscience which by degrees grows practically sightless as a result of habitual sin.

17. Hence man's dignity demands that he acts according to a knowing and free choice. Such a choice is personally motivated and prompted from within. It does not result from blind internal impulse nor from mere external pressure.

Man achieves such dignity when, emancipating himself from all captivity to passion, he pursues his goal in a spontaneous choice of what is good, and procures for himself, through effective and skillful action, apt means to that end. Since man's freedom has been damaged by sin, only by the help of

God's grace can he bring such a relationship with God into full flower. Before the judgment seat of God each man must render an account of his own life, whether he has done good or evil.

The words used in the last paragraph make a rather individualistic impression, but in paragraph 25 there is an important addition which is worded as follows:

Man's social nature makes it evident that the progress of the human person and the advance of society itself hinge on each other. For the beginning, the subject and the goal of all social institutions is and must be the human person, which for its part and by its very nature stands completely in need of social life.

In the chapter 'Man's activity throughout the world' there are again important observations on the meaning of man.

34. Far from thinking that works produced by man's own talent and energy are in opposition to God's power, and that the rational creature exists as a kind of rival to the Creator, Christians are convinced that the triumphs of the human race are a sign of God's greatness and the flowering of His own mysterious design. For the greater man's power becomes, the farther his individual and community responsibility extends.

35. Just as human activity proceeds from man, so it is ordered toward man. For when a man works he not only alters things and society, he develops himself as well. He learns much, he cultivates his resources, he goes outside of himself and beyond himself. Rightly understood, this kind of growth is of greater value than any external riches which can be garnered. A man is more precious for what he is than for what he has. Similarly, all that men do to obtain greater justice, wider brotherhood, and a more humane ordering of social relationships has greater worth than technical advances. For these advances can supply the material for human progress, but of themselves alone they can never actually bring it about.

It is undoubtedly true that the Bible witness speaks of an imbalance in man. It does not follow from the fact of knowing good that one possesses the power to do it. All this means that the expression 'men of good will' – which has found some currency in recent years in Roman Catholic circles – is dubious. It was not for nothing that Martin Luther King, in his well-known letter from prison in Birmingham, Alabama, wrote about the appalling silence of the 'good'. He added to it:

We must learn to realize that human progress never moves forward on the wheels of inevitability. It comes as a result of untiring efforts and persistent works of those people who are willing to be God's co-workers and without this hard work time itself is an ally of the forces of social stagnation.

Human life – and not only personal life, but also social life – is menaced by all this and it is a good thing to be warned against it. All experience points to the fact that we cannot maintain that there is a law which man does not impose upon himself but which holds him to obedience, let alone assert that there is a law always summoning him to love good and to avoid evil. Is it really in keeping with the biblical vision and with the reality of our daily experience to state that man has in his heart a law written by God? This latter does, it is true, link up with the concept of the godlike seed which is also mentioned once in the Constitution (*GS*, par. 3). The biblical data for this are scanty and the data of human history point in a different direction. Is not the Bible far more concerned with the dynamic power inherent in the definite announcement of the word of God in a concrete situation? Even then man obviously has great power for *dis*obedience and inertia. Paul knew all about this. In the letter to the Ephesians he speaks of 'grieving the Holy Spirit of God' (Eph. 4.30), and in the first letter to the Thessalonians he used the words 'Do not quench the Spirit' (I Thess. 5.19).

Therefore, I think it is much better not to say 'Man has in his heart a law written by God.' This may be a condition, but is certainly not a guarantee, of acting rightly. At most we may say that man is responsible for performing such actions as God expects from him. Man may indeed know quite well what is right, which still does not imply that he is willing to do what is right or even that he is able to do it. In the latter case he may be obstructed, for instance, by lack of will-power and perseverance; but possibly also by the structure of society itself. The static character of this picture of the human being means that there is insufficient expression of the need for a constantly renewed appeal to the creative faculties of man. The Bible shows us man as a creature who is again and again addressed by God. God creates man, not merely by making him as he makes the animals, but by speaking to him. It is from this vision that the God-given commission to uphold creation emerges. God summons man to take part in his creative work and he counts upon man's co-operation.

As already observed, the text of paragraph 17 gives an individualistic impression. Has it been sufficiently considered that there can in many cases be no question whatsoever of a knowing and free choice, since the external conditions for this experience of freedom have not been realized? We have here an utterance of a certain naïvety which suggests that man, working hard upon himself, is capable of planning himself. As if everyone has this under his own control! Many people, maybe very many people, are utterly dependent upon some other person or group or the whole of society. All this is indeed discussed briefly in paragraph 35, but the freedom concept is still insufficiently worked out. This freedom concept is the pivotal point today. People nowadays are finding it less and less possible to exercise their personal liberty without taking account of their responsibility to society as a whole. Being religious means that one realizes that the salvation of man cannot be divorced from the salvation of the world.

The encyclical letter *Populorum Progressio* speaks sober language in its pronouncements on man. The most important text is found in paragraph 15:

In the design of God, every man is called upon to develop and fulfil him-self, for every life is a vocation. At birth, everyone is granted, in germ, a set of aptitudes and qualities for him to bring to fruition. Their coming to maturity, which will be the result of education received from the environment and personal efforts, will allow each man to direct himself towards the destiny intended for him by his Creator. Endowed with intelligence and freedom, he is responsible for his fulfilment as he is for his salvation. He is aided, or sometimes impeded, by those who educate him and those with whom he lives, but each one remains, whatever be these influences affecting him, the principal agent of his own success or failure. By the unaided effort of his own intelligence and his will, each man can grow in humanity, can enhance his personal worth, can become more a person.

It seems to me that in this concise text a dynamic and creative vision of being human is portrayed. Speaking about the calling and destiny of every person and pointing to one's own responsibility (on which point the implicit quotation of Ezek. 18 is enlightening) are basic points for well-balanced anthropological thinking.

When the encyclical letter uses the words 'Everyone is granted, in germ, a set of aptitudes and qualities for him to bring to fruition', there should be a reminder that these aptitudes and qualities are not always directed positively. There is no purely natural goodness which will come to maturity in a process of education received from environ-ment, and personal efforts. Neither is man endowed only with intel-ligence and freedom. Then again the last sentence of the paragraph is incomplete. It is not intelligence and will that are decisive for growth in humanity.

The *Geneva* Report (we confine ourselves to the text of Section I) speaks very soberly about 'the human', constantly emphasizing that 'human purposes' must be served. By way of illustration we quote the following from paragraph 2. 'This means that Christian theology must expound and defend the understanding of the "human" as a criterion for judging economic and social change.'

In paragraph 50, too, there is an important text for our purpose which we quote in full:

For the Christian the basic impulse for constructive social change, for economic and social justice, is not a human product, but is the work of the Spirit of God. The Bible itself is in part a record of the changes brought about in human life as men responded to the call of God. In the law and the prophets, God laid upon man a solemn duty to care for his brother, a duty next to and inseparable from his duty to God himself. Above all in Jesus Christ the Church sees One who identified himself with the needs of man, material as well as spiritual, and who heals and transforms human life. As the Church preaches and teaches the good news that Christ lived, died and lives again that man may live in proper relation to God and to his neighbour it creates not only the most basic motivation for social change, but also the most enduring. It is tragically true that all too often churches have failed to live up to the fullness of their own Gospel, have been silent in the face of oppression, or have not heard the cries of those condemned to poverty and misery. But God's Spirit acts to arouse his Church, and to renew its faithfulness and obedience. It is to such faithfulness and obedience that he now calls us.

Lastly, we draw attention to paragraph 145.

In all countries, especially those which are or are becoming prosperous and highly organised, the churches should help to keep alive a deep concern for the human. The fulfilment of this task requires an understanding of technical and economic realities combined with sustained spiritual vigilance. In stressing the criterion of the human, we are aware that there is not full theological agreement on the meaning of our humanity in Christ, and the World Council of Churches could usefully invite a group of theologians and social scientists to pursue this question.

Within the World Council of Churches there is a strongly-felt need to arrive at greater clarity regarding the whole concept of 'human'. Our generation is again being challenged in a new manner to search biblical data and to set them against modern technological, political, economic and cultural data. As already stated, a study of this kind was decided upon at Uppsala. In Holland we are carrying out an experiment in this direction. The Christian Broadcasting Company has invited a group of theologians and of social scientists to prepare a series of lectures in which historical and biblical data will be reviewed. Social scientists have been asked to formulate their anthropological presuppositions. Before lecturing there has been a series of group discussions. The text of the lectures will be published in English and will be placed at the disposal of the World Council of Churches and the co-ordinator of the 'Humanum' studies.

The uncertainty as to the criteria for human actions is an obvious reason why the Geneva Report is worded in comparatively sober terms. It refers to embodying 'the belief that Jesus Christ is the disclosure to us of both true God and true Man', but does not elaborate the point. This may possibly also be connected with the fact that 'to seek to realize further possibilities of human life' is an exceedingly extensive and patient work concerning which, owing to the great diversity of human situations, one cannot speak in too detailed a manner. It is nevertheless certain that in order to obtain clear knowledge as to how we should act in order to preserve and extend the human element we shall need more specialized studies.[6]

In the Statement as well as in the Report of the Beirut Conference 1968 there are observations concerning the problem of man.

In the Statement (published with the Report) reasons are mentioned for the particular concern of the Christian community when contemplating world poverty:

Christians are totally committed to the unity and equality of all mankind under the headship of Christ, the Son of Man, and hence to unity and justice in the world society in which the human family lives. They believe in man's God-given responsibility to use his resources, to recreate and renew the face of the earth.

These basic points are further detailed in the *Beirut* Report. In paragraphs 2, 6, 7, 8, 10 and 12 the vision is fully expressed. The first sentence of par. 2 reads: 'God speaks to us in the demands of our fellow-men for bread, work, health, education – in short, for human dignity and justice.' We quote further:

6. We know the reality of sin and the depth of its hold on human beings, and on our political and economic structures; but we do not despair in spite of the resistance of men and structures, with all their delays and frustrations, because we know that it is God's will, and that in Christ there is forgiveness and a chance to begin anew every day, step by step. God wants the world to develop and he conquers and will conquer sin.

7. The hope of development is the human fundamental hope based on the fact of man as he is and will be, as he has been made and is challenged to grow, God working in him.

8. Men are made to be dynamic, forward-looking, imaginative, adventurous, creative. Our task in the twentieth century – the task of all men – is so to develop and share the riches of the world together that all men may benefit and come to their full human stature. True human development is the aim; economic and social development is a necessary part of human development. What we search for is the enrichment of the human spirit at all levels – in ourselves as in others.

10. Our standard is human dignity, human opportunity, human freedom, in short the fully human. We do not claim to know all that is in man, or that is involved in the fully human. We know that we have to learn from experts in all fields of knowledge, and to work with them. But we press for human development (and as part of this, economic and social development), because we believe that man's future is open – and that the future of many men should – and could – be more open than it is at present.

12. Why do we have this particular concern with men as men? With all men we are moved by our developing sense of human solidarity, and we believe that men have rights. Christians base their concern also on the faith that God in creation made men to be masters of the world.

These texts not only contain basic points for a balanced anthropology, but they provide an initial draft for an elaboration which is very promising, and with which Christians of different disciplines may perform very fruitful work.

At the beginning of the discussions in *Uppsala*, Section III, a number of participants made a request to the Chairman not to draw up an independent report. They were of opinion that the Beirut Report stated what had to be stated. They wished to confine the talks to discussing a plan of action for implementing the Beirut Report. The reader will notice that this Report has had a great influence upon the Uppsala Report. The contribution of Uppsala itself is mainly in its fifth chapter (paras. 29–48), to which we shall refer later. In the Uppsala Report there is comparatively little in the way of anthropological foundations.

3. Christians who know from their scriptures that all men are created by God in his image and that Christ died for all, should be in the forefront of the battle to overcome a provincial, narrow sense of solidarity and to create a sense of participation in a world-wide responsible society with justice for all.

20. The central issue in development is the criteria of the human.

III   *Analysis*

I restrict the searching of the documents with reference to my second point, viz. effective analysis, to the question of international social justice, though in *Gaudium et Spes* and the Geneva Report there are many other highly interesting problems under discussion. An analysis should contain more than merely a statement of reality. To be correct it should also give an indication of the forces which determine this reality and decide its course. Ecclesiastical history of the twentieth century has produced a document which I regard in all respects as superior and which may still serve as a pattern. I mean the Report of the Conference on Church, Community and State (Oxford, 1937).[7] From the recent documents we will now collect the respective analytical paragraphs and comment upon them.

Gaudium et Spes

63. We are at a moment in history when the development of economic life could diminish social inequalities if that development were guided and coordinated in a reasonable and human way. Yet all too often it serves only to intensify the inequalities. In some places it even results in a decline in the social status of the weak and in contempt for the poor.

While an enormous mass of people still lack the absolute necessities of life, some, even in less advanced countries, live sumptuously or squander wealth. Luxury and misery rub shoulders. While the few enjoy very great freedom of choice, the many are deprived of almost all possibility of acting on their own initiative and responsibility, and often subsist in living and working conditions unworthy of human beings.

A similar lack of economic and social balance is to be noted between agriculture, industry, and the services, and also between different parts of one and the same country. The contrast between the economically more advanced countries and other countries is becoming more serious day by day, and the very peace of the world can be jeopardized in consequence.

69. The right to have a share of earthly goods sufficient for oneself and one's family belongs to everyone. The Fathers and Doctors of the Church held this view, teaching that men are obliged to come to the relief of the poor, and to do so not merely out of their superfluous goods. If a person is in extreme necessity, he has the right to take from the riches of others what he himself needs. Since there are so many people in this world afflicted with hunger, this sacred Council urges all, both individuals and governments, to remember the saying of the Fathers: 'Feed the man dying of hunger, because if you have not fed him you have killed him.' According to their ability, let all individuals and governments undertake a genuine sharing of their goods. Let them use these goods especially to provide individuals and nations with the means for helping and developing themselves. In economically less advanced societies, it is not rare for the communal purpose of earthly goods to be partially satisfied through the customs and traditions proper to a community. By such means the absolute essentials are furnished to each member. If, however, customs cannot answer the new needs of this age, an effort must be made to avoid regarding them as altogether unchangeable.

85. The development of any nation depends on human and financial assistance. Through education and professional formation, the citizens of each nation should be prepared to shoulder the various offices of economic and social life. Such preparation needs the help of foreign experts. When they render assistance, these experts should do so not in a lordly fashion, but as helpers and co-workers. The developing nations will be unable to procure the necessary material assistance unless the practices of the modern business world undergo a profound change. Additional help should be offered by advanced nations, in the form of either grants or investments.

The harvest here is not great. A specific difficulty which occurs from time to time in Roman Catholic writings is that a description of an ideal state of affairs is given, and the reader is left reflecting that the reality is certainly very far removed from it. Paragraph 69 is a very good example of this. If it is true that the right to have a share of earthly goods sufficient for oneself and one's family belongs to everyone, then one cannot be content with recording the fact that the Fathers of the church have always taught this. On the contrary one must go on to say that people have not paid much heed to these teachings. The reality is in fact very far removed from this goal. An analysis of the forces that are responsible for this would therefore be appropriate but it does not appear in the Constitution.

In what way can the economic and political structures be changed so as to make it possible for individuals and governments to effect a genuine sharing of the goods, and to enable them to use these goods especially to provide individuals and nations with the means for helping and developing themselves? If it is recorded in paragraph 63 that an enormous mass of people lack the absolute necessities of life while some people, even in less advanced countries, live sumptuously or squander wealth, then we cannot be satisfied with merely recording these facts. We must ask ourselves in this case what the causes of this situation are, and what changes can be made for its amendment. Again paragraph 85 is very deficient. Hardly a word is said about the building up of the international economic structure. Another glaring deficiency is that nothing whatsoever is said about the failure of the first World Conference on Trade, Aid and Development which ended so shamefully in 1964. Henri de Riedmatten writes in his essay, 'Die Entwicklung als Weltproblem', that a passage in paragraph 86 contains an encouragement for UNCTAD, viz.:

> Let adequate organizations be established for furthering and harmonizing international trade, especially with respect to the less advanced countries, and for restraining the deficiencies caused by an excessive disproportion in the power possessed by various nations.[8]

This reflection, however, is indeed a modest one and shows little concreteness.

What do we find in the way of analytical observations in *Populorum Progressio*? With regard to the development problem, the main principle of social ethics is splendidly formulated. The quotation from St Ambrose about the resources of the world being given for the common good of all (see par. 23) is striking, but it is not followed by the necessary analysis for seeing how this principle can be made flesh. The text of paragraphs 47, 49, 54 and 57 does give indications of the direction in which the link-up point for action may be found:

47. Is each one. . . prepared to pay higher taxes so that the public authorities can intensify their efforts in favour of development?

Is he ready to pay a higher price for imported goods so that the producer may be more justly rewarded?

49. We must repeat once more that the superfluous wealth of rich countries should be placed at the service of poor nations.

54. Development countries will thus no longer risk being overwhelmed by debts whose repayment swallows up the greater part of their gains. Rates of interest and time for repayment of the loan could be so arranged as not to be too great a burden on either party, taking into account free gifts, interest free or low-interest loans and the time needed for liquidating the debts.

57. Raw materials produced by underdeveloped countries are subject to wide and sudden fluctuations in price, a state of affairs far removed from the progressively increasing value of industrial products.

The statements in paragraph 23 concerning the subordination of the rights of property to the common good are decisive for our problem, as is the remark in paragraph 49 that the continued greed of the rich 'will certainly call down upon them the judgment of God and the wrath of the poor'. But it is necessary to analyse:

(*a*) why the poor man exists and continues to exist;

(*b*) in what way his position can be remedied;

(*c*) what steps have already been taken in this direction and what effects these have had so far.

All this might link up with the condemnation of economic liberalism (par. 26). Merely to talk about the international imperialism of money does not get us very far. In the leading Western countries the evils of liberal capitalism (social and economic insecurity and instability, unemployment, concentration of economic and financial power), have been checked by intervention at the national level. But it is evident that these evils can still continue without obstruction in the *international* economic structures. Within national frontiers the governments concerned have accepted their responsibility by conducting a deliberate economic and social policy. In international relations there is no such political authority. This is a deficiency to which the Encyclical does not draw attention.

The *Geneva* Report is characterized by a far-reaching analysis of all the problems relating to development. It is utterly impossible to quote this text in its entirety. A very striking point in Chapter III of the Report (paras. 45 to 100 inclusive) is that an analysis is given of the developing countries themselves. I cannot but recommend the reader to take note personally of this statement drawn up mainly by the representatives of the poor countries themselves during the conference.

Paragraphs 102 to 114 inclusive are an analysis of World Economic Relations. It examines the structure of international economic co-operation and exposes the causes of the existing disparities between the two parts of the world. This analysis relates to the unfavourable balance of trade, the weak bargaining power of the poor (mostly countries producing raw materials), the systems of tariffs and other preferences which distort the pattern of trade, the transfer of financial resources, and the problem of foreign capital investments. The analysis is excellent and offers a large number of link-up points for concrete action.

In the *Beirut* Report the analysis is less extensive, largely because (unfortunately!) in the spring of 1968 one could still refer to practically every point in the analysis of Geneva, 1966. In this Beirut Report analysis is somewhat interwoven with the recommendations themselves. We find texts in both Chapter II and Chapter III. Particularly paragraphs 10 and 17 of Chapter II ('Obstacles to Development') show briefly but clearly where the shoe pinches. Chapter III, which bears the title 'The Strategy of Development', is a fine example of clear analysis, especially because its language and diction make it fully accessible to a large group of people who wish to take note of the gist of these problems. In this respect Beirut is superior to Geneva.

The *Uppsala* Report of Section III on 'World Economic and Social Development' again links up with the Beirut Report. It is, however, worthy of mention that Uppsala draws attention to the Charter of Algiers drawn up by the poor nations just before the second United Nations Conference on Trade, Aid and Development. This Charter contains an accurate statement of the development situation and of the questions which the poor countries were to ask at the New Delhi Conference. In the matter of analysis, the Uppsala Report gives little that is new after Geneva and Beirut. It would indeed be rather super-fluous to keep on making fresh analyses within such brief periods. Our examination of the five documents from the point of view of clarity of analysis shows that Geneva and Beirut are the best. Are there deficiencies running through all the documents alike? Yes, a critical analysis of our existing economic systems – both the mixed economy of the Western countries and the centrally planned economy of the East European countries – showing how we could reply adequately to the questions of the third world, is not to be found in any of the reports. It might well be a subject for a subsequent joint deliberation of the combined churches. This would enable the already established collec-tive institution SODEPAX to take the initiative. A link-up point for this discussion might be found in the following sentence from *Gaudium et Spes* (par. 86):

They [i.e. the advanced countries] have a very heavy obligation to help the developing peoples in the discharge of the aforementioned responsibilities. If this world-wide collaboration is to be established, certain psychological and material adjustments will be needed among the advanced nations and should be brought about.

iv   *The Next Steps*

Gaudium et Spes contains an important recommendation (par. 82) which deals with the problems of preventing wars:

The establishment of some universal public authority acknowledged as such by all and endowed with effective power to safeguard, on behalf of all, security, regard for justice and respect for rights.

This recommendation is missing in the paragraph on international economic co-operation (par. 86). This is one of the reasons why the whole set of recommendations remains rather vague.

Populorum Progressio has a chapter 'Action to be undertaken' (paragraphs 22–41). On the whole these have well-formulated principles, but the wording is far from a concrete description of political decisions to be taken. Nobody will deny the truth of the statements: 'Development demands bold transformations, innovations that go deep. Urgent reforms should be undertaken without delay' (32), or 'Programmes are necessary in order to encourage, stimulate, coordinate, supplement and integrate the activity of individuals and of intermediary bodies' (33). Nevertheless without any specification of the directions reforms and programmes have to take, people on the frontier remain somewhat empty-handed after reading this part of the Encyclical.

Paragraph 51 contains a very concrete recommendation. The Pope asks for 'the establishment of a great World Fund, to be made up of part of the money spent on arms, to relieve the most destitute of this world'.

In the previous section I came to the conclusion that there were some shortcomings in the analysis of the international economic order. Nevertheless there is a recommendation in paragraph 61 in this field: 'What holds for a national economy or among developed countries is valid also in commercial relations between rich nations and poor nations.' This is exactly the point that makes sense in the trade relations between the two partners. The countries of the European Economic Community think that they could improve their economic situation by abolishing their tariffs. This is what the poor nations are asking and what rich nations till now are refusing.

The *Geneva* Report is very concrete in formulating next steps. There is an excellent distinction made between steps to be taken in the short run and in the long run. Radical proposals dealing with trade and financial problems, with the problem of commodities and with institutional measures, are very well formulated in paragraphs 115–127. We give only one example by quoting paragraphs 115–116 and 127.

115. Economic aid, as it is now being given, is inadequate in both quantity and quality to accomplish the stated aims of both under-developed and developed countries. The situation might be improved by:

116. (*a*) a vast increase in the quantity of development assistance available to the developing countries. The World Bank has recently indicated that the developing countries can use effectively $3 to $4 billion more aid per annum. The developed countries should make continuous efforts to provide this immediately. Much larger national and regional programmes and projects will have to be organized in an efficient way. As seen at present, governmental contributions, not counting military aid, geared to these needs would range from 1 to 2 per cent of the aggregate gross national product of the developed nations.

127. Recognition of the ultimate aim: An international division of labour based on the specific contribution of fully equipped nations that trade with each other as equals.

The *Beirut* Report again is very strong in recommendations of economic and social measures to be taken. Chapter III, 'The Strategy for Development', is a very clear and important example of what I have in mind about the problem of next steps. Now, two years after the conference, the whole programme is still pertinent, alas! It is not unlikely that it will be so for the period of the Second Development Decade.

For Christians it is very important to have a yard-stick to compare the aims and instruments in both the documents. In some respects the Geneva Report is more radical than the Beirut Report, especially in the field of capital transfers. The Beirut Report states:

36. At UNCTAD II, in 1968, the developed nations adopted a target for such transfers of resources (including private investment) of 1 per cent of their GNP. (On this basis for 1966, such transfers would have been over $4,000 million larger than those made.) Even this target is less than the developing countries need and could use productively, and includes private investment, which though very valuable, fluctuates.

37. Hence, the developed countries should be pressed to raise official transfers alone to 1 per cent of GNP as soon as possible and preferably by 1971, and to review this target and increase it as feasible.

Maybe this lower percentage is connected with the growth target of 6 per cent annually of Gross National Product in the developing countries in the next years, mentioned in paragraph 2 of Chapter III in the Beirut Report. The participants of the Geneva Conference had in mind – without mentioning it in the Report – an annual growth target of 6·5 or maybe even 7 per cent. The Beirut Report is a step backwards in my opinion, because an ambitious growth target is needed to stimulate activities in the developing countries as well as in the developed countries.

The *Uppsala* Report has to be read – as mentioned before – in relation to the Beirut Report. It does not repeat the aid target of Geneva, although it sharpens the Beirut statement: 'as a *first* step, to increase annually the percentage of GNP officially transferred as financial resources to developing countries with a *minimum net* amount of 1 per cent *to be reached* by 1971' (par. 38. 2 [b], my italics). Uppsala rightly repeats the recommendation on the international political structure:

Creation of super-national structures to deal with regional and world planning involving the stabilization of the world market; an international taxation system to provide funds for development; increase of multi-lateral aid programmes (par. 18).

Uppsala is strong in the field of recommendations of next steps for what has to be done by Christians and churches. The pastoral and educational task, the service task, the prophetic and critical task and the political task respectively are very well worded. Also paragraph 43, in which the task of the individual Christian is spelled out, is very challenging as it pinpoints personal responsibility.

v *Final Remarks*

Some important items of the whole North–South problem are still lacking in the documents published so far by the churches.[9] I will indicate briefly what problems I have in mind, while expressing the hope that they will receive attention in the near future.

1. I have already stated that it should be ascertained much more precisely how far either the economic order or the economic policy of the Western and Northern countries should be modified in order to satisfy the desires of the poor countries. It is often said that the unconditional acceptance of a consumption society is the greatest obstacle to development. Is it true that a consumption philosophy in both Western and Communist countries is incompatible with concepts like solidarity, co-operation, participation and development? If so, what are the chances of changing this philosophy and what other economic systems are possible?

If one does not wish to modify the economic order one will need to ponder over the economic policy conducted up to the present. In other words, if the present systems are not obstacles, then the question arises: How can we radicalize and, above all, internationalize present economic policies?

2. *Populorum Progressio* says: 'Development cannot be limited to mere growth.' If we take this pronouncement seriously, and I think there is every reason to do so, two very fundamental and related questions arise:

(*a*) Is it possible to be engaged in increasing production with a policy aiming at a balanced distribution and with emphasis upon additional growth of the lowest incomes, and at the same time to be concerned with non-material welfare factors? Neither the Western nor the Communist countries have succeeded in finding satisfactory solutions to this problem. It would therefore seem reasonable to investigate in good time what conditions need to be fulfilled in order to balance these aims fairly.

(*b*) Will the developing countries succeed in overcoming poverty by rapid and effective economic growth without at the same time creating a thoroughly materialistic society in which money motives predominate.[9]

3. The large-scale operation with which the churches in affluent countries are being confronted in the coming decades is Development Education. World citizenship must take shape and form, and in this the churches have an obvious task. Further investigation of the conditions under which such a change of mentality can be effected is an imperative necessity. To end this the secretariat for Development Education of the World Council of Churches should draw up further detailed plans at once, and national churches should devote time and money to their implementation.

NOTES

1. *The First Assembly of the World Council of Churches: the Official Report*, ed. W. A. Visser 't Hooft, SCM Press, London, and Harper and Bros., New York, 1949, pp. 74 f.

2. Richard Dickinson, *Line and Plummet*, World Council of Churches, Geneva, 1968, p. 81.

3. *The Evanston Report*, SCM Press and Harper and Bros., 1954, p. 113.

4. Dickinson, *op. cit.*, p. 94.

5. *Study Encounter*, vol. IV, no. 2, 1968, p. 76.

6. A fine example is *Experiments with Man*, the Report of an ecumenical consultation, ed. Hans-Ruedi Weber, World Council of Churches, Geneva and New York, 1969.

7. *The Churches Survey their Task*, with an Introduction by J. H. Oldham, Allen and Unwin, London, 1937.

8. Henri de Riedmatten, 'Die Entwicklung als Weltproblem', *Oeconomia Humana*, Bachem, Cologne, 1968, p. 368.

9. This essay was completed in December 1969.

PART TWO

Towards a Theology of Development

It had been recognized that the search for a theology of development was a matter of urgent concern.

Professor J. M. Lochman, Chairman of Section III of the Uppsala Assembly, when presenting its report.

5

The Challenge of Economic and Social Development

ERICH HOFFMANN

In the last decade the Christian churches have been turning their attention with ever-increasing urgency to the problems surrounding the population explosion, the technological revolution necessary for dealing with it, and the rapid changes in social conditions which are a necessary consequence of it. Ecumenical conferences must give preference to enquiries and discussions on social and economic problems for the following reasons:

(*a*) The coming together of Christians from all parts of the world has helped them to become aware of the growing gap between the material conditions of life of the majority of nations which still have a pre-industrial economic base and those of the small but powerful group of industrial nations.

(*b*) The use of natural resources as a basis for material existence is becoming less and less possible in small self-contained economic units; instead it entails, with the growing division of labour in society, a strengthening of the mutual social interdependence of men both in the restricted economic sphere and on a world-wide scale.

(*c*) The rapid increase in world population and the changing social relations it is generating are no longer compatible with the stable predominantly agrarian social structure which has always been regarded as that divinely ordained and which has moulded the whole intellectual framework and literary style of the Bible.

(*d*) The scientific and technological outlook of the age in which we live no longer seems reconcilable with the traditional religious mission which has hitherto been considered to be the responsibility of the churches.

These and a whole series of other present-day trends are working together to bring about a world-wide change: the churches are being challenged to test whether their traditional teaching is standing in the way of the real meaning of the divine message which it has for thousands of years been the church's task to proclaim in the languages of every nation and epoch. In our endeavour to provide a theological interpretation of the development now being generated in human society we must remain aware of the shortcomings which always beset any attempt to formulate statements of belief in that truth which is Jesus Christ in a way which human understanding can grasp. The workings of God and his challenge to humanity must be given a more important place in present-day economic development; the scope of his revelation cannot be confined to nature and the history of nations as this was formerly understood.

From among the conclusions reached by the Geneva Conference of 1966 when it discussed the church confronted by these problems, the following were especially worthy of note, and were made the special concern of the Fourth Assembly of the World Council of Churches at Uppsala in 1968:

(*a*) The economic disparity between the rich countries and the poor countries is rapidly increasing despite the measures taken in the context of the first ten-year development period. It is imperative that the greatest possible efforts be made to reach a balance.

(*b*) Revolutions are seen as necessary whenever existing political conditions stand in the way of the progress of those hitherto weakest economically towards greater social justice and participation in the control of power.

(*c*) Humanity is progressing towards a responsible world community, but its realization is impeded by the resistance put up by hostile national interests which place self-assertion above responsibility towards the rest of humanity.

(*d*) The involvement of Christians in these problems is founded on that essential aspect of the gospel which H. Berkhof[1] formulated thus at Uppsala: 'The way to full humanity is not the way of self-assertion but of the *dying wheat*', i.e. self-abnegation.

Thanks to our modern communication systems the existence of hunger and plenty side by side amongst the same 3,500,000,000 people has become an open scandal, so much so that the consciences of all those aware of Matt. 25.42 are deeply troubled. To fit the present situation we may rephrase it thus: 'For we were hungry and you gave us alms instead of finding us work and buying the fruits of our labours at a fair price.' The statement which the Zagorsk Consultation drew up after the Geneva Conference on Church and Society contains the following conclusions:

By making it increasingly impossible to consider the present miseries of men as the fate of nature and by dissolving hierarchies which were traditionally considered eternal, technological and economic development has created all over the world a favourable environment for the outburst of this new awareness (III.1).

In the context of the demand of the masses for social justice, revolution means changing the social class holding economic and political power, mainly by the transformation of the system of property, with a consequent replacing of political leaders (III.2a).

In these quotations emphasis is laid on the sociological character which has been assumed by the poverty and underprivileged state of the greater part of the world's population. Now more than ever Christ's command that we should love our neighbour enjoins action in the fields of social economics and politics. But this means that we must also recognize the economic background which has contributed to these social injustices, so that not only the symptoms but also the causes may be eradicated. The declarations arrived at by the World Council of Churches conferences (Geneva, 1966, Zagorsk, Beirut and Uppsala, 1968) and contained in the papal encyclical *Populorum Progressio* have pointed the way to this end. But further studies are needed, particularly of the structural impediments standing in the way. For appeals to the conscience all too easily remain emotional; unless they are accompanied by an analysis of the economic context they can call forth no effective action.

1 *The Growing Disparity in the Economic Potential of the Nations*

World hunger is not so much the lack of food as the consequence of poverty. In a report on the world food situation at the end of 1968 it was shown that those underdeveloped agrarian countries which are densely populated and poor in purchasing power are having to rely on famine relief programmes, while at the same time agricultural production in countries with advanced economic systems has been so stimulated that they are amassing surpluses of agricultural products. In the past fourteen years the population of the world has increased by 25 per cent and food production by 35 per cent; but in Asia, Africa and South America agricultural growth at an annual rate of 5 per cent has only in the last two years caught up with the rate of population growth. Economic developments are produced to a particularly large extent by the pressure brought to bear by an ever-increasing population on the production of foodstuffs, clothing and housing which are imperative in any attempt to provide the wherewithal for material existence. In such situations the struggle to find space for pasture and housing was the same as we find described in the Bible amongst the peoples of ancient history, and as we can still observe today in the political conduct of nations. With an ever-growing population density even an increased deployment of manpower cannot hope to keep pace with the rate of consumption, because more of the necessities of life can only be obtained from the same amount of geographical space with yet more expenditure and more efficient methods of production. Only by increasing the productivity of available manpower can a growing population maintain an even standard of living if it has no further available space. The intensification of productivity can be attained through the progressive division of labour, which makes possible the introduction of technological means of production against a background of improved standards of technical skill. The evolution of humanity has been accompanied by this process ever since it ceased to be predominantly nomadic and made the transition from foraging and hunting to an economy based primarily on agricultural production.

The growth rate of productivity by means of the introduction of methods and techniques to increase output and save labour is determined on the one hand by population pressure and on the other by the opportunities for the formation of capital, i.e. the size of the percentage of the returns of labour which can be devoted to the provision of means of production rather than being immediately used up. The small self-supporting farmer undertakes these economies and investment himself, storing up stocks of grain and fodder and adding to the numbers of his livestock and to his farm buildings. The labour of the artisan, which is rewarded by his net profits from sales, brings about a transition to the accumulation of financial capital. Thus economic development is always accompanied by the formation of capital with a view to short or long-term investment in the means to stimulate productivity which, since the introduction of a market economy, are acquired in exchange for products from other economic units. In those countries with the greatest population pressure – in earlier centuries these were the European countries – this development took place most quickly and made them into the industrial economies in which the technological revolution had its beginnings.

The quicker the division of labour and the differentiation in the numerous branches of economy can lead to an increase in the returns of labour, the greater can be the surplus which is thus made available and which exceeds the need for consumer goods and services necessary for the simple maintenance of existence. This economic development is accompanied not only by the growth in the variety and number of consumer goods produced per head, but also by the opportunities for investment so vital for the broadening of the basis of production.

The industrial countries, which are predominantly those inhabited by the white races but also include Japan, did not of course have to solve the problem of population pressure solely by means of increasing the productivity of their own resources. Considerable proportions of their increased populations were able to emigrate to more sparsely populated parts of the earth, and furthermore raw materials from these parts were used to extend the basic elements of production in their own economies. North America benefited particularly from this influx of Europeans, because this thinly populated country offered excellent opportunities for development to the enterprising, in conditions not dissimilar – as far as climate at least was concerned – to those in their own countries. There, with the help of the forcible displacement of the indigenous population and the importation of African slave labour, the colonial agrarian economy could rapidly be converted into a dominant industrial economy. Thus relieved of their burden of overpopulation and given the added space of their overseas colonies to use, the countries of Western Europe could increase their productivity much faster than their population; they thus gained a continually growing advantage both in prosperity and in opportunities for the accumulation of capital for investment in technological progress. The extension of living space and resources to the other parts of the world politically controlled by the industrial countries held back these parts of the world from progressing towards any corresponding development because their population increase could be used to cheapen labour costs. It is rightly stated in the Report of Section III, Uppsala (par. 31): 'Undeniably, many of the developed countries owe their economic prosperity to the use of the resources and labour forces of the present developing countries.'

However, even in the industrial countries the need for investment for the development of technology, for the provision of new jobs and for the necessary training in the new techniques was so great that the burden of capital formation was at first inevitably borne by the profits from the labour of the peasant section of society and of the many people forced to change from self-supporting occupations to jobs in industry. The proletarization of a growing proportion of the population, which appeared with the beginnings of industrialization, accompanied the accumulation of national wealth which admittedly became economically effective in the hands of entrepreneurs. But social discrimination separates the owner of capital from the man driven out of his self-supporting peasant way of life into the position of a wage-earning worker without capital. In the last century population pressure within the European industrial countries and the creaming off of labour profits which was necessary for industrialization created so oppressive a social disparity that the revolutionary movements, under the intellectual direction of Marxism, denied the right of the individual to dispose of the capital built up on his profits, a right which depended on the principle of absolute ownership, and demanded that the right to the practical disposition of it should be conceded instead to society. The pressure emanating from these revolutionary movements took the form of a class struggle, as a result of which measures were obtained for the legally regulated redistribution of incomes, whereby the position of the workers in society could be improved by systems of social security and graduated taxes on income, wealth, and inheritance. In all this an important factor was the enlarged scope for the sharing out of the fruits of labour which had meanwhile been provided by increased productivity and by the colonial system. The Report (par. 2) calls the exploitation of men by men the core of social injustice and ascribes it to the reality of sin. But this hardly makes clear the connection between the necessity of diverting a proportion of the returns of labour in order to build up capital and the question of the right of possession of that capital. A moral condemnation of this process of diversion will do little to lead the way to a more rational method for the accumulation and direction of investment unless unconditional ownership and the right to dispose of the basic factors of production are called into question, and it is admitted that society should have the theoretical right to participate in them.

More and more the responsibility of society for a juster sharing out of the returns of labour is being recognized as a principle which must lead to further restrictions in the power to dispose of productive wealth, while at the same time society's right to participate in its allocation is no longer disputed in principle, even though it is seldom adequately realized as yet.

An analogous development has been taking place in the course of this century, as a result of which the social disparity between the nations has produced a situation similar to that of the class conflict. In the past the industrialization of nations with a high *per capita* domestic product was based both on the creaming off of surplus value in the case of the labour returns of the wage-earning worker and the peasant, and on the transfer of surplus value from pre-industrial countries caused by the importation of cheap raw materials. Countries with a low national product are not only contributing to the growth of the prosperity of highly-developed economic areas by their political dependence as colonies; they are also contributing to it by their economic dependence as the producers of raw materials whose export is controlled by the industrial countries owing to their market position as buyers. Thus states with pre-industrial economies find themselves in a position comparable to that of the proletariat in industrial countries. However they lack the opportunity to relieve their population pressure through emigration, and to facilitate their capital formation by means of colonialization. Furthermore the number of people affected runs into hundreds of millions and the rate of population increase is many times greater than it was at the beginning of the industrialization of Europe and North America.

The extent of this economic disparity can be observed in the figures compiled from the official statistics for the mid-1960s of a selection of typical states in the higher population range.

Table 1　Basic data of development in selected countries (about 1965)

| Country | Population | | Agricultural area per capita: hectares | Percentage of population active in agriculture | Gross national product per capita per year US $ | Percentage of agricultural origin |
	Millions	Rate of increase per year				
Low income countries						
Ethiopia	23	1·7	3·6	88	47	65
Nigeria	59	2·0	0·4	80	68	59
India	500	2·4	0·4	70	92	51
Brazil	85	2·6	1·6	52	232	29
Intermediate income countries						
Mexico	44	3·4	2·3	52	447	17
Poland	32	1·1	0·6	42	ca. 500	22
South Africa	18	2·4	5·6	29	557	10
High income countries						
USSR	233	1·2	2·5	33	ca. 950	22
Italy	52	0·9	0·4	25	1,040	13
United Kingdom	55	0·7	0·4	4	1,644	3
USA	197	1·3	1·7	6	3,500	3

This survey contains some typical examples for each of the three groups divided according to the size of their gross *per capita* domestic products. They reveal that the lower the percentage of people active in agriculture, the higher proportionately the domestic product. This percentage is an indication of the degree of socio-economic development, because it decreases as other branches of the economy make more claims on the labour force, thereby increasing their own share in the creation of internal economic prosperity. The rate of population increase is generally considerably greater in the pre-industrial countries; it is however not determined solely by socio-economic development. Moreover the size per head of the agricultural ground surface available for the production of food for a country's own population has no bearing on the domestic product, since the wide discrepancies in land fertility and intensity of cultivation make the significance of such statistics far from reliable. Moreover the return per hectare of the agricultural ground surface in the industrial countries is many times greater than it is in the agrarian countries, whose economies are managed with a much lower utilization of industrially manufactured means of production which would increase their output. This is why the agrarian countries, when densely populated, are hungry countries, whereas at present the industrial countries often produce agricultural surpluses even when they are densely populated. However, because of the great cost differences and the difficulties of transportation it is no easy matter to devote these surpluses to the alleviation of food shortages in the agrarian countries. A thickly-populated pre-industrial economy is unable to offer opportunities for jobs, and this is why subsistence-level peasant economies suffer from disguised unemployment: often less than 100 productive working days per worker per year. Taken together with these populations' natural methods of feeding themselves (a factor difficult to assess statistically) this accounts for their low annual *per capita* incomes of less than $100. A higher domestic product is only achieved by countries possessing non-agrarian raw materials (particularly oil) which can be sold to their advantage in world markets; nevertheless when such countries possess few or no processing industries the majority of the population has little opportunity to earn a satisfactory income.

Poverty and hunger resulting from a rate of agrarian productivity unable to keep pace with population growth can therefore only be overcome in these countries through industrialization combined with a progressive division of labour, with a differentiation of the economy, with the creation of a correspondingly efficient educational system, and finally with the integration of the various branches of the economy both internally and with the world market.

In this process the development of agriculture has priority in so far as it forms the dominant section of production in pre-industrial economies. From it a portion of the returns of labour must be diverted to the formation of capital and some of the labour force moved into those sections of the economy which need to be developed and which can make better use of these under-employed but potentially capable workers. This double pressure hits agriculture, which is economically less rewarding, all the harder the more this process is compelled to depend on the internal economy alone. In low-income pre-industrial economies the proportion of the domestic product available for investment, i.e. the investment quota, can only be small, for it would otherwise risk further decreasing the already low minimum subsistence level. If it is estimated that the amount of investment required to create a new vacant job is $10,000 and if only 5 per cent can be diverted to the formation of capital from the $100 typical of countries with a low *per capita* annual domestic product, it follows that 2,000 workers must bear the burden of these painful personal restrictions in order to create even this one vacant job. In industrial countries with a domestic product of $1,000, an investment quota of 20 per cent can easily be achieved, with the result that a diversion from the earnings of the same number of workers will provide sufficient investment for forty new vacant jobs of the same type or for a smaller number of jobs with considerably better conditions and productivity. This is why the disparity in industrial capacity between pre-industrial and highly industrialized countries is growing steadily greater.

At the beginning of economic development the rate of industrialization is therefore slower and the growth of productivity often lags behind the growth of population and its need for jobs and consumer goods. At a higher level of socio-economic development the rate of productivity accelerates very considerably, creating a surplus of capital and consumer goods which makes export imperative. The growing disparity in the prosperity of the poor and rich nations could no doubt be lessened by using this surplus, if the same principle of redistribution were acknowledged which in the industrial countries has already helped to reduce social tensions and has enlarged the market for industrial commodities by increasing the purchasing power of the mass of the population.

II   *The Unequal Position of the Nations in World Trade*

The disparity between pre-industrial and highly-developed economic areas is further aggravated by corresponding differences in their positions in world trade. The pre-industrial countries are confined to exporting the primary products of the raw materials produced by their agricultures and mines: this is an international division of labour which has given industrial countries a dominant position, even since the cessation of colonial rule, as exporters of processed products and manufactured goods which are in comparison more rewarding in the provision of work and capital. The industrial countries are able to buy their raw materials in the world market at prices which cover limited employment and a low wage level and which are subject to considerable fluctuations according to market conditions. On the other hand they are able to determine the prices of their industrial products in accordance with the greater purchasing power of their populations and their high capital and wage costs. The terms of trade, i.e. the relationship of raw materials to industrial products in terms of purchasing power, all tend predominantly to work to the disadvantage of the pre-industrial economic areas, especially since the majority of the latter are only able to offer a limited selection of commodities for export. The pre-industrial states are forced to depend on a very limited range of commodities not only because of their single-commodity agrarian systems which were developed during the colonial period, but also because of the narrow internal economic differentiations, with the result that three-fourths of a country's earnings from exports have to be earned with a single indigenous product. As long as they are unable to establish a more diversified economic structure entailing a sufficiently trained specialized working force and the production of export commodities by industries requiring more labour, these countries will remain in an unfavourable position as far as the exchange of goods and services is concerned.

The continued existence in world economy of this division of labour between the exportation of raw materials and of industrial products is in fact a concealed form of exploitation; it allows the industrial countries to achieve a high domestic product by the processing and marketing of commodities originating from countries with a low income level. Statistical evidence is unable to tell us the extent of this process whereby the wealth created by the raw material producing countries is drained off by the highly developed economies, or what it means in relation to the statistically demonstrable transfers of capital in the form of development aid. Since more than 70 per cent of the currency transferred from the industrial countries to the so-called underdeveloped countries comes from their export surpluses, it can be assumed that the total sum of the grants, subsidies and credits received by the latter under the general heading of 'development aid' is almost equivalent to that of the capital diverted from them to the industrial countries because of their unfavourable position in world trade. The balance of payments of those states dependent on the importation of industrial means of production for their own economic development is moreover further burdened by the rates of interest repayable on the loans they have accepted. Many countries find themselves having to pay more in repayment of debts and interest than they are receiving in 'aid'.

The Report of Uppsala Section III deplores (par. 7) the failure of the Second United Nations Conference on Trade, Aid and Development in New Delhi to respond to the proposals of the Charter of Algiers for better world trade conditions, and in paragraph 11 it demands radical changes in the institutions and structures governing the international economic relations. In judging this problem equitably the differences between various development policies must be taken into account, since some give priority to capital aid and some to expansion of trade.

The policies adopted by the industrial nations in the measures they are taking to assist the pre-industrial countries are politically conditioned by their endeavour to keep the latter within their own spheres of influence or to win them over. The capitalist states give precedence in their policy to visible transfers of capital in the shape of 'aid to underdeveloped countries', and consolidate their positions in world trade by the formation of larger economic groupings. The policy adopted by the socialist industrial states is one which meets with greater favour in the underdeveloped countries: it is expressed most succinctly by the slogan 'Trade not Aid'. The negotiations which took place at the second UNCTAD Conference clearly showed that the agreement of the countries of the Eastern bloc to diversify their range of goods bought from the developing countries and to arrange more favourable customs, duties and prices was accepted with greater confidence by the eighty underdeveloped countries, and seemed more appropriate to their own economic plans, than the capital aid promised but not made into a binding agreement by the capitalist countries, even though these devote much larger sums to their policy than do the socialist states.

The socialist policy towards the underdeveloped countries was formulated by the East German delegation at the first UNCTAD Conference as early as 1964:

International economic co-operation, and particularly international trade based on the complete equality of all states taking part, on mutual advantage and on non-interference in internal affairs, and carried out without discrimination or artificial impediments – these are the most important means whereby friendly relations can be fostered between all the nations of the world.

A sentence in the papal encyclical *Populorum Progressio* (56) cogently describes the mood of disappointment after the first decade of organized development policy and as it was felt at the second UNCTAD Conference:

The efforts which are being made to assist developing nations on a financial and technical basis, though considerable, would be illusory if their benefits were partially nullified as a consequence of trade relations existing between rich and poor countries.

For this same reason the conference of Christian churches held at

E

Beirut in April 1968 also demanded that measures be taken 'to make the markets of the prosperous countries more ready to accept the exports of the underdeveloped countries'.

Demands of this kind have, however, little prospect of being met if one considers the present distribution of economic and political power. On the contrary, development aid is at present being misused as an instrument of foreign policy and is being exploited to build up and defend the economic and political positions of the more influential industrial nations. We have a shameful example of this in the decision of the United Nations Economic and Social Council (ECOSOC), which was taken in February 1969 and according to which only West Germany was taken on to the preparatory committee for the second development decade; this gave the socialist countries a pretext to abstain from participating in this undertaking. Unless there is a fundamental change in the power structures which have evolved, historically speaking, out of the spheres of interest of the colonial powers and the imperialist results of both world wars, the disparity in living standards and world trade relations cannot be removed, nor can its continuing accentuation be lessened.

III   *The Technological Revolution Necessitates a Social Revolution*

More than any other economist, Karl Marx stressed the fact that the development of productive power entails an alteration in production conditions: by this he understood the relationship of those engaged in production to the means and the yields of their work. In the light of the particularly rapid rate of technological development today we can observe the influence it generates on inter-human social relationships all the more clearly in so far as these relationships are sanctioned by the legislation governing the control of the means and yields of production.

In the reports of the Geneva, Zagorsk and Uppsala Conferences the need for revolutionary changes is recognized with increasing urgency, but also with limitations that result from the dangers implicit in such changes for the very foundations of existence. As long as discussion centred on the ethical implications of the use of force, the problem of the concept of property and state sovereignty remained in the background. The report of the Committee on Church and Society of the World Council of Churches to the Assembly at Uppsala is alone in containing (Section 16.4) a demand for relevant studies to be made: 'The legal structures of ownership are especially in need of further scrutiny.'

The Marxist objections to property are still opposed as the negation of a right consequent on the dignity and freedom of the human being: this is because an insufficient distinction is generally drawn between personal ownership and the overall control of the bases of production. Although the gospel itself is most emphatic in stressing that man is endangered by possessions and is but the steward of what God has entrusted to his care, these reports do not do more than allude to the social significance of the prevailing laws of property. Social justice however requires a more varied solution of the problem raised by the control of the bases of production essential for the needs of society than is offered by the false alternatives between rights of ownership in the private and public spheres.

As the economic interdependence of those people engaged in co-operative productive labour continues to become a presupposition for the modern way of life, the laws of property we have taken over from the economy (literally, from the Greek, 'house management') of self-supporting farmsteads will become less and less valid as absolute principles of justice. Instead, accepted rights of disposal of property must be increasingly restricted, starting with land ownership, and then proceeding to other resources and finally to the essential means of production. The extent of participation in rights of disposal by which certain often not fully realized social responsibilities of ownership towards the material bases of production are brought into being, is decided by social structures and the legal principles recognized within them.

Socio-economic relations are at present predominantly decided by legal principles which attach the right of disposal over the material bases of production to ownership and, on the international level, to territorial sovereignty. The absolute validity of these legal principles cannot however be maintained any longer, now that social methods of production and world economic interdependence brought about by the technological revolution are both increasingly stressing the opposition towards exclusive limitations of this kind. The belief in unconditional rights of ownership is widely sanctioned by Christianity as is that in the independence of nations, often misinterpreted as eternal and divinely ordained; both offer the strongest resistance to the idea of adaptation to rapidly changing economic conditions, while at the same time both strengthen power structures based on economic factors.

It is therefore no coincidence that the movements of social revolution, which have been attacking both old and more recent political ascendancies with varying intensity ever since the industrial revolution, have therefore chosen to oppose the right to private ownership of the means of production as well. The disappointing results of the UNCTAD

conferences have clearly shown that the way to international settlement
of world economic problems is blocked by national rights of sovereignty.
The clash of economic principles with political structural ones
is one which those most penalized by it feel first and most deeply
even when they are not fully aware of the causal connections. Since
a peaceful adjustment of interests spontaneously worked out is apparently out of the question and since those privileged by the retention
of the traditional legal system are standing in the way of this process
of adjustment, the technological revolution is being followed by a
social revolution which will become increasingly militant the longer
the already overdue changes are delayed. If we use the term technological
revolution to describe the accelerated transformation of the machinery
of production and of industrial processes, it is logical to use the term
social revolution to mean the forceful alteration of political structures.
As M. M. Thomas[2] said at the Uppsala Conference:

> The essential element of revolution is the radical alteration of the power
> structure as the embodiment of social justice, and not violent action as an
> end in itself. . . . [Revolution is] a vigorous transformation of society which
> will allow for the truly responsible participation of the people in the centres
> of social and national power.

The theological group at the Geneva Conference on Church and
Society drew the conclusion:

> The Christian is called upon to say a radical No to the structures of power
> which perpetuate and strengthen the status quo at the cost of justice to those
> who are its victims. The task of bringing about effective social change, and
> of discerning in the protest of the poor and oppressed the relative historical
> justice at work, is especially his.[3]

Before this D. von Oppen had already stated the effect of a Christian
attitude to systems of justice even more categorically: 'Wherever the
gospel penetrated, it destroyed the time-hallowed and sanctified
polities of men.'[4]

Awareness of the forces generated by economic development and of
the static quality of power makes Christians of today not only able to
understand but also ready to participate in action when revolutionary
changes are being made in society. Christian involvement can only
be limited by the knowledge that revolution stands trial just as much
as the retention of the old order whenever it regards its cause as an
absolute and promises eternal salvation.

When it described development as the secularized man's version
of the Christian's expectation of the kingdom of God, the Beirut
Conference asked the question (Section I, par. 17):

Dare we leave the roads to justice and peace so completely blocked that men who look to the future have to resort to violence where other ways are possible? It is the work of courageous dynamic love to break through these rigidities. There can be non-violent revolutions. All our efforts must be directed to change without violence. But if injustice is so embedded in the status quo and its supporters refuse to permit change, then as a last resort men's conscience may lead them, in full and clear-sighted responsibility, without hatred or rancour, to engage in violent revolution. A heavy burden then rests on those who have resisted change.

The transition from an agrarian system consisting predominantly of self-supporting subsistence economies to highly differentiated and integrated industrial economic systems is a transition so fundamental that a corresponding transformation of political structures can scarcely be other than revolutionary. What strategies this social revolution should follow, whether it should entail civil war and complete upheaval or be non-violent, whether such revolution should be permanent or should provoke far-reaching reforms, all this depends on a multitude of historical factors and, last but not least, on the attitude of the social sections ruling at the time.

IV　*The International Redistribution of Prosperity*

The demands made by the eighteenth-century social revolutionaries were rejected by the churches in league with the ruling powers in the industrialized nations. They viewed the social order that had evolved historically as part of a divinely created order which they assumed to be permanent, a misconception which prevented them from comprehending the dynamic quality of social structures. Social disparity was met by moral appeals to those economically favoured and by charitable works to help those who benefited less from the differentiations engendered by society. Rarely did the Christian plea for social justice turn itself into actual participation in bringing about a fundamental change in laws and justice: a change which would have recognized the claims of those hardest hit by the creaming off of surplus value for some measure of reparation. But paternalistic charity is felt by the poor to be a failure of that justice to which they feel entitled.

Although the class struggles in Western Europe and North America did not lead to violent upheaval, the revolutionary strength of working-class movements was enough to overcome the opposition put up by those defending the principle of unlimited ownership and the existing power structures and hostile to any measures in favour of social equality. Capitalism has been led towards the creation of social states not by humanitarian motives alone; the economic compulsion to lessen the disparity brought about by economic expansion has forced capitalism in this direction in the interests of increasing mass purchasing power. Despite considerable inroads into the rights of ownership, the principle of the social redistribution of income and wealth is no longer really disputed in these so-called 'welfare states'. The social responsibility of ownership has progressed from being an optional ethical formula to becoming a lawful claim of the economically underprivileged. A partial collectivization of the rights of disposal of income and wealth and their legalized transfer in the interests of those without property has taken a firm foothold, even though the socialist economic system is rejected in principle.

The state regulation of social security systems was designed to deal with the serious risks incurred by inability to work, which in earlier subsistence economies had to be covered by family co-operation. Progressive taxation of incomes, wealth and inheritance and the responsibility taken on by society for all its members have in various forms become basic features of the industrialized states. The contributions levied in this way are transferred through direct or indirect subsidies so as to equal out social disparities. But although some social needs and grievances are thereby alleviated, it can scarcely be claimed that a comprehensive system of social justice can ever be achieved by such measures, particularly as they do not, either in theory or in practice, create any real partnership between the two sides as far as their economic relationship is concerned. The inevitability of bureaucratic machinery is as restricting when attempts are made to apply this process of secondary redistribution as it is when rights of ownership are officially equalized through the total conversion of the means of production to complete public ownership.

Now that social disparity between the nations has overtaken interclass tensions within nations in revolutionary intensity, it is obvious that the principles of redistribution of wealth and income and restriction of control over the bases of production should also be taken into account in the domain of international relations. The British Labour Party originally suggested that the industrial states should, as it were, tax themselves according to the levels of their domestic products so as to raise funds for the development of the pre-industrial areas of the world. This resolution was subsequently adopted by the Ecumenical Conferences in Geneva, Beirut and Uppsala as well as in the papal encyclical *Populorum Progressio*, and it is one which aims in principle at a redistribution of wealth. But its implementation will of course retain the appearance of charity as long as such redistribution remains voluntary and based on bilateral agreements.

The contributions actually made by the industrial states towards redevelopment cannot be assessed accurately because reliable and complete statistics do not exist, and because it is impossible to make clear-cut distinctions between transfers of capital genuinely intended for development on the one hand, and on the other political and military subsidies and commercial credits given in the interests of the nations lending them. The contributions to development aid agreed on by the industrial nations in fact amounted to sums which represented as much as 1·02 per cent of their national products in 1962 and only 0·88 per cent of their national products in 1966. Table 2 shows that the former colonial powers contributed more than the other industrial states.

Table 2   Agreed contributions towards development aid from selected countries, expressed as percentages of their national product (GNP)

	1962	1966
France	2·51	1·70
England	1·15	1·16
Germany (Fed. Rep.)	0·96	0·81
USA	0·94	0·76
Japan	0·62	0·69
Sweden	0·32	0·64

Although the national product of all these countries is increasing by more than 1 per cent per year, their contribution to economic development in the pre-industrial parts of the world lags behind this figure. The reduction in 1966 should not be attributed only to the temporary recession in these countries: it also indicates their growing reluctance to co-operate. However the 1 to 2 per cent often recommended (as in the Uppsala Report, par. 38) as a guide-line for development taxation is not too far from the contributions already sometimes made. The second UNCTAD Conference in 1968 was, it is true, given assurances by the Western industrial states that they intended to devote to this purpose 1 per cent of their gross national product, which is about 30 per cent above the net national product on which assessments were previously based. But their temporary concern with overcoming their own internal economic difficulties affords little hope that these proposals are going to be realized in full. Moreover, the capital aid provided during the first decade of assisted development was for the most part determined by bilateral agreements in which the payment of sums varying according to the urgency of the recipient country's economic requirements was hampered by political interests, by East-West tensions in particular, and also by the economic superiority of the donor countries. The same can be said of the bilateral trade agreements.

The need of recipient countries to curry the political favour of donor countries intent on furthering their own international positions puts

them in a humiliating situation. This provides a breeding ground for
revolutionary trends aiming to overthrow the very positions which
the donor country's politically motivated subsidies are supposed to be
defending. The fact that the threat of military complications has led
to defence budgets one hundred times larger, and subtracted of course
from the productive areas of the national product, has given rise to
a worsening of international relations and indeed to the danger of
another world war. How long the former colonial countries will remain
the battlefield for the conflicting interests of the great powers is something which they will certainly not be able to decide for themselves.

A redistribution aiming to bring about a peaceful eradication of
disparities ought to be founded on legally binding rules which would
determine the responsibility of the industrial countries to pay back the
wealth which, in order to build up their own economies, they have
diverted from the former colonial areas, the young nations of today.

Those in positions of authority in the industrial states will of course
hardly recognize such responsibility as the only motive for the task
which has befallen them, of providing the necessary investment which
those areas which have remained in a pre-industrial condition require
in order to catch up economically. But their keenness to find new
partners in world trade with adequate purchasing power, and their
justifiable anxiety to avoid the class-struggle threatened by the dispossessed, makes it possible for their governments to secure the
agreement of their parliaments and electorates to grant financial
subsidies. It would be quite unrealistic to imagine that the desire to
aid underdeveloped countries can be awakened simply by the demands
of altruism and social justice, and equally unrealistic to fail to respect
the essential part played by self-interest in economic matters in particular. Lefringhausen was quite right in pointing out that in general
Christian public opinion is easily misled by the following misunderstanding:

Development aid policy is concerned with two alternatives: the altruistic
(sacrifices, gifts) on the one hand and self-interest on the other. Yet it is
much truer to say that the real alternatives are temporary interest on the one
hand and long-term (i.e. carefully-considered) interest on the other. If we
examine these interests in the theoretical half-light of ethical principles and
of dubious or even illegal morality, we will make ourselves guilty too of
provoking outraged public reaction.[5]

As far as the gospel is concerned, the morality of the whole problem
becomes evident if we venture to interpret John 12.25 in this sense:
'He that makes sure of his life in the short term shall in the long term
lose it.'

Even within the industrial states redistribution did not develop as a charitable institution: only as the result of violent class struggles could it have been turned into reparation for capitalist creaming off of surplus value. But the advantage of alleviating social distress as a prerequisite for an expanding market was naturally a considerably more compelling motive for internal redistribution, just as it is today for redistribution on a supra-national scale. Thus an entirely altered relationship was of course brought into being as part of the general process of expanding production, a relationship in which provider and recipient become partners instead of confronting each other like rich benefactors and grateful paupers. In this connection let us quote the following passage from a document on the churches and development which was presented to the Assembly at Uppsala:

What is absolutely essential is partnership rather than paternalism – a partnership which acknowledges that both sides have something to offer, and that the perspective of each side is seriously limited and narrow.[6]

The effects of economic and political inequalities can be neutralized by a multilateral system of redistribution all the more effectively when the distribution of the funds available for development aid is entrusted to the authority of supra-national institutions.

The promotion of the controlled redistribution of wealth must not be a matter of international charity or of foreign policy in disguise; it must be a fair and just system corresponding in its structure to the increasing economic interdependence of nations which has led to the concept of world citizenship. If social policy is already an area of a nation's internal policy, it should also become the core of that global internal policy of which C. F. von Weizsäcker has spoken in his book on the conditions of peace.[7]

v *The Dynamic of the Structures of a World Community of the Future*

One of the most marked differences between the prerequisites for measures to reduce social disparities at home and on an international scale is that there is a lack of international institutions at present capable of exercising the same kind of authority as the Inland Revenue department of national governments. Every state has developed its own taxation system alongside its monetary system, and these have been able to function comparatively easily as instruments for ironing out social disparities. The right to levy taxes has always been regarded as a constitutive element of national sovereignty. This has led to the failure of every attempt made ever since the Geneva Conference on Church and Society to implement the demands contained in those resolutions

proposed by the churches which imply that national products should
be taxed on an international scale in order to further development,
and which therefore come up against the sacrosanct concept of national
sovereignty. One of the principal prerequisites for any change in the
structure of world economy must therefore be recognized to be the
gradual restriction of rights of sovereignty through international
agreements. Uppsala III (par. 36) therefore demands that the churches

should especially consider how the present economic structures in which
national sovereignty plays a decisive role can be transformed into a structure
in which decisions affecting the welfare of all are taken at the international
level.

The same applies equally to the possibility of developing an international
taxation system to raise funds for development (Report, par. 18) and
to the regulation of world trade relations on the basis of partnership.

But the significance and gravity of this problem should not be
underestimated. The industrial states have since the Second World
War been trying slowly and laboriously to overcome the impediments
which international frontiers present to their growing international
economic interdependence, by creating supra-national economic
units. But the young nation states are still compelled to back up their
internal economic integration with the psychological stimulus of
nationalism. They have just been freed from political dependence and
the magnitude of their effort to achieve economic independence is in
direct relation to the extent to which their weak economic position is
caused by their restricted openings for export. In societies such as
these, nationalism represents an indispensable integrating force,
because as a result of the artificial frontiers drawn during the colonial
period they lack ethnic unity. During the industrial expansion of the
eighteenth and nineteenth centuries this was also the positive side of
nationalism in Europe: but it could not save it from chauvinism in
the twentieth. Seen as the result of developments such as these, the
constructive and negative aspects of nationalism of which Uppsala,
Section IV speaks (par. 34) are easier for us to understand.

Nowadays the new nation states are intent on strengthening their
own sovereignty and their interests are consequently clashing with the
growing interdependence of world economy. Although their economic
expansion too can only be assisted by further integration in supra-
national economic areas, they are hampered by their natural attempts
to achieve sufficient autonomy to protect them from being subjugated
by their economic superiors. This anachronism is due not so much to
their lack of judgment as to the economic and political inferiority of
pre-industrial countries in comparison with the great power blocs

which exploit interdependence in order to dominate, and which refuse to recognize that a genuine partnership in world trade would be in their long-term interest. In this connection we can see a certain justification for the challenge offered by the Nigerian Bola Ige to the Geneva Conference on Church and Society: 'It is not the poor, it is the rich who are a world problem.' Sovereignty is what stands in the way of the objective of greater social justice between the nations, just as the ownership of the means of production is what divides the classes, when these two principles are held up to command our respect as absolute and organic elements in the fabric of society. The elimination of these impediments by means of the complete transfer of ownership and sovereignty to society itself can scarcely be regarded as the only or most reliable solution to the problem. Rather it is a solution derived from an over-abstract view of real living conditions. A variety of practical solutions is more likely to be found if the concepts of sovereignty and ownership are divested of the ideological connotations which endowed them with an almost sacrosanct and inevitable quality.

Various systems providing for society's participation have already made and will certainly continue to make the principle of ownership increasingly relative, and to lay greater stress on the obligations of society in using its economic power and resources. For instance, in many legal systems the ownership of land does not include the right to do what one likes with it; instead individual rights of ownership are often restricted and society is given a say in the form of mining and planning regulations laid down by local government authorities, water boards, public transport corporations, etc., or of co-operative development plans. In an analogous way, growing economic interdependence is effecting a reduction in national rights of sovereignty, though these are still virtually unlimited. In cases where rivers flow through several states, or in certain maritime areas (e.g. in the Dardanelles) and in the air, agreements to reduce or remove the rights of sovereignty of single states have shown themselves to be perfectly practicable. However, it is true to say that most states are still trying to increase their rights over territorial waters, for instance, which until recently were open to all nations that cared to use them, and most are still resisting the limitations which technological progress is imposing on their territorial sovereignty. Yet on the other hand, the realization is growing that these rights are becoming increasingly open to question, especially where their maintenance threatens the vital interests of other nations. The right of various parties to make use of waterways, access to which is a vital factor for their agriculture and power production, is something which has scarcely been legally settled as yet, but which is being practised on an increasingly wide scale.

The international redistribution of wealth can be achieved without entailing the complete abolition of national sovereignty, or the setting up of a world government. But nations will have to learn to limit still further their exclusive rights to natural resources and their use, and therefore also their rights to dispose of their national products: this is essential for international social justice. Such limitations are likely to come about in the fields of atomic energy and space research, but these are not the only spheres in which a limitation of sovereignty is desirable; economic interdependence, rapidly growing with the technological revolution, and the attempts being made to reduce increasingly dangerous social disparities, are also areas requiring similar limitations. The way towards a world community will be pointed first by a growing series of smaller or larger international groupings which will limit, if not entirely remove, rights of sovereignty. But it will become increasingly evident that voluntary participation is not enough to avert the dangers threatening humanity as a whole. The development of military techniques seems most likely to be what will force *every* nation to agree to a renunciation of individual sovereignty. In the sphere of production and resources the first to be freed from the absolute control of the nations possessing them will have to be either those essential for economic existence or those whose misuse represents the greatest danger to the lives of all the nations.

The essential elements in the structure of a world community striving after social justice may therefore be seen to be a progressive reduction in the rights to dispose of the resources essential to prosperity. Present-day international relations and laws are still far too rooted in conceptions of living-space which may well have been valid for nomadic tribes fighting for their grazing-grounds. Society's increasing and far-ranging control of the life of the world's growing population makes it absolutely essential to devise methods which will allow the control of the bases of existence to pass into the hands of society without reducing national rights of self-determination in other spheres. In this realization are founded some of the hopes which socialist ideas have aroused in our century.

VI   *The Role of Science as the Common Property of Mankind*

The positive meaning of science and technology for the prosperity of mankind, and their responsible utilization, have on several occasions been stressed at the Geneva and Uppsala Conferences.[8] But no mention has yet been made of one particular danger which needs to be carefully studied because it is proving a growing threat both to humanity and indeed to science itself.

In the technological revolution the productive power of science has acquired such crucial significance that it is increasingly outweighing the importance of material resources. Scientific and technological processes affect the utilization of mineral and other natural resources so decisively that the economic success of production and ensuing prosperity depends primarily on the extent to which the findings of science are made available.

Ever since the eighteenth century, or even earlier, science has been regarded as the common possession of all mankind. The publication of its findings led the way both to their becoming objectively proved and accepted and towards their practical application in every sphere of modern life. The right to intellectual ownership was limited to the recognition of the author's priority, and its effects were theoretical rather than practical. But from the moment when the profitability of production and both economic and political power began to depend above all on the possession of technically relevant scientific know-how, its publication has become restricted to an extent which carries with it very grave dangers not only for science but for the whole of society too. This development first became obvious with the military exploitation of atomic energy, but it had started earlier, when industrial research began to feel itself obliged to protect itself from competition. From the moment when scientific research is placed under military supervision, and research centres are surrounded with barbed wire and scientists kept under close surveillance as in concentration camps, the measures taken to keep scientific findings strictly secret become an open contradiction of the ideal that the achievements of the human mind should be made known to all and become the common property of all mankind.

This contradiction has become a matter of political concern as regards the question of the control of atomic energy; it is a further example of the need for recognizing that the limitation of rights of ownership and sovereignty is an integral part of the structure of industrial society. The rate at which the pre-industrial countries can develop into industrial states is today more than ever dependent on how quickly they can be brought to participate in scientific and technological progress. Of course international scientific contacts between individuals and research institutions can to some extent exert a modifying influence on this trend towards secrecy; but the dividing lines between scientific responsibility and the betrayal of commercial and state secrets are leading scientists into almost insuperable conflicts. These conflicts can no more be resolved by the individual ethical implications of Christian theology than can the problems of private ownership and state autonomy by those of social ethics. The

International Atomic Authority and similar institutions in other fields have made a start towards creating a sense of global responsibility; they can provide a preliminary basis on which world-wide codes of conduct can be built up.

VII *Problems Facing Christian Theology*

If the demand for social justice is the fruit of one of the two commandments on which 'hang all the law and the prophets', the deductions we have set out above require some further theological clarification. First of all we should ask what the connections are between mankind's hopes for technological, economic and social development and the eschatological hope of the Gospels. In his Uppsala paper on the Finality of Jesus Christ[9] H. Berkhof came to this conclusion: 'Therefore redemption includes development and excludes acquiescence in any status quo.' Is God's creation as a *creatio continua* at work both in biological evolution and in mankind's evolution from wandering nomadic tribes to sedentary nations and finally to an industrial world community? What justification has the Christian for believing that the increase in prosperity and its juster distribution is part and parcel of God's road to salvation, and that 'development' can be used as a synonym for hope and for peace in the sense of *shalom*? If development towards improved social relations is seen in this light, the question remains whether attachment to traditional systems should be equated with sin, which wants to be left untouched by God's will. What is the connection between the ambivalence of all man's actions, and his limited understanding of the increasingly complex background to the making of responsible decisions, and the Christian conception of man as the sinner whom God still loves?

In analysing the motivation of this demand for social justice Visser 't Hooft at Uppsala[10] pointed to the 'deep trouble, which lies underneath the political and economic level. The root of the matter is that at a time when history requires that humanity should live as a coherent responsible society men still refuse to accept responsibility for their fellow-beings.' If we contemplate the future course of humanity we become aware of the relationship between responsibility for fellow human-beings and responsibility to God. This obviously gives rise to far harder conflicts than does personal altruism, which is based on the encounter with God made man, because structurally organized love, such as was spoken of at Geneva, is in danger of losing sight of the human being behind the mass of humanity.

The consequences of the moral criteria bound up with individual ownership and national independence should be rethought by this industrial society of ours, already well on the way to becoming a world community. Thus we may avoid launching yet more moral appeals and turn instead to the consideration of the social and ethical basis for new structures and norms of justice.

Another question which deserves more thorough investigation by the churches is how far the furthering of development projects is their immediate concern: they should consider whether, like their charitable work in hospitals, etc., they should transfer it to the hands of modern secular society. On occasions when society fails to play its part, action on the part of the churches is an appropriate testimony of their mission. But since development strategy cannot be separated from foreign policy, the churches must be careful to remain aware of all the dangers inherent in equating church and state in an alliance reminiscent of that forged by Constantine the Great; this can only obscure the message of the gospel. At this point one of the central and most decisive problems of the Reformation makes its appearance in a new guise: namely, the relationship of faith in that forgiveness promised by Christ's death and resurrection to the works which man undertakes believing them to be God's will, and by performing which he thinks he can justify himself in his own eyes and before God.

Concepts such as the theology of development or the theology of revolution can only have meaning when, instead of attempting to sanctify human aspirations, they seek to do God's will. Indeed, may not God be hidden behind all these aspirations and insights formulated by human beings and therefore by their very nature prone to human fallibility?

NOTES

1. *Uppsala Official Report*, Appendix IV, par. 27.

2. Quoted from K. Lefringhausen, 'Uppsala am Vorabend des zweiten Entwicklungsjahrzehntes (Sektion III)', *Ökumenisches Rundschau* 18, no. 1, 1969, p. 61.

3. Geneva Report, p. 200, par. 20.

4. D. von Oppen, *Das personale Zeitalter*, Kreuz-Verlag, Stuttgart, 1960, p. 219.

5. K. Lefringhausen, *art. cit.*, *Ökumenisches Rundschau* 18, no. 1, 1969, pp. 53–60.

6. R. Dickinson, *Line and Plummet*, World Council of Churches, Geneva, 1968, p. 90.

7. *Bedingungen des Friedens*, Vandenhoeck und Ruprecht, Göttingen, 1963.

8. See the Report of the Committee on Church and Society presented to the Assembly at Uppsala, Sections 19–24.

9. *Uppsala Official Report*, Appendix IV, par. 30.

10. *Uppsala Official Report*, Appendix V.

6

Reflections of a Lay Economist from a
Developing Country

SAMUEL L. PARMAR

1 *New Trends in Ecumenical Social Thought*

The World Council of Churches does not as yet have a well-formulated theology of development. Indeed, it cannot, for two important reasons: first, because we are newcomers to the development discussion and second, because new issues keep cropping up in the development debate necessitating a re-examination of views held thus far.

Thus the word 'towards' in the title of Part Two of this book is the key word. We have begun a learning process in an area characterized by a rapid rate of obsolescence of ideas. To understand social processes one has to unlearn and discard some inherited and even recently acquired approaches. Consequently systematic theologizing can easily become an exercise in irrelevance. Any attempt to evolve a Christian understanding of the technological and social revolutions of our times has to be tentative and exploratory. A crystallized Christian view is neither possible nor desirable.

The ecumenical concern for development really began at the World Conference on Church and Society, Geneva, 1966. But in a short span of less than four years there have been significant changes in the perspective on development. For example, the emphasis at Geneva in 1966 was on international co-operation for development and a 'one-world' approach. Development enthusiasts took up the cry of 1 per cent aid from rich to poor nations. In fact some of the leading experts lent their support to a much higher percentage. The joint Roman Catholic/World Council consultation on World Cooperation for Development at Beirut in April 1968 reiterated this position. But it was too close to UNCTAD II to escape the growing disillusionment with existing forms of international economic co-operation. Later, at the

Uppsala Assembly, the emphasis seemed to shift to economic justice internationally and nationally. It was recognized that without a framework of justice transfer of resources from one country to another would prove ineffective. In recent discussions at the SODEPAX consultation at Montreal in 1969 and the first meeting of the full SODEPAX Committee in Switzerland in July 1969, a number of new emphases have emerged, such as international co-operation within a framework of justice and self-reliance, the primary need of radical change in the structures of society, development as being more than mere economic growth, and the importance of ideological factors.

Participants in these conferences may differ with the above assessment. That would not invalidate the point in question, namely that ecumenical thinking on development is diverse and characterized by continuous change in emphasis, priorities and perspectives. Therefore in any attempt to evolve a Christian understanding of development the fluid nature of the subject should be kept in mind. Otherwise a fragmentary view may be projected as a comprehensive one, thereby lending rigidity to the theological quest when the situation demands openness and flexibility.

In this quest two entities have to be held together in dynamic relationship. The first is the gospel with its message of hope for humanity. It transcends time, space and situations but at the same time bears on problems of the day concerned with the aspirations and struggles of man. Its universality must encompass the particularity of the contemporary, otherwise there will be a tendency to think, speak and relate only to the beyond. That would make the Christian message escapist and irrelevant. Men are involved in the problems and struggles of society, which is in the throes of revolutionary change. Here we have the second entity: the existing situation. To this the gospel speaks words of hope, and within this the redemptive work of God is seen.

If we start with the cardinal elements of our faith and apply our understanding of it to society without considering what is happening, we may have systematic theology but not a theology of society as it is. On the other hand if we only consider the situation without constantly relating it to a Christian frame of reference, we may have a satisfactory knowledge of contemporary events but will fail to be involved in it as instruments of hope and peace. It is necessary to illuminate the situation by the gospel; it is equally necessary to re-examine and reinterpret our understanding of the gospel in the light of human situations.

Correlating the message of the gospel and the situation is the task of the ecumenical theologian. Others, like the author, who have no pretensions to theology can contribute by reflecting upon the situation so as to focus on the issues that theologians should consider. That is the general approach of this paper. Hence it contains some reflections on the aftermath of Geneva and then picks out a few of the crucial issues in the development debate today.

II   *The Geneva Conference and its Sequel*

The World Conference on Church and Society, Geneva, 1966, had a special flavour. That should not be surprising. Some of its ingredients differed strikingly from those of previous ecumenical meetings on societal issues. Reference will be made to three: first, the composition of participants and its bearing on the orientation and total thinking of the conference; second, the nature of the contemporary situation wherein the interplay of the technological and social revolutions of our times was presenting new possibilities and threats to the human community; third, a significant breakthrough in the approach to theology.

Composition and its effect on content

According to the official report of the conference a majority of participants were laymen: professional men, economists, political leaders, social workers, businessmen, social and physical scientists; the rest were theologians and church leaders. Almost half were from Asia, Africa and Latin America. Such a preponderance of non-theologians with a high percentage of representatives from developing countries was bound to leave its mark on the deliberations of the conference.

A majority of lay participants were new to the ecumenical movement. Quite a number had no *official* links with local or national church organizations. They were, therefore, not of the 'establishment'. There are no clear criteria to judge an authentic layman. But non-exposure to the conventional ecumenical style of thinking, functioning and participating in conferences lent an undeniable touch of authenticity. Whatever the quality of the contributions of such newcomers, they are the ones with the right credentials to work at the concerns and expectations of the church in the world. Not infrequently the lay component of national and international ecumenical gatherings is a part of the in-group, and hence somewhat domesticated, if not completely broken in. This could not be said of the majority of the lay members of the Geneva Conference. They brought a new and refreshing type of voice into ecumenical deliberations and raised vital questions which a theology of man and society must deal with if it is to speak a relevant word to our times.

Some manifested an impatience with such little theological discussion as there was. This was, however, not a denigration of theology but a dissatisfaction with a certain kind of theology which has tended to be condescending towards the secular, categorical and triumphalist by turns, indifferent to social processes, individualistic and ingrown, and occasionally fomenting self-esteem and self-righteousness in the church. It is not that relevance is the only test of good theology. There is a danger that expediency or acceptability by society may be made yardsticks to judge relevance. If theology is about eternal truth it must be both time-bound and time-transcending. So we have to be careful when assessing relevance. Yet since theology embraces the deepest yearnings of man it must bear upon contemporary tensions, conflicts and expectations. Concern for development is part of the Christian concern for the whole man, which means man in terms of his total societal relations. He is not just a child of God whose spiritual well-being should be promoted, but also one whose body is involved in his spirituality and should, therefore, be adequately provided for. Hence we have to consider the values, institutions and structures of society, for these determine the extent of human freedom or enslavement. Poverty and dehumanization are not merely economic factors. They are more significantly a constellation of attitudes culminating in apathy and defeatism. They emerge from, and are conditioned by, the social framework that exercises dominance over men's minds and values. For these reasons we have also to look at man not just as an individual but as part of a community of relationships. A Christian view of society then becomes community- and structure-oriented.

The impact of the ideas and concerns of the 'third world' has brought a new direction to Christian social thinking. In previous ecumenical meetings from Stockholm to Evanston there was a dominance of Western theological and social thought. Some eminent non-Western thinkers also operated within a Western frame of thinking. Even New Delhi in 1961 did not come out with the perspective on social issues which could have been expected by its geographical setting. The Rapid Social Change Studies from 1955 provided the first wider drawing in of views from Asia, Africa and Latin America. But an over-arching influence of Western viewpoints remained. The term 'the Responsible Society', an approach which continues to have its adherents in the ecumenical family, was too evolutionary a concept to suit the urges of the developing peoples. Where structures have ossified into custodians of no change, nothing short of a radical transformation can meet the pressing imperatives of development. Perhaps the more developed nations have a built-in stability in their structures, which are flexible enough to accommodate change and even to initiate it (though recent events like the black revolution in the USA and the

ferment of youth in Western Europe would question this). However
the fact remains that without 'revolutionary change' the forces of
progress cannot make any headway in developing countries.

The variegated group assembled at Geneva succeeded by and large
in posing the problems of the 'third world' as seen, experienced and
understood by them and not as these might appear to people from
an external vantage point. We see development not merely as increased
production through a process that generates larger resources, but a
struggle for economic equality, new property relations, and the
elimination of exploitation nationally and internationally.

Since the Geneva Conference, churches and Christian groups in
many parts of the world have been stimulated to engage in a serious
study of social movements and to seek out ways of direct involvement.
It has become customary in ecumenical circles to describe the conference as a landmark. While this is a legitimate distinction within
the ecumenical family, it should not be forgotten that we are latecomers
on the development scene.

Most of the issues discussed at Geneva in 1966 and subsequent
conferences have been studied and analysed at greater depth in secular
circles over the last two decades. Problems of development and underdevelopment; structures of trade, aid and investment; possibilities and
problems of technology; the widening gap between rich and poor
nations; conflicts of ideologies and political systems; world peace;
international co-operation for development, are subjects on which
much thinking has been done at various levels in the post-war period.
In comparison to the available literature and expertise on these issues
the findings of ecumenical conferences are quite modest and may
not have broken any new ground.

Therefore we are neither trail-blazers nor pace-setters, but more
like dazed stragglers joining belatedly the mainstream of social thinking.
For this reason an important part of our Christian obedience is to
listen to the voices of the 'world'. No longer can we make pronouncements to the world outside. The era of theological pontification is
happily on its way out. This is the best thing that could have happened
to the Church. In all important documents of the World Council of
Churches it is stressed that we are speaking to the churches and not
prescribing for the ills of the world.

However, we need not bemoan the fact that our thinking on development is not of the trail-blazing variety. Looking ahead there is no
reason why we cannot keep abreast of progressive thinking on these
issues and occasionally serve as catalysts, creative dissenters and even
pace-setters. The present period may, in fact, be favourable to such
possibilities. Frustrations of the first development decade have dam-

pened enthusiasm for development through world co-operation. Hopes raised in the early sixties have been belied by time and events. There have been no significant changes in international economic relationships to ensure that the flow of resources from rich to poor nations will benefit the latter. On the contrary inequalities have increased, the trade pattern has become more adverse to developing nations, the rules of the game of private investment remain unaltered, and so on. Consequently there is on both sides a re-examining not only of the structures of international co-operation but of the whole concept of development through such co-operation. If existing patterns inhibit growth and increase burdens on developing nations it is natural that they tend to lose confidence in the whole approach of development through international co-operation.

On the other hand if all rational considerations lead to the conclusion that the abilities of the technological revolution can be harnessed to meet the needs of the 'third world', the case for international co-operation remains strong. Is it possible that ecumenical concern for development will show a way out of the present impasse? Many of the current difficulties arise because in the international economy there is a continuance of values and institutions of the nineteenth century while grappling with problems of the twentieth. Perhaps political, economic and military factors geared to the 'enlightened self-interest' approach may not force developed nations to work for more egalitarian patterns of international relationships. Why then should they initiate change which does not guarantee tangible advantages to them in the foreseeable future? One could argue that they should do this not because it is expedient but because it is right. That introduces a moral element in international decisions. Social scientists will fight shy of it. At this point Christian social thinking may provide some guidelines.

The revolutions of our times

Contemporary conditions provided the other ingredient which made Geneva 1966 qualitatively different from previous ecumenical deliberations on societal issues. Our age is marked by two on-going revolutions: the technological and the social. Although all nations experience their impact, the former is more evident in developed countries and the latter in the developing. In their positive expressions these could be complementary, with the increased productive power generated by the first meeting the rising expectations characterizing the second. It is being said that for the first time in human history technology gives to mankind the power to eradicate want and misery from the face of the earth. Economics, the 'dismal science', obsessed with scarcity, may now be based on potential abundance. That would outdate most of our 'conventional wisdom' and the policies and politico-economic structures built on it. If continuance of poverty is no longer to be accepted as a given fact of life, and yet we find that povery and inequality continue their tyranny, it only means that existing structures are regressive and incapable of actualizing the promise of technology. Such structures must go, constitutionally if possible, otherwise by extra-constitutional struggles. The social revolution becomes necessary to release the creativity of the technological revolution.

While acknowledging the positive aspects of these revolutions their inherent dangers should be kept in view. The same technology that provides tremendous potential for increased production also gives an over-kill capacity through monstrous devices of warfare. Its power to eliminate poverty is counterbalanced by its ability to destroy the world. It would be naïve to ignore the negative face of technology, for that has been more evident. The nuclear age was ushered in by the exigencies of the Second World War. This power was invented as an engine of destruction. Its symbol continues to be Hiroshima. It is the key factor in the balance of terror that is supposed to ensure world peace in our times. If it is to serve as an instrument of human welfare it has first to be civilized. So long as the original contamination persists one cannot sing paeans of praise to technology.

Technology is power. Power is never neutral, for it operates within a given framework and reflects the values undergirding it. Thus if the social framework contains elements of exploitation of the many by the few, technological power will strengthen the hold of the forces of domination. A radical change in the framework with new rules of the game becomes a necessary precondition for giving full play to the liberating and humanizing potential of technology. For that reason the values that determine and govern social relationships and pertain to social classes (such as property, organization of production, distribution of the social product) have to be changed. New institutions can be built only on new values. This is the major challenge of the technological revolution, and here again the response has to come from the social revolution.

Similarly the social revolution is a mixture of promise and threat. To the extent that it mobilizes the army of underprivileged to press for a new deal it is a bearer of hope. But predatory groups, with no commitment to social justice, can misuse the expectations of the people and continue to dupe and enslave them. In the name of change and progress oligarchies and anti-people dictatorships have come into power. Existing inequalities breed class tension and will explode in some form of conflict if the social order is not radically changed. But this very possibility gives power to organized reaction to manipulate popular discontent. How many 'revolutions' have petered out into 'revolts' with power passing from one selfish group to another, all engaged in crushing the aspirations of the people!

As we attempt to develop a Christian understanding of society the ambiguous character of the contemporary revolutions must always be kept in mind, lest we feel tempted to sanctify all that goes on in the name of technology and social upheaval.

Towards a new theological approach

Concern for development is helping the World Council of Churches to make a significant theological breakthrough. This may sound strange in view of a fairly widespread criticism (by admirers and denigrators alike) that Geneva 1966 and subsequent conferences on social questions have lacked theological content and depth. Such criticisms stem from a traditional notion of the place of theology in ecumenical conferences. Since Geneva the style has changed. Theological discussions are neither over-arching, nor alongside, but integrated with discussions of social issues. Those who are accustomed to an artificial compartmentalization between theological and societal fail to see the inherent possibilities of the new pattern. It has already encouraged new insights to some of which reference is now made.

1. The *laissez-faire* approach which was reflected (and still is) in much of Christian understanding of society has been replaced by a structure-oriented approach.

Christian understanding of society has been influenced by the social values of the milieu in which it originated. The dominant theology has been Western. In these societies social attitudes were conditioned by *laissez-faire*, gradualism and faith in evolutionary change. Personal piety, individual salvation, charity and good works, and acceptance of the social framework were emphasized. It was believed that if persons are good society will become good; if healthy influences are injected into a social system through education, welfare, etc., they will gradually spread and transform society; if human needs are met the beneficiaries will grow into responsible persons and initiate reform to eliminate poverty, and so on.

It would be unfair to criticize this approach as lacking in social responsibility, or being spiritualistic or other-worldly. It is very much concerned with existing human problems, and represents in fact a Christian response to them. It does not advocate withdrawal and non-involvement but assumes that through individual goodness society can be transformed and the kingdom of God extended. Thus personal piety becomes a means for social change. But since individual action provides the dynamic for social improvement there is no need to challenge the existing social framework. The traditional Christian approach to society was not indifferent to environment, but it operated with a philosophy which made structural change superfluous. The fault was in the presuppositions.

At Geneva and since we have been saying that the social framework prevents individual goodness from transforming society. Non-involvement with social processes helps to entrench and perpetuate injustice. Therefore our struggle has to be against inhuman structures also. Viewed from this standpoint the earlier individual-oriented theology becomes an anachronism in today's situation. And yet the fact remains that its intention was the well-being of the total community.

That again is in keeping with the *laissez-faire* tradition. In its original form its objective was maximum social welfare. Freedom of individual action, non-interference with market forces, unquestioned acceptance of the social framework were supposed to ensure progress. Unfettered pursuit of individual self interest was only the means for the pre-eminent objective, i.e. social well-being. History exposed the *naïveté* of such presuppositions. In pursuing self-interest individuals converted it from a means to the primary end, with obvious damage to community interests. Selfishness and avarice joined hands with thrift and industry. Efficiency became an instrument for increasing power over means of production. The privileged few dominated the disinherited many. Under such conditions the social framework helped to consolidate and perpetuate the suzerainty of dominant groups. Class tensions went deep and forced society towards regulation, state-interference and planning. Now it is recognized that without necessary alterations in the social framework society cannot be transformed.

However, the shift to structure-oriented theology should not minimize the importance of personal commitment. The arena for working out personal piety is society. Persons and processes have to be in creative relationship before radical change can be brought about. Failure to see this vital link may swing us from personal to social pietism, that is, concern for society without personal commitment. Our new approach, if it may be called that, is not a rejection of the earlier one but a discovery of the creative elements it had, which time and custom had obscured. A structure-oriented Christian understanding is a logical outcome of personal Christian obedience.

In subscribing to the new approach we are, of course, reflecting social values that have gained ascendancy and are being influenced by prevalent social values and attitudes. This was precisely the situation of the Christian advocates of *laissez-faire*. And yet in a significant sense there is a forward movement. We are progressing from a theology based upon the realities of a bygone age to one that is struggling to relate itself to contemporary social realities.

Once Christian social thinking is freed from its narrow individualistic orientation it acquires new dimensions. In dealing with human needs we cannot any longer confine ourselves to their surface manifestations but have to grapple with their fundamental causes. Hunger, disease, illiteracy, and various other expressions of deprivation are symptoms of the social malaise. If charity and good works are the total extent of our social involvement we become society's ambulance corps – providing limited assistance to victims of social processes but incapable or un-concerned about the processes themselves. The attack has to be against the structures of privilege and domination that generate and perpetuate poverty. For example, hungry and unemployed landless workers need immediate help. Let us provide that to the extent we can. But let us then join the struggle for land reform and an egalitarian social order without which the problem can never be solved. That would mean taking a stand against existing land legislation and its political props. In many Asian and Latin American countries a movement for land reform spells revolution, not in the sense of violent upheaval but as a radical change in economic relationships between social classes. Thus initial involvement at the micro-level should lead into involvement with the social framework, that is, at the macro-level. Short of that our well-intentioned Christian social service will merit the criticism that it provides temporary relief to the have-nots and blunts their indignation at the existing order. Consequently it becomes counter-revolutionary.

Social and economic change at the macro-level comes through governments. If a government is responsive to human needs and acts as a change-generator a new deal for the dispossessed groups is possible. But when it is change-resisting our commitment to serve the needy necessitates lending support to movements to reform or dislodge the power-structure.

Christian social action should see more clearly the relation between the sectional and the total. For example, in the context of international co-operation for development if it is assumed that capital resources or surplus food or techniques or skilled personnel or volunteers from outside will necessarily stimulate and sustain a process of development, we are falling again into the *laissez-faire* trap: that injection of this or that healthy force will somehow vitalize the whole system. The existing system has institutional rigidities that first resist and then neutralize healthy forces. Therefore, simultaneously with the insertion of healthy sectional influences an attempt must be made to restructure the social framework in such manner that total gains will be maximized. Take another example, that of education, which is generally accepted as an important determinant of development. In many Asian and African countries the educated have become the new *élite*, and hence part of the ruling class with a vested interest in the *status quo*. A potential healthy influence succumbs to the paralysing effects of the social framework.

2. There is a new awareness of the tension between order and justice. This debate has assumed considerable importance in recent ecumenical discussions. The primacy of justice is being recognized. Order and social organization exist to ensure justice. But quite often the contrary happens. Established authority provides sanction, legitimacy and power for unjust socio-economic relationships. Under its umbrella exploitation, hidden violence and human degradation flourish. Those who claim to be committed to justice have no option but to question and oppose such 'establishment'. An evolutionary, one thing at a time, approach is inappropriate. Gradualism tends to rationalize the *status quo*, and slow change approximates to no change. If it is part of our Christian obedience to be reconcilers by removing injustice which is the main cause of conflict, there is no escape from an involvement with changing structures.

3. The understanding of the lordship of Christ has acquired a new dimension. Certainly this lordship is over the hearts of men, bringing about a 'new creation' in their personal lives and interpersonal relationships. But in seeking the will of the Lord of history we have to take the 'principalities and powers' seriously. Just as there can be no separation between the individual and the social, neither can there be between the spiritual and the temporal. Many a time historical processes have challenged the church to its true obedience. Compromise with existing power structures stifles the prophetic ministry of the church. Only when we see how God is at work in the forces of change outside the church are we able to seek renewal.

4. There is now a clearer comprehension of the implication of Christian unity. The major emphasis of the ecumenical movement has been the unity of all churches. We have seen this as an essential part of Christian obedience. But there is a danger that unity may become an end in itself, perhaps as a new form of the *corpus Christianum*. Unity is for mission, and mission is to serve the whole of God's creation, within or outside the Christian fold. Real unity is, therefore, to be in community not only with fellow believers but with the whole inhabited earth. Our concern for development becomes an integral part of this mission. It is not merely social activism but a response to our calling. This should be the new sense in which we talk about the servant church.

5. We are gradually discerning our new vocation, that of a creative minority. Organizational unity may increase our numbers but the fact remains that in the post-Christian civilization of the West, as well as in terms of its officially small numbers in the rest of the world, the church is a minority. This should be a matter of joy. A majority church conforms to the values and ways of the ruling group. In its organized form Christianity has often been an appendage of the state. Theology has provided a rationalization of the policies pursued by the ruling powers. And this is not just a historical occurrence; it is happening in many parts of the world today. In the name of Christ feudal, capitalist and fascist views have been supported. Racism, economic and social inequality, colonialism, big-power chauvinism, have not lacked Christian apologists. The mission of the church has often become a projection of political and cultural domination. This kind of legacy is not easily given up. Perhaps the shedding of a majority complex with its overtones of triumphalism and self-righteousness will revitalize the church as it seeks to express a structure-oriented theology through its life and work.

III   *Issues in the Development Debate*

In the second half of this essay an attempt is made to pick out some significant strands of ecumenical thinking on development since Geneva 1966. As with previous sections, the analysis reflects the author's personal viewpoint without claiming to represent either the opinion of the 'third world' or a 'consensus' position of the World Council of Churches. The important thing to bear in mind is that these problems cannot be ignored by any theology of development.

The 'one world' approach: from welfare state to welfare world

Ecumenical social thinking continues to emphasize development through international co-operation. Assistance by developed to developing countries is seen as an extension of the welfare state policy beyond national frontiers. The social philosophy underlying this considers all nations as parts of a single human community.

Three cardinal elements constitute the welfare state approach. First, the resources of the nation should be used for the well-being of the total national community. Secondly, the relatively stronger sections should bear greater burdens in the interest of the weaker. Thirdly, the state should function as the agency to initiate and implement such policies. Both developed and developing nations subscribe (in varying degrees, of course) to such an approach in their domestic policies. Tax structures, price-support policies, selective subsidies, social security programmes, special rights to erstwhile underprivileged groups, etc., exemplify this. Improvement in the economic condition of weaker segments of the economy is recognized as an essential condition of stability and growth. Such policies are not institutionalized charity but a rational use of national resources to ensure optimum production and welfare. The interests of all sections are interrelated; weakness in any sector endangers the prosperity of all sectors.

On the basis of national experiences, especially of many developed countries, it is being suggested that this would be the most efficacious policy for the whole world. Seen in a global context, developing nations are analogous to weaker economic sections within a country. The logical basis for international economic co-operation would then be to move from a welfare state to a welfare world. This is certainly desirable; is it feasible?

To project the vision of a welfare world and attempt to shape international policies accordingly is a progressive step which merits our support, despite temporary setbacks. This would be the only way to bring together the possibilities of the technological revolution and the aspirations of the social revolution. But a number of obstacles impede its realization.

First, within a nation the government is the agency for promoting welfare state policies. There is no corresponding authority or power-structure at the world level and no likelihood of the establishment of one in the near future.

Secondly, the genesis of the modern welfare state has been some form of class-conflict. Owning classes have not given up their privileges by accepting rational arguments that their welfare was eventually tied up with that of the dispossessed. On the contrary they have waged last-ditch struggles to resist the granting of minimal additional facilities to the latter. It is only through organized resistance by trade unions, agrarian groups, etc., that the 'have-nots' have wrested some of their rightful share from the dominant class. No concessions have been given without sustained pressure. Applying this analogy to the relations between developed and developing nations, what pressures can the latter bring to bear on the former to initiate the move towards a welfare world? Economic pressure is negligible. In fact it is developing economies that are vulnerable to action by the developed. The same would hold for political and military factors.

Thirdly, the non-homogeneity of developing nations presents another difficulty. There is a tendency to put all these nations in one basket and assume that they have a common interest, a common approach and, therefore, common policies. Nothing could be further from the real situation. Even within a single nation class unity is seldom possible.

Social, cultural, ethnic and historical factors undermine it. How can it then be expected that the assorted group of nations constituting the 'third world' would easily weld into one class arrayed against the developed nations? Many of the differences between developing nations seem almost irreconcilable in the short run. As a result there is hardly any possibility of a united front of the 'South' pressurizing the 'North' to forgo some of its immediate advantages for the sake of future benefits.

Lack of social and economic homogeneity is a characteristic of developed countries also. A nation may be called rich but it has its exploited and submerged groups, e.g. blacks in the USA, migrant workers in Western Europe, and so on. Projection of such a welfare state pattern to the world would become, in effect, a projection of inequalities and unjust social structures. Therefore, before we apply the welfare concept to international relations we must recognize that its success rests upon the pursuit of social justice and egalitarianism within developed nations. Viewed thus, the struggle of underprivileged groups in any nation becomes a part of the larger struggle for international social justice.

Fourthly, the welfare-based 'one world' approach is evolutionary, while the problems of developing nations require radical solutions. Many factors invalidate gradualism as the basis of policies. Among these are the incessant pressure of the revolution of rising expectations; growing demographic burdens; problems generated by some welfare measures, such as the fall in the death rate and a consequent population explosion, or the diversion of resources from the high-income, traditionally saving group to the low-income, traditionally non-saving group; the whole dilemma of welfare versus growth; the fact that in contrast to the pre-development position of today's developed nations, the 'third world' has neither colonies and dependencies to draw upon nor labour-capital relations which would permit creation of capital by a pauperization of the working class; and a situation where two-thirds of the world is striving simultaneously to develop at maximum speed, so that no nation in the group has the advantage of being the only one to secure resources for development from others. Today's developed nations had achieved a fair degree of economic growth before their people became politically activated. It is the reverse in developing countries where intense political activism exists before any economic headway has been made. Such a combination contributes to a revolutionary climate. Under the circumstances proposals for a world tax for development, multilateralization of foreign aid, etc., are helpful but grossly inadequate to deal with the fundamental problems of development.

Fallacies in the 'enlightened self-interest' standpoint

Arguments for international co-operation based on enlightened self-interest are beginning to appear untenable. The emergence of the welfare state is supposed to have resulted from the enlightened self-interest of dominant economic groups. They saw that by paying higher wages to labour or ensuring better prices to the agricultural sector their products would be assured of a good market. Consequently economic depression, the bugbear of the owners of means of production, could be avoided. State action in the economic sphere was accepted because it helped to maintain effective demand and thereby guarantee markets and profits. Further, it was felt that a satisfied proletariat would be less inclined to create disorder. So both on economic and political grounds it was in the interest of the 'haves' to forgo some present gain in favour of future.

Extending this approach to the world economy it is argued that economic progress of developing countries would in the long run benefit the developed by ensuring better markets and outlets for investment. Improvement in economic conditions would also contribute to political stability in the 'third world', and hence to better prospects for world peace. At Geneva in 1966 two important slogans were: 'Poverty anywhere is a threat to prosperity everywhere' and 'The world cannot continue to live one-third developed and two-thirds underdeveloped'.

But the experience of the sixties casts doubts on such inferences. Developed nations are expanding trade and investment within their group and becoming less dependent for markets and investment outlets on the developing. Technology reduces the importance of developing countries as suppliers of raw materials, and low *per capita* income their importance as promising markets. The thaw in the cold war has opened glittering prospects of increased economic relationships between the 'West' and the 'East'. Certainly the economic self-interest of developed nations may not prompt them to come closer to the developing.

On the political side the portrayal of poverty-generated discontent in developing nations being a threat to the peace and stability of the developed nations is an overworked argument. All threats to world peace in the post-war period have come from the big powers, whether in Cuba, Vietnam, the Middle East or Berlin. Developing nations are not united; they do not dispose of economic and military power to endanger developed nations; they seem to be more busy fighting each other. In fact they provide the big powers with an opportunity to confront each other by proxy. Rather than clash directly to their mutual destruction these powers export their tensions to areas of conflict in the 'third world'. What happens to the enlightened self-interest argument in such a situation?

This is the set-up today. Economically and militarily the big powers are becoming stronger and will continue to do so. As their ideological differences decrease there is a convergence of their policies. Unless they are gripped by an uncontrollable death wish there will be increasing co-operation and collaboration between them. They are likely to maintain their stability and high economic standards without bothering much about the developing nations. Therefore, something more dynamic than enlightened self-interest must undergird the 'one-world' approach.

A more basic weakness of the enlightened self-interest approach is that it is a class doctrine. The interests of the privileged sections are made the basis of socio-economic policy. To say that erstwhile exploited groups should be helped to develop because this is in the interest of their exploiters is, to say the least, a callous approach to human and societal problems. Black Americans or outcaste Hindus and other disinherited groups resent such objectification. They demand their due on grounds of social justice and human rights, irrespective of whether this does or does not benefit privileged sections. The same applies to nations. Developing countries press for more equitable sharing of the world's resources on grounds of international economic justice and not because it may benefit rich nations also. Mutual benefits may be inherent in international economic co-operation. But that is incidental, not central. The vital factor is justice rather than enlightened self-interest. This dimension of the problem forces us to revise the nature and content of the 'one-world' approach which has gained currency in ecumenical thinking.

International co-operation must be built on internal change

If the national experience of developed countries or enlightened self-interest fail to provide a satisfactory rationale of the welfare-world approach, we have to find new underpinnings for it. This is provided by social justice. Development is a struggle for both economic betterment and equality. In fact the quest for equality motivates efforts for economic growth. Today mankind has resources and technology to eliminate material deprivation. Poverty is eradicable. And yet it continues. The basic reason is a maldistribution of economic and political power. Therefore, the problem is not one of enhanced production, because what society produces today is adequate to meet the basic needs of all, but of just distribution of economic and political power. Concern for development then becomes a struggle for more just political and economic structures, both within nations and in the international economy.

Despite the disappointments of the past decade we must continue efforts to promote international co-operation, but the real struggle has to be waged nationally, and this for a number of reasons:

Firstly, our immediate arena of action is our own country. Other things being equal, if we cannot make much headway in influencing national policies the chances of our influencing international policies are dimmer. In any case development is the responsibility of each nation. Help from others can accelerate the process but the major burden has to be borne by the people concerned.

Secondly, the nation state is a power structure through which egalitarian policies can be implemented. No such structure exists internationally. Rather than build from the top downwards, it is advisable to move from the national to the international.

Thirdly, pursuit of policies geared to social justice gives a nation the right to propagate similar policies for international relations. It is hypocritical and incongruous for representatives of developing nations to inveigh against the widening gap between rich and poor nations when in their own countries economic and social inequalities are on the increase; all the more when those who speak in international forums come from the relatively affluent groups in developing countries and are beneficiaries of the existing non-egalitarian process.

A new form of international class struggle may be in the making. Groups which fight for domestic social justice in developed and developing countries may become partners in a common global endeavour. The battlelines are no longer drawn between 'North' and 'South' but between the haves of the world and the have-nots, so that the struggle for social justice in any part of the world is linked with a similar struggle in any other part. International co-operation may not, therefore, be between nations as such but between fighters for justice in different nations. This does not eliminate nationalism as a vital factor in the growth process of developing countries, but supplements it.

Fourthly, once the primacy of action at the national level is recognized, we can see the positive aspects of nationalism. In developing countries a variety of parochial loyalties, tribal, linguistic, caste-based, sub-regional, etc., subvert development effort. Unity and community at the national level are essential conditions for fighting poverty. Nationalism symbolizes these and represents an outward movement from narrow to larger loyalties. It then corresponds to progressive movements among developed countries from welfare states to a welfare region, such as the European Economic Community, and the projected movement to a welfare world. In its positive form nationalism is not isolationist but outreaching, and hence an indispensable pre-condition for effective international co-operation.

It is true that the negative face of nationalism has been more evident in history, especially in that of today's developed nations. It has served as an instrument of aggrandizement, expansionism, colonialism and ideological domination. These dangers cannot be denied. But for developing countries in their present historical stage nationalism represents a progressive movement without which a social and economic breakthrough is not possible. The breakdown of monolithic communism, as shown by the Sino-Soviet ideological split, is a consequence of the nationalistic urges of a developing country. Monolithic ideologies are a threat to peace in a pluralistic world. We have, therefore, to recognize the existence of nationalism as an important fact of international life, and strive to purge it of its reprehensible elements.

The 'widening gap' / 'catching up' theory and the need for a new approach

Echoing the prevailing sentiment, ecumenical thinking on development considers the widening gap between rich and poor countries as the most serious threat to world peace. This is erroneous.

In the first place, world peace is threatened by the brinkmanship of big powers rather than by growing international inequalities. Secondly, where developing nations may pose a threat to peace it is only by conflicts among them or internal civil strife. These are independent of the widening gap. Thirdly, internal instability in developing nations results from domestic inequality. To the extent that they are a threat to peace the cause is a lack of social justice. Fourthly, in those conflicts between developing nations into which big powers are drawn, thus endangering world peace, the causes are ideological, racial, political, historical or linked with colonial legacies, rather than economic. One sees this in the case of Vietnam, the Middle East, Rhodesia, Nigeria, the Indo-Pakistan sub-continent, Cuba, Czechoslovakia, the Congo, and elsewhere. Why then hold the widening gap, which is essentially an economic phenomenon, as the Damocles' sword over humanity? If the intention is to frighten the 'North' into doing more for the 'South' it is a self-defeating argument. Fear cannot be the basis of long-term policies such as development calls for. If, however, the purpose is to condemn the widening gap as a denial of international economic justice, the present hysteria and sloppy sentimentalism in its advocacy should be replaced by sound, rational arguments.

All future projections about the world economy show that the gap between rich and poor nations will increase. This is due to the growing demographic gap which increases the burdens of developing countries, and the widening technological gap which enhances the productive

F

capacity of developed countries. By AD 2000 the present 1:30 ratio between the *per capita* incomes of India and the USA will increase to 1:100. The Indian economy is expected to have a higher absolute rate of growth than the USA economy and yet the gap will grow. Even if international economic relations are purged of their present inequities in trade, investment, and loan policies *vis-à-vis* developing nations, international economic inequalities will increase. So the whole 'catching up' emphasis needs re-examination.

Each developing nation has to compete with its own past performance. So long as it continues to do better than its previous best, if possible through assistance from other nations, it is achieving development, even though in terms of relative *per capita* incomes it may become poorer. Our present understanding of poverty and development does not incorporate such an understanding. That should prompt us to seek for a new meaning of development. Our yardsticks are essentially economic. But development is much more than economic growth. Developing nations should have the self-confidence to realize that they are rich in a number of ways that are non-quantifiable and do not fall within the purview of economic calculations.

On the other side developed nations are experiencing the poverty of affluence. Men feel like robots enslaved to a technological society. Structures manipulate persons who feel alienated and confused. A revolt against the tyranny of technology is growing. People wish to break free from the stifling influence of things, of an unending pursuit of material well-being. While a positive materialism is important for nations at a sub-marginal level of existence, they must see the debilitating effects of unbridled materialism. We are only beginning to recognize the need for a new understanding of development wherein human development overrides economic development. But it remains an unexplored territory which ecumenical thinking would do well to reconnoitre. We from developing countries must realize that we are operating with a Western understanding of development under which the harder we work the relatively poorer we become. Our quest for self-reliance should not be limited only to productive and technical processes, but more vitally to the discovery of indigenous concepts in keeping with our reality and ethos.

International co-operation for self-reliance: a new approach to aid

Ecumenical concern for development has done much to create public opinion in favour of 1 per cent GNP as aid to developing countries. This is a laudable effort. But it is necessary to see the aid question in proper perspective. Firstly, transfer of resources from rich to poor nations should not be seen in the traditional framework of charity and good works but as a necessary expression of international economic justice. One wonders how clearly some of the ardent supporters of the 1 per cent idea see this. Secondly, aid (most of which is through loans) is only one factor in a package deal which consists of structural changes in trade, foreign investments, and domestic production patterns of donor nations. In fact the structural factors should be given higher priority because resources can give desired results only if the right conditions for their use are created. Our preoccupation with aid may have changed for the worse the priorities within the package deal. Thirdly, aid should promote self-sustained growth, more correctly called self-reliance. By keeping these elements together we can have a dynamic approach to the whole matter; not otherwise.

The experience of the sixties points to basic weaknesses in the aid-trade-development relationship. The bulk of foreign aid is in the form of loans. The burden of debt repayments continues to increase, making heavy inroads on the hard-earned foreign exchange resources of many developing countries. What is earned through export promotion and saved through import restriction is often not enough to meet debt servicing charges and repayment of principal. Given the structures through which resources are transferred it is inconceivable that the situation could be eased in the foreseeable future.

The position becomes even more unsatisfactory when one links up the trade-aid process. Transfer of 1 per cent GNP from rich to poor nations, even if it materialized, would not improve the situation because debt repayment, adverse terms of trade and the restrictive trade policies of developed nations combine to take away more from the normal trade income of developing countries than the quantity of aid they receive. That is why we seem to have reached a point where aid as mere transfer of resources is self-defeating unless it is undergirded by new structures of trade, and a new international division of labour which takes account of the production potentiality of developing nations.

Rightly understood, aid is good if it leads to no aid, i.e. if it generates a process of production and exchange which makes the initial transfers self-liquidating. That is what one means by the self-reliance of recipient nations. It is not a plea for closed economic development on a self-sufficiency basis, but for international partnership where each injection of external resources strengthens the production and export capacity of developing nations. Existing international structures have not so far helped to strengthen such trends. We are then stuck with aid which increases domination of the giver and dependence of the receiver. It is help leading to helplessness, not to self-reliance; it increases international economic inequality. The time has come to cry a halt to such regressive aid, and we in ecumenical circles committed to world co-operation for development should press for structural changes in the international economy and in those of donor nations, through which alone aid can become dynamic.

From pragmatism to a new ideology

It is a truism to say that new values are necessary for new structures. The prevailing mood in ecumenical concern for development, while emphasizing structural change, leans towards pragmatism. By pragmatism is generally meant doing the best possible in a given situation. But that would be self-contradictory. The situation is responsible for the continuance of underdevelopment and social injustice. To achieve development the situation or the social framework has to be changed, and that radically. Thus pragmatism tends to become an ideology of the *status quo*. Then the only way to bring about change is to operate in terms of a new ideology opposed to the *status quo*. Our commitment to social justice, new economic relationships between classes, radical change, etc., is really ideological. One finds, however, that we in ecumenical circles are disinclined, even hostile, to see ideological nuances in our approach to societal questions. But there is no option if we mean what we say.

Development, disorder, revolution

In some recent ecumenical meetings Latin Americans and Asians have found themselves at loggerheads in a development versus revolution debate. Latin Americans say that talk of development and nation-building is reactionary because it does not see the prior need of change in the power structures of society. Asians say that too much talk of revolution is reactionary because it makes revolution an end in itself rather than a means for social justice, and projects a certain anti-institutionalism which appears to be a new version of *laissez-faire*. Both positions have some merit, but a synthesis is possible; what is more to the point, it is necessary.

Once we recognize that development cannot take place without radical structural change, we can see it as a form of revolution. Existing structures perpetuate old property relations, forms of production and social inequality. Vested interests obstruct the development process. The aim of development is to establish institutions that are change-generating. Therefore, it is bound to disturb the *status quo* and create disorder. In its essentials development is disorder and revolution. If by contrast we assume that the development process should adjust to given conditions, the charge that it is reactionary would be fully justified.

As for revolution, its stated objective is to assume control of the power structure in order to use it for building a new social order; it is goal-directed. Its objectives are the same as that of development: social justice, economic equality. Precisely for these reasons the idea of perennial revolution goes against the goals of revolution and thus becomes counter-revolutionary. At some point the revolutionary process has to convert itself into a building-up process. If our goals are development, a better deal for the common man, humanization, etc., how can these be achieved in a vacuum? The kind of anti-institutionalism reflected in many so-called radical movements in the West is a throw-back to *laissez-faire*; as if society can progress without organization. The tearing down process is the first part of a revolution but it must logically proceed to the next step, namely building up. Otherwise it is mere romantic anarchy, a luxury which pseudo-radicals in the West may like to wallow in, but which we in the 'third world' with our tremendous problems can ill afford.

An important issue arises here with reference to direct Christian action in development. We tend to operate in areas of development work approved by and acceptable to established governments. But if a government is change-resisting, we then become allies of the *status quo*. How do we include the dissenters and rebels who really represent the change-generating forces, in our policy-making and programme? This is a ticklish question but we can no longer avoid it. Compromising with existing temporal authority is endemic to the Christian approach to social processes. Our concern for development forces us to undergo an agonizing self-appraisal on this question.

Finally, revolution should not be equated with violence. Historically, violence and revolution have gone together. But in recent times we have examples of non-violent revolutions: under Gandhiji in India and Martin Luther King in USA. With modern technology tending to make war obsolete as a solution to human problems our choice is between non-violence and non-existence. There is a tendency to talk of a theology of revolution or a theology of violence in such a way as to seek Christian approval and sanctification of violence. But this would repeat the mistakes of earlier theology which sanctified order with its hidden violence, and just wars with their hidden injustice. Our goal is humanization and social justice. Like many other forces which we oppose, violence dehumanizes. How can we give a blanket approval to such force in the name of revolution and radical change? We certainly need to wrestle with this very difficult issue as we evolve a theology of development.

7

Introduction to a Christological
Phenomenology of Development

NIKOS A. NISSIOTIS

The short history of the ecumenical movement, as seen through the work of the World Council of Churches, and especially through the two movements of Life and Work and Faith and Order which led to its foundation in 1948, is characterized by a double emphasis. The one stresses the social action of the church and the other the debate on theological and doctrinal issues which separate the churches. This dual emphasis, however, should neither be understood as an opposition nor as two parallel lines of thought and action. I think that the positive element in this respect is that both of them through their organic co-existence and integration in the World Council of Churches, and in particular through their confrontation, have proved to be the backbone of the dynamic fellowship of all member churches of the World Council of Churches on their way towards mutual renewal.

It is evident that owing to an exaggerated enthusiasm for their special concerns both sides, through some of their spokesmen and only for the sake of these concerns, in some periods of ecumenical history accentuated their views in a rather exclusive way. This is usually seen as the main characteristic of the way traditional theologians dispute doctrinal issues, but during the last decade of the World Council of Churches' existence the 'social gospel men', the pro-activists and the theologians of 'the presence of the Church in the world' have succeeded in giving the impression to people outside the movement that they completely dominate ecumenism. The Uppsala Fourth General Assembly of the World Council of Churches in 1968, following upon the explosive Church and Society meeting in Geneva in 1966, was an indication of this.

This situation, however, seems to be quite natural if one pays attention to the different but closely related causes which provoked it. The first cause is the fact that the ecumenical debate centred on the renewal of church life for evangelistic and missionary purposes. This preoccupation turned the interest within the World Council of Churches towards social and practical issues and orientated the theological discussion in a more concrete way, namely on the presence of the churches in their world environment. The second cause is to be found in the expansion of science in the modern world and the explosion of the human mind in all spheres of knowledge. This situation made the task of a traditional type of theology, such as has been developed in closed systems without reference to the historical realities, almost impossible. We have to be conscious of the impossibility of such a theology today, because this crisis is creating a vacuum in theological thinking. Because of this vacuum it appears that theology in general is unable to offer a substantial help to the churches struggling amid all kinds of problems in their social and political involvement. And it is in this vacuum that radical activists are appearing to dominate the ecumenical debate and work.

On the other hand, it is true that though the Christian faith has played an important role in shaping modern societies and social structures, it seems today as if the same faith has abandoned its immediate involvement, being unable to fit in with the permanent change characteristic of modern societies and the pragmatism of science and contemporary man. The emphasis on the social aspect of the work in the World Council of Churches has therefore to be understood also as a corrective attitude to the churches' hesitation or incapacity to be fully and dynamically involved in social, political and economic affairs, as well as an exhortation to them to take this area of their responsibility more seriously.

Against this background I want to stress the point that the recent developments in the ecumenical movement, grasped so clearly at the Fourth Assembly, are positive with reference to church life and theology, and represent a very normal evolution of church ecumenical thought and action if we look at it from the angle of the World Council of Churches. One should not seek always to keep an absolute balance between pure theological trends and sociological thinking. There are times when the ecumenical movement needs a certain imbalance in ecumenical thinking and orientation for the sake of renewal in church life and an appeal to the churches to become aware of their responsibilities in areas which they have unduly neglected.

At the same time one has to bear in mind that one-sided trends of this type should not make church people lose the vision of their total life and work. When speaking about development, emphasizing the need of a church presence amidst the problems of the modern world, they should never forget that they are parts of the church and channels of the grace of God as bearers of his word in the world. It is in this sense that this essay is written as a contribution to the effort of all those engaged in the study and life of the World Council of Churches; all those who, whilst welcoming fully the new trends in the ecumenical movement, would like to see them appropriately appreciated and rightly connected with the life of the churches as such. It would be a fatal error if enthusiasts were to take these pro-activist trends as absolute and thus render the churches mere welfare institutions, forgetting their share in the church and her particular presence and mission in the world.

1   *Is there a Theology of Development?*

The word theology is very often used in the sense of a theological approach to a concrete phenomenon in the world concerning human relationship. In this sense one can definitely say that there is a theological phenomenology, inasmuch as one tries to find in God the deeper sense of a phenomenon in the light of one's faith in him and his relationship to historical events. I do not mean ethical or sociological thinking which elaborates principles of human behaviour on the basis of the Bible and Christian experience in contemporary society; this preoccupation could be named theology *for* development, and would have as its purpose the preparing of churches and individuals for action in view of today's developments. This theology for development is self-evident and essential for all churches today. In this paper, however, I am dealing with something that to my mind precedes this stage. It is the theological sense of development, namely that of looking at development through faith in Christ and his incarnation. A theological phenomenology of this kind seems to me to be absolutely necessary as the prelude to all social involvement on the part of the churches, and their responsible action as churches in the contemporary explosion of science and technology. To a great extent the church's role within today's continuing social change will depend on how we as Christians understand development in relationship to God's continuous creativity towards the completion of his creation. Only then can one speak of a theology of development in this strict phenomenological sense and in close relationship to what is basic theology.

Theology is not just phenomenology or communication. Etymologically it refers to a word about God, that is to say, systematic thinking about God and his revelation. In the narrow sense of the term one is obliged as a theologian to limit oneself within the boundaries that God prescribes; that is, after the incarnation of the Word of God, our word cannot remain an abstract philosophical reflection about God. It refers to the Word incarnate in history; and therefore the task of theology is to be a reflection on God's presence in history. Theology, then, is the thinking of God as he reveals himself to man and the world; it deals with God's being in time and in concrete personal action.

Systematic theology, then, signifies the systematization of the biblical revelation. No one can deny this fundamental approach of theology, but no one can pretend today that the task of theology – understood as the apprehension of the fullness of the reality of the incarnate Logos of God – can remain only within these limits. Not only Christian ethics or the philosophy of religion as extensions of dogmatics are necessary, but the whole concrete cosmos, its culture and civilization, its progress and evolution, the human condition and concrete historical events are inseparable elements in a theology of incarnation.

I want to insist, however, that all these are not additional or separate chapters of theology in a post-biblical era. Theological phenomenology, as a critical study of the historical phenomena in the light of the incarnation, is rooted in and inseparably linked with the substance of the historical personal revelation of God. This is important for two reasons: first, that no distance or opposition is introduced between the so-called vertical and horizontal lines, between the Word of God incarnate and the reality of this world; and secondly, that no substitute for the revelation itself and the biblical message of salvation is professed, as might be implied in the view which says that in a post-biblical era the agenda of theology is written by the world alone. Here we touch the crucial issue of today's ecumenical debate and we have to clarify it before we attempt any kind of theological phenomenology of development.

It becomes more and more evident that in a scientific age the difficulties of human reason in conceiving God in ontological terms or in accepting a transcendent element in his revelation in Christ cause many modern theologians to think that the current historical scene is sufficient background for the Christian faith. The secular, with its explosion, which fosters technical progress, is conceived as fundamental for the achievement of human dignity. Instead of trying to bring an element of judgment and a criterion from 'outside', God is conceived only with reference to the historical reality of human development. What is wrong in this attitude is not so much the point of departure, or the priority given to the world's data and development in relation to

F*

the transcendent element of the Word of God, but the exclusiveness of
this attitude which risks losing sight entirely of the distinctive historical
intervention of God in a concrete person and his distinctive operation
through a historic community that he has chosen.

The current historical situation is a first point of contact for a
theological phenomenology. But if we remain only at this point of
departure, without seeking to see its special meaning in the light of
the revealed personal God as a source of grace and judgment, then we
can no longer speak of a theology of development, but only of a new
type of humanism and natural theology. What distinguishes an authentic
theology of development from such a humanism or a natural theology
is not an abstract escape to a theistic God or to metaphysics or even
to a static concept of salvation understood as expiation from our sins;
but it is the ability to discern the signs of the times according to the
edifying and saving judgment of God, acting in Christ and present
in the Spirit through the church in all realms of the personal and
collective life of man. In other words, the attitude of the horizontalists
should not be corrected by a static theology of the Word or a separate,
remote and wholly transcendental (and therefore unattainable) reality.
It should be corrected by seeing things in themselves and in their
relationships as basic materials of complex historical events which are
brought under the judgment of God. We then have a theology *of*
development accessible through a theological phenomenology; namely
through investigating the logos (the cause and the reason) of being
and the purpose of phenomena, not only by one's own conscience,
experience, and intellectual possibilities of grasping the ultimate
realities of a transcendental order, but in God's judgment and grace.
In this way no opposition between verticalists and horizontalists,
between transcendentalists and immanentists is possible, because in
historical reality a Christian traces the dynamics of God and proceeds
to an evaluation of it in the light of Christ's presence.

Whoever grasps the distinctive act of God in Christ cannot but trace
it as an ongoing historical reality. The horizontal line for the Christian
faith contains the vertical, and *vice versa*. The one does not send us
for completion to the other, but they coexist as an inseparable whole.
The distinction between the two is made because they belong together
in Christ's event; it is also made in order to reaffirm the unity between
the two in an authentic Christian approach to a concrete historical
event, so that in each case we might operate with a realistic theological
discernment, preparing the churches for appropriate involvement and
action.

The question raised is, therefore, not What is development? but
What is its cause, its *raison d'être* and its goal in God's judgment?

If we call to mind the various definitions of development in general as 'the autonomous activity of man to achieve a higher standard of dignity and material sufficiency', or 'the totality of processes by which individual human beings and human societies seek constantly to realize their potentialities', then we are given a positive starting-point for grasping the theological meaning of this phenomenon in God. But we have immediately to make the following observations:

(*a*) Development is both material and spiritual.

(*b*) It is individual and collective.

(*c*) It is quantitative and qualitative.

In other words development concerns the whole man and his whole environment, and consequently one rightly speaks of a total effort of humanization. In Christ this effort finds its deepest *raison d'être* and purpose. It would be wrong to think of this effort as merely autonomous – though it is autonomous as a purely human operation – either in its functional reality or in its means for achieving the goal. A theological phenomenology of development does not question whether there is an autonomy of operation, but seeks the deeper sense of development in God as the Lord of history. Development is a God-given possibility to man for making him a collaborator towards the completion of God's creation, through man's link with God in Christ. This struggle of humanity towards its full dignity reveals that man and the world are created with a specific purpose, with a goal to be attained through a continuous process of change and renewal. That goal is the reality which has been revealed by God in this world in the person of Jesus.

Thus God affirms this process and at the same time gives it a sense and a purpose. The incarnation is not merely a static link between God, man and history, but sets forward in meaningful motion the whole of the creation. Further, it does not simply confirm the God-given possibility of the technical, economic and scientific development of man but provides a sound cosmological and anthropological basis for achieving it. For development comprises far more than economic progress, which concerns the material welfare of man; it requires man's responsible use of it as a steward and not as an owner of wealth.

On the basis of these preliminary remarks we can see that from the Christian point of view every aspect of development and every aspect of human progress cannot be exhausted by the mere registering that it is in fact taking place. We have to penetrate beneath the surface, beneath its simple functioning, and try to find its deeper significance for total human existence in a responsible society. It is in this phenomenological operation that the theology of development is operating for the sake of development itself. In each event, phase and aspect of it God's will is revealed in a special way for all men; it becomes manifest how God's will is incarnate and how Christ's regenerating power can be appropriated as the inner power of the world's history. God is no longer an abstract ethical principle guiding action from a distance. He is the heart of the event, the human person involved in a dynamic action for the progress of all creation. In this sense we should not speak of a theological phenomenology of development but of a christological one.

This inner power of development constitutes the backbone of history in the movement forward to its completion. It is the inner sense of life, the being of man turned towards the achievement of a higher degree of human personality. Christ, the inner sense of development, and the human being, all three are related through the concrete historical events. These events reveal the origin, meaning and purpose of the whole creation. Therefore one has to trace the reality and the meaning of all these phases of development and thus reveal their inner coherence. These are some of the significant aspects of a developmental event:

(*a*) It has international and universal dimensions and never merely national or individual ones.

(*b*) It abolishes discrimination between the privileged and the under-privileged.

(*c*) It poses the problem of defeating injustice in the distribution of the earth's goods and the fruits of technical civilization.

(*d*) It contributes to the maintenance of peace, by overcoming the fighting between oppressors and oppressed and the dependence of developing upon developed nations.

(*e*) It sets up new possibilities for world-wide education and the growth of human personality.

(*f*) It reveals the fact that all events involving human progress are not ends in themselves, concerning only material welfare, but that they are above all means for creating human personality and moving history forward for the sake of future generations.

It becomes more and more clear that the accumulation of progress and development through technological change in itself leaves many other problems unsolved. These are becoming more complicated the more development increases. A christological phenomenology has to detect the reasons why this is so by reminding us that development means more than progress seen as the result of economic relationships.

II   *Secular Meaning or Cosmic Reality of Salvation?*

Let us now investigate how a christological phenomenology of development detects the reasons for the problems caused by development. Usually Christian theologians in modern times operate a theology of development by extending the meaning of the incarnation in the secular realm. The incarnation is then understood as an event which refers not only to the church, as the renewed people of God which resulted from it, but also to the whole world and its history. This interpretation is not absolutely wrong, although from a theological point of view the incarnation cannot be used alone in order to approach the riddle of history. In other words, one cannot provide the necessary basis for a theology of development without the cross and the resurrection, as well as the foundation of the historical community of faith. A full reference is needed to all stages of the divine economy as seen christologically. The christological phenomenology of development, of which the premises are described above, cannot operate unless an appropriate understanding of salvation in Christ is used as the basic reality when we reflect on human progress in history. Salvation proves here to be the depth dimension of development which is the missing element in its simple function and completion.

But what do I mean by salvation when I speak in this way? I do not simply mean forgiveness of sins, or justification. I wish rather to point out its positive aspect which emphasizes the regeneration of the whole creation and the life of each man. I mean the transfiguration and transformation, in the broadest possible meaning, of the world. For the world is not simply created as an object without a personal relationship with God. It is not a *demiourgia*, in the ancient classical Greek understanding, but it is created as a *ktisis*, full of deeper meaning and purpose. It is created in order to be continuously recreated on the basis of the personal revelation of God in space and time. There is in the biblical understanding of creation a sense of salvation seen as a continuous recreation linked in an indirect way with the incarnation, cross and resurrection. It appears at a first approach to historical events that there is no connection between these two separate types of salvation. But a christological phenomenology reveals that God is not saving us only from sin; he sets forward his whole creation and recapitulates it in the person of Christ who is our expiation. On a personal level we understand through our faith that we are saved from our sins; and on a world level we see the love of God extended to his whole creation. In hope then we see that this creation as a whole is directed towards its end, its goal, its fulfilment in Christ.

Two remarks are to be made here. First, sacred and profane are not two opposed or separated realms. The sacred is the secular understood at a deep level. Secondly, the vision of salvation extended into the secular is based on the particular intervention of God in Christ, whose salvation reveals that every historical event contains a possibility of becoming an agent of this salvation if it acquires the broad dimension given to it by Christ's incarnation, death and resurrection. A historical event acquires its deeper significance in the eyes of a Christian only when it really assists in the restoration of humanity to all men according to the cosmic understanding of the reality of Christ's salvation. This is not automatically given to every historical event. A service to humanity as a whole is a highly complicated affair which cannot be reduced only to the limits of a welfare programme of economic and social change. There is always something missing in the eyes of a Christian phenomenologist. This can be captured only if the event is transformed into a service to man, i.e. if the event extends the salvation of Christ understood as a vehicle for the regeneration of history.

Cosmic salvation in this sense does not mean a mystical and speculative vision conceiving the whole creation as automatically saved because Christ died for all men. This is a vague generalization. In reality it does not do justice to specific historical events and the human responsibility in them. It eliminates the judging element which is at the heart of Christ's salvation. 'Cosmic' in my view points to a worldly and world-wide salvation through a strenuous, continuous process of inner transformation, conceivable only in the faith, love and hope given in Christ in a personal, concrete way. The cosmic vision is not possible without the cosmic reality of salvation as regeneration, as continuous change in order that every historical event comes under the saving judgment of Jesus. If it is to further development each historical event has to be seen in its appropriate function in order to serve man's personal transfiguration and society's total restructuring.

All events connected with development await their evaluation and, through it, their appropriate function in this cosmic understanding of salvation, which unites the personal and the social, the cosmic and the secular, the sacred and the profane. According to a Christian phenomenology of development Christ provides, through the faith of the man who acts in faith, the missing basis of development and enables it to make a more positive contribution to regenerating the world.

There is in other words a cosmic Christian vision of the secular and the universal; but this has very little to do with a theoretical, speculative and visionary interpretation of the salvation of all things in Christ. In reality the appropriate practice deriving from the universal salvation of Christ is a specific Christian contribution in all these historical events. Human activism and technological change do not solve the problems of justice, peace and universal partnership in development. There is no automatic presence of Christ in development. The more we develop human resources, the more we need specific Christian participation. The only generalized principle which can be applied is that Christians should approach the phenomenology of development with a positive mind and a concern for all that furthers material and economic growth at the service of man. They know that the judgment of God in history, through the regenerating spirit of Christ, is never annihilating, but constructive and saving. In Christ we and every event are judged. In him we know that justice and love are absolutely interchangeable, even though we cannot fully understand how this is so. Our concept of justice includes punishment as an inseparable part. We cannot conceive a loving justice in an absolute form as is the case with God; we cannot see now how the world's history can be saved in love and judgment by God.

One positive attitude to development and its origin in our Christian faith is based on this dialectics of salvation through love and judgment by God at the same time. This attitude approves and furthers development in every realm, and creates the basis for a deeper understanding of it. Thus it can really become a transforming element in persons and societies. At the same time this dialectics of salvation of God in history through love and judgment preserves the Christian vision and prevents the evaluation of development from becoming easy, superficial and over-optimistic. Love and judgment will always accompany all events of development according to a Christian understanding. There is neither an ideal solution of the problems raised by development nor a final stage which humanity can reach and live in happily for ever. There will always be tensions between purpose and achieved goals in development, between theory and practice, between individual and communal, between national and universal. This belongs to the nature of development. Realizing this we are not pessimistic but are filled with hope and our thoughts and actions are turned towards the future. It is the Christian hope which has to permeate all events of development. This hope prevents us from seeking immediate and permanent solutions to all the problems created by today's explosion of technological change.

The true regenerating contribution of the Christian to development has to be a balance between the extremes of easy optimistic cosmic visions of a 'secular' Christianity and of the welfare policies of affluent societies, and the pessimistic theologies of the sin of man, of his condemnation, of the vanity of history and the tragedy of the human condition.

III   *Beyond Monophysitism[1] in all its Forms*

When theology deals with problems of development or of relationships between the gospel and society it runs a permanent danger. Either it fails in an excessive concern for the active presence of the churches in the midst of today's social problems or it tends to withdraw entirely from the world scene. We experience such extremes today. Pro-secularists and fundamentalists exaggerate in their attitudes and confuse the very important issue of church and society relationships.

In the previous section of this essay I tried to show how a christo-logical phenomenology of development can help us to escape the dichotomy between a vertical and a horizontal line concerning the theological basis of the church's presence in the modern world. It is evident, I hope, that this phenomenology is founded on a solid christo-logical presupposition which carefully avoids any hidden monophysitism. It is very difficult to avoid it when one enters into thinking and action regarding development and church 'presence' in modern societies. Many of the suggested schemata of action in this respect betray a pro-humanist dominating element and a tendency to be one-sided. Against this attitude we have the well-known reaction of those who fight for preserving the purity and the uniqueness of the gospel.

In both these cases we find a crypto-monophysitic approach. It is not sufficient to say that Christ became man and therefore all men, inside and outside the church, are automatically saved, and that every historical event furthering progress and development is *ipso facto* in continuity and total identity with Christ's presence in and with the world. Equally, it is not theologically right to say that God is only intervening to judge and to save the few chosen and converted, and that the social action and presence of the church is a secondary ethical task of the individual Christian exercised through his professional life. No! The church is not immediately identical with the social, economic and political revolution of our times, nor with the process of develop-ment in general; there is a *sui generis* action of the church in these realms. On the other hand, the church is not only the agent, the channel of salvation in a narrow sacramental and individual way; there is a social and political involvement of the churches as such in their local situation and a definite responsibility in these realms.

There is no biblical message without social involvement and *vice versa*. Both belong together and the one validates the other. A christo-logical phenomenology of development can be authentically operated only on the basis of a christology which is beyond all these crypto-monophysitic tendencies. This christology does not simply affirm Christ's nature as equally human and divine in a way that leads to the conclusion that the human and the divine are identical, or parallel and operating on an equal footing. Then the pro-humanist monophysitic interpretation is present and a christological phenomenology cannot be arrived at; any analogy and image borrowed from human experience is totally excluded for understanding the incarnation. The only thing

I can say is that 'true man and true God' does not mean an equal footing regarding the initiative and origin of the incarnation, because it is the Word of God who assumed human nature through the will and sovereign power of God and not *vice versa*. It is God who comes to man humbling himself in the form of a servant, intervening thus in human history as he wills. There is an 'asymetry' in the origin of the incarnation which qualifies in a special way the event of the incarnation and preserves the qualitative priority of God.

This priority, interpreted in the right way by a christological phenomenology of development, can give to the Christian and the churches involved in social action the basis for their specific responsibility in it. The priority of God in the origin and realization of the incarnation does not give any priority or dominating power to the churches' contribution to development, seen from the human point of view. On the contrary it means that the churches are at the full disposal of the world for service in repentance and humility. This 'priority' is revealed through a christological phenomenology as the basis for understanding that human development is not, as such, the whole object and interest of the churches. A whole new dimension is brought by the churches through their presence and interest which helps to achieve a continuous process of transfiguration of man and of the conditions of life, which is not possible in a purely humanistic framework.

This 'special contribution' is not intended to be a continuous reminder to all people that they are sinners and have to be saved. The 'special' does not mean a repetition of old formulae from ivory towers, and a puritan morality. It signifies struggling together with the man of today for a world with more justice and for a higher standard of human living, without hidden proselytizing intentions to win him for the gospel, or for 'my denomination'. It is by struggling as a Christian and by discerning the signs of our times in all efforts towards development, through a christological phenomenology, that what is specifically Christian appears as 'special' in a given situation. Then it can express the loving and judging word of God, by itself. If it does not, then something is wrong in our involvement in development and in our discernment in all kinds of changing situations. We should not stand either as hidden missionaries or as completely identified with the secular humanists. If we do that the priority of God in the operation of the incarnation and the cosmic understanding of salvation will be misinterpreted and used by people who have not overcome their particular monophysitism. Thus, neither a theology of development nor a christological phenomenology is sufficient to help us to grasp the church's *total* responsibility in today's social changes.

IV   *World-wide Community and Church Unity*

It is absolutely true that the technological age has contributed greatly to all peoples wishing to unite into a world family. Furthermore, technical progress is facilitating communication, reducing distances and bringing people easily into contact. However, on its way to unification, this world has increased at the same time the separation between nations, divided in super-power blocks, and has made man feel lonely within the anonymous masses of the big modern cities.

From the Christian point of view, the tendency for the world to unite into a pan-human family has to be accepted as a positive sign. It is a God-given opportunity for all men to realize their purpose as one community within the creation of God. The regathering of peoples into one unbroken family is part of God's whole plan of renewing and regenerating his whole creation.

Rapid changes and development render peoples interdependent, though living in places distant from one another. Interests are no longer purely local or national. In a highly developed world all provincialisms are disappearing for the sake of creating a pan-human responsible community. There are signs already of this tendency. The young generation especially is becoming more and more sensitive to world problems. Indeed all of us are concerned with problems of a world-wide dimension. There are no internal affairs of one nation which cannot become problems for other nations if they have a bearing on the world's need to unite.

Here we face one of the most immediate good results of development, but here again we can trace an inner dialectics in all development events: as peoples and nations become more united in one way, their relations threaten to be disturbed in another. The most alarming sign today is the inability of all specialists in development issues to apply their good plans in such a way that they bridge the gap between developed and developing countries. It is most discouraging in this respect to hear those involved in aid and technical assistance state frankly that the gap is going to increase in the next ten years. Most disappointing of all is the realization that even though all the details regarding official action for establishing an equilibrium between affluent and poor societies are well known, it remains extremely difficult to apply these plans with full consistency.

A christological phenomenology of development has to grasp the immediate need for a special contribution of the church at this point. By nature the church has to be the supra-national, supra-cultural and supra-racial world community. The church is the *pars pro toto* and the nucleus of a real gathering of all men into the one family of God. In her all walls, all partitions are to be broken down and all discriminations overcome.

In the trend towards the progressive formation of a responsible world community resulting from today's development, the church has a paramount role to play. We are, however, faced with a strange phenomenon which discourages us further. The great majority of church activists in the realm of development are either reluctant to work for the unity of the church and, through it, for the progress of the pan-human gathering, or believe more in a world secular community than in the possibility of church unity. Clearly this attitude is caused by the failure to reach rapidly the reunion of the church, after the first period of intense ecumenical activity. Thus there is increasing bitterness, especially among young ecumenists. Consequently there is great impatience as far as long-term plans for church reunion are concerned. On the other hand those 'new theologians' who maintain that salvation is given everywhere and to everybody on the basis of a general christology regard the pan-human secular unity as a substitute for church unity.

Yet I think that the divisions still existing within the church should not make us lose hope in the possibility of a specific and distinctive regathering of all peoples through the historic community of faith. It may seem somewhat paradoxical, but even a divided universal church community has an important role to play, if it sees its responsible task in this respect. The church must also grow as one with the world. This is perhaps the 'secret weapon' for recapturing church unity within a world which seeks to establish a responsible world community. If non-theological factors have divided the church in the past, those same factors resulting from rapid changes in societies and the tendency towards a pan-human family, can now become factors working towards church reunion. Here the churches which act ecumenically – namely those which are renewed by their active membership in the new fellowship they form for the sake of their living presence in the world – have to become the axis of the emerging world community and offer their specific contribution in the effort of all nations to overcome every form of discrimination. The spiritual presence of such a community is more than ever necessary on a world scale where a highly developed minority is contrasted with a highly underprivileged majority of nations.

Thus a christological phenomenology of development today has to teach us as responsible people involved in the ecumenical movement the specific tasks of the churches within the manifold scientific and economic progress. The accent on the social presence of the churches in today's world, as has been strongly stressed in World Council of Churches' conferences and documents recently, does not imply any shifting of position or giving up of a theological basis for the sake of some pro-secularist church activism. It does not signify, either, a blanket approval of all sorts of revolution. This emphasis has been a constitutive element of the World Council of Churches' work from its beginning, but it is stronger now owing to the necessity of the times, and because the churches are not yet fully conscious of the urgency of the question and the need for their involvement. If one understands the present concern which the World Council's member churches have for develop-ment, then the whole theological task will acquire more power. Theology will then have to work out anew, in a clearer and more convincing way, the specific place, role and contribution of the churches in the universal effort to increase the standard of human living and raise the level of human dignity.

NOTES

1. Monophysitism was one of the views of the nature of Christ current in the age of the Fathers of the Church and condemned as inadequate at the Council of Chalcedon in 451. According to it the union of the two 'natures' (of God and man) in Christ resulted in a single 'nature' and that divine, which meant that Christ had no human 'nature'. (Editor)

PART THREE

Christian Hope

Our hope is in him who makes all things new. . . . In their faith in the coming Kingdom of God and in their search for his righteousness, Christians are urged to participate in the struggle of millions of people for greater social justice and for world development.

The Report of Uppsala, Section III, par. 4

8

The Christian's Secular Hope and his Ultimate Hope

ANDRÉ DUMAS

I   *The Anti-world which is Passing Away and the World which is Coming into Being*

The title, though I agreed to it, is a bad title. But it is valuable to have heresies and false perspectives so that we may recognize and resist them (I Cor. 11.19). It is valuable to have mistaken titles so that we may know whether we can find some better way of saying what they are trying to express, whether we are capable of regaining the veridical sense as contrasted with the false sense with which we always start, and the nonsense which ever threatens to overwhelm us. Christian hope does not in fact set its 'secular' preliminaries in opposition to 'ultimate' aspirations: that would still be a slightly temporalized version of the Platonic ascent from what is the confused, secular and tangible world of our experience towards the purified and ultimate world of the contemplative. Christian hope does not confront the world with an 'anti-world'. Christian hope is always concerned with the world, including both the experience of the ageing of the world and faith in its begetting, in its re-creation. For Christian hope the opposite of the old earthly man is not the heavenly man but the child. Thus the imagery with which apocalyptic hope is surrounded remains completely secular: there will be a city full of people and things, of assembled nations and of treasures, as though what was to come was not the garden of our lost innocence nor the desert of our burning refusals, but still and for ever an urban concentration characterized at the same time by conformity to human scales and measurements, by contributed wealth and by freedom of enjoyment (Rev. 21.17, 24; 22.2). What is to come will be in the fullest sense a world, with its new

heaven and its new earth, freed from the division between the provisional and the ultimate, because all the signs of the ultimate have
disappeared ('And I saw no temple in the city', Rev. 21.22) to give
place to the solidity of earthly provisionment ('the wealth and splendour
of the nations shall be brought into it', Rev. 21.26, NEB). To use the
titles of well-known contemporary books, the kingdom and the new
Jerusalem, which we mistakenly call the heavenly Jerusalem, for it
'*came down*' from heaven, from God (Rev. 21.2), will be a 'secular city'
and a 'metropolis', the world in its fullness. The ultimate is this new
world. Futility will have ceased to haunt human enterprises for,
strangely enough, the dream of eternity will give place to the validity
of time.

We know that the vocabulary of the Bible, the Hebrew of the Old
Testament as well as the Greek of the New, does not use two words
to distinguish and contrast time and eternity. *Olam* in Hebrew and
aion in Greek both serve, according to the words and phrases which
accompany them, sometimes for the present age as it passes, sometimes
for the new age which is coming. The fact that there is only one word
makes it clear that hope does not abolish the passing age here below
to replace it by the changeless eternity of beyond. In biblical language
eternity is still expressed in centuries: literally 'unto the ages of the
ages' (Rev. 22.5). Expectation goes ahead of the world. It does not
soar above it. 'Toujours' means 'for ever' and not 'nevermore'. Thus
we should be very near to biblical hope if we could succeed in reversing
our usual schemas of thought and imagination about the replacement
of the world and time by the anti-world of the eternal verities. It is
rather the anti-world of our ultimate fears and nostalgias which will
finally disappear, when the world of our real inheritance has begun.
The imagery of Revelation here chooses the parable of marriage, as
the prophets and apostles so often did, to make us understand and feel
the relationship between God and his people. The betrothal with its
romantic uncertainties will end. The marriage will take place. The
new Jerusalem is beautiful as a young bride adorned for her husband
(Rev. 21.2). The city and its God stay together. Eschatology is not
detachment from earthly affections. It is finally marriage between
the world and God, whereas by comparison the present time is still
the inarticulate groping of betrothal without action, decision or consummation. We do not then aspire towards a disincarnation of the
earth. We hope for its realization. We await, to paraphrase the Marxist
expression, the end of the pre-history of betrothal which will mark the
beginning of the history of marriage between God and humanity.

But this Christian apocalyptic imagery raises as many problems as
the Marxist attempts to describe the rupture between the pre-history

of alienations and the history of full humanization. What is really involved here? Have we a utopia which expects wasted time to turn into the fullness of time? Do we think we can know the why, the when and the how of the world's conversion? Have we faith in a revolution which would no longer contain a threat, still less the seed, of restoration of the old? A new time which would be other than time as we know it? Hope does not oppose the ultimate to the secular but the new to the old. If we minimize this contrast we obtain the notion of progress, or rather of development, to use the current word which has replaced the eighteenth-century 'Enlightenment' and the nineteenth-century 'Progress'. We shall speak of the advancement of peoples ('*Populorum progressio*'), or of Economic and Social Development (the title of Section III of the Fourth Assembly of the World Council of Churches at Uppsala). But if we sharpen, if we maximalize, the contrast, we obtain in Christian language: judgment and salvation, eschatology and parousia; and in Marxist terminology revolution, classless society, total man. The difficult problem which confronts us seems to me not, as I have already said, the relation of the secular to the eternal, but the relation between development and salvation, both secular; development depending, however, on a progressive revolution, and salvation on a decisive rupture. I imagine that Marxists in their language and convictions are conscious of a similar difficulty when they emphasize sometimes the science of economic infrastructures as Marx analysed them, and sometimes the prophecy of the effects of revolution upon humanity as the Communist thinkers see them.

But let us concentrate on the Christian difficulty: does biblical hope proclaim the development of man during the course of the technological, social, political and cultural improvements in the world, or the salvation of man at the moment of his conversion to faith? In very simple and striking sentences D. T. Niles asked at the end of his opening sermon to the Uppsala Assembly,

Should Jesus ask us now what we would have him do for us, what would we ask? Justice among men? Yes. Freedom for all from fear and want? Yes. Peace between peoples and reconciliation between individuals? Yes. The unity of the Church and the renewal of its mission? Yes. But above all, would we not ask for that which is the direst need of the human heart, and which he alone can supply? 'Show us the Father, and we shall be satisfied' (John 14.8).

In other words, does the Christian hope give priority to the development of humanization on earth or to the knowledge of eschatological salvation, also come upon earth? Are there two expectations? Let us try to understand the connection between them theologically. Then let us see whether or not this Christian hope comes close to the other human hopes of our time. In conclusion we will think about the interactions between development and salvation in contemporary ecumenical thought.

II   *Short-term Expectation and Long-term Expectation*

Let us first be clear about the precise biblical meaning of the word expectation. It carries hope within it like a certitude which requires both tension and patience. 'To expect' is to remain alert in awareness that the *kairos*, the propitious moment, must not be missed. Expectation is indwelt by hope which believes without seeing, 'for in this hope we are saved. Now hope that is seen is not hope. . . . But if we hope for what we do not see, we wait for it with patience' (Rom. 8.24 f.). This is expectation, attention, not waiting on events; controlled passion, not relaxed passivity. It lies in wait for the opportunity. It does not shipwreck in doubt. It forges faith. It does not beget scepticism. We have taken the life out of biblical expectation by making it bear upon the distant in time, leaving the near future empty and static. As so many contemporary theologians, from Johannes Weiss to Albert Schweitzer and from Karl Barth to Jürgen Moltmann, have shown, though without all drawing the same conclusions, the New Testament is as much a story of expectancy as the Old. Jesus Christ, who accomplishes everything, does not bring anything to an end. He inaugurates. He is the firstfruits, the promise, the first-born among many brothers, the initiator of the new world, the herald of his second coming, destined to reappear just as, when risen, he in fact disappears instead of staying to build up the kingdom. Messianism, we might say, is brought to life again instead of being destroyed by the first coming of the Messiah. Jesus Christ created expectancy, because he makes actual in fact, partially and temporarily, the new humanity which by rights should be universal and durable if it is really what it claims to be. There is no expectancy when there is no sign of germination; neither is there expectancy when the harvest is in. Expectancy whether in relation to the birth of a child, the sprouting of a plant, or the march of history, requires an unfulfilled promise. It stands in the gap between annunciation and realization. It retains what it holds already without yet possessing it. Expectancy knows that what is given still remains hidden. It is the breach made by hope in the record of insufficiency. It inaugurates a race of men who march forward without pretending to consolidate. Without expectation faith would be a closed affirmation, as moreover without faith expectation would be an aspiration without content.

Contemporary theology has given significance to the power of expectation introduced by Jesus Christ into history. The nineteenth century saw in him the preacher of the most perfect moral ideal which extends the conscience to the utmost extreme of purity. But the twentieth century, first in exegesis and then in dogmatics and ecclesiology, has rediscovered another Jesus, less close to us as rational spirits, for he seems often to be an eschatologist on the frontiers of the apocalyptic, but also nearer to us as participants in universal history when he reveals himself as the stick of dynamite which splits the eternal order of things and opens the breach for a global advance. The eschatological perspective of the New Testament is without doubt the deepest factor which is held in common by the various twentieth-century theologies, whether they emphasize an intratemporal eschatology, with the problem of the delay of the parousia (Schweitzer for example), or a continuously supratemporal eschatology with the other problem of the substitution of existential historicity for real history (Bultmann for example), or an eschatology of the future with the third problem of the distinction between the exaltation of futurism and the christological expectation of a return (Moltmann). I do not need to develop these various problems here, but only to emphasize how all the great theologies of this century have rediscovered in eschatological expectation not an appendix infected by unhealthy curiosity, but a global horizon and a profound aspiration.

The Bible in teaching us faith injects expectation into us. It discovers hope in between these two other attitudes, ignorance and knowledge, which are so much more natural to a man. Indeed we can never say too emphatically how foreign hope is to us. It would be so much more normal either not to expect tomorrow to be really different from yesterday or to endeavour to prove that the present has already radically transformed the world. The first attitude is called wisdom, serene as with Goethe ('the present is nature's eternity'), or tragic, icy and jubilant as with Nietzsche ('to desire the eternal return of the being's assent'). The second attitude is called 'signs and wonders of the times'. Some see them in the technological, others in the politico-social, others again in the psychological and cultural fields. But hope is no more a part of the visible world of change than of the invisible one of reflection.

For Jews demand signs and Greeks seek wisdom, but we preach Christ crucified, a stumbling-block to Jews and folly to Greeks, but to those who are called, both Jews and Greeks, Christ the power of God and the wisdom of God (I Cor. 1.22–24).

Hope is an abnormal kind of expectation. It horrifies those who want to see the world changed. It exasperates with its irrationality those who are convinced that the new will only be the old in disguise. Hope is a category ignored equally by those who confuse it with the mutations of history and by those who bury it in the permanence of being. It has its place in the crucifixion of Jesus Christ, where history looks most like a permanent procession of unjust suffering, of irreparable errors and of sterile misunderstandings, but also where the being of the world receives a most decisive shock, since here death will not be final, since this forgotten man will be listened to for century after century, and this ultimate misunderstanding will become the Light which inspires relationships between God and man, between man and man, between man and the world. As the place of biblical hope, the cross will become not an impasse, but the crossroads where our insufficient knowledge and inexcusable ignorance meet with the knowledge and the strength of God. Put more concretely, the cross begins when we think it terminates. It begins because it implants the reappearance of the new, the risen, in the manifestation of the ancient, the superseded. In this sense, it touches the two sides of our problem: it is fully within historical time and it is the rupture of this time, when it is followed by a new time, both terrestrial and complete, the strange time of the resurrection, which partially inaugurates in Christ on earth the universal hope of God for the earth.

We are now equipped to distinguish what I have called short-term expectation and long-term expectation. Let us make it clear at the start that the two adjectives are not distributed, the one to development and humanization (the short-term and this-worldly expectation), the other to salvation and eschatology (the long-term, ultimate expectation), but that development as well as salvation both live in the two dimensions, short-term and long-term, of the expectation which hopes and the hope which expects. Jesus Christ in history heals *and* saves, saves *and* heals, and the gospel narratives give no chronological nor systematic priority whatever either to healing or to saving. Quite unpredictably in his encounters Jesus begins with one or the other, as though sometimes faith made restoration to life possible and sometimes restoration to life called out faith. Healing has taken on the modern name of development. It gives the body a stronger use of its potentialities, when it satisfies hunger, makes the ill well again, restores a lost sense (to the blind, deaf or dumb), renews a useless limb (the paralytic and the lame) and sets free those not in control of themselves (the possessed and the demoniacs). It also gives the spirit a lost relational dimension, when it fights unjust discrimination (Samaritans, tax-collectors, women and children) or when it breaks up sepulchral segregations (the learning of the scribes, the discipline of the Pharisees, the power of the mighty, the wishes of the disciples), when it thus renews a humanity liberated from arrogance as well as from possessions. Finally it gives the heart a knowledge of what is really happening (parables, discourses, interpretations of scripture, the birth of new writings which will reflect the events lived through). To develop man means this restitution of the body, of society and of meaning, for we are flesh, collectivity and culture. What then is salvation, if development is already all this? Nothing else, quite certainly, than the conviction of the truth of what is done, said, given and commanded. Salvation is the interiorization of development, the moment when I know that in my healing I have met the 'why' of my existence.

You will notice the terseness of the gospel statements about salvation, whereas the details of the healings are told at length. Let me take a few examples from a narrative section devoted to ten miracles in Matt. 8 and 9. 'Jesus said to the leper: See that you say nothing to any man, but go, shew yourself to the priest and offer the gift that Moses commanded, for a proof to the people' (8.4); to the centurion, 'Go; be it done for you as you have believed' (8.13); to a disciple: 'Follow me, and leave the dead to bury their own dead' (8.22); to all the disciples: 'Why are you afraid, O men of little faith?' (8.26); to the paralytic: 'Take heart, my son; your sins are forgiven' (9.2); to Matthew: 'Follow me' (9.9); to the woman with a haemorrhage: 'Take heart, daughter; your faith has made you well' (9.22); to the two blind men: 'According to your faith be it done to you' (9.30); and lastly to the disciples, in the presence of the weary and distressed crowd: 'The harvest is plentiful, but the labourers are few; pray therefore the Lord of the harvest to send out labourers into his harvest' (9.37–38). Each time there is no detail about the content of salvation, but either before or after a work of healing comes the command to believe, to make his own the strength that has gone into him, to grasp the message implicit in the deed which has been accomplished.

Salvation is there when man takes what God gives in the development of the world, when he takes it as a gift and an appeal, instead of letting it pass unnoticed as his due, something which is soon forgotten. Salvation is thus not the ultimate truth to which healing and development are but the secular foothills. Salvation is the ratification, the recognition and acceptance, by the man's faith of the opportunity which comes to him. Without this ratification development and healing alike remain lost opportunities, a relief of little significance, not because it is nothing to have healed and improved, but because man remains only the object of external development until he becomes the subject of personal salvation. Development and salvation in the gospel perspective are related to one another as the works of healing are related to the acts of faith demanded. We have noticed in the examples from St Matthew that we generally know the nature of the healing acts which are performed, whereas faith remains secret, guessed at or unknown:

'Go! According to your faith be it done to you' (Matt. 8.13; 9.30).
One can develop mankind. But none can believe on behalf of another.
That is why I say, echoing but modifying the closing words of D. T.
Niles, 'What do we ask? The fullest possible development for body,
mind and spirit of each and every man? Yes. But above all, that each
and every man may believe, which is to say, hope.'

The acts of healing and the acts of faith, the development and the
salvation of which I have been speaking up to now, are short-term
expectations. Reading the gospels one is struck by the absence of any
long-term programming. Jesus seems to organize the objectives of his
ministry much less than, for instance, St Paul. He comes and goes,
he walks by the lake, withdraws to a hill, enters a synagogue, accepts
a meal, performs or refuses to perform a cure, sends out, shocks,
explains or is silent, according to the whims, apparently, of an extremely
work-a-day life. We know how difficult it is to reconstruct from the
four gospels a coherent framework for the duration and geography
of his activity. But expectation exists everywhere. Men await an action
or a word. Jesus looks for obedience or understanding. These two
expectations are immediate, in proportion to the absence of programmes
for tomorrow to catch up the missed opportunities of today. These
paths will not cross twice. There is no haste, because there is no visible
planning, but there is urgency because it is here and now that God keeps
his promises, when the kingdom which is to come is in the midst of us.
'Today, if you harden not your hearts . . . the kingdom of heaven is
at hand. . . . He who has ears, let him hear. . . .' Throughout the gospels
resounds the imminence of short-term expectation. It quickens its
rhythms when the trial in Judaea succeeds to the walks in Galilee.
Realized eschatology is short-term expectation made up both of the
unpredictable disorder of daily life and of the urgency of acts of
development and of faith which speculate upon no tomorrow. It matters
little whether it concerns collective situations (crowds, so often present)
or individual encounters (passers-by, so often distinguished); in both
cases the expectation is immediate. It disposes neither of time nor
means. Jesus always leaves people free, but is clearly himself always
pressing on. He has no ivory tower wherein to analyse, prepare or
train before acting. The first eschatological premonition of the gospels
is this immediacy, symbolized by this short period of three years
attributed to the ministry of Jesus of Nazareth. It explains why acts
of healing (which I have called development) are instantaneous and
partial, pointers rather than programmes, just as salvation (which I
call theology, dogmatics, catechism, creed) is rapid and, in the deepest
sense of the word summation, summary!

This first aspect, day by day and in no sense programmatic, of the ministry of Jesus, seems to me essential. It gives validity to our own everyday life, threatened in its faculty of hope by the keen awareness of its limitations. Short-term expectations legitimize the fragmentary acts and the ephemeral appeals, provided that they are void of pretentious haste, but rich in ready urgency. The short-term element here is, in the first place, the favourable moment. Thus, far from prostrating hope in helplessness, urgency pushes Jesus to work while it is day. What is short-term also is the smallness of the hope entertained: a multiplication of loaves, not a world campaign against famine; one man healed, not a World Health Organization; a centurion, not a United Nations Organization; twelve wavering disciples, not the World Council of Churches nor the Vatican. . . . The last short-term feature is the unwonted obscurity of the witnesses: he himself was born at Nazareth and not at Jerusalem, belonging neither to the priestly caste, nor to the pious laity, nor to any recognized ascetic brotherhood, nor to revolutionary youth, choosing his disciples with a fair proportion of mistakes (the young Hegel deplored the fact that Jesus was not able to recruit a Plato as Socrates did!), interrogated by nobles but dialoguing with unknown people, to end too soon and too badly an unfinished task. In every respect the gospels are full of short-term eschatology devoted to daily chances, to a limited time, to restricted space, to minor personalities, to failure close at hand. Yet they are still concerned with eschatology, for Jesus sends sounding through all the everyday occurrences the power of healing which develops man, and the call of faith which identifies man, giving him his 'wherefore' as well as his 'how'. What is short-term is also complete, strong and decisive. To use the expression dear to Kierkegaard, the instant is certainly here the best analogy for eternity, or should we rather say the new world which is coming. Short-term expectancy plays its role within the moment. Thanks to it the everyday becomes essential, the dark becomes shining clear, the tiny becomes fundamental, the brief irrevocable. An act of development is concentrated in a gesture, not in a programme. An act of faith is summed up in a confidence, not in a theology. Hope feeds upon the instant, when it can give to and respond to the instant. Surrounded by ignorance, which makes one sceptical, and by knowledge, which makes one prudent, hope behaves like a child. It seizes the moment of play or of tears, of praise or of blame, of Galilee or Judaea. It knows that time never comes back. It reflects enough to rejoice in the presence of the bridegroom while he is still there. It does not reflect so long as to kill the present by memory or foresight. The first dimension of the eschatology of the New Testament is its short-term realization, as much in the field of development as in that of faith.

But the gospels vibrate also with a second eschatological expectation which I shall call long-term. From time to time Jesus of Nazareth becomes the Son of God who, according to Daniel 7, judges the world and has dominion over all powers of the universe, on the earth, under the earth and in the air. We often reserve the word eschatological, meaning last, for these moments of vision and proclamation. It would be better to speak of long-term eschatology, characterized by a global event, a programmed achievement, a cosmic duration, solemn reversals and re-creations, by the glory and the reign of the Lamb. This is the exact opposite of what I have called short-term eschatology, with its disorder, its smallness, its urgency, its instantaneousness, its insignificance and its obscurity.

Faced with this prolonged and grandiose transfiguration of the earth it seems to me that theological reflection yields two interpretations, neither shedding much light on the idea of hope. The first takes the end of all things literally. But then we break the thread which joins our expectation in time to our expectation beyond time. Fear, curiosity, and still more easily absurdity, then replace hope. The wave of a magic wand, terrifying and bewitching, succeeds the acts of healing and development, of faith and of self-possession, so ordinary, so human, of which the gospels speak. Eschatology becomes apocalypse. And the more definite the apocalyptic programme becomes, with its series of perfect figures, the further we penetrate into the secret language of symbolism, which drives us back to the ancient cultural mentality of the author of the Revelation and takes us further from our current historico-scientific mentality. In the extreme case there is no longer any real expectancy when we are informed about the fantastic programming of the future, as though it were a forecasting enquiry. What is too fully described is no longer hoped for but is already possessed like a reassuring fantasy. It would be just the same for Marxism if a revolutionary programme were devoted to the description in anticipation of the perfect society. The act of healing and developing, of believing and of grasping, like the action of seizing power, is killed by a futurism in which knowing comes too long before risking. For this reason long-term eschatology only remains a cause for hope when it stays in the category of faith, without being swallowed up in those of vision and of knowledge.

There is a second possible interpretation, but this also seems to be fatal to hope. Convinced that the apocalyptic setting is purely a cultural expression, this interpretation renounces not only the outworn expression but also the length of expectation which it conveys. Only what I have called the short-term expectation remains in fact truly of the gospel, the instant of healing and of love, of decision and of faith. As for the global future, we ought to know from contemporary science that it cannot secrete any decisive mutation because it is rationally devoted to evolution and to entropy, growing complexity and extinction, as much at the level of civilizations as at that of the universe. Hope is here an existential opening. It cannot nor does it any longer wish to be a universal expectation. It is honest if it admits to meeting another being who frees me from my solitary self-sufficiency and from my egocentric despair. It is dishonest if it extrapolates this experience of the I confronting the Thou in a fresco of Us confronting the world, and the old world confronting the new world which is to be. Eschatology, as Albert Camus the agnostic used to say, teaches us that 'the Last Judgment happens every day'. The pure gospel would then forbid us to speculate on the future of a last day, speculations which are the residue of a mentality which is apocalyptic, imaginative, curious and, let the big words come, supranaturalist and supra-historic. There is undeniably more truth in this second interpretation than in the first. But it raises an objection. It suppresses so many gospel passages where the excitement of a long-term hope adds to the excitement of the short-term hope. I select one example:

The seventy-two disciples returned full of joy saying: 'Lord, even the demons were subject to us in your Name!' Jesus said to them: 'I saw Satan falling like lightning from Heaven' (Luke 10.17).

If all that is left is the short-term hope (the demoniacs healed) without the long-term (evil driven out) the gospel (I quote Camus again) is like the message of *La Peste*. Men will always be raised up to heal, to develop, to recall to faith, to take possession, but always inexplicably, irremediably, plague and evil will return to assail the town. Hope is only the perseverance of Sisyphus when he rolls the rock up the slope of the mountain whence it will soon roll down again. Is the hope of Easter the hope of a tombstone which will never roll down again? Short-term expectation without long-term expectation is courage without hope, love within the limits of good-will and faith within the limits of pure reason. I use the Kantian terminology because Kant himself asked the question about long-term expectation in his little treatise on 'The End of All Things', and because he explicitly reserved the question of hope for this long-term expectation, after the two questions about power and knowledge: What can I know? What ought I to do? Finally, what have I a right to hope? It seems to me that the gospels divide hope between two phases and that every synchronization of the long phase with the short makes hope catch her breath. We must admittedly pass through the narrow gate of the short-term, but the open city of the long-term is announced. Let us then look for a

G

third interpretation which stands up to the curiosity of futurism and the instantaneity of decision.

In fact the gospels are never curious about the future, but neither is their view limited to the present. Healings as well as faith, development and salvation, also have a long-term dimension. Of development we only experience the healing acts, not yet the resurrection. Of salvation we only experience the reconciliation, not yet the redemption. Of history we only see the betrothal, not yet the nuptials. This second expectation, the long-term expectation, has consequences for our present hope. It restores the collective value of centuries and of peoples, often considered too unreal in relation to particular instants and individuals. It breathes into our anticipation not curiosity but hope. It makes us admit that the future age which overwhelms us still belongs to our responsibility and our expectation. It depersonalizes the better to humanize, it massifies the better to personalize. It knows that faith is sufficient for life, but that to live is also to expect, as faith does. All is begun. Nothing is finished. Jesus is the corner-stone of a world which is not yet built. We can only make people hope if healing announces a new state of health. The doctor of the short-term expectation is only a patcher-up. Only the doctor of long-term expectation is a herald. The preacher of the short-term expectation only bears a call to repentance. Only the preacher of long-term expectation bears a promise, a benediction. The first says grace, the second says glory. Between the two there is neither confusion nor rupture.

The astonishing thing in the gospels is the link between the two expectations which do not conflict with each other but support each other, as the everyday secretes the universal and the universal enlarges the everyday, as the psychological pledges the political and the political establishes the psychological, as man engages humanity and humanity manifests man, as the present moment chooses whether the past and the future are living, while the past and the future marry the present moment to history. Thus I think it is much truer to say that long-term eschatology universalizes short-term eschatology than that it is a futurist apocalyptic. Between Jesus of Nazareth and the Son of Man there is the same relationship as between my neighbour and our future. It is God alone who knows, said Jesus, when and how the transition will be achieved from faith into glory, from our partial developments to our universal humanity. For we are called Adam and not Sisyphus.

III   *Christian Hope amidst all the Human Variations on Hope*

This contribution is written in the context of Western theology.

It is complemented by an Eastern contribution. I shall therefore restrict myself to some contemporary currents of thought as they have emerged in recent years in the West. As I enquire into their position in relation to man's hopes, I make no attempt to trace a complete picture of contemporary ideologies but only to reflect on the variations brought out by the concept of hope.

We may hope, it seems to me, from three different motivations. First, we hope cumulatively. Humanity develops. It improves its technical skills. It refines its conscience. It organizes its struggle. Man's work provides a richer starting capital for his successors. As Pascal said in his 'Préface pour le traité du vide', 'the whole succession of men throughout the course of so many centuries must be thought of as the same man, who still goes on living and is continually learning'.[1] Man's works follow him and survive his individual death. Inventors disappear. Inventions remain. The memory of mankind registers his instrumental and cultural acquisitions. We are born heirs and we leave an inheritance behind us. There are endless examples of this hope which is linked with progress: in production, medicine, science, and in some respects also in the arts and cultures.

But our century has less faith in progress, it seems to me, than the two previous ones. Why? I see two thoughts which cause the crisis of progress. First of all, can we extrapolate from technological to human progress? Is it certain that, having more power and more knowledge at his disposal, man will be of more worth? Neither growth in production nor even development in education can guarantee the progress of culture, for example. We have no convincing proof that technological expansion encourages social justice, nor that social justice establishes the value of the human being. What is valid in one field does not necessarily hold in the same sense and automatically in all the rest. That is the first objection to the link between hope and progress. It is an objection to the abuse of lateral growth, for the human advance is not achieved on one front alone. The use of electricity and transistors does not in itself bring education with it, neither do education and learning in themselves produce art or sensibility. A second objection seems to me more alarming still: can there be hope through a cumulative process? The heir is never the actual inventor. Enjoying is like neither discovering nor hoping. The Pascalian and Cartesian idea that the whole succession of men may be considered as one man leaves out, for the sake of a generic and anonymous diagram of humanity, the specific and personal density of an individual face. At whatever stage of global progress chance decrees that we make our appearance, each of us has in fact to live these unique and never cumulative experiences – to be born, to learn, to love and to die. It would be an error to think that collective progress diminishes the intensity, the risks and the opportunities of each of our private histories. In a word, because humanity does not consist in the development either of a technological potential or of an abstract concept, but in a multiplicity of psychological choices and living consciousnesses, there cannot be an accumulation of hope. True, one should not deny the importance of the economic, psychological and cultural material available to us at the start. Still less should we deny that contemporary human sciences (Marxism, psycho-analysis, linguistics . . .) teach us how much the structures of our inheritance precede the moment when we are conscious of using them. It remains true nevertheless that to link hope with inheritance is in fact to give up hope – to be caught between illegitimate profit and overwhelming determinism. Hope cannot be capitalized because it springs from interiority, whereas capitalization (whether collective or private) always remains exterior. To link hope with progress is then to risk taking no account of multiplicity and of the disparity between the various domains of existence. It is also to forget that though humanity may be universal each man is unique.

The second possible motivation then is to link hope with encounter. Here the antagonistic replaces the cumulative. I hope, because I become both actor and audience, creator and admirer. The child is more capable of hope than an adult just because, having not yet become aware of the cumulative processes which forge him and drive him, he has this native spontaneity without which one no longer hopes or expects, one only possesses, but without joy. We are here at the antipodes of progress in a continually critical area where hope is connected with finding oneself when one is lost, with coming to life again when one feels dead, with opening out when one feels closed up, with existing instead of insisting. If the technological field is the most favourable for progressive and cumulative hope, the psychological, aesthetic and spiritual fields are the most favourable for existential and explosive hope.

But this second type of hope is itself terribly fragile though not in the same way that progress is. It is linked with the transcience of a problematic ecstasy. It lives on perpetual hope under perpetual menace. It has hardly time to blossom before it begins to fade. It is a flower-hope, which does not recognize its seed and never comes to fruition. The unforeseeable is its germ-cell, the established its decay. The two great names which have illustrated its current popularity are Kierkegaard and Sartre. They are equally opposed to any religion of progress, equally intent, the one on the instant of faith, the other on the pre-reflective spontaneity of conscience, probably equally incapable, as a result, of extending hope into a promise kept, a faithful partnership. Nobody has spoken better than they of the upsurge of hope, of the miracle of faith and the wonder of freedom. But how is the miracle to be repeated in the course of history? In Sartre's *Being and Nothingness* we see the being who exists, that is to say who hopes, for ever caught by the gluey mass of the world which precedes him, by the antagonistic freedom of the other who entices and reduces him, only finding his time and place in a project perpetually threatened by relapses into the opposite of hope which is immobilism. In *La critique de la raison dialectique*, by Sartre again, the collective hope of liberation is as fragile as was the individual hope of freedom in *Being and Nothingness*. A group which hopes (Sartre is speaking of a group in revolutionary fusion and quotes the example of the taking of the Bastille) exists very briefly between the anonymous, heterogeneous series which precedes it and the institutional, authoritatively homogeneous process which follows it. Hope has a very fugitive life at the level of the destinies of man as at the level of the destinies of peoples. It is impossible to see how these single instants could ever be connected together to form a global hope.

To connect hope with progress is to simplify abstractly, impersonally, the real concrete history of men and of each man. But to connect hope with the wonder of encounter is to atomize hope into a disconnected series of flashes too quickly extinguished. The man of progress forgets that one cannot make people hope from the outside of consciousness, by feeding it with products and slogans, with statistics and publicity. Hope asks to be aroused by the sensitive fingers of truth and conviction, of happiness and desire. But the man of the encounter forgets that consciousness requires also to live an outward-going existence, that it seeks to relate its expectancy to friendly realities and sustained achievement. Hope asks to be upheld by the strong hands of constructiveness and faithfulness. The plan is not enough. It needs the promise.

After cumulative and progressive hope, after instantaneous and explosive hope, I now embark upon a third attitude of contemporary thought on the subject of hope, which seems to me radically to challenge the preceding two and to reject the pretensions of subjectivity as much as the illusions of progress. According to this third attitude hope is a false question, and is moreover the cause of man's unhappiness. The novelist Samuel Beckett has given a savage but serene illustration of this point of view: 'Hope is the infernal condition *par excellence*, contrary to what has always been thought. Whereas to see oneself endlessly relapsing fills one with contentment.'[2] To learn to think and live outside the category of hope would be at one and the same time to purge oneself of disillusion and to concentrate upon rightful occupations. If nothing more is promised us, then everything remains lawful. The world does not give any sort of sign corresponding with a supposed meaning and purpose in history. Lives are not threaded with sudden wonders. Man is only an intelligent animal, who arranges his universe in coherent systems and also talks, producing many complex noises. We must no longer reason in terms of hope, but strain to be satisfied with the architecture of our knowledge. For hope is still a theological fantasy from which modern agnostic man has not had the courage to free himself. Having renounced God, he has projected hope upon history, and being disillusioned with history he has taken refuge in encounter. And why should we reserve a place for hope when we have been deprived of all promise? This third attitude, note well, rejects despair with as much force as its twin brother hope. Despair, it says, lives on the deceits of hope. Banish hope, and along with it you will banish despair. There will still be enough fields for man to exercise his astonishing faculties as a talking and thinking animal, a craftsman and engineer, a maker of words and objects.

Naturally, this third attitude is the hardest for us to accept, the most provocative. Does a man still exist, if his knowledge and ability are forbidden to think in terms of hope? If it is true that progress deludes us when it claims to offer us hope, if it is true that subjectivity goes wild like a compass without a magnet between the marvellous and the absurd, is the banishing of hope and despair a real possibility of behaviour or a verbal wager? Does the abandonment of hope mean the attainment of a non-historical and non-subjective serenity, or is it, whatever its claims, the discreet façade of a deeply tragic situation which has lost not only history and self-consciousness but man himself? 'I lack nothing', wrote Kafka, 'except my own self.'

I have tried to characterize briefly and partially without so far naming them the attitudes to hope of the three great currents of contemporary thought: Marxism, existentialism and structuralism. Equally briefly I should like now to set Christian hope in the midst of them.

Does history, in the Christian view, contain a certain progress which is the fruit and the seed of the hope of faith? The answer in the first place will be vigorously positive. Is it not from the 'progression' of the history of salvation that the notion of 'progress' in secular history was born? It is well known that the Greeks had a different view of history. They thought of it as going in cycles, earth time modelled on astral time which brings the planets back to their first position after the time of their regular revolutions. Our weeks moreover combine biblical and Greek origins. Their liturgical duration is connected with the history of salvation, the terminal sabbath and the initial resurrection. But the names of the seven days are derived from ancient thought about the astral cycle: Sunday (the sun), Monday (the moon), . . . Saturday (Saturn).[3] Our weeks are thus Hebrew and Greek, progressive in duration and cyclical in name. The Greeks also thought of history regressively. Beneficent time, that of Chronos, which unfortunately we do not live in, would be time which could be wound back to its origin. Maleficent time, that of Zeus, in which we are, unwinds and flows away to its fall, to its decadence. On the other hand biblical time is the advance of creation towards an eschatology, of a seed towards its blossoming, of a promise towards its accomplishment. Biblical time is neither cyclical, nor regressive, but messianic. Luther uses a good parable when he compares secular time with giving birth. It is well known to midwives, he used to say, that once the head of the child is through, the rest of the body will easily follow. It is the same for humanity, when Christ is the head and Christmas the giving birth. At first sight then Christian hope implies a global progression. It is nearer the idea of the cumulative tide of alliances and accomplishments than the instantaneousness of encounters or the agnosticism of non-hope.

But does messianic hope mean progression? I shall make at least three comments. The Bible recognizes no simplistic view of progress as unique and multilateral. It is possible for a king to be powerful, wise, and completely wicked. David, the ever-threatened king, is better than Saul the despot or Solomon the luxurious. Often, but fortunately without the reverse being inevitably true, it is interior ruin which accompanies outward progressiveness. Did not the greatest 'progression' in the history of salvation happen through the cross, which is a total failure according to the history of secular 'progress'? The Bible does not speak of a cumulative advance but rather of a repetitive and innovating one. It knows nothing of the capitalization of gains. It invites either the repetition, the *anamnesis*, of what has been given, conquered and concluded, or the hearing or the prophesying of what is to come. Biblical progression is effected by crises. I should have mentioned moreover that the most profound feature of Marxism, which distinguishes it from a naïvely constant and cumulative progressivism, is also its theory of crises and revolutions, especially when we reflect that the modern idea of revolution (historical, innovating, and no longer astral and reactionary) came to Marxism by way of Hegelian negativity, which itself arose out of speculation upon the cross and Good Friday. Finally biblical messianism always speaks of a double progression, that of man which is related to faith, and to hope, and that of God which is related to his sudden, unforeseen intervention. Unlike progress, messianism thus remains an unforeseeable encounter. To the immanence of events it adds the transcendance of judgment and of grace. History is not its own final judgment on itself. Actualization never becomes its proper norm, or history would be reduced to the necessity of its own future.

True, without the progression of salvation there would have been no human reflection on progressive development We see this clearly in the upsurge of cyclical and archaeological reflections as soon as we really get away from any Jewish or Christian reference.[4] At the same time, biblical hope is not to be confused in any sense with cumulative progress. The retention of an eschatology is what separates the progression of salvation from any ideology of progress. For the true role of eschatology is not to satisfy our curiosity about the future, but to maintain the freedom of God in face of the unfolding of history, which also means to assure man, the image of God, of a fundamental freedom as he faces his destiny.

Let us now see whether in the Christian view hope culminates in an encounter. Here again the first answer is an eager affirmative. What are short-term eschatology and long-term eschatology if not definitely encounters? The Christian hopes that he will hear and know as he believes himself to be known. He hopes to know what to do, to learn why he must suffer, to receive what is proclaimed and, above all, to see the face of him of whom so far he knows no more than the name. Here too, certainly, secular reflection on the interiority and the subjectivity of consciousness starts from meditation on the status of faith, one of the most striking illustrations of which is the relationship of Kierkegaard's existence to Sartre's existentialism. The Greeks were not hoping for an encounter. They were looking for the ultimate foundation which overhangs or underlies reality. Their theology aimed at fitting the word to the world, the logos to the cosmos. They did not yearn to see God's face. For the Greek gods have still the face of Janus, which makes them simultaneously marvellous idealizations of man and impenetrable masks of fate. The fact that the highest hope that I can form is of an inter-personal encounter is therefore an echo, in contemporary feeling and culture, of the trinitarian theology, which has decisively transformed the foundations, the hypostases, of Greek thought into living persons.

But are hope and faith relations between subjects? Here again it is important to define certain limits, as we have just done for the progression of salvation and the progress of history; for Christian hope is not personalist existentialism. The vocabulary of the Bible strangely applies to God not only human expressions such as face, arm, hands and heart, but also non-human words such as rock, cloud, spring, rampart and buckler. Is this not a pointer to the fact that for biblical hope God is at once like man and yet not only man? Unlike human consciousness, God has a relationship not of manufacturer nor of consumer, but of Creator, with the uncountable and subjectively inaccessible world of life and of matter. If God were only a subjectivity, although super-eminent, he would share this fragility in which existentialism has so admirably demonstrated the essence of the existent. He would share our admirations as well as our eclipses. But how would he also be the God of the universe, whose immeasurable exteriority has been made greater for us by the conquest of the moon? I see no other outcome of secular existentialism than an absolute dualism between consciousness, the being-for-oneself, and things, the being-in-itself, which implies, I also think, a second irremediable duality between the individual and humanity. 'Man', writes Proust, 'is the being who cannot get outside himself, who only knows others in himself.' Indeed, in spite of all his efforts, has Sartre ever said anything else about the nature of consciousness? Now biblical hope seems to ignore these two dualisms inasmuch as it applies to a God who created not only man but things. Man is of course the central animal of creation, since he is the image of God and the partner of his inter-personal alliance. But yet, according to the myths of Genesis, man is still merely one of the animals created on the sixth day of the cosmos. How could he who only hopes in terms of intersubjective encounters also have hope for the whole of humanity and for the universe? The function of the doctrine of creation is not to inform us about the initial causalities of our emergences, but to say to faith that the dualism between the consciousness of the existing and the opacity of the universe is a mistaken dualism. The doctrine of creation does not answer our curiosity about origins. It crosses the existentialist abyss between anthropology and cosmology.

Finally, have we the right and the duty to hope? I shall try here also to begin by showing where there is an initial agreement with those who deny us this right and this duty. Biblical thought destroys illusions and pretensions. We know how firmly it refuses to speculate upon the two great sources of religious aspiration, procreation and death. To beget, according to the Bible, is not to participate in divine fecundity, but only to bring into the world a man child. To die is not to return at last to a blissful beyond, but to see the bond loosened between breath and body. If hope is the fantasy of immortality conveyed in a soul not yet instructed in reality, the Bible deprives us of any such hope. The Bible clearly sees man's vocation without hope or despair in these tasks of work and love, both of which are made up of words and actions. The Bible is not metaphysical nor supernatural, but physical and natural. In all these respects perhaps structuralism is one of the numerous secular echoes of the biblical war against 'religion'.

But I do not see man remaining man without hope. The missed appointments with God, with history or with consciousness do not destroy the idea of a given appointment, which some call a meaning, others a mystery. Biblical hope believes that man questions himself about the 'why' of a word as well as about the 'how' of a language. The human animal is certainly the manufacturer of words and of things. He is also the recipient of words and of things. With them he makes not only more or less well regulated systems but also more or less well understood stories. The biblical doctrine of the Word is not aimed at giving us a revelation descended from heaven, but at establishing men upon earth as listeners and answerers. To hope is to breathe expectancy. The extra-human creation 'sighs'. We men ourselves 'intercede', which is to say that we have the permission and duty to ask (Rom. 8.22, 27). Whoever asks, hopes. Could a man still be man while eliminating all petition from his action and his speech?

I have run rapidly through some contemporary variations on the theme of hope, from progress to encounter and to non-hope. Neither arrogantly challenging nor allowing myself to be passively intimidated, I have asked how Christian hope can live with these ideologies which disturb it and turn it upside down, even when they have been indirectly nourished by it. It remains to say simply that short-term eschatology and long-term eschatology which together, as we have seen, constitute Christian hope, have extreme difficulty in relating themselves to the hopes and non-hopes of contemporary man. Short-term eschatology seems to them to have been a fleeting ray of good-will, and the place of long-term eschatology to remain the permanent dream of an un-attainable kingdom. It rests with every man who wants to be a Christian to hold the taut bow of his obedient hope between the two, so that development does not deteriorate into ever inadequate good-will, and salvation does not ebb away, alike a deceptive and deceived mirage. That is what I shall attempt to say as I conclude with a few remarks on the Report of Section III of the Uppsala Assembly, 'Economic and Social Development', the theme of this symposium.

IV   *Hope, Development and Salvation*

The Uppsala Report states that we live in a period of immense changes due essentially to the growth of men's possibilities, but that these changes do not necessarily in themselves give grounds for hope because technological progress is not accompanied by social justice, equality and freedom, and also because changes often destroy without rebuilding; because, in short, development is a too exclusively economic concept (growth) without political, psychological and cultural reper-cussions. There are great changes but there is little hope. On the other hand the gospel confronting this situation describes small changes accompanied by great hope. Hence the question which breaks through the whole of the Report: how can we relate development to hope? How can we avoid the disillusionment of the developing countries which see their difficulties increasing and have good reason to expect more from revolution than from development? How can we avoid recriminations from the industrialized countries who doubt the usefulness of their contributions, reduce their efforts towards world solidarity from year to year, and are tempted by their own wage demands and financial difficulties to shut themselves up in a neo-isolationism, not seeing that their economy of incessant growth and planned waste is a deep-lying factor in the world's division.

Christians are far from existing alone in the world. On the contrary, we live in an age when Christianity, as well as the old sacralization of Christendom and the old colonialism of the West, seems to be on the defensive. Other ideologies have put forward other hopes: the revolution of Marxism, the freedom of existentialism, the know-how of the social sciences and of structuralism. What is remarkable is the speed with which the breath of hope brought by these new acquisitions and theories is exhausted. Difficulties quickly arise to challenge the solutions they offered. Marxism, spreading enthusiasm when it is mobilizing the masses against underdevelopment and in the cause of the dignity of man, fails, when it is established, to give birth to a really new man. Existentialism, in spite of its longing to be committed, finds it difficult to emerge from individualism. The social sciences, finally, are passionately keen on study but exclude any exhortation. For this reason our world on the whole knows very little about hope. The various youth protests are certainly directed against this lack of hope, as though development in itself could not be an objective, since it provides a richer life but not a life enriched in meaning. Christians themselves doubt the adequacy of their faith to meet the needs of contemporary humanity. Some persevere in the perpetuation of the churches, which are more or less cut off from human expectation. Others share human expectations but without seeing how their faith also is anything other than humanism.

In this situation I shall underline four points in connection with the Report:

1. Hope is *universal*. Man does not save himself alone. This is the meaning of the church. Jesus Christ is at once the 'first-born of all creation' and 'the head of the body, [that is, of] the church' (Col. 1.15, 18). Human solidarity needs to be built on as deep a foundation as possible, at a time when in spite of the superabundance of information we live everywhere like fragments of humanity in heterogeneous blocs, races and cultures. Solidarity founded on good will is shaken when this good will is suspected or ill rewarded. Solidarity founded on

utility is shaken as soon as interests diverge. Solidarity based on affinities creates its own enemies. Lastly, solidarity based on understanding frays at the edges as soon as we come up against foreign mentalities. Only to an 'ontological' solidarity, 'christological' to Christians, is given the strength to follow through. This conviction questions the provincialism of development, either on a world scale or in a particular country. This conviction demands reparations which are not charitable compensations but just equivalents. There will be no hope, so long as the privileged close their ears and so make the underprivileged unwilling to listen. Short-term eschatology as well as the long-term eschatology of the gospels are both universal. Although he has never given up his solidarity with his people, Jesus through his words and his actions has instituted a universal solidarity. Similarly, Christian solidarity, without giving up solidarity with the churches and with the church, has no meaning unless it is continuously related to non-Christians.

2. Hope is *global* in the sense in which we speak today of a global economy and a global architecture. Development is not only concerned with the revenue but also with the political régime, with daily life, with customs and with ideals. We do not know a people, nor indeed a man, if we only calculate his budget and ignore his habitat, his family, his reading and his myths. One of the present difficulties of the churches in relation to this global development comes from the fact that they are rarely communities, but only places and occasions of religious assembly, of theological training, which shuffle off the multiplicity of the secular at the door of the sacred world. But whereas the 'religious' man sets himself apart in a provincialized sector, the saint mixes with the whole world to restore to it direction and hope. Reforming themselves on their own initiative in this respect and so speaking more convincingly to the world, the churches ask that the idea of development should not be restricted to economic considerations which always take for granted the superiority of industrialized societies. A technologically advanced society is often politically dead, culturally sterile, emotionally underdeveloped. Just as there is no multilateral progress, but it is diversified with excesses and deficiencies, so development is not measured by the average *per capita* income of its inhabitants. Economic superiority gives no ground for satisfaction, nor economic backwardness for contempt. Indeed there is no society which is a very impreesive model of global development.

3. Hope is *active*. The New Testament as we have seen is familiar with a short-term expectation and a long-term expectation. Only action can relate one with the other without short-term expectation being satisfied with isolated gestures and reformed prototypes, or

long-term expectation being reduced to an eschatological passivity or a millennial revolution. The man who hopes also acts. I should like here to quote two sentences from secular leaders; Ben Bella of Algeria: 'We should never have rebelled if we had not had *dreams*', and Sukarno of Indonesia at the opening of the Bandung Conference: 'In your discussions do not be guided by fear, but by hopes, by resolves, by ideals, and also, yes, by *dreams*.' One can certainly act without hope. Courage and obedience do not need hope. The darkness of the night often makes their greatness. But I do not think the New Testament is mistaken in linking together love, faith and hope (I Cor. 13.13), for love without hope is pity and faith without hope is absolutism. Hope does not measure itself against the chances of success but against the chances of communication. Hope gives action its flavour, as action gives hope its seriousness. Work for universal and global development requires men rich in hope, realistic, energetic and not discouraged, as Christ on earth was not discouraged (Heb. 12.3 f.).

4. Lastly, hope is *eager*. By itself the word development indicates a task never finished. I have compared it with Jesus' acts of healing, for manifestly these do no more than relieve unless they also express this other action: salvation to be believed in and grasped. The word salvation has been emptied of its human substance when it has been equated with a magical transition from perdition to deliverance. In French the word 'salut' for salvation is also a greeting, the acknowledging of a presence. In the eyes of Jesus, a man is saved, if he himself welcomes what is happening to him. To develop preserves an external consonance with to educate, to encourage to grow, to instruct, to feed, to heal. To save, to greet, or to salute, on the other hand, indicate a man's personal presence in his words and actions. As we have seen, it is a false choice to offer development or salvation, technical aid or evangelization, as alternatives. For the gospels contain both, the act of healing and the summons. But it would equally, it seems to me, be a false solution to identify them. To develop oneself, to be developed, or to develop someone else, this is still not to salute him personally. Salvation, *salut*, is the 'yes' which is required of us, the 'amen' which suddenly intervenes, before or after the development, before or after the healing. We must be thirsty if we are to drink the water. The man who is not thirsy will never speak the welcome. The gospel came upon the earth to contribute amongst other forces to the development of humanity, but also to teach us to salute, to greet one another. Mary welcomed the news that her son would come to fulfil the hope of Abraham and develop the earth (Luke 1.47–55). A salutation will always make the heart of man leap for joy more than any assistance, however adequate. Thus the church does not magically 'save' the

world. She 'salutes' it in the name of God, the Creator, the Companion and the Expectation of the earth.

NOTES

1. 'Préface pour le traité du vide', *Oeuvres complètes*, ed. J. Chevalier, Gallimard, 1954, p. 534.
2. *Molloy* (Les Éditions de Minuit, Paris, 1951), p. 206.
3. This does not quite work out in English since some of our names of days have come by way of German mythology, but the point remains the same. (Translator)
4. E.g. in Nietzsche and Freud and in structuralism.

9

This World and the Other

PAUL VERGHESE

I *Clarifying the Question*

The method

Christians have not always maintained the dialectical tension between the secular and the ultimate in the Christian hope. It has too often been much easier to put the major emphasis on the one, and to give but lip-service to the other, and thus to live without tension.

An objective study of the writings of the apostle Paul in the New Testament would show that he lived in tension. But it was not the tension between the demand for radical reconstruction of Roman society here on earth and the expectation of the kingdom of God to be established beyond history. St Paul did not seek to draw the contours of the future society, nor did he attempt to relate the coming kingdom to the reorganization of society outside the church. His tension was between living in hope here, and entering into the fulfilment beyond the veil of time.

Our approach today in social ethics has to take the New Testament affirmations about the Christian hope fully into account. We cannot, however, expect to find the New Testament speaking directly to our situation.

It is the very nature of the Christian faith to place us before certain choices, and to help us by the Holy Spirit, which operates through the tradition of the eschatological community, to discern the direction and pattern of the future of human society.

In this paper, therefore, we do not begin with New Testament exegesis. For the present writer and for his tradition the theological method which attempts a pure hermeneutic of the scriptural revelation already given makes no sense and falsifies the Christian understanding of the role of the Spirit and of the eschatological tradition of the community in making theological choices.

Our method here will be to use as much of the insights and understandings of man in the Christian tradition as can be mustered and related to the present situation of man, within the scope of such a short paper. This must be done by the power of the Spirit, which always uses the Bible as the unique and primary document within the Christian tradition.

The question

Certain extreme types of Christianity have tended to regard Christian salvation as primarily related to the salvation of the soul in the life after death. Such concepts of salvation are basically individualistic and other-worldly. They have shown but meagre interest in the transformation of society here on earth.

At the other extreme are certain forms of Christian humanism, which lay their main emphasis on the 'secular city', and would like to drive out all elements of mystery and sanctity from human existence. These theologies tend to overlook the problem of death, and glide over some of the fundamental questions that man has always asked about his ultimate existence. They would, for example, reduce the difficult and delicate problems of christology to very simple sociological questions.[1] Some would even go so far as to say that the Christian faith is concerned only about this world and no other.

Both these extremes, along with many varieties in between, seek to derive their basis from the Christian scriptures. And it is hardly possible to arbitrate between these two views solely on the basis of the Bible. Neither would it be fruitful to try to neutralize the difference by easy compromises.

Our question in this essay is not set in terms of these alternatives. It is rather more complex than a simple choice between this world and the next. Our setting for the question is the new concern for world development seen as a responsibility of man. We need to begin the process which the Conference on Church and Society at Geneva in 1966 neglected to initiate – theological reflection on the meaning of social change and on the development of man.

There are certain basic elements in the Christian's ultimate hope: that good will triumph over evil and destroy it; that death will be overcome by a life that is beyond its reach; that righteousness, love, joy and peace, freedom and wisdom, will characterize the human community; that we shall be transfigured into creatures of light and be able to approach the God of light in more direct apprehension and adoration; that we shall be with Christ, in a new resurrection body.

None of these elements we expect to be fulfilled within history – individual or corporate. It is beyond death, and through death, that we must enter the world of ultimate reality in its fullness – not only personal death, but perhaps also the death of history, when this world shall have passed away. If history is to be saved, it must also be through death and resurrection. What the author of the second epistle of Peter says with such clarity belongs to the authentic tradition of the church and constitutes the eschatological foundation of that tradition:

But the Day of the Lord will come; it will come, unexpected as a thief. On that day the heavens will disappear with a great rushing sound, the elements will disintegrate in flames, and the earth with all that is in it [history] will be laid bare [*heurethesetai*]. . . . But we have his promise, and look forward to new heavens and a new earth, the home of justice. (II Peter 3.10, 13, NEB.)

If that is what is going to happen, then what meaning can our development activities have upon the earth? This seems to be the question which many theologians seek to avoid, by calling all that mere myth.

The question has been raised by Fr Karl Rahner with unusual clarity in a recent article: 'Is the world which man creates only the "material" for his moral testing, remaining in itself morally indifferent? Will the world simply disappear when the definitive kingdom of God arrives?'[2] What is the relation of our development projects to this ultimate 'new heavens and new earth'? Rahner raises the question whether the human world is to be compared to the rush baskets which the ancient monks of the Egyptian desert wove and unwove every day to keep themselves from sinning. Are development programmes merely an exercise in moral training, a preparatory school to enter the college of heaven?

How is the Christian's ultimate hope related to his 'secular' activities upon earth? Does the nature of his ultimate hope nullify the significance of his activities to build a society with justice, dignity, freedom and love upon earth in history? Or does the former give some orientation, some meaning and some ultimate purpose to man's efforts to develop the earth which is entrusted to him?

The terms 'ultimate' and 'secular'

What precisely do we mean by the 'ultimate' and the 'secular'?

The secular, at least for the purposes of this paper, means 'confined to historical existence', both personal and social. It is not to be contrasted with 'sacred' or 'religious'. Its counterpart is rather the 'eternal' or trans-historical. We shall in this paper try to steer clear of the usual dichotomies between natural and supernatural, sacred and profane, church and state, etc.

By ultimate hope we mean the expectation of the final fulfilment of the kingdom of God beyond human history, beyond time.

By secular hope we mean the expectation of the progressive fulfilment of the same kingdom of God within human history.

To what extent are we justified in holding on to the ultimate hope in the context of our current knowledge of the universe? This is a prior question which needs to be answered before entering upon a fuller discussion of the meaning of the terms secular and ultimate.

The Bible makes a basic distinction between this age and the coming age (*ha-olam ha-zeh* and *ha-olam ha-baa* or *ho aion houtos* and *ho aion ho mellon*, Matt. 12.32). The emphasis on the end of this world and the promise of a coming new world are central in the teaching of Jesus (Matt. 13.39, 40, 49; 24.3; Mark 10.30; Luke 18.30; 20.35). St Paul also operates in the same framework (Rom. 12.2; I Cor. 2.6 ff.; 10.11; Gal. 1.4; Eph. 1.21, etc.).

Like man, the present world is also subject to death (Rom. 8.19 ff.; I John 2.17; Rev. 21.1; II Peter 3.10 ff.). Like man it is to be reconstituted (Rom. 8.19 ff.; Rev. 21.1 ff.). The two resurrections, that is, of man, and of the creation, are interconnected, according to St Paul in Rom. 8.

There is a world of the resurrection, to which man and the present creation can enter only through death. This is a world where there is no time, for time is the interval between birth and death, and in that world there is no death and therefore no need for marriage and birth (Matt. 22.30; Rom. 6.9; 8.2; I Cor. 15.21 ff.; II Tim. 1.10; I John 3.14; Rev. 20.6, etc.).

We are certainly not yet in a world without death and birth, without funerals, marriages and baptisms (for centuries the mainstay of the clerical class). On the contrary, death and birth (sex) are our major obsessions, as our literature and poetry so clearly bear witness. The kingdom is yet to come in its fullness.

The apostle Paul says quite clearly and unmistakably (I Cor. 15.19): 'If it is for this life only that Christ has given us hope, we of all men are most to be pitied' (so the New English Bible). The Revised Standard Version, 'If in this life we who are in Christ have only hope, we are of all men most to be pitied', does not fit in the context of the passage at all. Even the strained explanation of the Interpreter's Bible does not make it fit. The real point, whichever translation we take, is this: If our hope of the resurrection is not to be fulfilled, or if we have no hope that goes beyond this world, all the martyrdoms and sufferings are sheer folly. St Paul's sentences are directed against those Christians in Corinth, who like some today, believed that there is to be no future resurrection. St Paul discountenances such a secular interpretation of the gospel in no uncertain terms; all the more pity therefore when translators and exegetes try to do violence to the very sentence in which he attacks such an interpretation.

The New Testament leaves us in no doubt that the fulfilment in Christ is to be completed, and manifested as complete, only on the 'Last Day' which is still in the future. The imagery in which this last day was described by Jesus and the apostles may have to be understood in a poetic sense. But it seems quite unfaithful to the scriptural documents to interpret them in a totally 'realized' sense, as if all fulfilment were in the past and there were nothing to look forward to in the future.

That future day can come only when death is removed, evil disappears, and suffering ceases. To fix a date for it is to misunderstand the meaning of the word 'day' which is unlikely to be a day on our calendar, but is something at the frontier of history where there is a radical transition from time to eternity. And that is why we prefer to call that day 'ultimate' rather than 'last' because the latter refers to the final member of a series, while ultimate refers to a different dimension altogether.

So long as man groans, the creation groans, and the Holy Spirit himself groans with wordless prayers in the hearts of the believers (Rom. 8.18 ff.), the end is not consummated. And any secular theology which overlooks that fact is not faithful to the central insights of the New Testament.

The secular hope then refers to the experience of man in seeing God's purposes and promises increasingly fulfilled in personal and human history. For the individual it is primarily a *pre-mortem* (before death) experience. For mankind it is historical experience in a time-continuum.

The ultimate hope refers to a *post-resurrectionem* experience, where sin and death, law and suffering are totally removed, where the good life in freedom and joy becomes abundantly available.

Are there two worlds?

It seems misleading to speak of two different worlds, this one and the coming one, as if they were two sets of universes, one here and one hereafter, or in more sophisticated Platonic terms, one perfect world of forms above, another imperfect world of particulars here below.

Our current scientific knowledge does not permit us to think in terms of two different universes, unless one were to use the concepts of universe and anti-universe. Scientists tell me that the very question about the unity of the universe is meaningless. At the immense and near-infinite scales of the universe as now known to physical and mathematical science, the very notion of continuity (which is after all a time-space notion) loses its validity. The universe at that scale becomes a series of possibilities – many possible universes. The universe we now know seems to be undergoing 'periodic' cycles of gravitational collapse and expansion.[3] What we regard today as 'physical laws' or 'laws of nature' may turn out to be but parochial phenomena limited to our particular corner of space and to our particular time in the expansion-contraction cycle. If we are now in the expansion half of the cycle, all the laws could be reversed when we get to the contraction-side of the cycle.

The ontology of the universe, as far as modern science has gained access to it, reveals a high degree of indeterminacy, both at the micro-level 'inside' the particles, where time ceases to exist, as well as in the 'spreading ripples of super-space' where 'before' and 'after' have no meaning, where there are only the 'quantum mechanical couplings by probability waves', and where something determined called 'the' universe ceases to exist. If that is so, then the relation between 'this world' and 'the next world' could be conceived in terms of a probability of the present universe, and not as a totally different one.

Even if the universe were given, with a fully regular and predictable constitution, as far as we are concerned, we have to deal with this universe in terms of our own equipment of perception. It is a notorious commonplace of high school psychology that perception is an extremely selective process. A good share of the data pounded in by the senses has to be eliminated first in order that the mind can build the rest into a coherent and meaningful picture.

Further, the very sense data that come in are far from complete. Our sense equipment is severely limited in range and depth. The air we breathe is full of different waves and particles of light and sound and smell with which our equipment is simply incapable of coping. There is so much that goes on on our little planet of which we are blissfully ignorant. It is literally true to say that we 'see only in part' even that which we think we see. What is invisible to us may constitute a very significant aspect of the reality around us. With our present structure of mind, if we were able to see all, we would not see at all. Only by filtering out much can we make sense of our experience.

The point of all this digression about perception is simply this – our present universe is constituted by our sense-equipment, and by the ancillary equipment which we have been able to make for ourselves by technology. Change our sense·equipment and brain-structure, and we will have a different universe. Look at the paranoid or the psychedelic. Is the universe of his experience the same as ours? And which is the 'true' one? For our equipment ours is true, for his, his is true. And if all were paranoid or psychedelic, we would have a totally different universe.

As the post-Kantians are so eager to tell us, there are as many universes as there are systems of perception. The bee has its world, the spider and the bat have each its own, depending upon the particular perception system of each. Change our sense-equipment – this world disappears, and another one takes its place.

Thus the question of one world or two worlds or many worlds becomes academic. We still have no idea of what 'the universe' as such is. And that will always escape us, says Kant. Time and space are our forms of perception and when the system of perception changes, these too may cease.

Orientation for a theology of development

Our task in theology is to find some orientation to our life and work and prayer in this world. Certain thinkers among us, following the line of thinking best characterized as 'secularization', insist that we should understand the gospel in terms of this world and no other. Granted. But are we to assume that this world is subject only to the forms of change peculiar to time and space, and to our technology drawn from our notions of time and space? The Christian's ultimate hope speaks in terms both of the dissolution of the body (death) with its time-space equipment and of the passing away of this world. A proper Christian theology of development has to take into account the temporary nature of our bodily and earthly life. That is an integral part of our understanding of 'this world and no other'. We cannot, as Christians, subscribe to a theology of development which seeks all fulfilment within the confines of the *pre-mortem* personal history and of the time-space world of history.

Someone may ask: but is it not this universe, given to us by our present sensory system, that is the object of development, especially scientific, technological and economic development? The answer is, no.

It seems necessary to shout at the top of one's voice that the object of development is not the universe, but man. Once we lose sight of that fact, all our thinking is bound to go wrong. If we want to develop this world, it is not for the world's sake, but for the sake of man, and the full manifestation of his being, which is after all the image of God, and redounds to the glory of God.

This man is mortal man, in time, caught in the meshes of evil, suffering and death. Man's emancipation must therefore rescue him

from the power of evil and death. Man and the universe have both
to be freed from their present evil- and death-bound existence and
introduced into a world without evil and death. Christian theology
has to play her full role in this deliverance.

The notion of 'ultimate' is fully biblical. But it has a special and
somewhat complex meaning in the Bible. The Greek is, of course,
eschatos, and it is used primarily in connection with a day or an hour,
which is the time of settling accounts and of renewal.

In the fourth gospel, this 'last day' or 'ultimate time' is identified
with the future day of resurrection,[4] which is also the day of judgment.[5]
But in the first epistle of John we are told that it is now already the
last day.[6] The first epistle of Peter maintains this same tension. In 1.5
we are told that the fullness of salvation is faithfully kept in store for
us to be manifested fully only 'in the ultimate time'. In 1.20 we are
told that the resurrection of Christ has already taken place 'in these
ultimate times'.

It is this tension that upsets all our circular or linear notions of
history, and radically questions our 'this worldly' or 'other-worldly'
notions of development. Theology seems still to be in the elementary
fields of plane geometry and arithmetic.

Our logic has to be more sophisticated. Neither the circular nor the
linear notion of history can do justice to the complexity of the time-
eternity relation. For after all the ultimate was in history, and is now
in it.

The ultimate is not necessarily all beyond history; neither is it fully
in history, which is certainly a *pre-mortem* experience for man.

We are promised a fullness of salvation which is our living hope
(*elpis zosa*) grounded on the resurrection of Jesus Christ.[7] We hope
to come into possession of 'an inheritance, not subject to disintegration,
uncontaminated by evil, which will never grow dim and uninteresting,
faithfully conserved for us in the heavens, for all who are guarded by
the power of God through faith'.[8]

In other words, the three major problems of our existence – namely
death (or time that is always running out), sin (evil, the absence of the
good), and boredom (all pleasures grow dim and turn to dust and
ashes) are to be overcome only 'in the heavens', i.e. in a mode of life
into which we cannot enter except through death and resurrection.
There death will be no more, life will triumph. There sin will be wiped
away, righteousness will flourish. There boredom will be swallowed
up; joy will bubble forth in an eternal spring.

It is this hope which is the foundation of the Christian faith; God's
love and his promise are the bases on which we cling to this Christian
hope, however unfashionable or scandalous it may appear to the

mythical 'modern man', who seems in any case to be less sceptical than Celsus[9] in the second century.

Our question then is: *If this world is to be dissolved, and our ultimate hope is a fulfilment beyond history, then what significance can human history and human development have?* The answer to this question lies in the direction of understanding (*a*) the meaning of man's existence and his vocation, and (*b*) the relation of what is done in history to the ultimate hope.

II   *Answering the Question*

Man and his vocation

The Eastern tradition understands man and his vocation primarily from the perspective of the biblical concept of the image of God. The Western catholic tradition often makes the same affirmation, though the concept has been given a much less central place in the West than in the East.[10]

Among the Fathers of the Church the two who have paid the most detailed attention to the nature of man as image of God are St Gregory of Nyssa (*c.* 330–*c.* 395) and Maximus the Confessor (*c.* 580–662).

Gregory of Nyssa draws his materials from the scriptures and from classical erudition, but as it comes out after a process of gestation in his consecrated mind, Gregorian anthropology is neither pure biblical exegesis nor a summary of Protagoras and Plato, Diogenes and Aristotle. Attempts have been made in the West to brand him a neo-Platonist, an Origenist, and even a semi-Pelagian. (Pelagius may well have acquired the material for his half-digested thoughts from Gregory of Nyssa, to whom freedom was the inner essence of man as well as God.)

The meaning of human development has to be understood in the context of three fundamental and related concepts – the image of God, the freedom of man, and the kingship of God.

For Gregory man's constitutive essence is that he is created after the image of God. In all his numerous treatises, this concept occupies a fundamental place. His brother St Basil had given the same importance to the concept at the end of his ninth homily on the six days of creation, and promised a full series of sermons on the concept. Basil concludes his *Hexaemeron* thus:

If God permits, we will say later on in what way man was created in the image of God, and how he shares this resemblance. Today we say but only one word. If there is one image, from whence comes the intolerable blasphemy of pretending that the Son is unlike the Father? What ingratitude! You have yourself received this likeness and you refuse it to your Benefactor! You pretend to keep personally that which is to you a gift of grace, and you do not wish that the Son should keep His natural likeness to Him who begat Him.[11]

What was promised by St Basil was delivered by his younger brother. One can take almost any of Gregory of Nyssa's treatises and find the concept of the image of God at the centre. Take for example the *Treatise on Purity (Virginity)*:

> This reasoning and intelligent creature, man, at once the work and the likeness of the Divine and Imperishable Mind (for so in the Creation it is written of him that 'God made man in His image'), . . . being the image and the likeness, as has been said, of the Power which rules all things, by reason of possessing inner freedom (*autexousia*) of choice, kept also this likeness to Him whose will is over all. He was enslaved to no outward necessity whatever; his feeling towards that which pleased him depended on his own private judgment; he was free to choose whatever he liked.[12]

Here are two of the crucial aspects of being man – freedom in two senses: (*a*) the liberation from external and internal constraints and (*b*) the capacity to discern, choose and create the good.

The development and the freedom of man

This freedom of man is the substance of our hope. Our ultimate destiny is to enter into the fullness of the image of God. Completely freed from the impulses of passion and the constraints of externally imposed structures, be they legal or conventional, corporate man is to become a powerful, wise and loving being who spontaneously discerns the form of the good in wisdom, chooses it in love, and creates it by power.

This is who God is, and this is what man has to become. The two fundamental differences between God and man, as Prototype and image are these: (*a*) God has his being in himself; man's is derived from God; (*b*) God is what he wills to be, and wills what he is. For him change is not a necessity. There is no gap in God's case between what he is and what he ought to be. Man, however, is not yet what he ought to be. So change is a necessity for him, a necessity that will ultimately lead him either to the freedom of being or to the bondage of non-being. He is placed in time, which is the structure of change, i.e. between a beginning and an end. That end can be the beginning – of true, free and spontaneous being, or of a non-being which by its very nature as false being becomes a bondage.

The time (the secular) between the beginning and the end can thus determine to a certain extent the nature of the new beginning after the end (the ultimate), both in a personal sense and in the collective sense of the whole of humanity in history.

Maximus the Confessor follows basically the same line, though he makes the careful distinction, characteristic of Origen, between *image* and *likeness*. Image, according to Origen, is the gift, a status, a dignity conferred by God. Likeness to God, on the other hand, is man's destiny, to be achieved in part by his own acting in conformity with God. The image is thus a dynamic entity tending towards the likeness. Life on earth is a time when the image can consciously choose the likeness.

This Origenic view does not belong to the general patristic tradition. Maximus the Confessor picks it up and develops it. The distinction itself could be read back into the Hebrew text of Gen. 1.26: 'Then God said, Let us make man (Adam) in our image, according to our likeness.' For a modern interpreter, however, it is much simpler to explain the phenomenon in terms of 'Hebrew parallelism' and to see *tselem* and *demuth* as synonyms. But for Maximus the distinction implies a difference. The image, for him, means primarily the capacity for reciprocity between God and man, man's being endowed with reason and spirit. The likeness of God, however, is the consequence of the incarnation and the adoption of man to the sonship of God. God makes himself by nature man, that man may by grace become God. This basic patristic formula is now applied to the concept of 'likeness'; man's mind, reason and sense become transformed by the contemplation of God. This process leading towards 'theosis' or divinization is what Maximus calls spiritual development leading to divine likeness. This process of 'theosis' takes place through divine-human reciprocity. God becomes man; man is now able to live face to face with God because of his being adopted in Christ. He can now turn towards God without fear in worship and thus be transformed into God's likeness.

For Gregory of Nyssa, the image is the original perfection, which man is now enabled to regain in Christ through the disciplined practice of virtue. Man was created as perfect, and salvation means mainly undoing the harm brought in by sin. For Maximus, however, the original state of man included 'ever-being', but not necessarily the perfection of all goodness.

In the creation itself God gives to man both being and ever-being. But goodness and wisdom are acquired, according to Maximus, only through the disciplined life in time. Goodness and wisdom belong thus to the likeness, but being and ever-being belong to the image. Image is ontological, while likeness is moral, though such a distinction does violence to patristic categories.[13]

The idea of development

The patristic tradition thus has an embryonic notion of development, whether it be from image to likeness, or from the reality of the image to its fullness. The tradition sees this development as a divine-human process in which man has to respond to God in worship and has to discipline himself to practise virtue.

It would appear, however, that the Fathers laid major stress on worship or contemplation and the practice of good deeds or virtues. Though generally accurate, that statement does not do full justice to someone like Gregory of Nyssa. For him the body was fully part of the image of God. His upright form and the use of his hands are specially emphasized as belonging to his sovereignty over creation. 'The hands cooperate with the bidding of reason', says Gregory in *On the Making of Man*.[14]

It is this point of mind and hands that needs further elaboration today. The ancient Fathers were not forced by their circumstances to see it. We must see science (mind) and technology (hands and their extension) as part of the way in which 'theosis' itself takes place.

I say part of the way, advisedly. The contemplative or liturgical aspect of worship is the other part, which we shall not discuss in detail here. It is only the combination of the life of worship with the life of science and technology that can take man to a new stage in his development.

The point of both is precisely what the Fathers called *theosis* – the practice of 'virtue' by human effort surrendered to God. In monastic life in the past there has been too much emphasis on the contemplative and the personal. Today we need to combine, in the life of the layman, the aspect of worship and prayer on the one hand, and that of science and technology on the other. If the body, soul and spirit all belong to the image of God, then a harmonious development of all three seems necessary. The spirit of man must commune with God and love his fellow-men; without that the mind and the hands will be pushed in the direction of evil. The mind must be liberated from all fear and anxiety in order to discern in wisdom the truth of God and to communicate it to his fellow-men in word and art. The hands must develop the skills and the strength to transform the creation and to adorn it with all beauty and goodness.

This is the full development of man. The spirit of man must become like God, who is love. The mind of man must become like God, who is wisdom. The hands of man must become, like God's, full of power.

But not in an individualist sense alone. The corporate worship of the Eucharist must become the reality of eternity breaking into and transforming time, deifying corporate man and filling him with the love of God. The corporate wisdom of man must seek and share knowledge, so that mankind becomes all-wise with the wisdom of God. The political, economic and social life of man in the world as a whole

should be so organized with the aid of technology that human power
is shared and used by all in such a way that all can create and contribute and none need suffer want and loneliness or lack of dignity.

It is this development of mankind as a whole of which the apostle
Paul speaks, though here he restricts it to the church, in the epistle
to the Ephesians:

So shall we at last attain to the unity inherent in our faith and our knowledge of the Son of God – to mature manhood, measured by nothing less
than the full stature of Christ. We are no longer to be children, tossed by
the waves and whirled about by every fresh gust of teaching, dupes of
crafty rogues and their deceitful schemes. No, let us speak the truth in love;
so shall we fully grow up into Christ. He is the head, and on him the whole
body depends. Bonded and knit together by every constituent joint, the whole
frame grows through the due activity of each part, and builds itself up in
love. (Eph. 4.13–16, NEB.)

III *Conclusion*

There is both continuity and discontinuity between the Christian's
ultimate hope, and his proximate or secular hope. One analogy which
the scripture often uses is that between the plant and the seed. Our
life on earth is a seed planted, which must bear fruit and be harvested
on the 'last day'.

Whatever a man sows, he has to reap. He who sows [life] with the desires
of the carnal flesh must reap the fruit, i.e. the corruptibility of the flesh.
He who sows [life] with the desires of the spirit will from the same spirit
reap the life that triumphs over death. Let us who practise the good not be
discouraged. For in due time we shall harvest our own beings as indestructible.
So, in this season of seed-time let us practise the good towards all, especially
to our kinsmen in the faith (Gal. 6.7–10).

It is thus the source and motive and direction of our actions in this
(*pre-mortem*) season of sowing that determines the harvest of our
post-resurrectionem being. Elsewhere St Paul puts it this way:

There can be no other foundation beyond that which is already laid;
I mean Jesus Christ himself. If anyone builds on that foundation with gold,
silver, and fine stone, or with wood, hay, and straw, the work that each man
does will at last be brought to light; the day of judgment will expose it. For
that day dawns in fire, and the fire will test the worth of each man's work.
If a man's building stands, he will be rewarded; if it burns, he will have to
bear the loss; and yet he will escape with his life, as one might from a fire.
(I Cor. 3.11–15, NEB.)

The *post-resurrectionem* structure of a person's being is determined
thus by the fact that he has the foundation which survives death (the

life of the risen Jesus) and by the *gestalt* of personal history he has
built up on this earth through his *pre-mortem* actions. This is further
elaborated by St Paul in I Cor. 15.35–49. The fire introduces the
element of discontinuity, in that it destroys what is worthless or evil.
But the person and all the good that he has done goes through the
fire and arrives purified on the other side.

The same applies *mutatis mutandis* to the corporate history of mankind. A great deal of that history is but dross and a great deal more
positively evil (if evil can ever be positive). But humanity as a corporate
entity is now established in the person of Jesus Christ, and sanctified
by the presence of the community of the Spirit therein. Through the
fire of history's death, through the painful termination of time, mankind
as a single entity must pass into eternity. When the new heavens and the
new earth have been established, the kings of the earth will bring their
treasures into the heavenly Jerusalem, and the nations will walk in
the light of the Lamb (Rev. 21.24).

In history, mankind can build war and oppression, hardness of heart
and deceitful cunning; the fire must burn it out on the last day, and
we shall all suffer the loss. But whatever we build for the sake of love
and wisdom, and for the sake of the loving and wise use of power and
creativity, will endure. That much in our secular hope will carry over
into the ultimate hope.

The orientation given by the ultimate hope to the secular hope may
be summarized thus:

(*a*) Those who are established in Christ will be able to stand firm
both in the secular and in the ultimate.

(*b*) The worthless and the evil in both personal and corporate
secular existence will be destroyed by fire which will be painful to
individual men and to humanity as a whole.

(*c*) The achievement of God's image by man is the orientation for
development. This means:

(i) individuals must become liberated both from the tyranny of the
passions (internal bondage) and from the oppression or constraint
of others (law, structures, etc.).

(ii) humanity must together grow in love, wisdom and power and
be able to co-ordinate all three in true creativity of the good.

NOTES

1. A good illustration of this tendency to mistranslate traditional theology
is in Harvey Cox, *The Secular City* (Macmillan, New York, and SCM Press,
London, 1965), p. 111: 'Is Jesus God or Man? . . . When the problem was

discussed in the language of Greek substance philosophy, the formulation of the Council of Chalcedon held that Jesus was fully God *and* fully man. When the same discussion is translated into the vocabulary of contemporary social change, the issue is whether history, and particularly revolution, is something that happens *to* man or something that man *does*.'

2. 'Christianity and the New Earth', to be published in German in *Schriften Zur Theologie VIII* (Zurich); Eng. trans. in *Theology Digest*, February 1968, pp. 70 ff.

3. See the brilliant article by John Archibald Wheeler, 'Our Universe, the Known and the Unknown', in *The American Scholar*, Spring 1968, pp. 248–74.

4. John 6.39, 40, 44, 54; 11.24.

5. John 12.48 (cf. James 5.3).

6. I John 2.18.

7. I Peter 1.3.

8. I Peter 1.4 f.

9. Author of *A True Discourse*, against whom Origen wrote his *Contra Celsum* more than half a century later.

10. *The New Catholic Encyclopaedia* (McGraw Hill, 1967) for example devotes less than half a page to the subject while acknowledging: 'In fact, "Image of God" is the theological definition of man that is the only basis for an authentic Christian Anthropology' (Vol. 7, p. 369).

11. IX. 6 (Eng. trans. from the *Library of Nicene and Post-Nicene Fathers*, 2nd series, vol. VIII, p. 107).

12. XII. 2 (Eng. trans. from the *Library of Nicene and Post-Nicene Fathers*, 2nd series, vol. V, p. 357, slightly altered).

13. For a full discussion of Maximus' anthropology see Lars Thunberg, *Microcosm and Mediator*, Gleerup, Lund, 1965, esp. pp. 133 ff.

14. VIII. 2 (Eng. trans. from the *Library of Nicene and Post-Nicene Fathers*, second series, vol. V, p. 393).

PART FOUR

The Human

The central issue in development is the criteria of the human.

The Report of Uppsala, Section III, par. 20.

IO

The Concept of the Human

DAVID E. JENKINS

The report on World Economic and Social Development as adopted
by the Assembly at Uppsala indicates (par. 20) that the central issue
in development is the criteria of the human. I wonder why? This
seems like a typical piece of bland and metaphysical preaching which
one would expect from a church body. Such a body has professionally,
so to speak, to struggle to keep alive vast questions of a profound and
abstract nature which suggest that we are part of a mystery which has,
obviously and necessarily, religious dimensions. A practical man, a
man who lives in the actual world where decisions have to be taken
and who has to share in taking those decisions, may very well know
differently.

There is no such thing as 'development' which has to be reflected
on, decided about and acted upon. There are only developments in
developing situations which have to be responded to by assessment
and action. These developments and these situations may be capable
of classification because they show similarities and have recognizable
inter-relations, but these classifications and recognitions are themselves
abstractions made for the purpose of assisting decision-taking and
action. To talk about 'the criteria of the human' as being 'the central
issue' in 'development' is to compose a sentence relating one very
high level of abstraction to another. And the trouble about high levels
of abstraction is that they fall very far below the threshold of usefulness
for the assistance of those who have to act, suffer and react.

Living in developing situations requires decisions, and decisions
concern choices of alternative courses of action in particular circumstances and situations. This remains true whether the likely effects
of the decision are small or great, whether what is involved is deeply

H

personal or merely trivial. It is always the actual situation presenting itself which has to be dealt with, the decision has to be made between the concrete possibilities which are the only ones present or the only ones perceived, and what can be done and what has to be done as a result of the decision is always, inevitably, specific. Hence any decision must always be related to the facts of the case. This is, always, in fact the case. A decision which attempts to ignore relevant facts or is made in ignorance of relevant facts is none the less shaped both in its taking and in its effects by those facts. Hence it is clear that decisions have to be taken in relation to the facts of the case.

When, therefore, we move from some purely general consideration of decision-taking (like inquiring about the 'criteria of the human' in relation to 'development') to consider the responsible making of decisions in a social, political or professional context there seems a great deal to be said for the view of what I am calling 'the practical man', that the *basis* of decision should be and will have to be the facts of the case. For where else is it safe or reasonable to base one's decisions. The facts are absolutely relevant to the situation and therefore to the decision to be taken and the facts form a firm and objective given on which to base one's decision. But, what precisely, is covered by 'the facts of the case'?

There is an apparently simple and sufficiently practical answer to this which has to be taken very seriously. The facts of the case are all that, and only that, in the situation which is appropriate as data for the appropriate scientific approach and discipline. Thus, in a case of sickness, the facts of the case are the medical facts as recognized and dealt with by medical science. In the case of a development situation, the facts of the case are the economic and social facts to be analysed and organized by economics and sociology. This assumption and understanding put into practice enables one to take decisions scientifically, that is to say in an objective manner in relation to facts scientifically determined and observed. The ideal to be aimed at is to refine one's techniques of observation, to develop one's techniques of analysis and to expand one's techniques for processing data to the point where all important decisions can be computerized or where, at least, the result of computerized handling of information will become the major factor in any decision.

This type of decision-taking, it can surely be argued, is both necessary and desirable. It is necessary in order to eliminate, as far as possible, errors of subjectivity and distortions caused by cloudy and imprecise notions which are very problematically related to reality. Ideological distortion of the recognition and assessment of facts is notorious and notoriously dangerous. Reality is precisely that which is amenable to scientific treatment and measurable or organizable by scientific methods. The rest is emotion, prejudice, belief and fantasy. To take a realistic decision it is necessary to expose the facts of the case in as scientific a way as possible so that reactions and responses shall not be clouded or confused.

This also makes it clear why scientifically based decision-taking can be held to be so desirable. It permits and promotes that action which is most in accordance with facts and which will, therefore, be the 'best' action. It is clear that unrealistic action can only, so to speak, go against the grain of the facts and such going against the grain must produce factual disaster or, at least, increasing factual disharmony. To be scientific is to be aware of and to act in accordance with the facts; to act in accordance with the facts is to fit in with reality; and to fit in with reality is a good thing. Hence the proper basis of decision is the facts of the case, and the proper way to arrive at the facts of the case is to apply the most refined scientific techniques available.

This approach appears to offer an attractive simplicity, an attractive opportunity of knowing exactly where you are and hence an attractive appearance of practicality. Moreover, it seems to offer some chance of an agreed basis of approach to men of vastly varied creeds, cultures, perspectives. While I shall later argue that the view of things implied in this approach is logically untenable, practically impossible and actually undesirable, it none the less seems to me necessary to be clear about the strength and plausibility of the case for making scientifically determined data the basis of our decisions. To plunge into a discussion of the concept of the human in relation to the happenings of development seems to me to be far more likely to be profitless than profitable. Why choose one starting-off point rather than another for one's jump into the whole field of the subject? And why choose one part of the field rather than another into which to jump? One can always talk. To talk relevantly in relation to actions actually required and required by the actualities of situations is quite another matter. It is scientific development with its products of technological change and technological know-how which have made the developments of the developing situation and situations possible. It is certain that a very full use will have to be made of all the resources of science, technology and research if problems of development are practically to be dealt with at all (cf. e.g. the population problem and the food problem). Science provides the one really universal language and universal method which the world knows. Is it not therefore possible that the scientific method of discovery and analysis of the facts of the case is our best hope as a fundamental basis for approaching and dealing with (not just thinking about) the problems of development?

I do not think that this suggestion can be easily put aside as a naïve reversion to a nineteenth-century type of 'Scientism'. In the latter half of the twentieth century one would put this sort of suggestion forward not with the confident hope of an earlier century nor with any easy assumptions about progress. But one might quite reasonably put it forward as a possible hope and quite possibly the only hope. It is not *prima facie* obvious from past history that ideas, values and beliefs have played decisive and consistent roles in helping men forward to happier and fuller lives. And even if it be held that deeper investigation will show that it is ideas, values and beliefs which have hitherto been decisive in preserving and promoting what can be claimed to be the distinctively 'human' quality of the life of men, women and children it will not be easy to get general agreement about *which* ideas, values and beliefs. Further, *all* the old ideas, values and beliefs are now radically challenged, and very widely seen to be radically challenged, by scientific and technological developments and the presuppositions and assumptions which make them possible.

And still further, and finally, the actual problems involved in development situations manifestly demand scientific treatment, as has already been remarked. On the basic problem of food production, for example, development of agricultural research and the application of scientific techniques is clearly a *sine qua non* of any positive deveolpment. No matter what your values, metaphysical ideas or religious beliefs, malaria and kwashiorkor and the like are to be eradicated only by the application of scientifically arrived at and scientifically guided drugs and techniques. To remove such things no amount of either prayer or saintliness can be effectively substituted. To face the squalors and terrors of over-population chastity is not only clearly not enough, it is also cruelly not enough. Science may well not be *all* that is required but it is quite clear that, even if not sufficient, it is certainly necessary. This is not at all so clear about agreed values, overall ideas or religious beliefs. It may be possible to make a case against writing off Christianity on the grounds that 'It is not that Christianity has failed, it has never been tried'. It is surely much more plausible to say of science and the scientific method that 'It is not that science is insufficient, it has never yet been sufficiently applied'.

Hence it does not seem to me at all easy to take it for granted that ideas of, values concerning, or beliefs about 'the human' and the consequent criteria for this are the central issue in development. Nor does this become any more obviously obvious if our attention is directed to those great signs of our times, the struggles of the 'third world' (allegedly for liberty), the fight of the 'coloureds', especially, the blacks (allegedly for equality), and the protests of youth (allegedly for fraternity). Certainly these are human struggles, fights and protests for they are the struggles, fights and protests of human beings, and they are manifestly important and arguably distinctive phenomena of the present behaviour of the human species or, rather, of some of the present members of that species. But that the central issue in our understanding of and responses to these struggles is that of the criteria we adopt for understanding or judging about the human is not, on observation and reflection, self-evident. For while they are human struggles, it is not clear that they are struggles for or towards the human. A common descriptive base (these are all activities of suf-ficiently large groups of the human species) does not automatically imply, guarantee or justify the assumption of a common prescriptive aim (all these men are seeking to attain 'the human' which is common to them all and provides criteria applicable to all their activities).

Moreover, although 'seeking to obtain the human' or 'being concerned with humanization' or 'making a central issue of the criteria of the human' sound important and significant, what do phrases of this nature in fact mean? They do not directly reflect the facts of the varying situations to be met with in countries of the 'third world' or in blacks struggling against the effects of white racism or in youth protests. They represent rather the reflections and judgments of certain persons or classes of persons about those situations, struggles and protests. These situations and struggles are described as having a significance, a context, an aim beyond themselves and the assumption is that this is a common significance, context and aim. Human beings in their various struggles are examples of, say, 'man struggling to be human'. But what does this add to the situations? Or what are the grounds *in* the situations for this addition? And what help does such an addition give or what help could it give to the people in the situations?

My point here is twofold. Firstly, I am trying to draw attention to the fact that a commonly and readily agreed description of developing situations and 'the development situation' which is plainly supported by the facts of the case (and of the cases) will not go nearly so far as is often too readily assumed. And, secondly, I am arguing that, despite the highly prestigious and respectable nature of traditions of talk about 'the human' and 'liberty, equality and fraternity', it is likewise not at all clear that such talk is really helpful or what it is really helpful for. Clearly people who are suffering from the pains of hunger, disease and oppression, once it is clear to them that these pains are not inevitable, will struggle to be free *from* them. Likewise, black men will want to enjoy what they see white men keeping to themselves. If classes of young people experience environmental *malaise* they will react against this in various forms of 'protest'. How shall we know that all these various reactions are all part of one human reaction with one human aim? And what would such (doubtfully available) knowledge enable us to do?

This seems to me to be the central worry to which I have to find something positive to say before I can contribute any paragraphs, let alone an essay, on 'The Concept of the Human' to a book on 'Technology and Social Justice'. I am impressed by the *particular* nature of man's problems which seems to go with the particular nature of men's actual living. Certain features may be *observed* as typical of life in a country of the 'third world' or of the experience of blacks confronted with white racism or of youth in affluent societies, but they are not *experienced* as such. Experiences are the experiences of persons, of individuals. It is true that these experiences are immensely influenced (some would argue wholly conditioned) by the group to which individuals belong, and that the environment of these groups is in turn immensely affected by a network of inter-relationships between the groups. Further, it can be very plausibly and almost certainly correctly argued that developments in the world are such that the network of inter-relationship which observably affect each and every human group is rapidly extending to include the sum total of inter-relationships contained by the whole world, as a physical entity. That is to say that the model of 'the global village' could probably be given an observed and pragmatic descriptive reality if the available information could be collected and organized enough. But even so there is not and could not be 'a global consciousness', or 'the awareness of man' or 'the experience of humanity'. 'The globe', 'man' and 'humanity' do not experience. It is men, women and children who have experiences.

Conversely, there is no such actuality as 'the problem of man' or 'the question of humanity' (? or 'the criteria of the human'). There are problems which particular men have to face and there are questions which particular human beings have to meet. It is, however, worth remarking at this point, and with a view to further reflection and discussion in the last part of this article, that if there were a God and if there were grounds for believing him to be at least personal (however much it was necessary to avoid thinking of him as a person), then it might be literally the case that there was something in reality corresponding to phrases like 'the experience of man', 'the awareness of humanity'. This something would lie in God's experience of a relationship to the experiencing and experiences of all men. Similarly, there would be something corresponding to 'the problem of man'. That would be found within the love of God as he set himself to work out his creative and redemptive purposes for all men. But such an understanding of and faith in such a God has clearly got to face up to, and measure up to, the challenges of the particularities of human situations. Otherwise the utterances of such a 'faith' will occupy a particularly prominent and shameful place among those rhetorical abstractions which men use to conceal from themselves what they really have to face and what they actually have to do.

We return therefore to the particularities, to their interlinking and inter-relating. What we know about, what we experience and what we have to deal with are these particularities. The central issue in development, as in any other broad field which covers distinctive current aspects of the living process of human beings, may well be the study of these particularities and their inter-relationships. It may simply be a mistake belonging to the unscientific stage in the development of man to suppose that generalizations about common aims, common bases, or common 'humanness' are of central importance. This dependence upon and high estimation of generalities and abstractions could be said to belong to a time when we had no hope of knowing the facts or of handling them if and when we knew them. Now we are increasingly in the position of being able to replace vague and ill-based abstractions with organized tabulation and storing of the immense range of particular facts involved, and careful study and analysis of the complexities of their actual and possible inter-relationships. Our central concern should perhaps be, not with an abstract and subjective overview of some quite insufficiently surveyed field, but with the careful building up of processed information factually based, analysed statistics and computerized predictions of possibilities and alternatives. The outraged protests of those who insist on retaining the rhetoric of values, aims and talk of 'the human' may be the equivalent in this century of those who vainly and self-destructively rioted against the introduction of technological advances into industry in the last. It is no use smashing the machines or refusing to use them. Their proper acceptance and use is the only way by which development develops.

It seems to me, therefore, that it cannot be taken for granted that a discussion of the concept of the human or the criteria of the human is a useful or necessary discussion with regard to technology and society at this juncture in human development. It is not *prima facie* obvious that we are really called to face *the* problem of humanity or *the* question of man. On the face of it it seems much more likely and reasonable to act on the assumption that it is a series of complexly inter-related problems and questions of a basically factual nature which we have to face and that what we have to work on is techniques for facing these questions.

Certainly, whatever else we might have to attend to, we shall have to work out techniques for facing and dealing with these questions if the human race is to survive at all. The trends which are already clearly established towards a population explosion, towards increasing urbanization and towards pollution of the environment (to mention a non-exhaustive list of sufficiently empirically established features of current human living) make it sufficiently clear that men must find ways of dealing with the problems which their own present development is causing if the human race is not to produce an environment which is decisively inimical to its own survival. Thus, however much rebellion against or opting out of present aspects of society there may be or need to be, if these rebellions and protests are also against the organization of technology by society and the shaping of society with the help of technology, then the rebellions and protests are, in effect, demanding race suicide, however much they may be held to be 'for the sake of humanity'. Or it may be that it makes some sort of sense to say that *human* life is of such a peculiar quality that the conditions necessary to ensure its physical continuance could make that life so 'inhuman' that it would be 'more human' to choose extinction than continue in so 'inhuman' a way. But here again we would be forced into the consideration of some oddly 'transcendent' quality to or possibility of human life. And we are doing our best to avoid the introduction of such a notion unless and until it is plain that such a notion cannot be avoided.

What is at least plausibly and, as a matter of mere observation, clear, therefore, is that the present situation of the human race is such that an empirical approach to the complexly inter-related matters of fact which build up into a series of broadly definable problem areas is an urgent, and probably an absolute, necessity if that human race is to struggle into an environment which promotes its survival rather than its disappearance. Now, *the* empirical approach to complexly related matters of fact is the scientific method, just as it is the scientific method which has produced and has been refined by the various techniques and technologies which have made both present developments and their control possible. It might seem wiser, or at least more in accordance with the facts of the situation, to conclude that the central issue in development is not the criteria of the human but the application of scientific method and scientific techniques to the problems of development. At any rate, if we are to have grounds which will stand examination which eventually compel us to reassert the central importance of the criteria of the human, these grounds will have to include some indication that talk about the criteria of the human does enable, or can enable, a real and useful difference with regard to those problems which require at least a scientific and technical approach to them. Further, if we want to use 'human' as a value word (presumably with some basis in the actualities of the human species) why should we not hold that the most 'human' thing about men is their ability to develop and use science and technology? Certainly science and technology are the most potent causes of the present situations and an indispensable means for dealing with them.

Perhaps, then, our concept of the human has emerged from our attempt to examine the situations and problems which appear to be most distinctive of, and decisive for, the existence of the human race at the present time. It is the development of, use of and responsibility for science and technology which is that which is distinctively human. And this concept of the human is put forward as being descriptively accurate. Prescriptions are to be drawn from this description. And in every situation where a prescription cannot be drawn, then we must refine the description until we see what is and can be done. Decisive decisions are not related to vague abstractions called 'values' but to precisely delimited and organized particulars which constitute the facts of the case.

We have, of course, or at least many of us have, a very strong feeling that this is not enough and we long to turn to the 'really human' things–values, love, enjoyment, purpose, significance, worthwhileness, and the understanding of *these* things given us by and in the gospel. But how shall we turn to these 'greater' things effectively? And how shall we know that our turning is a turning to reality and not away from it? It seems to me clear that our concept of the human must be related to, must include, and must take fully seriously the concept which I have arrived at and sketched out in the previous paragraph. If the concept of man as a science-evolving and technology-producing animal is not to be *one* of our criteria of the human then, I should judge, we have decided to fly in the face of the facts of the case as it stands today with regard to the evolution of the human species.

This decision, however, we can take. Indeed, this is just the decision which certain religous and philosophical traditions would seem to urge us to take. Facts are precisely what we must pass beyond. Or to put it another way, the basic and fundamental insight is that all facts are illusion. The very fact human beings can thus get above, and pass judgments upon, their judgments of fact (i.e. about their very status, not about their correctness as matters of fact) itself warns us that it is not very easy to establish a matter-of-fact basis for our matter-of-fact approach if we probe deeply. But must we 'probe deeply'? Why is pragmatism not enough? The matter-of-fact approach has enough facts to go on and enough to do. Do the people who 'probe deeply' contribute to human happiness and development or do they just enjoy a private human luxury of 'thinking deeply'?

But there is a presupposition contained in the way this last question is formulated which can be exposed and questioned by asking 'What is wrong with enjoying a private human luxury?'. Might not this be a 'very human thing' to do? Quite possibly so, especially if my earlier observation is correct about the particular nature of human living and experiencing. My experiencing of the 'private luxury' of thinking deeply could well turn out to be one of the characteristically human things – one of the criteria of the human. The way of formulating my original question about people who 'probe deeply' betrays the assumption that if there is a choice between 'contributing to human development' and 'enjoying a private human luxury', then the former is to be preferred or chosen. In most discussions of development, justice, the human and so on, this *is* taken for granted. But it is by no means clear why it should be. It is also pretty clear that most people most of the time may *say* they make this assumption but they do not very consistently act upon it and very often seem persistently to act against it. This frequent lack of correlation between people's declared values and faith and actual behaviour is one more reason for being attracted to the analytic pragmatism of the scientific method as a basis for approaching human affairs. Claims about the centrality of values, of the criteria of the human and the like are so very hard to establish in practice. Why then should we make them?

I can myself, at present, see only two reasons for this which, if valid, would be quite sufficiently decisive despite all the difficulties to which I have been drawing attention. Our grounds for being concerned with the concept of the human and the consequent criteria for the human are that firstly we cannot avoid it and secondly that we could not possibly wish to avoid it. We cannot avoid it because a completely pragmatic approach to the neutral 'facts of the case' is quite impossible. We could not possibly wish to avoid it because we have been offered glimpses of possibilities open to human beings going so gloriously beyond the present 'facts of the case' that to abandon anyone to nothing but the situation as it is would be a self-evident betrayal, a self-authenticating blasphemy. The first impossibility arises from the nature of the situation with regard to 'the facts of the case'. The second impossibility arises from the preaching of the gospel. The first impossibility we must face with all men. The second impossibility we can only bear witness to before all men. Further, neither of these impossibilities, whether singly or in combination, which prevent us from resting with a pragmatic approach and the application of scientific methods, license us to get away from responsibilities for and to facts. The difficulties of entering effectively into a consideration of what it is or can be to be human which has any effect on, or in, the actual situations of human beings remain immense. It is my conviction about this which has forced me to turn this essay somewhat tediously into what is largely prolegomena to considering the concept of the human rather than considering that concept. It is now the fashion to talk much of this concept. A fashion in talk can be relied upon to breed talk. Great care has to be taken for it to produce application and action.

But none the less, I am suggesting, we are forced into talk about 'the human' and consideration of its relevance to our concerns and actions. We are forced into this talk firstly by the impossibility of resting in an approach based firmly and solely on the assessment of the facts of the case and the facts of the inter-relationships of all the relevant cases. This is so because logically speaking any concept of 'the facts of the case' and how they are arrived at involves either an explicit decision concerning how 'facts' shall be defined and selected, or a decision on such matters which is implicit in the tradition and practice within which one is operating. That this is so can be sufficiently indicated by reflecting on the way in which concepts like 'scientific method' and 'scientific data' interlock with one another in a circular manner. What one accepts or looks for as a medical fact depends on one's view of medical science and the practice of medical methods which one has accepted. In the economic and sociological fields the influence of presuppositions is even more immediately obvious. Scientific data are those which are amenable to scientific method and scientific method is that which is appropriate to dealing with scientific data. It is necessary to touch on the logical untenability of this position of 'let us base our decisions on the scientific facts', because it is a position which seems to offer so attractive a haven from the uncertainties and difficulties of any other basis for decision, because it is a position which is, in practice, very widely held, explicitly or implicitly, and because other 'positions' so frequently turn out to be incapable of either definition or application. However, logical considerations do make it clear that it is not a possible position even as an ideal. The 'facts of the case' are not the absolutely indisputable and to-be-taken-for-granted bed-rock they are often assumed to be. Any assemblage of facts already involves and implies two decisions. One of these decisions is general and is implied in the perspective, the way of looking at things, the general stance involved in the tradition which is being employed to perceive and evaluate facts. The other decision is particular and is expressed in the selection of these particular facts as constituting the relevant assemblage. (The particular decision is shaped by the general tradition within which the observer and would-be decision-taker is operating.)

The concept of 'the facts of the case', therefore, does not provide a neutral and determining basis for decision and cannot be fallen back on as such. Further, it is clear that in practice any decision which I take involving another human being implies my assumptions (decisions) about 'what it is to be human'. That is to say that, in any significant instance, my decision about the facts of the case and what is to be done in relation to them reflects my views or implicit assumptions about two interlinked matters of fundamental importance. The first matter is my understanding of who 'I' am that is deciding. I am reflecting my understanding of my responsibilities, my relationships, my possibilities and resources. I am secondly reflecting how I regard the person or human object with regard to whom the decision is being taken. Thus my decisions in practice reflect how I regard myself and how I regard other human beings. The question of the human, then, is implied by and in human activities precisely because at least some of these activities have an element of decision in them. That is to say that human activities are not always just reactions to stimuli but, sometimes at any rate, are guided reactions, which guidance comes creatively from within. Men have some opportunity of and some responsibility for shaping their responses and therefore contributing to the shape of that to which they have subsequently to respond. It is because men have some opportunity of making their own life that they cannot escape the question of the shape and shaping of that life, i.e. of 'the human' not in a purely descriptive sense (what shape or shaping *is* there) but also in the prescriptive sense (what shape or shaping *should* there be?). Indeed, I would argue that the main reason for the 'question of the human' coming into such general and urgent prominence at the present time is that the accelerating development of the powers, possibilities and effects of science and technology is bringing about a situation where it is clear that man is to an increasing extent creating his own environment and therefore creating himself, whether he is conscious of this or not. As consciousness of this develops, so it becomes clearer that he must face the question of how he creates his environment and himself.

We do, therefore, find that if we examine the human situation (in the descriptive sense of 'human', i.e. the description which an inspection of what is going on in the human species leads us to give), then we are faced with the question of the human in the prescriptive sense. Hence we cannot escape reflecting on the concept of the human and the criteria of the human. None the less, the fact that we are forced to this reflection does not appear to imply that we are forced to this reflection relevantly, practically or helpfully. We cannot escape the question (of the human) but it is not at all clear that we can answer it, not least because the repetition of what various faiths, traditions and philosophies have held to be answers to this question seem, on examination, to be so much rhetoric and nothing else. It is for this reason that it seems to me necessary not to rush too quickly into refurbishing our 'concepts of the human', declaring we have discovered new ones or reiterating that the old ones are now ripe for re-revelation. The present crux for the problem, concept and criteria of the human lies not so much in facing the question 'What concept shall we, can we, must we, have?', but in facing the question 'How shall we relate any concept or criteria we have to the actions and sufferings, the possibilities and impotencies which we are actually experiencing?' Unless we face this latter question with some degree of success we live in a dichotomy and a dualism. On the one hand we act, suffer and attempt to act with regard to the actual situations we are experiencing whether as ordinary citizens, the oppressed, the decision-takers at some level of organization and influence or what you will. On the other hand we (or some of us) talk about the human significance or possibility of these doings and sufferings. If there is no effective connection between the two, then it would seem that talk about the concept of the human is simply one of the drugs (evolved, perhaps, by natural selection to 'enable' the human race to survive) which enable human beings to face their situation by concealing that situation from themselves. Our slogan, perhaps, should be: 'There is no God and Sartre is our prophet.' The truth about the human situation is that it is not human. To retort to such a formulation 'But that is absurd!' would not be to refute the formulation but to confirm it. The important question, therefore, is not whether we can entertain any concept of the human or what concepts we should entertain, but whether entertaining concepts of the human makes any difference to the human situation, and this implies facing the question how a difference is made.

It seems to me extremely likely that there can be no definitive answer to this question, just as there can be no decisive answer to the question 'Do decisions decide?' Here there is the underlying doubt whether our decisions are creative things or simply resultants of other elements in the situation. And even if we can dismiss this there is ample evidence available that our decisions are hardly ever (never?) taken for the reasons we suppose or have the effect we expect. As a working procedure I am at present inclined to the view that the best we can do is to endeavour to see to it that these questions are constantly faced and kept as questions. That is to say that we must keep constantly in touch with the situational, experiential 'facts of the case and cases' questions about doing, suffering and deciding, and be constantly attempting *in relation to these questions* to face our need of criteria for the human, and to make use of whatever criteria of the human we believe to be available and possible in whatever way we can.

For the upshot of this whole discussion seems to me to be that in relation to the human situation we cannot avoid the question of faith but that the biggest question which is put to any faith is how that faith can be related to the actual human situations and not be an escape from them. What view shall we take about there being the possibility of any eventual answer to the problems posed to us, of the possibility of living with unanswerable questions without denying them if these questions are posed to us by our living, and of the hope of finding a living way of denying the dichotomy of the Absurd (see p. 217)? It is here that we return to my assertion (p. 214) that as Christians we raise the question of the human, not merely because we have to, but because we want to. For it continues to be our conviction that the things leading up to and stemming from Jesus Christ offer glimpses of the possibilities open to human beings which constitute a glory and a gospel which demand repeated attempts at expression and application, no matter how great a gap seems repeatedly to yawn between fact and faith. It is with some sketch of this understanding and hope of faith that I must attempt to close this essay, but I must repeat that it seems to me possible to come to any expression of faith about the human and the criteria of the human only against the background of the intense difficulties about the use of any overall or general understanding and picture; and only if we propose to make a constant, always unfinished and always imperfect attempt to relate the talk and the meditations of our faith to particular doings and sufferings in situations directly experienced and analysed in a matter-of-fact way. The concept of the human must always fully reckon with the aspect of particularity in being human and with the human manifestations of science and technology.

Thus, in the understanding of the believer who bases his faith on the God whose living reality and activity is the basic concern reflected in the Jewish and Christian scriptures, the world and human life within it is always to be seen, received and responded to in a perspective of openness. This is because the basic fact about the world is believed to be that it is 'created'. This belief in Creation is an understanding of the basic nature of the stuff which makes us up and with which we have to deal. It is held that a living God, an active possibility, a personal purpose, has been encountered in the historical experience of a continuing and developing people and in the experience of individuals within that people. This experience of personal purpose and possibility in history, and for the men who both as a corporate whole and as individuals are the subject of that history, has been held to embrace the stuff of nature which is the material basis of the possibilities of history. Hence it is held that the stuff of the universe is at least capable of being related to and fitted in with an overall purpose and pattern of activity which is rightly to be described as personal because it is not indifferent to the development of what we call persons. Hence the possibilities of the world, as far as human beings go, are not to be seen as necessarily indifferent or inevitably determining and destructive. Rather the world always has this perspective and possibility of openness to a further development of any particular situation in a personal and humanity-promoting direction. The 'facts of the case' as seen from the limited and limiting (although reasonable and authentic) perspective of the sciences, physical, biological and social, do not state all there is to be said about the human situation and need never have the last word about the possibilities of a situation from the human point of view. The most extreme and yet typical expression of this type of faith is the belief in God as giving resurrection to the dead, a belief established and vindicated through the resurrection of Jesus Christ. Whatever else this may mean it is a concrete and symbolically powerful way of representing the conviction that the possibilities and perspective of human living are not to be received, understood, responded to, or defined by the inevitable fact and limit of death. That I will die does not determine the scope of my responsibilities and possibilities. That he will die does not define the value of my client, my patient or my neighbour, my enemy, my friend, my oppressor or my deliverer.

In the light of a faith of this sort men, both as social beings and as individuals, are understood as being *in fact* organisms in whom the potentialities of matter and the determinations of the environment go beyond themselves in the direction of a relationship and response to the reality who is God. God is understood as the reality who is other than the directly observable realities, in the sense that he is neither confined to them or limited by them but he is known in and through these realities. Indeed, belief in the world as 'created' precisely reflects this conviction that the materiality and process of which men are part and to which they can be analytically reduced is in fact the object of and material for divine action and possibilities. This means that mystery is part of the facts of the case with regard to the human situation or a human situation.

Mystery is to be very carefully and rigorously distinguished from any notion of mystification or of muddle. The point is that men are material organisms emerging as human persons with potentialities in the direction of the divine. Since we are dealing with emergent organisms developing personally in a world which we have to understand more and more as in process, it is clear that we cannot know in advance how the human/divine possibilities are to be related to the actualities of any situation. To have all our answers cut and dried or all our material for decision-taking neatly stored up and categorized in advance, is to suppose that the whole process with which we are involved and of which we are a self-conscious part is, so to speak, of a 'routine' nature, wholly determined in a mechanistic way by some objectified and hypostatized set of conditions which might be called, perhaps, the 'qualities of matter'. It is also to suppose that there is no real newness open to men. Such suppositions are quite impossible for believers in the God of the Bible who is understood as the Father of Jesus Christ. He stands against the reduction of possibilities to anything like 'the qualities of matter' or 'the possibilities of the environment' and he represents an open future of infinite possibilities for those emergent products of the created process who have possibilities of conscious and responsive relationships with one another and with him. Hence the element of mystery which represents the necessary and, as it is believed, built-in element of openness and free possibility waiting to be discovered, which is always part of what it is and will be to be human. This is no excuse for, or encouragement to mystifications and muddles about the facts of particular cases. To refuse to face facts is to set up a barrier of muddle, distortion and withdrawal which can stop human reactions and responses long before they approach the threshold of the mystery which is the given context of really human development and fulfilment. But an approach to 'facts alone' which does not seek to take the mystery into account is likewise distorting inadequate and ultimately destructive.

A further important practical feature of any faith which is shaped by the understanding of God which is reflected in the Jewish and Christian scriptures is that man is not merely understood as having this context and element of mystery. God is not simply understood as an overall perspective and a constantly present possibility. It is believed that he is known as himself active to promote the realization of the mystery and the achievement of the possibilities to which men are or can be open. Thus God, who is known as the mystery who is the context of man and the world, is known also as providing resources for being human and as being concerned with human response and fulfilment. The understanding and expectation of faith refers to this aspect of the possibilities of human living by such words as grace, prayer, worship and love. Grace is a reference to the experience of the possibility of resources beyond our own resources which infuse into situations a way of dealing with them, responding to them and living through them, which can keep them open, hopeful and renewing or restore them to openness, renewal and hope when 'for all practical purposes' they seem to be dominated by the inhuman or anti-human. Worship refers to the awareness of an existent worthwhileness which is always there, always available and always to be aimed at no matter how bewildering, nihilistic or simply uncertain and directionless any circumstances or set of circumstances may seem. It is the response to that which fulfils humanity in an existence which towers over and goes far beyond the present actual conditions of ourselves in our distortions, difficulties and partialities. Prayer refers to the possibility of intimate communication with and direct personal awareness of this transcendent and gracious reality who is God. Although far beyond us he is to be known immanently in the core of our own being and the stuff of our experience. And so love refers not just to a human emotion, a social relationship and a moral ideal of activity, but to a dynamic at work in us in response to the active reality who is at work beyond all things, in all things and despite all things.

Hence it is held that men must not be and need not be reduced to a function of, or merely a component part of, their world seen either as material process or as history. They have the potentiality of standing out from, that is of becoming transcendent over, all that which might be thought, at the level of scientific observation, to condition and determine them. Men have, therefore, a real opportunity, built into the wider nature of things, to be themselves. The worth of any human being is to be seriously and factually seen as that of an emergent person, and must never be devalued by taking decisions as if the person or persons concerned were a means to something else than themselves. It is inhuman and contrary to the nature of things to take it for granted that all human beings may be primarily considered, for example, as means of furthering research or developing the interests of the state or as advancing economic development, although all those three types of aim may be perfectly legitimate and indeeed necessary for proper human expansion and fulfilment. The ultimate basis for decision, however, must lie in an understanding of the worth and reality of human beings as being a function of their own existence as persons in relation to one another.

Such an imperative and directive with regard to the basis of our human decisions may indeed seem too difficult at both the practical and the theoretical level. Actual decision-situations are under such pressures and limited by such realities that there is neither time, space nor energy for humane decisions at so lofty a moral level. Moreover, it is extremely difficult theoretically to square such an understanding of the overall nature of things with the way we actually experience, or with the apparently necessary theoretical bases of, our various disciplines and procedures. But this is where faith comes in to struggle with the gap between the perspectives glimpsed and the ultimate possibilities offered on the one hand and the actual limitations experienced on the other. Faith is the struggle of holding in tension the elements of the duality and dichotomy referred to earlier (p. 217) and refusing to accept this duality as ultimately true and decisive.

Our faith has to be related to the way in which we come to terms with the contradiction between the elements and possibilities of present situations and the understanding of and hope for the human which we dare to maintain. The perspective and hope which faith provides operates directly and indirectly. Directly our faith requires that whatever evaluation is made of a situation or implied by any policy or decision this evaluation must take account of the fact that God is the only sufficiently adequate human perspective. That, of course, does not mean that our responses and responsibilities can be safely limited because the wider issues can be 'safely left to God'. It means, on the contrary, that a responsibility tempered and extended by awe, reverence and humility must be allowed both conscious and unconscious play in our approach to our decisions. However tempting the limited perspective and the approach of keeping reactions in neat compartments may often be, it must be quite clear that to make a policy or habit of such an approach is to betray the humanness of oneself and of one's fellows.

Further, the practical evaluations that are made with regard to possibilities of action (including one's evaluation of one's own ability to sustain the tensions of attempting to operate in the wider perspective) can and must be related to faith's understanding of what resources are available for directing and re-directing human action. These resources are not limited to the technical uses of know-how, techniques and ever more elaborate ironmongery. There are resources also of grace, reconciliation and forgiveness which can drastically alter the direction in which a situation is developing or the manner in which those principally involved react to it, and so are shaped by it and so, eventually, make their contribution to the shaping of it. There is, further, the understanding of what in fact (because of the underlying nature of things) and in the long run are the most hopeful types of power and the most humanly productive directions for policies. Here the understanding which faith gives of the possibilities and direction of love is of fundamental importance. Is one to base one's decisions on the assumption that in the long run nothing really gets one anywhere but aggression, self-centredness, and defensiveness or, even, that in the long run nothing gets you anywhere? Or is one to operate in the faith and hope that the important and decisive thing is not to get anywhere but to be and to become more human in relation to other human beings, and that this is a real possibility because of the reality of God and therefore of man's situation in the world?

Here the immense importance of the possibilities of the Christian understanding of the human in relation to suffering and to sin need to be realistically related to, illuminated by and set free to give illumination to, the situation with which we have to deal and in face of which we have to live and attempt to make a human response. Whatever ultimate view of the human we may struggle to maintain, receive or apply we have to face and suffer the monstrous facts of inhumanity, the violence done to men by men (as one example, why not call this book 'Technology and Social *In*justice'?), the indifference of the natural world to men, the constant and frequently cruel contradictions between men's aspirations and men's actions. So much suggests that the human situation is not merely absurd but wickedly and brutally absurd, and that it is man who contributes actively and constantly to that brutality. I believe that a faith which focuses on a crucified man and a tradition of faith which constantly portrays positive and reconciling attempts to overcome the recognized sinfulness of man, provides criteria for the human which can take full account of undeniable and apparently inevitable inhumanities and remain realistically available for recognizing and promoting a humanity in and beyond all inhumanities.[1] Here, more than ever there is urgent need to sketch a concept of the human which relates the insights of faith to the actualities of living.

In all this it is probable that our understanding and attitudes of faith will be related to and reflected in our decisions as much by indirect influence as by direct application. Because of our faith about the fundamental human situation we shall see it as a necessary part of human living to promote and practise activities which will in themselves enhance appreciation of the necessary perspective and proffered hope. Worship might be described as both the promotion and the practice of the basic perspective of faith in God. Both corporate and individual experiences, related to religious understanding and living, of the kindling of hope, of the receiving of forgiveness and of the discovery of renewal will be related to a developing sense of the hope in which human affairs are to be tackled. The fact that much so-called religious practice neither stems from faith nor promotes faith, with consequent failures in the promotion of perspective and the development of realistic hope, is a matter for urgent consideration elsewhere. But while the deadliness of much of church life has led to many exaggerated rumours about the death of God we may still look for a development of true faith and real religion if we focus on the implications and demands of the human situation in an open and hopeful manner.

The sort of thing that this might mean in practice with regard to decision-taking can, perhaps, be illustrated by way of example by considering decisions about the planning and running of a hospital. On the basis of our understanding of the human it clearly cannot be right merely to acquiesce in and accept an organization and practice which treat patients as simply the objects of medical science and technology (still less as a source of income). In practice, as anyone with any experience in this field of course knows, it will be necessary up to a point to work with such an organization, for this is the type of organization which has evolved and one has to get on with the job of doing the right thing (caring for the sick) even in the wrong way and for the wrong reasons. But, in fact and for the sake of developing humanity, one has to undertake the immense strain of taking into account both the limitations (religious people would say 'the sinfulness'!) of *all* the persons involved (i.e. practitioners, patients, nurses, administrators, relatives, etc.) and the human needs and possibilities of all these persons. This is the question of perspective.

Further, account must be taken in practice of the fact that there are always more resources available for reform and change, for taking being human more seriously, than either appear or are admitted. This is the question of hope, and one's overall policy needs to be within this perspective and informed by this hope. But one has to be clear that while one is seeking to base one's decisions in this perspective and hope no single question can be settled by perspective and hope. Every single and particular question has to be decided in the light of the scientific and administrative knowledge and know-how available, taking into account the possibilities and persons involved.

But faith is clearly required both to challenge what have become accepted and yet inhuman institutions and to inform and direct persevering action. Criteria for the human cannot be read off from some concept of the human which is, as it were, a blue-print of the men of the future. 'It doth not yet appear what we shall be.'[2] The central issue in development, as in all significant areas of human experience and enterprise is, therefore, not so much the criteria of the human as the struggle of faith to bridge the gap between the observable and experienced realities which must be faced with all the resources and all the accuracy at our disposal, and the glimpsed possibilities which have been seen in the gospel and have been believed to be offered in Jesus Christ. This gap can be bridged only in hopeful action which is always ready to receive and to give correction and which is never afraid of suffering. For we do not follow a concept of the human but an embodied human being who bridged the gap between human realities and divine possibilities in his own service, obedience and suffering. It is in following this pattern only that we can hope to bring together what our faith encourages us to believe are revealed insights and proffered human possibilities, and what our observation assures us are urgent human dangers, needs and opportunities.

NOTE

1. For some attempt to sketch out an approach which might support this belief see my and other essays in *Man: Fallen and Free*, ed. E. W. Kemp, Hodder and Stoughton, London, 1969, and 'The Suffering of God' in *Living with Questions*, David E. Jenkins, SCM Press, London, 1969.

2. I John 3.2.

I I

Theology or Ideology?

ALEXANDER SCHMÉMANN

I

It is impossible for a theologian, and in this particular case, for an Eastern Orthodox theologian, to 'reflect' on a document like the Report of Uppsala, Section III, without making first an attempt to place it in a wider theological and ecumenical perspective. We cannot avoid a preliminary yet crucial question: Is the 'social and economic thought' of the World Council of Churches (presumably expressed in this document) based on a consistent theology, i.e. an all-embracing vision of God, man and the world, or is theology in relation to that social and economic doctrine thought of as an *a posteriori* justification of positions and attitudes agreed upon without any serious theological search and analysis? It is a crucial question because in both cases the whole future of the ecumenical movement is at stake, as is – speaking *pro domo sua* – the question of the Orthodox participation in it.

A careful reading of the document leaves, it seems to me, no doubt as to the nature of the answer to these questions. Whatever 'social and economic thought' we find in the Report, its theological presuppositions and 'whereases' are not only remarkably vague but, what is even more alarming, 'heterogeneous' in regard to the long sequence of very 'practical' and even detailed ('political lobbies are essential . . .') pronouncements and prescriptions that make up the Report and shape its general tone and style. To be sure, we find scattered throughout the document sentences one could term 'theological'. For example: 'In Christ, God has entered our world with all its structures and has already won the victory over all "principalities and powers". His kingdom is coming with his judgment and mercy'; 'Christians know from their Scriptures . . . that Christ died for all . . .'; 'food is a resource which belongs to

God', not to mention the recurrent leitmotive about God 'making all things new'. But the presence here and there of such and similar sentences does not in the least give the entire document a theological 'key', or relate it to a recognizable theological framework. One cannot help thinking that these sentences do not truly 'belong' to the body of the Report. They are not essential to it either as its theological 'infrastructure', as the basis on which everything else depends, or as a unifying, ultimate vision supplying us with clear and transcendent criteria for the understanding of our present 'situation' and its needs. It looks as if Christians having already and for 'non-theological' reasons accepted as self-evident and normative such notions as 'development', 'revolutionary change', 'human dignity', etc., felt the need to relate them as quickly and as generally as possible to some familiar 'symbols'. These symbols, however, serve neither as a *terminus a quo*, i.e. as a basis, on which the Christian 'social and economic thought' could be built, or as a *terminus ad quem*, the ultimate vision of the 'just and human society' for the elaboration of which we are called to work. In fact, they destroy the unity of style of the document which was obviously meant to serve as a set of very practical and concrete guidelines. They remain thus extrinsic to the real substance of the Report, and one has the feeling sometimes while reading it that it would be better if rhetoric about 'releasing God's children from bondage' and the advice concerning the lifting of the economic blockade of Cuba were not parts of the same text.

Nor are the invitations to theological reflection very useful. We are told, for example, that there is an urgent need for a 'theology of development' or for the clarification of the 'criteria of the human', yet at the same time all these terms are used throughout the whole document as clear and self-evident in their 'semantics'. Nowhere is an attempt made to define the crucial term 'newness' (God 'makes all things new') which is used nevertheless as the obvious justification for all these 'liftings of blockades', 'powerful political lobbies', etc. In short, then, the document may have, and in my opinion obviously has, an ideological unity and consistency but certainly not a theological one. Willingly or unwillingly – and again my guess is, willingly – theology is reduced to a vague minimum of mottos or slogans considered as sufficient to justify the ideological option of the World Council of Churches. The fact that Christians may, and in reality do, violently disagree on the nature of 'newness' of all things in Christ, or on that of the 'bondage' of millions of God's children, is nowhere even mentioned and the impression is thus given that there is simply no other way – except that of a 'practical heresy' – to understand these tremendously complex theological notions, no other solution but to dissolve them within a secular ideology which becomes thus an inner norm for theology. *Theologia ancilla ideologiae.* . . .

II

It is the whole point indeed that if the Uppsala Report subordinates in fact theology to something else, this 'something else' is precisely an ideology, i.e. a view of the world's situation and needs based on a specific understanding of man, his relationship to society, history, matter, etc. There is no need for us here either to 'label' this ideology, although it would be rather easy to describe its various sources and its development in Western thought, nor to analyse it in depth. From the theological point of view the following basic characteristics must, however, be mentioned.

In the first place it is a *world-centred* and a *world-oriented* ideology. By this we mean that it *de facto* excludes any transcendent dimension or at least considers it irrelevant and unnecessary even to allude to it in dealing with notions like 'justice', 'freedom', 'responsible society', 'abundant life', etc. That the Report adopts this understanding of the 'world' is made abundantly clear by the lack of a single reference to the transcendent destiny of man and of the world itself. Even where such reference could have been made, namely in paragraph 2 where the Report states that 'In Christ, God entered our world with all its structures and has already won the victory over all the "principalities and powers" ', and that 'His Kingdom is coming with his judgement and mercy' – it is absent. Both the nature and the coming of the kingdom remain ambiguous. Is it the consummation of all things in God? Is it the 'new heaven and the new earth' implying an ontological mutation: the 'end' of 'this world' and the inauguration of the new one? Or is it simply the establishment of a 'world-wide responsible society', the end of hunger, oppression and exploitation? God's purpose is defined in one short sentence: 'abundant life for all men' (par. 34), and man is to live 'creatively' (par. 27) because people have achieved a 'new sense of the human' (par. 46).

Not once is it said that the basic need of man is for God and that the 'abundant life', as proclaimed in the gospel, is the antithesis not of hunger and exploitation but, in the first place, of a life without God, of a life which indeed is death. If only all these evils—poverty, oppression, exploitation, racism—were condemned as obstacles to man's ascent to his transcendent vocation and self-understanding! If as Christians we would say that we join in the struggle against all this because, without a certain degree of freedom from oppression and hunger, from exploitation and racism, man cannot start his real human search for

God and his eternal kingdom. But as said above, the horizon of the document is limited, without any loophole, to a 'world-wide responsible society', as if Christians had nothing else to offer and to contribute in the midst of the world's material and spiritual crisis. That Christ not only 'entered our world and all its structures' but, according to Christian faith, also ascended into heaven with his deified humanity, revealing thus the ultimate vocation and destiny of man as 'participant in divine nature', that his gift to us is, above everything else, life eternal and that this life eternal is knowledge of God, communion with God, 'the joy and peace in the Holy Spirit', all this is obviously not considered as relevant to the 'economic and social thought' of the World Council of Churches. Thus its plain surrender to a non-transcendent ideology becomes tragically evident.

III

Being world-centred, the ideology which underlies the Report of Uppsala Section III is also *utopian*. Utopianism has been one of the basic characteristics of Western 'ideologies' since the Enlightenment, but it is the first time that a Christian document dealing with the world and its social and economic problems seems to accept and to adopt it not only as a 'working hypothesis' but as a theoretical framework. From the theological point of view, utopianism is based on the rejection by secular thought of the Christian notion of evil and sin. Evil ceases to be a mystery, rooted in the irrational depths, but is rationally identified with certain 'structures' which, once changed or improved, will result in a 'dream become reality'. And it is indeed highly characteristic of the Report that after an ambiguous reference to sin at the beginning ('we know the reality of sin and the depth of its hold on human things'), sin is no longer referred to, but is systematically replaced by 'structures'. It is no longer the whole creation, it is the 'political and economic structures' that 'groan under the burden of grave injustice'; and that 'grave injustice' is presented not as the dark power of hatred and irrational mutual alienation of human beings alienated from God, but again as the interplay of impersonal and objective 'structures'. The world is good and full of new and 'exciting prospects'. If, at the same time, it is full of defects, it is because of defective political and economic structures. These structures can and must be changed, and to achieve this 'Christians are urged to participate in the struggle of millions of people for greater social justice and for world development'. What is implicitly and explicitly absent is thus the soteriological dimension and content of the Christian faith, its insistence on *salvation*, and not only on improvement and 'the solution of problems'.

The secular action of the churches is disconnected from the soteriological perspective, is neither evaluated nor presented in the light of the doctrine of salvation and redemption. How exactly is Christ's 'death for all' (par. 3) related to the participation in a 'world-wide responsible society with justice for all'? What does his death mean for all human concepts of justice? What are the 'principalities and powers' over which he has already 'won the victory'? And what is the nature of that victory? Is it possible simply to transpose – without any word of explanation or qualification – all these soteriological notions, implying a radical and ontological change ('trampling down death by death') into an entirely 'this-worldly' perspective, to see in this world alone the stage for making 'all things new'? That the two levels or orders may be related to one another, that Christian soteriology and eschatology are by all means to inform, inspire and shape the Christian *praxis* in 'this world' is a perfectly valid theological assumption. That this can be done without distinguishing these two levels, as if 'all things new' meant 'a world-wide responsible community' seems, above all, an irresponsible theology.

IV

The Western ideological utopianism is, first of all, a naturalized eschatology. Its true idol is history viewed primarily in terms of an irreversible progress towards the *eschaton* in the form of a 'just society'. The Report instead of evaluating this 'naturalized eschatology' in the light of the Christian understanding of history and of Christian eschatology, simply accepts it as its own ideological framework and term of reference. We see this acceptance, in the first place, in the non-qualified claim that ours is a *new* world and that what happens to us in it, happens 'for the first time in history'. This reference to the 'new' world combined with the recurrent leitmotive about God 'making all things new' is meant probably to give the impression that our situation, being radically 'unprecedented' justifies also a radically 'new' approach on the part of Christians, places them in a kind of *kairos* in the biblical sense of that word. The implication here is, of course, that by means of this 'new' world we, Christians, are to 'discover' something we have not known or believed before, to go through not only a quantitive but also 'qualitative' re-evaluation of Christianity itself. It is indeed very characteristic – not only of Uppsala but of the entire trend of Christian thought to which it belongs and which it expresses – that it never refers to Christian tradition, to the teachings, experiences and vision which the church has preserved during two thousand years of her unbroken history. The entire ethos of the Report, its enthusiasm and emphasis are in the present 'newness' and the possibilities it opens for the future. 'Our hope is in him who makes all things new. He judges our structures of thought and action and renders them obsolete. If our false security in the old and our fear of revolutionary change tempt us to defend the *status quo* or to patch it up with half-hearted measures, we may all perish (par. 4). Once more, if this is a *responsible* Christian statement, what does it mean? What are the '*status quo*' and the 'old' referred to? And why is it that Christians have to accept the 'revolutionary changes' at the risk of perishing? And what is a 'revolutionary change'? One is forced to think that the authors of the Report have accepted a revolutionary ideology, which has obviously no precedents in Christian thought and spiritual experience, and in order to justify it seek its roots in the eschatological notion of 'all things new'. That such is indeed the case is made clear by the following statement (par. 15):

The building of political structures suitable to national developments involves revolutionary changes in social structures. Revolution is not to be identified with violence however. In countries where the ruling groups are oppressive or indifferent to the aspirations of the people, are often supported by foreign interests, and seek to resist all changes by the use of coercive or violent measures, including the 'law and order' which may itself be a form of violence, the revolutionary change may take a violent form. Such changes are morally ambiguous. The Churches have a special contribution towards the development of effective non-violent strategies of revolution and social change.

The 'revolution' is seen here as the eschatological event which, fulfilling the 'aspirations of the people', partakes of 'all things new' and is transposed from secular into Christian eschatology. By the same token it is deprived of its transcendent character and limited to the horizon of human history.

Accepting the 'naturalized eschatology' of the contemporary ideologies centred on 'revolution', the Report accepts of necessity the reduction of history to 'struggle', a reduction typical of that ideology. Christian participation in history is seen uniquely as participation in 'the struggle of millions of people for greater social justice and for world development' (par. 4), 'the struggle of oppressed people for economic justice', etc., this struggle being always and evidently on the side of the 'masses' and the 'people'. Not only is a Marxist understanding of the dynamics of the historical process adopted here without one single word of Christian qualification, but no attempt is made to elucidate, in Christian terms, the notions of 'masses', 'people', 'oppressed people', etc. Nowhere is the gospel of reconciliation and *love* mentioned, nowhere is to be found the hope that Christianity may transcend the divisions of the world. It is obviously assumed that the new commandment of love has no place within the framework of 'social and economic thought' which knows no other rationale than interest, conflicting aspirations and therefore 'struggle'. There can be no doubt therefore that the fundamental ideological presuppositions of the Report are overtly Marxist, and that this was accepted as a self-evident basis for the approach to the socio-economic area as a dialectical view of history centred on the notion of 'struggle'.

V

The document speaks of 'churches' and is addressed to the 'churches'. But there is no *church* in it, at least in the meaning given that word by centuries of Christian thought and experience and whose rediscovery was one of the most decisive fruits of the ecumenical movement. In the perspective of 'social and economic thought' the 'churches' are seen as mere agencies for the promotion of specific ideas and programmes. The fundamental nature and vocation of the church as being *in* the world but not *of* the world, the basic biblical dichotomy church-world, the church understood as the very *locus* of that 'newness' to which we are called, all this is simply ignored in the document; and its ideological categories, its entire orientation leaves no room for that ecclesiology. The implications of this are extremely serious. For it means, in the first place, that the church's self-understanding as an organism transcending the world and its 'fallen' logic is denied any specific function in the very elaboration of the 'socio-economic order'. The latter needs no 'grace'. It means, in the second place, that the church is no longer viewed as the 'means' by which God 'makes all things new', is not ultimately the bearer, the epiphany of the new humanity and of renewal. And it means, finally, that the Christian *paradosis* does not inform and illumine from inside the programmes and strategies elaborated on the basis of our empirical and theoretical 'knowledge' alone. 'Theology' we are told, 'has also to come to grips with the meaning and goal of peoples all over the world who have awakened to a new sense of the human. Indeed, the interaction between technology and social justice is a crucial issue of our time' (par. 46). Thus, apparently, the entire Christian experience, unique in its depth and vision, the experience of God and Trinity, of Christ and of theandric mystery, of the Holy Spirit and the sacramental life, of the church and sanctification are thought of as not a sufficient basis for the understanding of the 'meaning and goal of peoples all over the world'. Implicitly, the document makes its own the modern obsession with 'relevance' which implies as its presupposition that the entire development of Christian thought has probably been 'irrelevant' to the radically new 'needs' of the radically 'new world' of ours. As everything else, the church is reduced to 'history' and is entirely dissolved in the various aspects of 'development' and 'radical strategies'. On two occasions, it is true, *repentance* is mentioned – 'the Church is called to work for a world-wide responsible society and to summon men and nations to repentance' (par. 29). But in the biblical context, is not 'repentance' (*metanoia*) primarily the possibility of seeing the world in a new way and thus being liberated from its 'fallen' logic, dichotomies, imperatives and dead-ends? Has not the same Christ who 'has entered the world and all its structures' proclaimed a kingdom which is *not* of this world, although in the midst of it? Is not the church precisely the place where the world can be saved all the time by being transcended and referred to that kingdom? Of all this there is simply nothing in a document which calls the 'churches' to a new self-awareness. But ecclesiology, in the last analysis, is based on cosmology. It is, in fact, a doctrine and an experience not so much of the 'church' but of the world itself, for the church is the icon of the world as redeemed and made *new* by Christ. And no failures or betrayals by Christians can abolish that vocation of the church. The world in which the church is reduced to the level of an 'agency', and is ontologically subordinated to it, ceases to be a world transparent to Christian evaluation and action. It is for this reason that one can say without any exaggeration that there is in the Report *no* Christian vision of the world, but a totally secular ideology which the 'churches' are requested to accept as such, justify *ex post facto* theologically, and make the basis and the goal of their own strategy and action.

VI

The final proof of this ideological 'reduction' is the absence from the Report of the fundamental Christian emphasis on the 'person', of Christian 'personalism'. The document deals abundantly with 'masses', 'nations', 'peoples' and 'societies' and very little with 'persons'. There is a reference to the 'encounter' between human beings as one of the goals of 'development' but this idea is given no explanation or elaboration. One could argue, of course, that the areas of the economic and the social are *par excellence* areas of collective, supra-personal interests and realities and that therefore the personalism of Christian experience, being not explicitly denied, has no reason to be stressed in this particular document. But is it so? Is not a radical reduction of man to the economic and social the very essence of those secular ideologies whose basic categories, vocabulary and 'world-view' the Uppsala Report seems so obviously to endorse? And if it is so, is it not a self-evident duty for Christians at least to make some reservations as to that reduction?

Granted that Christian personalism was much too often identified with non-Christian individualism, was it not urgent to clear that matter? Is not the Christian vision in which, on the one hand, the whole world exists for one man and, on the other hand, man fulfils himself only by becoming in Christ man-for-others, the specifically and uniquely Christian response to the tragic reduction of human existence to either demonic selfishness or ant-like collectivism? Not only do all these questions remain unanswered, they are not even mentioned, such is the blind surrender of the drafters of the Report to an ideology in which there is simply no room for the personal and their fear of not being sufficiently 'social'. And yet, how can one speak of a 'responsible' society without founding it, first of all, on the responsible human being, and thus on his transcendent freedom and spiritual nature? How can one speak of 'development' without even mentioning that for Christians the goal of all development is not 'society' but man in his unique and eternal *hypostasis*, and that only because of the experience of that uniqueness can the 'economic' and the 'social' become themselves problems of a spiritual and human order.

VII

In conclusion it remains for us to outline, briefly and tentatively, those 'criteria of the human' which stem from the Orthodox doctrine and experience and which, such is my deep certitude, are altogether absent from the entire perspective of the Report. These criteria are to be found in the three fundamental dimensions of the Christian faith itself: the cosmological, the ecclesiological and eschatological. I am sure that it is the failure of contemporary Christian thought, on the one hand, to distinguish these three levels or dimensions and, on the other hand, to see them in their mutual interdependence that is responsible for the various 'reductions' and 'surrenders' of which the Report is, alas, a truly tragic example. For ultimately there have always existed three fundamental types of 'heretical temptations' for Christian theology, all of which consist precisely in the 'reduction' of one of the dimensions or realities mentioned above to another, or an undue confusion among them. By reduction I mean here the viewing of the Christian 'event' in terms either of the world alone, or the church alone or, finally, the kingdom alone. If today we seem to live through the 'worldly' reduction, there have existed and there still exist, to be sure, the 'ecclesiological' and the 'eschatological' reductions of Christianity, which provoke, in turn, violent reactions and obscure and mutilate the truly Catholic vision and 'wholeness' of the Christian experience. What makes each reduction truly 'heretical' (and 'heresy', we ought to remember, means precisely 'choice' and thus, reduction) is that it mutilates and deforms that very reality which it seems to exalt and to place in the centre of Christian preoccupations and concerns. A Christian vision and understanding of the world is simply impossible without it being seen in the light of the church and the kingdom of God. An ecclesiology that is not rooted in cosmology and eschatology is a radically wrong one. And finally, the ultimate reality of Christian faith, hope and love, the kingdom of God, cannot be 'known', and thus believed in, hoped for and be the content of our love, except by means of 'this world' and the church. The living and personal principle both uniting and yet 'distinguishing' these three realities is Christ whom we confess to be the Logos and the Redeemer of the world, the Head of the church which is his Body, and the King of the kingdom which is to come and in which he 'fills all things with himself'. These, however, are not three separate 'functions' or ministries of Christ making possible three different and independent levels of theological investigation, three self-contained 'treatises' but, on the contrary, the 'epiphany', the revelation and gift of one all-embracing 'mystery'.

The 'content' of that mystery concerns the world, the church and the kingdom. In Christ who is its Logos, the Life of its life, the world has its ultimate destiny and fulfilment in the kingdom of God, in the transfigured reality of the 'new heaven and new earth', in the consummation of all things in God. Having rejected this destiny and alienated itself from God, the world was redeemed by Christ, by his incarnation, death, resurrection and glorification and made the stage of a new communion with God. Concerning the church, the 'mystery' is that she is the epiphany and the presence in it of the kingdom which is to come; and, finally, concerning the kingdom, that in Christ it has been revealed and communicated as grace, knowledge of God, communion with him and eternal life.

These, indeed, are the 'criteria of the human' because here is revealed the fundamental 'sacramentality' of man, his total belonging to and dependence upon the world, on the one hand, and his power to transcend that dependence and to transform the world itself into communion with God, on the other hand. The world is given him as his life, but it may become his death. It is life when it is recognized and used by man as 'means' of his communion with and knowledge of God, a matter so to speak of a 'sacrament' uniting man with God. It is death and communion with death when it is seen and accepted as an autonomous end in itself.

It is then this 'sacramental' approach to the world and to society that constitutes of necessity the basis of a Christian understanding of the 'social' and the 'economic'. In 'this world' it is the church and she alone that not only reveals to man the true nature of the world and its destiny, but gives him the grace necessary for the fulfilment of his sacramental vocation. The church, the Body of Christ and the temple of the Holy Spirit is precisely the 'sacrament' assuring in each man the passage of the old into the new, relating the world to the kingdom, transforming the reality of the one into the glory of the other. The real task of Christian theology is thus to study and to reveal the implications of the 'sacramental' for the social and the economic. For the task of theology is always to refer the human reality to the *beginning* and to the *end*, i.e. to the ultimate root of all things and to their ultimate destiny. It is not quite sure that Christians can become, as the Report suggests, experts in highly complex and debatable matters of economy, development, justice, etc. But it is the duty of theology to refer these matters to those transcending values, without which they are always under the threat of becoming new idols, leading as all idols to new tragedies and to death. In Christ and his Spirit, the Christian not only knows *about* the world, the church and the kingdom, he knows *them*. This knowledge requires a tremendous effort, intellectual and spiritual, personal and ecclesiastical, to be transformed into 'action'; and Christians and churches are guilty, to be sure, of neglecting and even suppressing that effort. For this, but this alone, they truly must repent. Yet their repentance, inasmuch as it is true *metanoia*, will lead them not into the 'human, all too human' jungle of secular ideologies with their limited, distorted and often simply demonic horizons, but to that unique source, which in spite of all betrayals, the church has preserved in her *paradosis* —Christ and, in him, to the true understanding of the world, the church, and the kingdom.

12

The Status of the Human Person in the
Behavioural Sciences

DAVID MARTIN

1 *Preliminaries*

The prime focus of this essay is upon the various images of man employed in the 'behavioural sciences', with some reference to the interrelation between these images and philosophical anthropology. It will be argued that anthropology conceived in the widest manner as the positive science of man, and anthropology conceived as a philosophical estimate of man, his nature, dignity and destiny, have both a certain autonomy of each other and a complex interdependence. Even if it were held that studies of a limited scope in scientific anthropology can avoid any overt concern with philosophical anthropology it is the experience of most practitioners that certain pervasive images of man derived in part from a philosophical base do broadly inform the style and fundamental assumptions of research as well as the construction of theory. It is likewise true that one cannot pursue most of the prime questions of philosophical anthropology ignorant of and indifferent to the sciences of man. The exploration of this complex interdependence is undertaken in the opening and concluding sections of this essay, beginning with certain assertions of philosophical autonomy and concluding with a review both of the types of statement about man which might require an empirical aspect and those which manifest philosophical autonomy.

Clearly the most complex problem which arises is that of man's freedom in the face of biological and cultural determination. This problem cannot be discussed except in a cursory and very inadequate manner: all one can do is indicate the dimensions of the problem,

I

assume that readers are willing to look at the vast literature on the subject and assert that the problem is as unsolved, perhaps as unsolvable, as ever it was. The partisans of freedom and of determinism exist in 'the behavioural sciences' as elsewhere and in principle the range of argument among them does not differ from the various traditional stances available.

This essay is *not* about what is happening to man in modern society. It is *not* focused on the impact of alienating influences in the work situation, on depersonalizing factors associated with the growth of secondary groups meeting on a largely instrumental basis, or on the problems of admass, mass communication and mass society, the growth of a consumers' as distinct from a producers' style of living, exploitation within and between nations and so forth. However it is true that what is happening to man in modern society is clearly connected with how the behavioural sciences view him, in that (say) in a given society which tends to treat man as a thing, a scientific image of him as a mere object acted upon by external forces may gain greater currency. The two enterprises remain nevertheless analytically separate.

One further preliminary word is necessary. The very term 'behavioural sciences' is redolent of a positivistic tradition with which the writer is not in sympathy, at least in so far as that tradition asserts that *only* experiment, quantification and prediction deserve the name of science to the detriment of the tradition which also concerns itself with the 'looser' processes of hypothesis and empathy at the level of meaning and intentionality. From now on the term 'behavioural science' will be dropped: it is part of a depersonalizing vocabulary and approach to which the sciences of man, taken as a whole, give no warrant, except as a selected tactic in particular, limited contexts. It is true that those who specialize in such contexts, such as (say) the psychology of perception, may come to feel that such a vocabulary is appropriate not merely for special limited purposes but can acquire general applicability. Such limitations of perspectives belong to the professional deformations consequent on the division of scientific labour. For a sociologist, however, the nature of his discipline usually involves him in activity at every possible level from 'behaviour' conceived in terms of conditioned reflex to the adaptive capacities of units in an organism to the phenomenology of inter-personal being, meaning and purpose. Part of the essay will illustrate the range of levels available both in psychology and in sociology, and will argue that none of these levels excludes the others. Those concerned to view human beings as persons and not as things may perhaps be comforted to know that the most recent developments in sociology have emphasized the place of an analysis which operates at the level of personal interaction and shared meanings, so much so indeed that the lawful nature of social phenomena as conceived in the positivistic tradition has been somewhat neglected. Such fashions are ultimately irrelevant but they do illustrate a continuing tension within the human sciences and the resurgent capacities of the different levels of analysis and of the different images of man appropriate to them.

The alternative perspectives on man achieve a comparable variation in strength not only at different analytic levels within subjects but between them. Those academic disciplines which concern themselves with the bodily nature of man more naturally employ notions of stimulus and response than those which are concerned with man's culture, though even the former share organismic notions with the latter and both are (for example) increasingly interested in cybernetic models of self-regulating systems. Nevertheless, the subjects do differ: an interest in what used to be called 'instincts' or 'prepotent reflexes', for example, tends to notions of man's nature which are universally applicable, whereas an interest in the cultural channelling of these 'instincts' tends to emphasize the protean variety of the human and the plasticity of the human substance. Here again, fashion is evident in a recent swing from nurture to nature signalized in the growing science of ethology, with its emphasis on certain given constants in human patterns of behaviour. It is interesting, however, that both universal approaches to man's 'innate nature' and the particularistic approach stressing his infinite cultural variety may be either optimistic or pessimistic about ways in which that nature may be changed. The sections which are concerned with these differences of approach will try to bring out the ways in which either the limits operating on man may be emphasized or alternatively new potentialities and undreamt-of freedoms.

The sequence of discussion then is as follows: first, the elements of autonomy in philosophical (and theological) views of man; second, the various approaches found as *between* disciplines, ranging from 'biological engineering' to cultural anthropology and sociology; third, the *levels* of analysis available *within* disciplines, in particular sociology, but to some minor extent psychology also; finally the extent to which different classes of statement and perspective on man may or may not be affected by the progress of the human sciences.

II *Philosophical Anthropology and Human Science*

We turn then, first, to the logic of the relation between the sciences of 'man in culture' and philosophical anthropology, in which part of the more immediate aim will be to make a preliminary assertion of autonomy for certain philosophical views of man. Indeed, there are those who hold that philosophical views of man are not merely logically autonomous (or, if you like, that it is in the nature of any view properly described as philosophical to be autonomous) but further that such views penetrate into the substance of cultural studies by acting as pervasive and often unstated assumptions, particularly at the meta-theoretical level. At any rate, the logic of the relation between the study of man in culture and philosophical anthropology involves a two-way traffic: (1) How far and at what levels of statement are assertions about man in principle either autonomous or open to empirical verifiability and falsifiability?, and (2) how far and at what levels of statement are generalizations and insights about man in culture undergirded (or ideologically coloured) by broad assumptions derived from philosophical anthropology? Naturally, one can only indicate a very broad position in principle on so vast a subject and, as stated above, the discussion of levels of statement is largely relegated to the final paragraphs of the essay.

There *is* an autonomy from the human sciences which philosophical anthropology shares with metaphysics in general, as well as ethics and aesthetics. For example, to take a statement at the highest level of generality, if one affirms that man is infinitely precious in the eyes of God then that statement is not susceptible either to empirical verification or falsification. This is so in spite of the fact that by introducing 'God' into the statement it might be argued that certain empirical consequences for the condition of man ought to flow from the alleged friendly orientation of the Deity which do not in fact occur. However, one can affirm that human beings are infinitely precious without reference to God and in such a case the impossibility of verification or falsification is quite clear. I would argue that both from a theistic or humanistic viewpoint affirmations at this level of statement are based on an existential choice: one declares a choice about a view of man just as one chooses to prefer honesty and abhor murder. Naturally, one may then proceed to argue that these beliefs are to this or that extent socially 'useful' (for which one may need to produce evidence), but the criterion of 'useful' will, when the argument is pushed far enough, turn out to be based again on a value existentially chosen. All doctrines of man at *this* level are in the same logical condition, whether theistic, or humanistic, or asserting (for example) in Marxist fashion, that man's true 'nature' is currently obscured by alienating structures. I am not saying all these three statements are precisely parallel – they are not – but that they do share the same logical autonomy.

Not all doctrines of 'man' enjoy this autonomous freedom and some of those which may not can now be indicated in a very general manner. For example, if one asserts that 'man is inherently aggressive' or 'communism is against human nature' one is making statements which may have a wide validity, but which still refer to *particular* expressions of human nature within certain varieties of cultural pattern; and, moreover, such statements belong to the class for which one contrary instance might seem to provide adequate disproof.

However, there is a second line of defence available for those making such assertions. This is that any instance seemingly contrary to the generalization represents a violation of man's *real* nature, which has been overlain or repressed by conditioning, or by cultural channelling, or by sublimation, to use three different terminologies within which such a point may be made. Thus one could argue that the famous example of the Arapesh amongst whom the impact of the cultural pattern resulted in a very attenuated expression of aggression involved a distortion of man's real nature which could not but express itself in some other form.[1] To take a parallel instance, the apparently deviant case of a non-mating group such as a monastic fellowship (which differs of course from the Arapesh in being self-selected) can also be held to involve distortions of inherent 'natural' sexuality which cannot but express themselves in varieties of displacement.[2] Alternatively or in addition it is asserted that such groups arise from distortions rather than themselves being responsible for them. Whether one holds such views sometimes depends on one's general feeling towards the groups and values cited in the argument: in some milieux, for example, it would be appropriate to see the Catholic or Buddhist monastery as involving a distortion of man's 'nature' and the Arapesh as an object lesson in what might be done with appropriate cultural channelling. And indeed, it is possible to contend that sexual activity is part of man's 'true' nature whilst aggression is not, though the argument would be complicated by the plausible contention that aggression and sexuality are inextricably linked.

The argument is unresolved, partly because those who wish to locate a displacement due to a violation of what they regard as man's true nature can usually satisfy themselves that they have discovered just how such a displacement takes place. The criteria for these assertions about displacements and for counter-assertions are disagreeably loose, but not in principle unscientific; and in any case there is a further stage in the argument which even claims to identify 'genuine' displacements as distinct from other kinds. At this point the controversy about man's true nature becomes even more clearly fused with valuations of the psychological and social phenomena under examination. A certain kind of primitivistic might both assert *qua* scientist that e.g. aggression belongs to man's nature, and also proceed to evaluate positively the contribution made by allowing that aggression adequate expression to the 'healthy' condition of the 'self'. Many doctrines about the supposed 'need' for self-expression do indeed rest on just such combined scientific and evaluative premises.

The discussion is not closed: the central point here is that at least one important sphere of the discussion is and will be open, in principle, to scientific adjudication. It is not simply a question of an evaluative philosophical anthropology. Furthermore, the scientific argument is not confined to providing the empirical basis for what kind of self it is that 'demands' expression but also extends to providing evidence which can be used to sum the 'costs' of such expression in terms of the social nexus: who, if anybody, has to 'pay' for it and how much. This means that the evaluational process interlocks with the scientific not only with respect to man's 'needs' and the value judgment made with respect to the worth of self-expression, but also in terms of how the impact of self-expression proliferates empirically through the social system, notably in so far as it impinges on other people's self-expression, let alone on necessary disciplines for this or that type of task.

The examples just provided are useful in that they also enable one to see something of the other aspect in the two-way traffic between philosophical and cultural anthropology, viz. the way in which certain 'images' of man do inform and shape one's view and overflow into one's scientific work. Thus in the above instances a mixture of primitivism (Gauguin illegitimately abetted by Margaret Mead[3] if you like) and liberal notions of the self might easily give rise to predilections for one set of assumptions about man's 'needs' and about what constituted 'genuine' displacements as compared to another set. But these predilections are at the level of psychological predispositions and value-judgments in particular social scientists, and do not disturb the analytic and logical distinction between what are evaluational and what are scientific elements. However, the problem still remains somewhat more complex and it is not enough to allow a simple restatement of the logical distinction to stand as adequate. Some indication must be given as to the content of that distinction.

To approach the problem let us for a moment return to such a broad philosophical position as that illustrated in the assertion concerning the infinite preciousness of man. It was suggested that this class of statement is autonomous in that the conclusions of the science of man did not impinge on it. But does *it* impinge on *them*? The answer is that it does so only in so far as a person imbued with such a conception might choose fields for research which he regarded as clearly devoted to the good of humanity and might also have scruples about the ethics of certain experimental methods in so far as these involved human beings. He would have to sum the gains and losses of such methods in terms of his overall love of humanity; similarly with the application of the results. But it is not easy to see how his philosophical position impinges on his scientific role beyond that, except in so far as it might give him a preliminary preference for asserting that a science of persons conducted in terms of 'the personal' was at least a viable enterprise – even if he himself chose to concentrate at some other level. The present author certainly takes such a position and is reasonably convinced that a Christian background has provided him with just such a predilection, and has even prevented him forgetting what contemporary Marxists and phenomenologists are eagerly rediscovering. All the same, such broad orientations do not enter into the logical status of the scientific work in which one is engaged, which operates in terms of criteria of controlled observation, hypothesis and generalization.[4]

Again, let us take the sort of assertion involved in statements about the alienated condition of man under this or that social system. Such a view would inform one's critical perspective and almost certainly motivate one's political activity, but it would remain an unassailable and unverifiable philosophical vantage point. On the one hand it remains philosophically autonomous and on the other one's social science could exist quite apart from it consistent and entire. It can confer no privileges on one's empirical propositions, apart, perhaps, from the illegitimate aura it might carry with those who already agreed with one on philosophical grounds. It is true one might wish to operationalize the notion of alienation by specifying its differential distribution in time and cultural space or by devising measurements of such supposedly derivative psychological conditions or feelings as powerlessness, but then to go on and describe such conditions as fundamentally 'inauthentic' or rooted in 'false consciousness' necessarily involves the reintroduction of a philosophical perspective about what constitutes full humanity.[5] Such a perspective is no doubt based on experience, in that one empathizes 'the human', but the judgment *qua* judgment remains a philosophical choice. Similarly so even if one postulates that the condition of alienation is unverifiable *precisely because* the essence of being alienated is an inability to focus on the 'real' nature of one's dissatisfactions. At this point one is involved in an interpretation of 'distortions' of focus and 'displacements' where the border between science and philosophy is very poorly marked. That the classical concept of alienation will shape one's theory of 'displacements' and one's notion of 'genuine' as distinct from 'inauthentic' responses to the supposedly alienating structures seems inevitable. Perhaps all one can say, without going into an immensely complicated discussion, is that statements about the occurrence of displacements are probably susceptible to loose empirical criteria whereas judgments to the effect that a given response is 'inauthentic' are not. Obviously this whole question parallels the discussion above about man's genuine 'need' of self-expression in this or that respect.

Maybe at this point it will be easiest simply to quote a contemporary work on the social sciences which indicates the impact of values and broad philosophical positions on work in those fields and then to make one or two final comments. In *The Political Sciences* Hugh Stretton refers to our 'knowledge of causes' as involving

a selection of causal chains, terminated at *selected* points, including many causes *chosen* because they determine *selected* effects, which are chosen because they are *imagined* as possible and often *valued* as important.[6]

One notes in such a sentence the kind of qualification involved in preferring 'many' and 'often' to 'all' and 'always'. One also recollects the traditional distinction between the psychology of scientific work and the 'logic of justification'. If one were to deny the possibility of an objective public 'logic of justification' in relation to one's scientific arguments and propositions one would either fall over oneself into total relativism, so destroying the force of one's own position, or else one would have to state that some elements are objective whereas others are ideologically and psychologically coloured, in which case one presumably believes in objective criteria for making just such discriminations.[7]

So much then for necessary preamble on the philosophical issues raised in relation to the impact of the human sciences on our view of man, and the impact which our views of man (along with philosophical positions in general) may have on the human sciences. It is now appropriate to examine the various levels at which work on man proceeds and what type of view of man characteristically derives from them.

III   *Universal Biological Nature*

I begin with the biological level of approach, which can be separated into four sub-heads: biological engineering, an emphasis on the neurological and endocrinological aspects, the structure of mind and/or the brain, and ethology. When I speak of a 'biological level' in this context I mean what traditionally would be called 'the body' and which we see as providing a universal 'context' within which man 'produces himself' in all his varied cultural particularity. Even to attempt to indicate such a distinction already trespasses on the endlessly disputed sphere of the mind-body relation, on arguments as to whether or not man is a 'ghost in a machine' and so on. However, all I wish to do is to point towards an area of contemporary development in the sciences of man which lays relatively high emphasis on the *given* properties of man as distinct from those which are culturally acquired during the processes of socialization, or which interprets those processes in a highly mechanistic, biologically based manner. To some extent these developments also stress what man has in common with other animals, other primates in particular, either by extending presumed human characteristics down the evolutionary scale or presumed animal characteristics up. The most important point for my argument is their universality in that they point to a common 'nature' of man.

Clearly no attempt will be made to survey the four heads referred to as fields in their own right. It is simply necessary to indicate them as contemporary tendencies which in some cases carry certain very broad implications for our understanding of man. The first sub-head of 'biological engineering' will be discussed in some detail to bring out certain issues which inform the succeeding heads.

By biological engineering I mean both the possibility of determining the character of the next generation in advance through progress in genetics, and the possibility of altering the character of this or that person by operations or by drugs. These are rather different and need separating to some extent from each other.

In the former case certain very broad components of character, like (say) the level of aggression might be altered in such a way that what a man brought with him at birth into the socialization process altered the whole concatenation of his response to others and their response to him, so that he emerged as a somewhat different 'type' of person. The same would be true if a genetic decision were made in favour of high intelligence: this would have immense ramifications for the formative experiences of the person concerned and affect his capacity (on the average) to reach this or that level of social status and achieve the image of the 'self' associated with that status. A great deal would depend, of course, on the stress laid on intelligence in the society concerned as to how profound the ramifications of this decision would be for 'character', but it is quite likely that a society making a genetic decision in favour of high intelligence would also value it highly.

Certain points need to be made about the implications of the above possibilities. They involve a change from 'spontaneous' processes to processes partly governed by human decision. In principle this is not at all novel, since we know that on the average one can produce people with (say) higher intelligence by appropriate mating, and presumably people have been making such decisions in their mating habits for some time. What may be happening now is an extension of the process: the area of decision is widened and the intervention becomes less indirect. However, there is something rather new and disturbing in preparing a person for the world rather as one might assemble a kit, or deciding that the general characteristics of person A might be appropriately multiplied so many times as compared with those of person B. The process is full of unknowns, so far as the character of the human beings so produced is concerned and with respect to the relation between such interventions and the social nexus. Some of these may usefully be spelled out.

If, for example, genetic decisions were made in favour of low levels of aggressive potentiality, one neither knows how this is linked to sexuality nor how this decision would affect activity in relation to environmental challenges in general. No doubt it is possible to see that human aggression is 'too high' in relation to certain environmental challenges and problems of type X but it may equally be too low for challenges and problems of type Y. And the point which a sociologist might appropriately make is that society tends to socialize for the *particular* challenges it encounters (or maybe for those encountered just recently), building up or toning down certain broad potentialities in relation to the *contexts* in which they are 'programmed' to receive a certain type and degree of expression. It is *this* level of decision which will prove crucial both for the 'character' of the human beings concerned and for the viability of aiming at certain social consequences, such as (say) aggression in relation to the 'challenge' and specific context of war.

At this point the problems become immense, partly because those taking the decisions either in favour of a certain level of aggression in given persons or the levels of aggression built up as proper in specific social contexts are themselves people or social groups with particular proximate interests and values which are not necessarily identical with the long-term interests of mankind as a whole – even supposing one can give any content to so nebulous a concept. Further than that, one cannot realistically decide that any *type* of conduct is *per se* undesirable or desirable apart from the context in which it is to occur. Every society so far has tended to socialize into a certain level of aggression in general, but forbidding it expression in this context and permitting it in that; and although one might agree in terms of broad values that it is *usually* better to have a certain general level of 'aggression', or that it is better to channel aggression in a relatively harmless direction (say) sport rather than war, one could never be certain that one might not at some point require a high level of aggression for this or that social exigency. Maybe, of course, given the techniques of modern warfare, coldly indifferent decisions would need to be made without any significant affective element. Even so the problem would remain in so far as a given *type* of action or activity cannot be ruled out in advance as inappropriate. After all, once a decision was made in favour of low aggression the low aggression society might be immediately overrun by a high aggression society. This is one reason why societies officially dedicated to 'peace' socialize their populations *both* in a strong attachment to the word 'peace' *and* in a universal antagonism to societies defined and stereotyped as non-peaceful.

This is particularly true in the type of socialist society where *decisions* are taken as to how the population shall understand its attachment to the word 'peace', and as to which other populations or social systems are defined as non-peaceful. Capitalist societies also do this, but by not centralizing to the same extent and by leaving some social processes at a less conscious, less directed level they acquire substantial areas of uncertainty (i.e. dissent) as to how people understand their attachment to the word 'peace' and as to which other groups are responsible for war and therefore defined as appropriate objects of aggression. To put this discussion in a non-contentious context, what should the society dedicated to low aggression do in terms of biological engineering or in terms of programmed socializing *vis à vis* a society dedicated to high aggression? The answer must be that such a society prepares its population for a certain type of 'aggressive' response in the context of that particular exigency.

The discussion of the above example has been prolonged simply to underline certain issues which will underlie the succeeding sections. Firstly, it has been suggested that knowledge of techniques for altering 'character' introduces not so much a new element into our thinking as a new and rapidly increasing scope for conscious decision. This in itself is neither good nor bad. Secondly, it has been suggested that these decisions are fed into so complex a social matrix that one cannot be certain (or even attain a reasonable degree of likelihood) as to how they will operate. Thirdly, the 'programming' of these decisions in terms of the socialization process must be 'contextual'. Fourthly, decisions will be made in terms of the values and interests of certain groups and to the extent that these are centralized the chances of alternative characterological styles flowering are diminished. The point about the values of 'certain groups' underlines the characteristic danger in capitalist society, whereas the point about centralization underlines the characteristic danger in communist society.

Most of the above digression can be transferred to the issues raised by the other aspect of biological engineering which consists of altering 'character' when already formed. The most obvious and most frequently publicized example is that of pre-frontal surgery. All that needs to be said perhaps is that all 'engineering' of this type does arouse deep anxieties in relation to notions of 'character' either as fixed or, alternatively, as changeable by the human decision of the person himself *qua* person, not by the decisions of others. It seems peculiarly difficult to accept that a person can be altered in what we like to think of as his 'essential being' (a notion after all quite close to that of 'soul') by decisions which are *external* to him and processes which are also 'external' in that they do not require 'him' acting as a person. Yet this is only a rather pointed instance of what is always true, that we are what we are at least in part by the decisions of *others*, and to be rendered less brutal by an operation is perhaps not so different from being brutalized by the day-to-day pressures of a particular sort of emotional environment. And we are all aware of what processes of senility and the changes of role consequent on enforced retirement can do to 'character' without any crudely external *intervention*. In other words, this is only a particular case which points up in a sharply defined way the facts of common observation that our 'character' is a fragile possession built up within external constraints of all kinds, both biological and social.

The second sub-head is concerned with an emphasis on endocrinological and neurological aspects and it links easily with the preceding section. It also looks forward to a discussion below based on the development of Freudianism as a discipline originally rooted in neurological study. The main focus at this point ought to be on the notion of the conditioned reflex, since this is a central concept to a very influential school of human science oriented towards biology.[8] This focus concerns itself with the building up of 'character' not in terms of genetic decision made *ab initio* nor in terms of a decision made to use a particular drug or employ an operation at some point in a person's characterological development, but in terms of the continuous on-going process by which the 'person' emerges. Since the previous focus has been on the notion 'character' it may be useful to shift the focus a little on to that aspect of a man's character which we call 'conscience'. Whereas we have looked at biological engineering and 'character' we may now consider conditioning and conscience.

What is a conditioned reflex? How does it link with the notion of conscience? Above all, does the concept of conditioning constitute a level which gives an *exhaustive* account of the notion of conscience? In order to deal with this succinctly I intend to utilize an approach adopted by H. J. Eysenck together with certain broader issues raised by Michael Argyle.

In his book *Crime and Personality* (Routledge, 1964), Eysenck argues as follows. First, he distinguishes between learning and conditioning. In learning, what is pleasurable and rewarded will be learned whereas what is not pleasurable or rewarded will not be learned. This process is one of trial and error and is amenable to teaching. Conditioning, however, proceeds not through trial and error but through association by contiguity; and, furthermore, it is related to the autonomic nervous system, the activity of which tends to be *in*voluntary. Conditioning works in the following manner. The child misbehaves and is punished on each successive occasion until the conditioned response is sufficiently 'fearful' to inhibit recurrence. This rather specific conditioning eventually becomes *generalized* to all activities grouped by the conditioning agents (usually parents) under a particular head such as 'bad', 'naughty', etc. The result is a repertoire of conditioned fear responses: 'as burnt child shuns fire, so punished child shuns wickedness'. Eysenck goes on to argue that our inherited nervous systems vary in their capacity to mediate the establishment of conditioned responses so that those who are too readily conditioned fall prey to anxiety and obsession while those who are not so readily conditioned fall prey to the law.

Clearly there is more to conscience than this, for example the psychoanalytic processes of introjection and the way in which moral feeling relates to the growth of an ability to take the role of 'the other' and sympathize with his point of view. These involve different levels of approach and remind us that the level of the conditioning is not necessarily exhaustive. However, whether the process be conceived as one of conditioning or introjection, certain consequences follow for the notion of conscience and for the ways of dealing with 'moral failure' which Michael Argyle has neatly summarized.

Guilt feelings, he argues, are not accurate indicators of moral failure because often the wrong people feel guilty about the wrong things.[9] Those with the strongest conditioned responses (or superegos or consciences) feel most guilty, and they do so in terms of those childish misdemeanours to which their parents responded most sharply. Some people are more able to resist 'temptation' because they have been reared differently and (to reincorporate Eysenck's point) because their nervous systems are more easily conditioned. Hence it is in Argyle's view an entirely lawful and predictable matter whether a person will fall into temptation. Praise and blame are therefore inappropriate with respect to the past, though they may be used in varying proportions to help modify future behaviour, depending on the particular psychological make up of the person concerned. It seems fairly clear what this implies for notions of free will and responsibility: *except* that once delinquents or neurotics are socialized to see themselves as the pawns of entirely predictable patterns, they are more likely to remain as they are. In other words, the assumption that people are determined is not pragmatically viable. This paradox is at least suggestive, though there is no space to consider the range of problems which it opens up.[10]

The next sub-heading, under the general head of universalistic approaches, is concerned with what is fashionably called 'structuralism'. In this field the most well-known protagonists are Levi-Strauss and Chomsky, particularly with regard to their work on the structure of myths and of language. Only two points need to be noted here. One is that both in linguistics and in the analysis of symbolic structures such as myths it is held that the kaleidoscopic variety can be reduced to a few basic elements, constantly combining and recombining but nevertheless persistently exemplifying certain preferred paths of interconnection rather than others. The most obvious of these basic structures is the 'binary discrimination', i.e. sets of simple alternatives, on/off, yes/no, etc. The other point is that these notions are related to a revival of Cartesian ideas, or perhaps more properly Kantian ideas, about the properties of the human mind (and brain?) determining the way in which our view of the world is structured. This leads some people to compare the human mind to a computer programmed in a certain way, maybe with certain limits which are built in, including limits to science itself.[11]

The structuralist position is worth mentioning, partly because it roots man in a universal structure which is his nature and transforms all the diversity of cultural forms into a universal grammar. It is in essential contrast to the kind of empiricist view underlying the concept of conditioning and links interestingly with certain tendencies in sociology to construct sets of basic alternatives (e.g. Parsons' 'pattern variables') although these are rooted in ineluctable social exigency rather than the structure of the mind or physiology of the brain. So far as Chomsky is concerned one finds interesting ideas both about human creativity and human limits which are a part of the contemporary ferment about man. The point about limits to science has already been mentioned, but Chomsky also speaks of 'fixed rules' and 'restrictions' governing the innate structure of language and presumably these operate as limits, albeit as ultimate rather than immediate ones. On the other hand, the possibility of permutation between the 'deep structures' is held to be an indication of the possibilities of human creativity and the role of human intentionality in organizing such permutations. At any rate, the emphasis both on innate organizing principles and on the role of intentionality in permutations of the structures (however 'restricted') does point to the *activity* of the human mind in a way which corrects the behaviouristic view of the human mind as a *receiver* of sense impressions and as *product* of conditioning factors – a mere network of associations and habits.[12]

The final sub-heading, ethology, also relates to innate elements, to universals and to restrictions on humanity's freedom to invent creatively.[13] It is part of a reaction against the extreme emphasis on the range of cultural variability and on human plasticity, pointing rather to certain constants built up in the vast process of evolution which both link man firmly to the animal kingdom and persist into the present to create universal patterns as, for example, the persistent pattern of 'male bonding'. Thus, to give a concrete instance, the all-male society of the rugby club is seen less as an associational form dependent on a highly specific cultural pattern, limited in time and cultural space, than as one version of a universal tendency to 'male bonding' which proved functional in the earlier stages of man's evolution and which even now acts as a restraint on the range of inter-sex association which feminism might hold to be appropriate.[14]

The links between man and the animal kingdom are forged in a number of ways. At a very broad level the distinction between mechanical response and intentional behaviour is held to be partly eroded, and human reason and capacity to learn and animal 'instinct' are no longer contrasted in a simple way. Animals, too, are capable of learning and even pass on the fruits of it to the next generation. Animal societies in similar species vary in social organization according, for example, to the functional requirements of living in different parts of a forest. More specifically psychological phenomena and social phenomena from the two realms are treated to some extent in the same frame of scientific reference. W. J. M. MacKenzie summarizes these briefly and well in chapter 11 of his *Politics and Social Science* (Penguin Books, 1967). There he indicates concepts like territory, aggression and dominance which are applicable in societies whether of birds, animals or humans. Within territories a hierarchy of senior and junior will develop, and to the extent that numbers increase and territory is not available with adequate food resources then fighting will break out which restores the broken balance between population and resources. W. M. S. Russell has attempted to treat human warfare within a similar framework of analysis.

The dangers are obvious, since it is not at all clear that the common concepts used to describe the behaviour of men and animals do not conceal vital differences. This suspicion is increased for concepts like 'ritual', especially when these are related in the human context to complex theologies. Too many ethologists leap from the explanation which seems to fit certain phenomena in animal societies, such as fighting, to explanations at the human level, ignoring all the mediating levels of social structure and history.[15] Edmund Leach reminds us also of certain crucial distinctions which need to be set against the plausible analogies. Thus he points out that 'Human speech is a message-bearing and information-storing device of quite different kind from that possessed by any other animal'.[16] Whereas animals adapt to their habitat man 'is a creature with a *uniquely* versatile technical versatility for modifying his environment . . .'.[17] We can overstress the difference between men and animals just as we can overstress the difference between men and machines,[18] but distinctions of the kind just made remain vital and important.[19]

IV   *Universal Psychological Nature*

So far approaches have been reviewed which emphasize man's status as a part of biological nature and the universal characteristics which follow from this 'nature'. Throughout the discussion there has been a counterpoint between the creative possibilities open to man and the inherent limitations which operate upon him. It is now appropriate to turn to man in culture, which means recovering the emphasis characteristic of contemporary anthropology and sociology, and in particular illustrating the different levels at which man may be conceived within the sciences of culture. However, there are certain approaches within cultural studies which still emphasize universal patterns rather than cultural variation *without* relying on a biological orientation, and these form an appropriate bridge passage between the biological and social. The most important of these are associated with the names of Jung, Pareto and Freud. The two former need to be referred to only briefly, but the problems raised by Freud and the subsequent developments towards an existential psychiatry are of paramount importance in the context of this essay.

The Jungian notion of the collective unconscious barely needs exposition, except to suggest an interesting comparison with Levi-Strauss in so far as there is a common stress on mythological and symbolic constants. Both of them hold that beneath the welter of culture there are certain underlying, universal patterns, but for the one it is based on the structure of the brain, for the other rooted in a universal psyche. And just as Jung may be linked to Levi-Strauss, so Pareto may be linked to Freud, in that Pareto postulates certain sets of ideational constants ('residues') of which the endless variety of notions, ideologies and attitudes ('derivations') are the expression.[20] His basic concept of 'derivation' is indeed cognate with the Freudian concept of rationalization, as well as with the Marxist concept of ideology. And whereas neither Jung nor Levi-Strauss would stress a fundamental irrationality in man, both Pareto and Freud are profoundly aware of the irrational. This combines with their emphasis on universals to give their analyses of man a certain distance from specific time and cultural place, since for them so much of history is the perpetual revolution of these same universals: the wheel revolves and irrational man like a somnambulist turns with it.[21] Their horizon of hope is dim and in Freud, for example, barely extends beyond the possibility of achieving stoic self-possession. Yet there remains a genuine revolution in Freud which is not merely the changeless turning of the wheel but a new estimate of self-hood in so far as he made 'legitimate self-concern the highest science'. This orientation away from the active urge to save others towards self-manipulative contemplation represents an estimate of man which is at least superficially at odds with Western Christian traditions and perhaps capable of being linked to the interest in Eastern religions characteristic of many contemporary people.[22]

Freudian psychiatry was, of course, rooted originally in a background which tended to reduce psychiatry to neuropathology and it might therefore be affiliated to the biological approaches discussed above. Yet just as we noted earlier the pragmatic importance of treating man *as if* he were free even from the behaviouristic viewpoint, so in the development of Freudian therapeutic *practice* it has become necessary to treat man on the level of his concrete, unique, personal existence. In other words it does not *work* to regard man either as totally determined or to view his psyche as epiphenomenal. The history of this development is of considerable importance, since it illustrates certain key issues in the human sciences in general and links with a widespread movement in those sciences to recover man in the phenomenology of of his personal being. One of the principal figures for this process in psychiatry is Binswanger and he provides an appropriate focus at this point.[23]

According to Binswanger, Freud's man was *homo natura*, dominated by a natural force, the libido, calling forth 'every assimilative and constructive impulse or else every disintegrative, regressive and destructive impulse'.[24] Man in Freud is reduced to a purely hedonistic creature, and what a man may conceive *himself* as his interhuman experience and on-going *personal* history must be unmasked and reduced to the *natural* history of various libidinal transformations. This is, if you like, the universal transformational grammar underlying all the rich diversity of innumerable personal histories. Thus the human subject easily becomes the 'object' of analysis, depersonalized and objectified in a manner appropriate to a natural science of man, whereby 'I' and 'You' are transmuted into my 'Ego' and his 'Id'. Binswanger points out that whereas theology had conceived man as *homo aeternis aut caelestis* and philosophy as *homo universalis* the 'decomposition' of man assayed by Freud involves the reduction of him to *homo natura*. It was this concept that he opposed with the concept of *homo existentialis*.[25]

Freud's attempt at reductionism – which his own practice did not

fully exemplify – ran into the fundamental problem of human science:
the antinomy of antecedent cause and present purpose, to which belong
the related antinomies of man as passively acted upon and as positively
grasping, as subject to a natural history and the personal centre of an
inner story, as experiencing outer 'events' and endowing them with
singular, unique meaning. Neither set of antinomies is properly dis-
regarded in the whole science of man.

We are confronted then with a whole series of levels at which man
may be understood, and each of them demands its appropriate methodology and interpretative mode. This is not to say, of course, that each
level is insulated from the others: while affirming one particular modality
it is not possible to ignore its interpenetration with others. Thus the
contention of some contemporary linguistic philosophers that our
human understanding can be insulated in such a way from natural
history as to make *understanding* of man's inner story equivalent to an
exhaustive *explanation* of it is a deformation as dangerous as the reductionism and epiphenomalism of those who affirm the supreme
relevance of natural science models.[26] The complexity of human science
arises precisely because of this interpenetration of levels. It is now
possible to turn to these levels as illustrated in the development and
contemporary practice of sociology.

v   *Man in his Infinite Cultural Variety*

How does sociology conceive of man and at what levels does it attempt
to analyse and understand him?[27] Man has no species-specific environment in the sense of an environment firmly structured by his biological
organization. He adapts to his environment and adapts it to his needs,
so that he has a uniquely variable geographical habitat. The human
organism is plastic, his drives highly unspecialized and undirected.
Indeed one may say that from a sociological perspective there is no
'human nature' except in so far as man exhibits 'world openness' and
a plastic instinctual structure. The process of becoming man takes place
in an environment which includes a cultural order mediated by 'significant others'.[28] Man constructs his own nature and produces himself
in a joint social enterprise. Because of his plasticity he must externalize
himself in activity. However, there are limitations, partly those of his
sensory and motor equipment, partly those deriving from the exigencies
of life[29] in society, partly those due to the fact that his 'openness' is
always pre-empted in some degree by a particular social order. Thus
sexuality may express itself in an almost limitless number of modalities
but in a particular culture tends to be more or less well structured.

Man is always subject to some kind of structure based on institutionalization and habitualization. Institutions are inescapable.

The most well-known studies illustrating how a culture selects from only a small segment of the wide arc of possibilities are those associated with Mead, Benedict, Du Bois, Linton and Kardiner. Every sociologist is aware of the definitions of male and female sexuality found amongst the Tchambuli studied by Margaret Mead, amongst whom the roles and characteristic personality traits normal in Western society were reversed. Similarly the Kwakiutl and the Zuni studied by Benedict exhibit totally variant attitudes to aggression, the one glorifying competition, the other specializing in a personality type which is dignified, affable and never attempts to lead. The fact that individuals of 'powerful personality' are punished among the Zuni does suggest, however, that aggression and competition are far from completely malleable traits, but nevertheless it is clear that socialization can 'reduce the occasions for aggression, eliminate its motivations, disqualify its stakes' (Aron). It does *not* follow of course that such socialization is easily brought about in modern societies, which are in fact exceptionally competitive.

All that has just been said also follows for national character,[30] for social class and for the vast variety of sub-cultures, including the criminal sub-culture. Here the analysis tends to incorporate a strong Marxist component in so far as the characteristic social psychology of different social classes is held to reflect in part their position within the relationships of production. Studies like that of Adorno on 'The Authoritarian Personality' suggest particular lodgments for this psychological syndrome within the status system, and the lower middle class have been frequently selected for exemplification of 'authoritarian personality' (Fromm), though the working class has not been exempt.

The point about particular psychological constellations found *on the average* in sections of the social system has implications when we examine a notion like that of the criminal sub-culture.[31] These implications are as important for our use of praise and blame and for the strategy of dealing with crime as the kinds of approach by Eysenck and Argyle referred to above. Indeed, if we also incorporate the approaches initiated by Durkheim we may need to see crime and lawfulness as existing in a necessary symbiosis whereby the criminal's activity acts to stimulate the majority's conformity to legal norms. The main point is that whatever may be true about differential conditioning and criminality it is certainly true that some groups are positively inducted into criminal norms, and it is not easy to apply straightforward praise and blame with respect to their obedient conformity.[32] The same consideration applies to the differential incidence of marital breakdown in terms both of its class and status distribution and the variable likelihood of certain constellations of personality type and circumstances predisposing to vicious circles of marital infelicity and break-up, while others equally predispose to beneficent circles.[33] Crime and divorce and a host of other social phenomena so often the object of simple-minded blame on an individualistic basis are fundamentally *structural* in their incidence. Sociology gives additional force to the injunction 'Judge not'.[34]

vi   *Levels of Analysis*

We now turn to a closer examination of the levels of analysis in human science, beginning briefly with a glance at certain types of assumption employed for limited analytic purposes, such as the concept of *homo economicus*, and then at the fundamental shifts of perspective basic to sociology.[35]

The kind of assumption about man employed in economic theory is marginal to the theme of this essay since the concept of *homo economicus* is simply an isolation of a certain aspect of humanity relating to market behaviour. It does not carry any implication about the essential nature of humanity as such but merely states what would happen, other things being equal, *if* one assumed that human beings acted to maximize their gains. Such conceptions enable the analyst to construct internally consistent theoretical systems which can be quite distant from actual behaviour. Indeed, all theories depend to some extent on a degree of abstraction, but economic theory is more abstract, logical and deductive than most, and becomes perhaps for that reason more susceptible to mathematicization and prediction than other branches of social science.[36] More complex assumptions are made in sociological theory about such areas of human action as voting behaviour where notions about the essentially 'interested' character of voting achieve a closer empirical fit because they are based more closely and inductively on data and feed in other assumptions about habit, tradition, cultural conditioning, patterns of differential association and so on. But again, little follows for our estimate of man. The same applies in such analytic exercises as (say) the reduction of diplomacy to the dimensions of game theory: nobody supposes that human behaviour is being exhaustively described by treating actions *as if* they were part of a complicated game of chess.[37]

It is not easy to isolate the fundamental perspectives on man employed in sociology, and to some extent I rely on the schema proposed by Gibson Winter in his *Elements for a Social Ethic* (Collier-Macmillan, 1966) where he distinguishes four perspectives based respectively on causation, function, motive and intentionality. This is an analysis which runs parallel to the developments in psychiatry described earlier and is concerned to emphasize the propriety of studying man not only in terms of cause and function but also in terms of his concrete existence within the world of lived experience. Winter's orientation derives in particular from the prior work of Alfred Schutz. This work is extremely wordy and Germanic in style but the essential basis has provided a platform for all those who wish to retain a humanistic perspective on man, as indeed also for all those who see man in the even wider perspective of theology.

In his preamble to the main argument Winter suggests that American pragmatism loosened the hold of mechanistic models of man by emphasizing his *activity* in attempting to understand and master his world rather than his subjection to externally determined forces. Along with many others of like mind Winter finds in Mead the principal link between pragmatism and contemporary sociology. In common with Berger[38] he asserts that the kind of anthropology found in Mead based on the notion of the self intersubjectively produced is a superior base for phenomenological exploration to that found in Freud, due to the tendency already noted in Freud for the self to become largely a product of unconscious libidinal forces.

In Mead's view the self arises intersubjectively through the interpretation of its acts by 'others' who are significant to it – hence the term used above 'significant others'. A gesture or communication becomes significant for the self by partaking in what it means to the 'other'. Mead also put forward the notion of the 'generalized other' through which the self took on the *mores* of society. Now, as Winter suggests, such conceptions – baldly summarized to the point of vacuity – at least establish the sphere of an internally related process, but at the price of over-emphasizing a 'social self', a socially determined 'me' as distinct from a creative 'I'. This is indeed a persistent tendency of sociology and social psychology to treat the person as the sum of his roles, thereby neglecting the way in which the 'I' may distance itself from its roles.[39] In other words, sociology is puzzled how to incorporate the element of personal transcendence involved in 'I' in its account of the social world. It is constantly tending to see the individual as a palimpsest of the social networks in which he is implicated. Partly this is because of the process of abstraction already noted whereby sociology must work with 'typifications' rather than with the immediacy of experience.[40]

Winter presents his different fundamental perspectives within the context of this tendency.[41] The first level is that of behaviourism in which the fundamental notion is that of the conditioned response, either to instinctual forces producing calculable effects or external forces producing internal effects. Control is brought about by the manipulation of sanctions, i.e. a field of force is given which calls for accommodation from the structural unit. Such a view approximates the kind of conception already noted in Eysenck, and in a rather different sense some aspects of Freudianism in so far as the social world is conceived as the sublimation of the *real* libidinal forces.

The second level is that of functionalism, in which a totality of organism and environment is postulated in terms of a moving equilibrium. Part-processes are evaluated as they contribute to the maintentenance of the whole and the increase of mastery over the external environment. The ordering principle is not adjustment to a field of forces as in the behaviouristic style but functional adaption within the postulated equilibrium. Conflicts within the system tend to be seen as 'structural strain' rather than as involving substantive incompatibilities of interests and values.

The third level is what Winter labels 'voluntaristic', and he associates it primarily with Weber, though it clearly has an affinity to Marx as well. The basic categories of this style are rooted in a political conception: conflict, compromise, influence, domination. The stress is on the variability of interest and perspective according to milieu and on the role of struggle in social change. Whereas functionalism sees 'power' as a 'facility' the interest theorist sees it as an instrument of domination.

It is important to note that in each of these styles man's 'reason' is conceived somewhat differently. For behaviourism reason is a set of associations produced by external forces, for functionalism it is the consistent calculation of means to given ends, and for voluntarism it is an expression of interests and values within the perspective of a particular social location.

The fourth level is that of 'intentionality', which broadly approximates a phenomenological viewpoint. Whereas the other levels dealt with cause, function and interest respectively, conceiving man and his rationality within the nexus of such concepts, the fourth level attempts to locate man at the level of his personal intention, or if one prefers existentialist vocabulary, of his personal projects. The focus is also 'projective' in that man is viewed projecting himself into the future. Society comprises the 'sedimented project' which is its common culture. Man is understood in terms of the way in which the world as he lives it (Lebenswelt) is constituted. Clearly enough, such a level of analysis becomes misleading if it ignores fields of forces, compatibilities within functioning systems, or structures of domination, struggle and interest, but it does recover man *qua* man, in his personal immediacy, transcending the totality of the forces which act upon him or the constellation of roles which form the essential substratum of his being. This is not to say that he steps outside his 'circumstances':

indeed he rests upon them in terms of the necessary and calculable predictability of forces for the ordering of social life and the absolute necessity of locating himself firmly in a structure of roles. If existentialist ideology attempts to overleap this essential grounding then it misunderstands the nature of man's freedom. Man is more than his roles, but he requires them both as the base of his freedom *and* as the restrictive perspective within which he exercises it. A role is the necessary focus of a man's freedom.

VII   *The Nature and Destiny of Man*

In this final section it is appropriate to indicate what classes of statement about man are the autonomous declarations of a philosophical or theological anthropology and what classes of statement are in principle affected by the sciences of man and culture. Such indications cannot be fully argued, although most of them will be based on the foregoing discussion. For example, questions relating to 'freedom' and 'responsibility' have been touched upon at several points in the central substantive section of the essay. Different groupings of such statements are indicated by *a, b, c, d*.

(*a*) To begin with, social science has not provided us with any agreed moral psychology. The moral psychology of a Bishop Butler or of a Freud both lack a scientific imprimatur. Butler's 'Conscience' and Freud's 'Superego' are clearly cognate and yet exist within different intellectual universes: science seems unable to choose between such universes. The same holds for those two vital elements in Christian moral psychology: freedom and corruption – or sin. Social science can indicate the *limits* on the concept of responsibility in terms of all kinds of cultural and biological determinations, but it is part of the nature of freedom that it is built up upon a structure of determination, just as creative work in the arts depends on hierarchies of conditioned responses and sharp restrictions on viable ranges of interpretation. Moreover every increase in knowledge of determination is a potential increase in freedom.

The corruption of man's projects in which are included his 'bad faith' and his 'false consciousness' depend upon a philosophical perspective on which social science cannot pronounce. Sin, bad faith and false consciousness each derive from ways of viewing the human situation and are in no way dependent on a subjective recognition – guilt – empirically located by sociological investigation. Indeed if a man recognizes himself as sinful, or in bad faith or as affected by false consciousness, he is, in terms of these philosophical perspectives on the human situation, already on the road to salvation, personal or social.

Isaiah knows he is sinful precisely because he has seen the cherubim
and the seraphim.

(*b*) Science, philosophy and religion each affirm in varying ways
the unity of mankind. Again there is here no conflict, because that
united affirmation occurs at different levels: the unity of the species,
the common rationality of the human, the brotherhood of men before
the fatherhood of God. What science may say about the nature of man
is not in contradiction with what religion may say about his destiny.

(*c*) We cannot say of any institution or type of personality that it is
'natural'. Science cannot for example underwrite monogamous marriage
or self-fulfilment. It can show in what ways monogamous marriage
solves a particular social 'system-problem', and what are its dis-
advantages and advantages and chances in a variety of social contexts.
It can count the *costs* of various types of personality ideals, in terms of
the dynamic economy of the psyche and the consequences of such
ideals for social organization: it cannot adjudicate between them.
Self-fulfilment, self-control and self-abnegation all have their opportunity costs which can be counted: their relative value is not a scientific
question.

(*d*) Nor can the science of man deny in principle any form of human
transcendence, religious or secular. It can define all kinds of limits
in terms of conditions but it does not contradict in principle the active
transcendence of humanity over forces, systems and limiting cultural
perspectives. Indeed it is interesting that among social scientists
themselves certain forms of secular transcendence are of increasing
interest. The three following are of particular importance. There is,
for example, the transcendence associated with science itself, which
provides freedom for man through knowledge, without however adequately considering the perspectives and forces which may channel
the use of that knowledge. There is the transcendence of political
utopianism, notably Marxism, which calls men to rise above the one-
dimensionality of their incorporation into this or that social sysem,
and which unfortunately does not adequately consider the extent to
which all alternatives also involve opportunity costs and cramped
dimensions. There is the transcendence of those psychologies which
seek to release the creative imagination of men, and which sometimes
pursue all the techniques of expanding consciousness, without appropriate consideration of the norms which must govern viable social
existences and even the disciplines of mystical exploration. Moreover,
each of these forms of transcendence rests on assertions of ontological
superiority, whether for the meritocratic scientist, or for the political
rebel, or for the drop-out and Bohemian.[42] As one observes the forms
of arrogance and corruption stemming from precisely these secular

forms of transcendence, then it becomes easier to understand that strange form of transcendence which declares in favour of the poor in spirit, since they too, it seems, are heirs to a kingdom.

VIII *Postscript*

It may be that these forms of secular transcendence persistently deny *and require* each other and in turn properly deny and ultimately require the religous transcendence. One affirmation has warred against another and the status of the human person is constantly recovered by reviving one or other form of transcendence against that particular form which happens to be compromised and incorporated in the exigencies of social systems.

The religious affirmation cannot avoid some persistent reservations about secular transcendence or let go its continuing sense of the irony which attends every human achievement, including man's religious aspiration. Irony is an important category in the religious criticism of secular faiths, particularly as these establish themselves as accepted orthodoxies (and accepted unorthodoxies) in concrete social structures. A Gibbon observing our civilization today might well be a Christian. Yet irony is not enough, even though it is part of the Christian 'humour' in every sense of that word. The fruits of the Spirit are love, joy and hope – *gaudium et spes* – and irony is too often the perspective of those who have given up hope. It seems to me that there is a dimension in the human enterprise which is not exhausted and may even be betrayed by any proximate hope or secular city, and that ultimately man turns himself, frail and rejoicing, towards a City whose builder and maker is God. At any rate only the shallowest of positive philosophies and nothing in positive science forbids us to think in terms of what is man's chief end or to answer that his chief end is to know God and enjoy him forever.

NOTES

1. At one time some people were inclined to cite (say) the psychological advantages deriving from uninhibited sexuality at certain periods in the life cycle among, for example, the Samoans as indicating how man's 'true' nature ought to express itself and to advocate parallel developments in our own culture. The argument against this is not only that one does not know this true nature, but also that the costs must be summed up as well, and above all, that what may have one consequence in cultural *gestalt* A may have a totally different consequence in cultural *gestalt* B. In other words, one cannot combine the argument from human plasticity with the argument about man's

true nature to suggest and prescribe what might be done in any given modern society, for reasons which are both scientific and philosophical.

2. Some scientists hold that there is no voluntary celibacy among the animals. Leaving aside the precise force of 'voluntary' in such a context, this clearly suggests that celibacy is peculiarly human, and one's evaluation of that depends on which meaning of 'peculiar' one prefers to employ. Science does not help either those who automatically side with the animals any more than it comforts those who automatically side with the angels: after all man is half beast, half angel according to some influential anthropologies.

3. So far as I know Margaret Mead has no primitivistic leanings.

4. The relationships *between* these three is another and different controversy.

5. Cf. J. Horton, 'Alienation and Anomie', *British Journal of Sociology*, vol. XV, no. 4, December 1964, for a critique of attempts to operationalize such global concepts into sets of discrete measurable traits.

6. H. Stretton, *The Political Sciences: General Principles of Selection in Social Science and History*, Routledge, 1969.

7. Cf. T. Kuhn, *The Structure of Scientific Revolutions*, Phoenix Books, 1962, for a discussion of the way certain very broad paradigms may inform our way of doing research and of the manner whereby one paradigm may supplant another, and I. M. Lakatos and A. Musgrave (eds.), *Criticism and the Growth of Knowledge*, Cambridge University Press, 1970, for an alternative view.

8. For a discussion of the current estimates of the endocrinological aspect, one might consult the forthcoming book by Philip Bradley on the chemistry of the body and personality. For a sociologist there is particular interest in the viability of the endocrinological contribution to studies of criminality.

9. For a discussion of the methods of cure following from this level of analysis (aversion therapy, etc.) see H. Freeman 'Behaviour Therapy: A Possibility', *New Society*, no. 7, 15 November 1962.

10. Michael Argyle, 'The Psychology of Morals', *New Society*, no. 52, September 1963, p. 8.

11. Cf. the contributions of N. Chomsky, S. Hampshire and A. MacIntyre to *The Listener*, 30 May 1968. A good summary of structuralism is provided in the Introduction by R. Poole to C. Levi-Strauss, *Totemism*, Pelican Books, 1969, and in E. Leach, *Claude Levi-Strauss*, Fontana Books, 1970.

12. For some of the philosophical implications cf. E. Gellner, 'On Chomsky', *New Society*, no. 348, 29 May 1969. Gellner argues that Chomsky is really attacking all interior *verstehende* explanations of our human linguistic competence, replacing them by highly ordered 'deep structures' not entirely available to consciousness. Gellner also notes that Chomsky's attack on behaviouristic analyses of linguistic competence (e.g. in terms of association) and on analogies with animal communication in favour of 'deep structures' seems to run counter to the modern attempt to establish the unity of man with nature and suggests a radical idiosyncrasy for man. George Steiner in a magisterial essay on the status of man (*Encounter*, August 1969) certainly applauds Chomsky for doing just this.

13. For a recent critique cf. J. Lewis and B. Towers, *Naked Ape or Homo Sapiens? A Reply to Desmond Morris*, Garnstone Press, 1969. Ch. 5 is particularly relevant.

14. Thus Lionel Tiger in *Men in Groups*, Nelson, 1969, where he further argues that the pattern of male bonding is the backbone of the community (pub, political meeting, club, football match, secret society) and underlies all organized political and social activity. Cf. also D. Morris, *The Naked Ape*,

Jonathan Cape, 1967, *The Human Zoo*, Cape, 1969, and V. Reynolds ,'The Animal Society IV: Social Bonds' in *The Listener*, 27 April, 1967.

15. Cf. R. Aron, *Peace and War*, Weidenfeld and Nicolson, 1962, for a superb exemplification of the range of explanation appropriate to human warfare. Pages 339 ff. are especially appropriate to this context.

16. E. Leach, *Runaway World*, Reith Lectures, BBC, 1968, p. 21.

17. *Ibid.*, p. 23. Cf. also E. Leach, *Levi-Strauss*, p. 43: 'Animals of all kinds respond mechanically to appropriate signals; this process does not entail "symbolic thought". This involves the ability to distinguish between the sign and the thing it signifies and then . . . to recognize that there is a relation between the sign and the thing signified.'

18. Leach in *Runaway World* points out that analogies between men and machines do not rely on comparisons with pieces of complicated metal but on such notions as that a machine 'is a structured system which works'.

19. With regard to language, see for example Sol Tax, ed., *Horizons Anthropology*, Allen and Unwin, 1965. In ch. 7 Susan Ervin suggests that human language is unique not so much in its particular features as in its combination of them.

20. The status of Pareto's residues is disputed: Werner Stark refers to them as 'physical, animalic' and describes Pareto as 'blinded by the timelessness and universality of mechanical regularities'.

21. Cf. P. Rieff's article in B. Mazlish, ed., *Psychoanalysis and History*, Prentice Hall, 1963.

22. Cf. P. Rieff, *The Mind of the Moralist*, Gollancz, 1960, ch. 10. The same author's comments on Jung in *The Triumph of the Therapeutic*, Chatto and Windus, 1966, are extremely perceptive.

23. I lean here on the account given by D. Cargnello, 'From Psychoanalytic Naturalism to Phenomenological Anthropology', in *Human Context*, ed. Paul Senft, vol. 1, no. 1, August 1968.

24. D. Cargnello, *op. cit.*, p. 79.

25. Cf. R. D. Laing, *The Divided Self*, Tavistock Publications, 1960, particularly ch. 1 on 'The Existential-Phenomenological Foundations for a Science of Persons'. I understand that an important text for assessing the variety of possible approaches is J. Bowlby, *Attachment and Loss*, vol. 1, Hogarth Press, 1969.

26. It seems to me that the notion of different 'conventions' within which something is 'understood' results in a conception of each separate culture as essentially a floating island, neither interconnected with other cultures nor rooted in the various sub-soils of the natural world. Cf. P. S. Cohen's cogent summary of this controversy 'The very idea of a social science' in I. M. Lakatos and A. Musgrave (eds.), *Problems in the Philosophy of Science*, Collier-Macmillan, 1969.

27. I rest here on P. Berger and T. Luckmann, *The Social Construction of Reality*, Allen Lane, 1966, pp. 65–70. The work of these two sociologists is of particular importance for the recovery of a humanistic and phenomenological understanding of man, although I think it fair to say that in Britain, the home of empiricism, the humanistic perspective has been constantly maintained. In this respect British culture retained enough tradition to be abreast of the future!

28. For an expansion of this notion, see p. 257.

29. These are usually termed 'functional prerequisites' by sociologists. A neat statement is provided by D. F. Aberle *et al.* in *Ethics*, January 1950. He

indicates such prerequisites as a pattern of sexual recruitment and socialization, role differentiation and role assignment (adequately legitimated), a communication system, shared cognitive orientations, shared goals, regulation of means of emotional expression, and so on.

30. Cf. M. Ginsberg, 'National Character and National Sentiments' (1955) in *On the Diversity of Morals*, vol. 1 of *Essays in Sociology and Social Philosophy* (1956), Penguin Books, 1968. Cf. also W. J. H. Sprott, *Social Psychology*, Methuen, 1952, ch. 10.

31. Cf. T. Morris, *The Criminal Area*, Routledge, 1957, the first part of which clearly summarizes the history and approach of the ecological school in criminology.

32. L. MacDonald, *Social Class and Delinquency*, Faber, 1969, shows, for example, how crime increases with each decrease in educational level.

33. Cf. J. Dominian, *Marital Breakdown*, Penguin, 1968, for a clear statement of the social patterning of divorce and breakdown by a Catholic psychiatrist.

34. It is important to mention here the subjective aspect of objective structure found in the 'interactionist' approach exemplified by E. Goffman, H. Garfinkel and D. Matza. Interactionism concentrates not on the objective structural predispositions nor even on the motives of the agent towards a given line of conduct, but on the pattern of action and perception arising from mutual labelling and typing. In this view deviance is not 'an act' but a process of exposure to typing by others (and by the deviant himself), which results in an increasing assimilation of the self to the preferred label and the adoption of a particular sort of 'moral career'. Cf. E. Rubington and M. S. Weinberg, *Deviance: the Interactionist Perspective*, Collier-Macmillan, 1968.

35. In the original plan of this essay I also intended to indicate the various levels of approach in psychology in relation to the moral development of the child, ranging from (1) 'conformity-learning' to (2) 'identification-guilt' to (3) 'the development of judgment' approach associated with Piaget. For a succinct summary cf. J. D. Halloran, *Attitude Formation and Change*, Leicester University Press, 1967, Appendix A.

36. Cf. G. Homans 'On Bringing Men Back In' in *American Sociological Review*, December 1964. It is interesting that Homans tries to import the essentials of *homo economicus* into sociology. The result is an increase in abstraction, an apparent increase in rigour and a swing to deductive principles.

37. Cf. W. J. M. MacKenzie, *Politics and Social Science*, Penguin, 1967, pp. 120 ff. A great deal of 'peace research' operates on this type of principle, not to mention the operations of the CIA.

38. For a useful statement of Mead's social psychology, cf. P. Berger and T. Luckmann, *The Social Construction of Reality*, pp. 151 ff. In n. 7 on p. 270 they point out that Marxists would find more congruence in Mead with their notion of 'man as a self-producing being' than in Freud.

39. It has been suggested that the ability to achieve freedom by distancing oneself from one's roles varies with status position. In other words at a certain level human freedom is not universal but variably distributed in terms of different social contexts. We need a statement of the levels at which freedom is variable and the levels at which it is universal. Cf. J. Ford, D. Young and S. Box, 'Functional Autonomy, Role Distance and Social Class', *The British Journal of Sociology*, vol. XVIII, no. 4, December 1967.

40. In the work of Schutz these are labelled 'secondary typifications' as distinct from the 'pregiven typifications' of everyday life. For an account of

Schutz, cf. chs. 4 and 5 in Winter and the Introduction by George Walsh to Schutz, *The Phenomenology of the Social World*, Northwestern University Press, Evanston, 1967.

41. Winter, *op. cit.*, ch. 6.

42. For an affirmation which involves all three forms of secular transcendence and therefore the more rigidly contradicts the religious affirmation, cf. L. Trotsky, *Literature and Revolution*, Allen and Unwin, 1925, pp. 249–56, reprinted in C. W. Mills, *The Marxists*, Penguin, 1963, pp. 277–81.

PART FIVE

The Human as a Criterion

For the first time in history we can see the oneness of mankind as a reality.

The Report of Uppsala, Section III, par. 1.

13

Racism or Christian Faith – the Categorical Choice

J. ROBERT NELSON

I

The problem of prejudice becomes increasingly acute as the human population becomes more numerous and compacted. There was a time in most lands when persons of different racial groups who disliked each other could simply maintain separate spheres of living and thus avoid conflict. Such deliberate isolation is more difficult to achieve in the present time, when rapidly growing populations have a high capacity for mobility. Migrating with ease from country to country, and generally disposed to settle in great cities, they have caused homogeneous societies to become rare and obsolescent. No longer is it only the seaports which are mixing bowls of races and nationalities, but the inland cities and towns as well. Whereas in former times a foreign visitor with differing facial features and colour of skin may have been treated with polite curiosity and a certain respect, the presence of large numbers of foreign intruders now causes feelings of suspicion and resentment. Thus are seen the signs of new racism in Great Britain, especially, and in some countries of Western Europe. Australia is trying to prevent the difficulty by maintaining a policy permitting only white immigrants. The United States, in spite of its declaration that the equality of all men is a self-evident fact, has for many years maintained discriminatory laws which tell some people that they are undesirable. But racism is not a new phenomenon, of course. Despite their apparent similarities, as seen by occidental eyes, the differences between Chinese and Koreans or Japanese or Vietnamese have been sufficient

K

to cause instinctive hostilities and conflicts for many centuries. The British have only recently experienced serious racial tensions in their own small isles, but during the era of imperial extension over Africa and Asia they have given ample expression to their feeling of distaste for the 'lesser breeds' of mankind. And so have the Spanish and Portuguese and Germans and Belgians and Dutch. The unparalleled diversities of racial and ethnic groups migrating to North America have accounted for some of the most vicious and complicated patterns of prejudice, made all the more horrendous by the melancholy history of Negro slavery and the century of suppression and exploitation following the annulment of legal slavery by the Civil War. Receiving lesser attention until recently have been the irreparable injustices and atrocities visited upon the indigenous peoples of lands seized, conquered and settled by Europeans and British. The Indian tribes of North and South America, the Eskimoes of Canada and Alaska, the Aborigines of Australia, the Maoris of New Zealand, the indigenous peoples of Southern Africa have been so brutally treated for so long a time that few white people even pause to consider their plight.

This brief sketch of the dreary landscape of racial prejudice is sufficient to remind us that it is a primary problem for ethics and hence for Christian theological understanding. What is the generating source of this power of prejudice? Is it simply inevitable that human beings of one race should try to wreak indignities upon others? Must we accept the fact that economic exploitation and political suppression will always be imposed upon powerless peoples, along with social segregation, limitation of educational opportunities, and other restrictions of human rights?

Scarcely any nation, ethnic or religious group, or well-defined social class has been free from the attitude and practice of prejudice. But this nearly universal scope of human discord affords no comfort to the minority of the earth's population who are called Christians. More than any other religious faith, Christianity has been presented to mankind as a way of forgiveness, love and uninhibited community. These virtues are not lacking in other religions. But neither Judaism not Islam nor Hinduism nor Buddhism has been commended for its universalism to the degree that Christianity has. It is all the more humiliating to Christians, therefore, that they more than other religious adherents are vulnerable to the charge of the greatest excesses in the practice of racism. This is a primary reason why the Christian faith has been discredited in the eyes of millions of persons today, and why many of these who would not be attracted to other religions have chosen to espouse no faith other than the ideologies either of democratic humanism or Marxism. It is why many of these people, who devote their energies to the task of eliminating racism, can disregard the insights and values proposed by Christians and find their norms for human equity and justice in the realm of philosophies alone.

A serious theological problem, then, is precisely that of the impotence of faith and theological statement in respect to racism. Perhaps it is sheer illusion to think that there is a consistent sequence of cause and effect which begins with the attitude of faith in the God of love through the figure of Jesus Christ, stirs the believers to commit themselves to the welfare of all men, and empowers them to cast off all prejudice and to seek liberty and justice for all. If such thought be illusory, certain corollaries present themselves to the mind. One is that Christian faith itself is an illusion. Another is that virtually all Christians are guilty of hypocrisy or lack of seriousness about the ethical mandates of their faith. Or a third, as some have insisted, is that the faith is relative only to matters of personal spirituality and salvation rather than to human relations and social morality.

None of these three is convincing, even though each contains an element of truth. That is, there are *interpretations* of Christian faith, accepted by some at least, which are illusory. Belief in human perfectibility or in a predictable and apocalyptic second coming of Christ would serve as examples. That *many* Christians are hypocritical cannot be denied, but not so many as to render all professions of faith meaningless. Also, the personal dimension of Christianity as a way of salvation for the individual is indispensable, but it by no means excludes the relevance to corporate life and social well-being. The reason for Christianity's impotence to suppress and overcome racism is different from these three.

It is a blend of several elements: they are negative, not positive; they are deficiencies rather than undesirable possessions. One is a widespread lack of knowledge of the Christian teachings which lie below the cultic conventions and perfunctory practices of church membership. Another is the insufficiency of commitment in faith to the self-sacrificing style of discipleship, which is concomitant with devotion to Jesus Christ. A third is the limited and astigmatic vision of many Christians in regard to the consequences of Christ's life for the reconciling of human beings to one another and their mutual caring. When this triple defect is considered in the light of the prevailing egoism and acquisitiveness of the human being, as well as the pervasive influence of the *mores* and traditions of one's own society, culture and nation, it is all the more understandable – not excusable! – that racism survives and even flourishes in nominally Christian societies.

There is a further factor in the apparent failure of Christians in their totality to live up to what the world legitimately expects of them. It is

more a description than an explanation. This is the variability of
sensitivity to what is primary and urgent for the Christian life, as one
generation is compared to its predecessors. What is tolerable in one
generation or century becomes wholly intolerable in another. From
the same biblical source and from the same fund of traditional teaching
come diametrically opposed convictions in the succession of centuries.
Heresy-hunting, witch-burning, Jew-baiting, Negro slavery and slave-
trading, exploiting the labour of women and children, monarchical
autocracy, ecclesiastical erastianism and caesaro-papism have all been
condoned by churches in the past; but all are condemned in the present.
Yet ostensibly the same Christian faith has been professed in past
and present. Is there no constancy in ethical mandates? Or does historical
relativism decree that there are no perennial mandates?

Excessive preoccupatjon with these flaws in the fabric of faith can
so unnerve an individual or a group of Christians as to paralyse their
assaults upon the attitudes and institutions of racism. Both the past and
present defects of Christian performance have to be admitted, as well
as the fact that changing time and circumstance affect our estimate
of ethical priorities. If Christians of South Africa or South Carolina
or Southampton argue that the Bible and theology support their
policies of white supremacy and racial segregation, it is quite obvious
that their thinking has been strongly influenced by social and economic
factors which are of strictly secular origin. But secular factors of another
kind lead other white Christians to contrary convictions favouring
civil and social equality for members of all races. Is there no effective
authority by which perplexed Christians can be led away from this
dilemma?

The problem of a credible moral authority to be heeded and obeyed
is far more acute for Protestants than it is for Roman Catholics and
Orthodox. But recent disputes over another moral issue of first magnitude, namely birth control and the population explosion, have demonstrated beyond doubt that even the word of the Pope, as the teacher of
faith and morals, does not command the assent and obedience of all
Catholic Christians. These dissenting Catholics are demanding precisely
the same kind of guidance to which most Protestants have been long
accustomed, namely, that of representative synods or councils which are
convened on the principle of collegiality.

The nearest approach to such an authoritative body for non-Roman
Christians is an assembly of the World Council of Churches. Stress
is laid upon the words 'nearest approach' because the World Council's
constitutional authority over the churches is negligible. Nevertheless,
it is the body with the widest diversity of Christian representatives,
who bring to its deliberations the greatest variety of concerns, view-

points and convictions. It is highly important for all Christians, therefore, that the World Council of Churches (and its preceding organizations of the ecumenical movement) have consistently and with increasing intensity denounced all forms of racial discrimination as contrary and inimical to the gospel of Jesus Christ. The Council has not been content with its solemn rhetorical denunciations, however. It has encouraged the churches, and has directed some of its own modest agencies to undertake specific actions to oppose racism and promote inter-racial understanding, justice and reconciliation. Yet it was fully evident at the Uppsala Assembly that these actions have been too paltry and timid, and that the Council and the churches must speedily multiply their efforts to salvage from the many scenes of tension and conflict what remains of opportunity for creating tolerably just societies.

What are the theological resources for sustaining an approximate consensus on the evil of racism and the urgent need for eradicating it? There are at least four. They are: the conception of human identity, the meaning of reconciliation through Jesus Christ, the inclusive character of the church, and the practical exercise of love, power and justice. A critical examination of these four resources constitutes the main portion of this essay.

II   *The Conception of Human Identity*

Not man in general but a man in particular is the first datum for a theological inquiry into racism. It is he who is the discriminator or else the victim of discrimination within the broad social milieu. He belongs to a variety of concentric and overlapping social circles, wherein racial prejudice takes effect. But the primary locus of that effect is not the circle, but himself as the centre of it.

By introspection he knows that he possesses intelligence. He may never have heard of René Descartes, but he is aware of the dependence of his existence upon his ability to think.

He knows further that he is an individual, a unique person, an irreplaceable ego. He may never hear of Adolf von Harnack, but he senses that the value of his life – to himself and to God – is infinite.

Nature and human society place upon him all manner of restrictions and restraints; but despite these inherent or imposed necessities, he rejoices in a degree of freedom. He himself can determine what he will think, what choices he will make, and what actions he will take. He may not have read Immanuel Kant, but he understands that his identity requires his freedom.

Always lurking in his mind is the thought of his finitude and mortality. His religion and his culture may teach him to regard death in a manner different from the attitude of other people. But he does not need a brooding philosopher like Ecclesiastes (Koheleth) to tell him that eventually he must die.

Meanwhile he lives the days of his years upon the earth, in relation to his family and friends, dependent upon both nature and civilization, experiencing in varying measure both enjoyment and suffering in spirit and body. He may not be consciously either Hellenic or Hebraic in his concept of man, but he is well aware of the symbiosis of body and spirit and their unity in his person.

These are among the elemental ingredients which make the human animal to be the human person. These are the definite and universal elements shared by every man, which are known by experience: more concrete than the *imago Dei*, which is acknowledged only by faith. Whatever the pigment of epidermis, the shape of eye-sockets and nostrils and lips, or the texture of hair among the varieties of mankind's millions, each one is a person because he has intelligence, freedom, individuality of spirit and body, and a knowledge of death.

It ought to be as simple as that. Every human being ought to be regarded with due respect by every one who meets him, and that respect diminished only by the unrespectable behaviour of the person himself. But racism or prejudice is the contradiction of that oughtness about human relations. It is the denial of a fellow human being, not because of his personal identity nor his behaviour, but because of his racial identity.

To disregard, minimize or ignore racial identity is not the way to eradicate prejudice, however. This has been the unintended error of good-willed white people who describe themselves as being 'colour-blind'. By pretending that races do not actually exist or that they have no particular importance, such people not only insult others who find beauty and cause for pride in their races; they also implicitly deny the goodness of creation and thus the goodness and wisdom of the Creator himself. It is as disrespectful towards God for them to give him no credit for the varieties of mankind as it is for racists to blame him for causing this distress.

It is well known to anthropologists, of course, that racial identity is no easy thing to ascertain. Where is the line of critical demarcation between white and non-white? Or is 'white' a meaningful racial designation at all? Probably not. Today there is much talk of 'black identity', especially in the United States. But black is not literally a description of the skin colour of all Negroes, since many come of mixed parentage and are exceedingly light of skin. Neither are all persons of truly black skin, such as some Dravidians of South India, properly called Negroes.

Such problems of classification are of interest to geneticists and anthropologists, but not to theologians who are troubled by racism. The blunt fact is that many people of white skin look with condescension or disfavour upon those who are tan, brown or black, and they do all things possible to discourage the latter from securing financial and political power as well as social acceptability and equality in their white societies. In so doing they pour contempt upon the racial groupings to which these others attach themselves either naturally and inevitably or else by deliberate choice. They regard it as self-evident that the racial type called Aryan, Caucasian or white is superior to all others, and indeed is the norm of human excellence. To vindicate such pretension by appeal to revelations and insights which inform the Christian faith is an attempt doomed to failure. Christianity neither suggests nor permits such racial pride.

However inexact may be the delineations of races, it remains true that no individual exists in isolation without some racial identity. There is, naturally, a spectrum of evident identity: many are of 'pure stock'; many are of moderately mixed ancestry but with one strain clearly dominant; and some, as notably in Hawaii, represent such a genetic *mélange* that it is virtually impossible to classify them. Again we say that this question is of interest to empirical anthropologists and geneticists rather than to theologians, whose concept of anthropology (or doctrine of man) is more concerned with the marks of universal humanity as found in each person than with the external and secondary characteristics. Nevertheless, the theologian must be cognizant of the fact that racism, which is a denial of the truth of his 'theological anthropology', springs from human prejudices which are caused precisely by these differentiations of external characteristics. It is his vocation as a Christian thinker to demonstrate that the varieties of human types are manifestly good as a part of God's good creation; that self-conscious awareness of belonging to a particular race or of having biological derivation from two or more races is natural and unobjectionable, since no human being can be free from some racial identity; but that ideas and dogmas of racial superiority and inferiority are wholly unwarranted.

This last assertion about superiority is supported not only by theological insights but also by a wide consensus of scientists. For example, there is a popular notion that the attainment of higher levels of civilization and technological skill is determined by an innate racial quality. But a group of internationally recognized experts declared in a report for UNESCO that 'current biological knowledge does not permit us to impute cultural achievements to differences in genetic potential'. It is their studied conviction that the obvious varieties of mankind's cultures – a concept which begs for definition yet defies it – are not due to genetic, but to environmental, factors. This judgment brings comfort to those who for religious and ethical reasons espouse the belief in the unity of mankind and the undifferentiated equality of diverse races. It is a basis upon which can be constructed strategies and plans for developing a fully integrated society. And as will be shown, it is especially congenial to Christian understanding of inclusive community.

It is ironical, however, that this interpretation of the divorce between race and culture is most unwelcome to many Negroes, especially in the United States. Representing only 10 per cent of the population, wanting to have full and equal opportunity as citizens, and yet dreading assimilation into the predominantly Anglo-Saxon/American culture, they deliberately insist upon the integrity of their Afro-American tradition and way of life. Having been forcibly deprived of this by the slave traders who bought their ancestors, contemporary black Americans are striving to recapture and assert what they regard as their own black culture. Think black, sing black, study black, eat black!

This is no question of superiority of either black or white people. Only those who are most prejudiced against Negroes would question the ability of members of that race to live as responsible participants in the culture of a predominantly white nation. This has been demonstrated many times, not only by Negroes but also by Chinese and others. But this is not the important question. More urgent is the question of whether it is desirable and just for a majority of white citizens, whose cultural roots are British and Continental European, to expect the minority of African or Chinese ancestry to conform in all ways to the majority's way of life. The same kind of issue now confronts white British people with respect to the 'coloured immigrants' from India, Pakistan and the West Indies. And a similar problem, though not quite the same, has been experienced by many countries in relation to the Jews. The simple alternative to social and cultural assimilation was invented centuries ago: the ghetto. First devised to contain Jews within a limited quarter of a city, it was later adapted under the name of Chinatown or New York's Harlem. But the justification for these confining urban enclaves is neither clear nor uniformly applicable. While not so different physically from the white Gentile majority, the Jews have had an ancient and distinctive culture, a particular language, and a strong religious identity which marks them as God's particular people. Anti-semitism and the persecution of the Jews are not, then, strictly speaking expressions of racism. The Chinese have likewise been maintaining their solidarity in occidental societies because of their traditional linguistic and religious bonds, but also because of racial homogeneity. But the black ghettoes are due primarily to the racial factor, to which cultural patterns are secondary.

It is argued by short-sighted or prejudiced Anglo-Saxons that 'they' really prefer to live to themselves. The 'they' can pertain to any racial, ethnic or national group other than themselves. And certainly in a democratic society 'they' ought to be free to choose where and how they wish to live. But the issue is by no means so simple, of course. It is ambivalent for all concerned. All people, both 'we' and 'they', desire to spend their lives with the people whom they find congenial; or if congeniality and community seem less important to some, they wish to live where and how they please. But the all-important factor is the free choice, in contrast to the brutal coercion applied by those who are economically and politically powerful and who nourish prejudice against other races and peoples. Some Jews may prefer the ghetto, but should be free to join the diaspora. The same with Chinese and Negroes in Europe and America, or with Indians in East Africa, Algerians in France, etc. In every case the freedom of movement and location depends upon the prior concession by the powerful majority of the full civil rights and opportunities of all persons in the nation; and the freedom is obviously conditioned by the economic means to exercise it.

When the fair-minded, objective UNESCO experts rejected the necessary correlation between race and culture, they had ample reason to believe that their judgment was happily in the best interests of the oppressed races. Nor did they intend to deprecate such recognizable cultural patterns as are usually associated with certain races, such as those of Polynesians, Japanese, Indonesians, or the Africans of Zambia, Jamaica, or New Orleans. They did not mean that this correlation is impossible, nor judge it to be undesirable; they said it is not necessary. There is nothing in this thesis which is incompatible with a Christian theological understanding of man and his relation to his fellows and to the rest of creation. It gives support to the belief in the equal worth of all human beings, and thus undercuts the basis for inordinate esteem of a particular race for itself. However, it does not reject the legitimacy of recognizing how diverse cultures have developed among people of diverse races. And it tacitly permits the hope that there can be in the same country a pluralism of races and cultures without the distressing attitudes and practices of racial discrimination.

The foregoing discussion of human identity emphasizes the universal quality of humanity in all persons as well as the inevitability of each one's finding further identity in a particular race. These are data which can be discerned by scientists; they can also be interpreted by theologians as the consequences of the creation of man by God. But there is an aspect of man which is more evident to the theologian than to the scientist, and which has considerable bearing upon the problem of racism. This is the brokenness or contradiction within the human identity, which biblical faith candidly designates as sin. It is the dynamic and demonic power of alienation which is at work in every person. Every observer can see how it sets a man against his brother or his neighbour. A believer can attest that it sets a man against his Creator and Lord. To employ the biblical concept, mankind as a whole, and thus every single member of it, is fallen. He is fallen from a putative state of righteousness, which need not be posited as a once-upon-a-time condition of earthly man. It is, rather, the real but inexplicable contradiction between what a man is and what God's intention for him is.

The symbolic patrimony of Cain, who wilfully slew his brother, has been inherited by all. It is commonly expressed in the myriad daily attitudes and acts of selfishness, aggression and hostility which characterize the lives of men and women. Apart from a serious consideration of this human defect, by whatever name known, there can be no adequate inquiry into the insidious phenomena of racism.

Still avoiding the literal acceptance of mythical language in the Bible, we can take seriously what it says about the 'demonic powers' and corrupting forces which are manifestly at work in the world today. Perhaps they are best described as the uncontrollable inclinations to malevolence, which are precipitated by the suspicion and distrust of one's fellow human being. Man's whole history is marked by the destructive actions arising from xenophobia. The fear of what is strange and foreign puts one on guard against attack and danger; then in order to eliminate the danger before it strikes, an offensive blow is delivered. In the realm of human relations, and especially between races, these blows need not always be physical and kinetic. They may take the form of verbal insults, injurious subterfuges, subtle strategies to deprive the other of his advantages or powers or human rights. Xenophobia is likewise expressed in dermaphobia, the fear or rejection of a different skin.

The 'demonic powers' are manifest not only in the hurtful inclinations of individuals and groups, but also in the movements, organizations and institutions which get out of hand and become uncontrollable. Industrial and commercial enterprises which profit by exploiting cheap black labour gain irrevocable momentum; racist laws are enacted in times of fear or panic, and they defy amendment or repeal; processes of deterioration and decay in city slums outstrip the resources and actions available to correct them; popular movements for reform are transmuted into anarchical and violent uprisings.

Somehow the human identity is linked to this mystery of iniquity.

Not only with respect to racism, but in many aspects of existence, people are thus ensnared in a net of irrationality and malevolence, from which the extrication is literally a divine work of salvation.

III   *Reconciliation through Jesus Christ*

Many people who are not Christians have clear ideas about the nature of man, his relation to race and culture, the evil and corruption at work in human society, and the need for justice and peace. These may be adherents of other religions or of no religion. They may be democratic humanists, existentialists or Marxists. And they have a great passion to eliminate racial prejudice and racist practice. Sharing this concern with Christians, they often assume that the Christian perspective (in so far as it is not corrupted by the well-known distortions expressed by church members) is virtually the same as their own. In fact, it seems that in the struggle for racial justice there are many agnostics and atheists who are 'better Christians' than some believers in Christ.

Is there any significant difference? Yes; for the Christian, if true to his professed faith, draws his guidance *explicitly* from Jesus Christ. It can be argued successfully that many a non-Christian is *implicitly* following Christ. But the Christian knows whom he believes and is expected to act accordingly.

What does Jesus Christ have to do with racism?

The relevant reports of the Uppsala Assembly do not make this very clear. Those dealing with social and economic problems (Section III) and world peace (Section IV) mention that 'Christ died for all', that he 'has already won the victory over all the "principalities and powers",' and that he has come to reconcile and make peace. These familiar words communicate deep meaning to those who already understand them theologically, but for others are puzzling and annoying because of their elusive vagueness. Section I dealt with the church's catholicity, within which it included an appeal for the end of racial segregation on the basis of Christ's work:

The unity of man is grounded for the Christian not only in his creation by the one God in his own image, but in Jesus Christ who 'for us men' became man, was crucified, and who constitutes the Church which is his body as a new community of new creatures (par. 21).

This confession, too, is pregnant with theological meaning for the informed believer; but it does little to demonstrate how Jesus the Christ actually effected the new condition of human unity. Can the 'work of Christ' be made more explicit? How does it affect our situation of racial divisions and tensions?

Racism as we know it now is a relatively modern phenomenon. We should not expect to find in the New Testament the concrete answers to our questions, which were not asked in the first century. However, there was at that time in the Roman Empire a kind of absolute separation of human beings which was due more to legal than to racial distinctions. The Roman citizen could reject, despise or mistreat any Jew or Greek or barbarian or African who did not enjoy the privilege of citizenship or the right to own slaves. It was the civil law which gave him his power and sense of superiority. For the Jews, however, it was the religious law which determined that they should have few dealings with the uncircumcised Gentile. The stronger the devotion to Torah, the wider the separation from all others who were unclean.

Both the civil and the religious grounds for separation probably aroused feelings of discrimination similar to those felt by racially prejudiced people in the modern era. These constitute an ancient analogy to our present problem. So it is instructive to note how Jesus addressed himself to the condition of segregated persons, employing both his words and actions to combat the prejudices and to make peace. Indeed, in the broadest consideration of Jesus' ministry and mission it is rightly said that he came to establish *shalom* between God and men, and thus among men. His verbal and active defence of the despised of society, the outsiders and the unclean, are recorded in the gospels. Because of the brevity of these writings, we cannot know how much else he did to reprove the strictly exclusive Jews for their closed minds and hard hearts. But the gospels tell enough to convey the sense of scandal and outrage which Jesus provoked. In his first appearance as a teaching rabbi in the synagogue at Nazareth, his own city, he incited the Jews to an attempt to kill him because he emphasized how God had favoured non-Jews such as the widow of Sidon and the unclean leper of Syria (Luke 4.26–27). He taught the universal mercy of God, falling as sunlight and rain upon the just and the unjust, and thus insisted upon prayers for one's persecutors and enemies (Matt. 5.44–45). In his decisive parable of the good neighbour he exalted the merciful Samaritan over the priests and Levites (Luke 10.33); and when Jesus passed through Samaria he broke the rules of law and custom by drinking water with a Samaritan woman and conversing intimately with her (John 4.9). He even paid tribute to a centurion of the hated Roman army of occupation, saying that this Gentile had more faith than anyone in Israel (Matt. 8.10).

It is often declared that Jesus' words were events or deeds in themselves. They were effective signs of what it means for the reign of God to be breaking into man's present history. The gospels record no carefully reasoned discourses of Jesus in which he tries to persuade his fellow Jews to change their attitudes; neither do they report any rousing exhortations, in which Jesus appeals to abstract principles of justice and equality. His words and deeds have power for two main reasons. First, because they are concrete and unmistakable. Second, because of his personal identity as the doer and speaker.

Christians would pay little attention to these instances of 'xenophilia' in Jesus' ministry if they did not believe him to be the Anointed One of God, the Messiah or Christ. It is for this same cause that the event of Good Friday and Easter is of highest significance for the appraisal of racism today. It is not the genius of the Christian gospel to promise that men's lives are changed, peace established, and salvation effected by the persuasive power of Jesus' teaching alone. The symbol of faith is a cross, not a parchment scroll. The vicarious Christ-figure has had profound impact upon human ethical and spiritual sensitivity, both in visual art and literature, precisely because the real Christ died a real death for the sake of all human beings. 'Christ died for all' is thus the corollary of 'God created all'.

The implications of the death and resurrection of Jesus Christ are inexhaustible. They have challenged the wisdom and interpretative skill of believers for many centuries. But two emphases, which were already perceived by the New Testament apostolic church, are especially meaningful for today's struggle with racism.

One interpretation of his work employs the language of conquest and victory over demonic or satanic forces. The other is that his radically obedient life, his vicarious death, and his triumph over death are not only exemplary for his disciples, but effectual for creating community of all sorts and conditions of human beings. Each of these speaks powerfully to Christians who are in any way involved in racial divisions today.

Attention has already been called to the reality and pervasiveness of corrupting and destructive powers at work in the world. However they may be demythologized and by whatever name they may now be called, they represent the irrational and uncontrollable forces of evil, which frustrate the best plans and hopes of men. Now it would be inexcusably naïve, and indeed an evidence of pretension, to claim that all the corrupting powers at work in the world today have been rendered ineffectual by Jesus Christ. Their continuing effects are too well known to allow such a claim to be taken seriously. What, then, was accomplished by his self-sacrifice?

First, the true nature and identity of evil was exposed, stripped of its secrecy, for all to see and understand. As the very incarnation of divine love, he had been brought to humiliation and death by allegedly the most righteous and legally just people. His death vindicated his earlier teaching, that compliance with cultic regulations and per-functory religious obligations is hypocrisy or worse so long as the will and spirit of a man are corrupt. The pure white sepulchre is filled with dead bones. The corrupt tree cannot produce good fruit. Not only the secret sins of the heart, but the murderous acts of violent men were epitomized on Golgotha as they brutally killed the perfectly innocent and uncomplaining Jesus. So the cross on the Jerusalem hill has been for all mankind the epiphany of human acquiescence to evil powers, such as those, for example, which have caused the enslavement and suppression and exploitation of certain races.

Second, the imperfection and vulnerability of evil, and even the limited power of death itself, became evident in the resurrection of Christ. For Christian faith, rather than for empirical observation, this Easter event is both the supreme meaning of Christ and the best hope for mankind. If death, as annihilation and final destruction of life, represents the final work of evil, then there is hope in the faith that God has placed limits upon it by raising Jesus from its lethal bonds. Thus, all those attitudes, movements, institutions and powers which today we call 'de-humanizing' and deadly are placed under the judgment of God in Christ.

Finally, as a consequence of the whole dedicated life of Jesus Christ there was let loose in the world a power of opposition to the evil which works for man's destruction. This is the movement of love and recon-ciliation, the aim of which is *shalom* between man and God and man and his brother, the price of which is man's free choice to be a follower of this way, and the power of which is the presence of God's Spirit. The conscious bearer of this way of love is the community of Christ, the church; although any who live by love are unconscious bearers of it; and many in the church membership have shown gross infidelity by ignoring the mission of his love for all men.

The second emphasis in interpreting the effect of Jesus' life, death and resurrection is that the natural and historical barriers to human community were dissolved. The apostles themselves found this to be a literally miraculous happening. In a time when it was believed to be inconceivable and impossible that Jews and Gentiles could accept one another mutually in religious community, this very thing took place. There was at first considerable tension and even hostility within the growing apostolic churches. We cannot really feel the anguish of the Jewish Christians who discovered to their dismay that the same God of Israel was now claiming Gentiles to be members of his people and sharers of the covenant. The agony felt by, let us say, a convinced white supremacist when he first experienced a situation of full social equality with Negroes is comparable. For a time, Peter was so agitated over the revolution taking place that he would permit himself no fellow-ship with Paul (Gal. 2). But when conditions became such as to show that 'there is neither Jew nor Greek', since believers 'are all one in Christ Jesus' (Gal. 3.28), this was regarded as a manifestation of God's eternal will for man, his 'mystery' which was revealed and made operative through Christ's work (Eph. 3.3). The best explanation the apostle could suggest was that the ancestral religious and ethnic barriers had been abolished by Jesus Christ on the cross. Divisive laws, ordin-ances, prejudices, patterns of segregation were abolished in his flesh, by the giving of his life's blood for the sake of reconciliation (Eph. 2.14–17).

It was not mere rhetoric, then, when the Uppsala Assembly de-nounced racism because 'it denies the effectiveness of the reconciling work of Jesus Christ'. This is equivalent, of course, to calling racism the very nemesis of Christian faith. It is apostasy, taking one's stand apart from Christ. Because of the gravity of such language, it should be used with sobriety, which means with the determination to eradicate racism as the condition from which Christ's influence is excluded.

Founded on faith in what Jesus Christ has done for human recon-ciliation, an exceedingly persuasive 'Message to the People of South Africa' against any kind of racial discrimination or segregation on the part of Christians was issued in 1968 by the South African Council of Churches. (It can be read in *The Ecumenical Review*, January 1969.) With much fervour and, in that land of *apartheid*, much courage, the Council urged Christians to remember what the gospel includes. It proclaims Jesus Christ as Reconciler, not a general notion of human equality in creation nor idealistic principles of brotherhood. It tells how the ministry, crucifixion and resurrection of Jesus Christ defeated and negated the powers of human divisiveness by reconciling men first to God. Segregation, or separate development of races, is thus condemned as a contradiction of the gospel. This bold message is a model of the application of the explicit work of Christ to the current situation of racism.

Turning from the traditional concept of Christ's work of reconcilia-tion to that of his person, we find that the results of the hard-fought christological debates of the fourth and fifth centuries still have much to say about the reconciling of races today.

The historic confession that Jesus Christ was both true man and true God was not intended to be just a pious speculation. Neither was it just a doxological statement used to promote praise to Christ. Rather, the confession is a statement of belief and understanding about the meaning of humanity. Christians who either intentionally or unwittingly allow their mentalities to be racist should reckon with the fact that Jesus Christ assumed the humanity of all persons of all races, both of the discriminator and the victim of discrimination. To ignore or despise or hate persons of other races, or indeed any persons, thus means to show the same inimical attitude towards Christ.

In asserting that Jesus Christ is at one with all humanity we do not minimize the importance of his particularity as a first-century Jewish rabbi. Many people find symbolic value in portraying Jesus as a member of their own ethnic group. A Chinese Jesus stills the storm on the Yangtze River; an Indian Christ meets a low caste woman at the village well; or a Black Messiah purges a church belonging to white people. These conceptions constitute a needed protest against the long-accepted distortions in European and American Christian art, which present Jesus as an Italian saint, an Anglo-Saxon prophet, or even a Teutonic deity. But the effect of such ethnic depictions is also negative and misleading, making people forget that the individual and historical form of Jesus' humanity was clearly that of a Jew. Anti-semitism and white racism are equally reprehensible; although due to differing causes, they are both incompatible with authentic Christianity. Still there is particular poignancy in the anti-semitism expressed by prejudiced Christians, for by it they are rejecting in fact the Jewishness of Jesus of Nazareth. Had he been born in China or the Congo, inheriting the characteristics and culture of either of these lands and peoples, the same observation could be made. All humanity without discrimination was assumed in the Incarnation of the Word of God; but his earthly life began as the son of Jewish Mary under the particular circumstances of Israel's tradition and Mediterranean history. Thus it was first to Israel, and to the church as its successor movement, that Jesus entrusted the message and task of reconciling all men everywhere in each generation.

The other dimension of the christological confession tells of the hope to be found in Jesus Christ for the realization of full humanity for men and women in all times. The apostle Paul took the familiar belief in the image of God in all men and transposed it to a higher plane in Christ: from creation to incarnation. Christ was in 'the form of God' (Phil. 2.6), 'the likeness of God' (II Cor. 4.4), 'he is the image of the invisible God' (Col. 1.15). The human import of these ascriptions of divinity is that 'we all . . . are being changed into his likeness from one degree of glory to another' (II Cor. 3.18).

Reflective persons have always sensed the incompleteness of themselves and of all human beings, both as individuals and as members of the human race as it exists in this present stage. Without now becoming involved in the questions of human evolution and emergence, whether discussed by micro-biologists and anthropologists or by so rare a thinker as Pierre Teilhard de Chardin, let it be emphasized that Christian faith sees Jesus Christ as the really humane being. He is not only a great figure of the past to be imitated, but the pioneer and prototype of the man of the future, beckoning us to be conformed to himself.

Christians have no cause for ignoring or despising the secular philosophies which militate against the common enemy of mankind's well-being, which is racism. Appeals to democratic and humanistic principles of human equality, dignity, inalienable rights and justice are valued motivations for action. However, as shown in this exposition of the meaning of Jesus Christ for human reconciliation, there are still deeper roots of motivation for Christians. As for the current efforts and programme to eradicate racism and promote concord among races, it is right that Christians should work with all who share the same objectives. But it is both a theological and strategic question whether Christians understand explicitly why they have a special vocation within this struggle. Are they consciously and faithfully carrying on the work of reconciliation which God initiated in the person and achievements of Jesus Christ? Indispensable to a response to that question is consideration of the place of the community of Christ in history, the church.

IV *The Inclusive Character of the Church*

Only by deliberately avoiding the common knowledge of history can one boast about the peculiar role of the church in combatting modern racism. For the past two centuries or more the churches have often been giving support to the imperial and colonial expansions of European nations in Asia, Africa and the isles. Inevitably joining political control to commercial exploitation of indigenous peoples, the white nations have continued in varying manners to the present time to acquire material profit in exchange for the imposition of indignities. Only in a relatively small way have the churches had the insight and courage to raise protests against this whole process in modern history. The many good actions and brave words of some individual Christians and churches have been commendable and in keeping with the proper character of followers of Christ; but they have been largely obscured from the world's attention by the more obvious complicity, either silent or manifest, of churches in the oppression of non-white peoples.

Nevertheless, it remains as a token of hope and promise that the church, as the people of God and followers of Jesus Christ, is by both nature and vocation in direct opposition to every form of racism. The critical question remains, whether the millions of Christians can find the will to make their theological convictions prevail over economic, political and psychological influences which support and stimulate racism.

It would be less than useless, and even debilitating, to spin out here the webs of ecclesiology which constitute the abstract and idealized church as found in many books. Ecclesiology *is* of primary importance, provided the connection with empirical, historical reality is not lost.

Begin with the familiar element of community. The unity of all people is often proposed on the basis of belief that every created human being is made for community. It is not good that he should live alone. This is true; but it is difficult to apply specifically as a condemnation or curative of racial segregation. The community may simply be defined by the kind of people one chooses to recognize.

More helpful than this general doctrine of creation is the authentically biblical one, which stresses the realization of divine-human covenant as the purpose of human creation in the image of God. The covenant of Yahweh with his people was made through the representative patriarchs Noah, Abraham and Moses. It was this concept expressed in the formula ,'I will be their God, they will be my people', with all of its rigorous ethical mandates and its promise for the future, which has given the Jews their sense of identity for three and a half millennia. It was this same basic covenant-concept, reinterpreted and made universally inclusive, which was ratified by the blood of Jesus Christ, and which has given the church its sense of identity.

Among the hundreds of millions of church members, relatively few are consciously aware of the way the church's existence derives from the old and new covenants. If they had such knowledge and held it in faith, they would know that their fidelity to the God of covenant makes them brothers in a particular way with all who share this faith. Their fraternal community is not intended to be rigorously exclusive or sectarian. On the contrary, admission to it is literally 'by faith alone'. No factor such as race or ethnic origin, language, nationality or physical peculiarity can of itself be a cause for one's being excluded from the community. Neither should any such factor constitute a reason for one member's refusing to recognize and accept any other as his brother in Christ.

The Christian sacraments of initiation and communion are of highest importance, therefore, in respect to the overcoming of racist tendencies. Whatever one's colour of skin may be, when he is baptized as a disciple of Christ he becomes a permanent member of the covenant community, which is supra-racial and universal. Membership is not nominal; it is actual and integral. Discrimination against a brother, or fellow member, is more reprehensible than the violation of an abstract theory of human equality; it amounts to a wilful denial of the validity and integrity of the community itself, and hence a denial of the covenant made with God through Jesus Christ. The New Testament abounds in statements which support this categorical condemnation of discrimination. It is the ultimate rejection of the bond with one's brother and with God as symbolized in baptism. In the same manner, discriminatory attitudes and policies on the part of church members do violence to the essential purpose of the sacrament of eucharist. What is this sacrament if not a solemn commemoration of the covenant effected by Jesus Christ for the reconciliation of human beings to God and with one another? What is it if not a graceful means of continually renewing the covenant and purifying the reconciliation?

In view of the earlier warning against an abstract and idealized theory of the church, it must be maintained that these implications of baptism and eucharist for human community are not mere theories. They represent the power of God's love itself at work within and among men by the Holy Spirit; they are indispensable, indeed literally essential, to the church. And they have an immediate experiential and sociological relevance which every person can recognize.

Despite the contradictions between faith and practice in matters of community, Christians have been able to keep before them the image of a church which tolerates no divisions or separations on account of race. The fully inclusive church, free from either enforced or voluntary segregation of races, has been strongly advocated for two reasons: first, because this is consistent with the church's own being; second, because the mission of Christianity to all men and nations is credible only to the degree that the churches can manifest publicly that all are one in Christ. The formula seems simple and of a commanding logic.

The logic is resisted, however, and the simplicity of the formula is made complex by the present state of the churches in various countries, where the majority of members are white and the minority black or coloured. For most of these the norm remains one of solidarity and mutually acknowledged brotherhood in Christ. But the fear has arisen that the sincerely held concept of an inclusive, non-discriminatory community might prove to be a demonic device in angelic form. Racial minorities assimilated fully into the structures and life of a dominantly white church might still be subtly suppressed by the majority. This fear has assumed the form of a policy of voluntary separate existence for some black Christians, notably in the United States. This is defended as a necessary but temporary expedient. It is a provisional suspension of the striving after full integration so that, in a longer period, the black Christians will have a stronger sense of their own identity, a clearer conception of their vocation in the church and contributions to it, and also the political leverage needed to persuade hesitant or recalcitrant white Christians to live up to the implications of the covenant community. For a time, therefore, it is preferred by many black churchmen that their congregations remain homogeneously black, that only black clergy serve them, and that deliberate efforts towards integration be postponed. What may prevent this policy from being another form of racism infecting the church is the emphasis which falls upon the word 'temporary'. Without specifying the time required, whether a few years or a generation, they hold this plan to be necessary until conditions for full mutual acceptance and responsibility are met through changes in the attitudes of white members.

The virtue of this policy is neither self-evident nor unambiguous. Perhaps it is a dangerous course to take, since the racial disharmonies may thereby be aggravated and the divisions made more lasting than ever. Certainly such risk is involved. Those who pursue the policy in America or elsewhere must consider the risk in relation both to the existing condition of prejudice and discrimination and the desired situation of a true community in Christ with all of the personal and social benefits of life in the church and society. If there is good hope that all members of the church, black and white alike, may be delivered from the existing situation into the realization of what is desired, then the risk may be commended.

In Africa, however, and especially in South Africa, this policy of separate life and development in the churches must be resisted and rejected. For this is precisely what many of the white majority are favouring anyhow, and the hope for transcending the present pattern of segregation is scarcely enhanced by having it favoured by the large non-white majority.

There are church members in South Africa who sincerely believe that it is impossible to follow any system other than *apartheid*, or separate development. For every white person there are more than four non-whites. The white minority possesses the education, production skill, wealth, and political power. It is manifestly dangerous to belong to a minority in power when the great majority of the powerless feels a rising exasperation, indignation and eventual hatred. But within this dangerous situation, many whites say they believe that separate development will provide the maximum chance for black Africans and 'coloureds' to develop their societies. All efforts to legitimate this pragmatic policy by appeals to Christian theology or biblical guidelines have, however, enjoyed little support by most of world Christianity.

In terms of faith and theology there is no equivocation or room for dispute about the unity and the community of all members in Christ. And further it is clear to all that Christians must keep open at all times the invitation of the Lord to join his fellowship on earth. Whosoever will, let him come! Nevertheless, we would be wholly unrealistic and irresponsible not to recognize the need for diverse and sometimes contradictory strategies for the expression of this fellowship in the many nations and socities of the earth.

v *The Practical Exercise of Love, Power and Justice*

Anyone can see that there would be no problem of racism if the love of God were actually operative among men in the manner described and exemplified by Jesus Christ. Likewise, there would be little worry over racial distinctions if the ideal of justice were realized everywhere. Since human sin and perversity are only moderately inhibited, however, any longing after love and justice in inter-racial relations is merely sentimental unless the constructive uses of power are known and applied.

The circuit of connection between love and justice, justice and power, and power and love carries the energy which impels and informs most human relations. All three factors are required in the struggle against the deleterious work of racism. Power may be the way to justice, if its motivation is love; then love prudently uses power for the just end. But the condition of justice may in turn become the relationship among men which makes possible the exercise of higher degrees of love.

In many countries it is economic power and political power which determine the policies and forms of racist oppression. These are of course fed by the powers of thought and prejudice. But the process of eradicating racism from society cannot achieve success by the use only of the powers to influence minds and dispositions. In addition to these, the powerful weapons of economics and politics need to be turned against the discriminators. When a favourable degree of equitable distribution of economic and political power has been achieved in a society, then the talk of justice becomes plausibly realistic. Then, too, the expressions of love may become fraternal rather than paternalistic, straightforward rather than condescending.

The Report of Uppsala Section III rightly declares (par. 23) that 'The Church must actively promote the redistribution of power', if racism is to be effectively opposed. Yet it would be inexcusably naïve for anyone to think that the institutions and corporations and individuals holding major economic power are voluntarily going to distribute their wealth and their means of acquiring wealth in response to an appeal from the churches. Neither will political parties composed mainly of white persons be willing to redistribute their power to control governments, national or local, unless made to do so by the leverage of a strong political movement or by inducements which promise them continued security in office. This is a matter-of-fact recognition of the way men hold and wield power in society. It is not repugnant to Christian faith. It simply points to the truth that racial groups which feel the squeeze of economic and political oppression, whether they be minorities as in the United States or majorities as in Rhodesia and South Africa, are doomed to second-class citizenship or peonage so long as they possess no power in these realms.

The concept of 'black power' in itself is, from a Christian standpoint, unexceptionable. It has had a sinister connotation, implying racism in reverse with acts of retribution against whites; and in America there have been numerous acts of violence which vindicate that fear. Even so, as a strategic concept it is perfectly legitimate and undoubtedly necessary to put in operation. Power at the polling place and money in the pocket may seem unattainably remote to millions of black Africans; but in America these are attainable. As black citizens acquire them more and more, with as much help as the churches can provide, the prospects for justice in the land will gleam more brightly. But it would be either stupid, cynical or malicious for white people to tell the blacks that they must wait for powerful whites to experience moral conversion and subsequently to redistribute their power.

Black power is seen by many to be the successor to both the strategies of justice and of love. Justice was sought by appeals to legislators, by testing unjust law in civil courts, and by urging a civilized citizenry to recognize the discrepancy between democratic theory and prevailing practice. But only a small amount of justice was added to the black community's civil status. Love was then employed through the witness of non-violent protest; stolidly, passively refusing to honour unjust laws and customs, bravely accepting the consequences of humiliation, brutality and imprisonment or even death, the black protesters hoped that a loving response would be elicited from white breasts. The response was too small and too slow. Inevitably, understandably the impatience of the Negro people became more intense. The last alternative was power. But how to get it? By means which are just and loving? By rational suasion? By social disruption, or by ruthless seizure?

The phenomenon of America's black revolution in the decade of the 1960s has placed an unbearable strain upon the structures of theological and ethical thought, by which Christians have tried to support their concern for racial reconciliation. The primary problem among others has been, and remains, the justification of violence.

Violence has more than one meaning. It is violence when people burn shops, smash windows, steal merchandise, throw home-made bombs, or use clubs and fire-arms. Most Christians find it difficult to justify such actions by reference to a desired but not visible eventuality, such as a just society; others find it impossible to do so. A prooftext appeal to Jesus cleansing the Jerusalem Temple is a spurious support for incipient anarchy and unchecked destructiveness. Certainly no Christian should enjoy violence. But can any rightly condone it?

More dependable as a guide for Christians than an isolated event in Jesus' ministry is the whole style of his life, the consistency of his preaching of love, and his specific manner of handling the prejudices of some Jews towards the minorities and outsiders of the time. In all these it is suggested that both the attitude of non-violence and the employment of it as a means of moral persuasion are appropriate to those who follow after Christ. Thus the Report of Uppsala Section IV commended 'non-violent strategies of revolution and social change' (par. 33).

Exasperated Christians still ask, though, whether the absolutely necessary black power can be secured by non-violent strategies only? Should sympathetic white Christians advise their brothers to go the way of the cross, accepting violence of word, law, attitude and action at the hands of white people, in hopes that the power will somehow come into their waiting hands? Since such advice would be gratuitous, to say the least, the words could acquire integrity only to the extent that the white advisers themselves subjected themselves to the same kinds of humiliation and violence. Only in such a way can there be honesty in the Christian commendation of vicarious love and redemptive sacrifice. But even after the second mile has been walked, the cloak given away, and the vicarious cross carried on some *via dolorosa*, there may be no assurance given that the economic and political power for black people will have been secured.

Avoiding a piously frivolous attempt to resolve this dilemma, we can perhaps delineate a moral basis for action which is coherently Christian and practically effective. It is in line with Jesus' admonition to be as wise as serpents and as harmless as doves. It means using every available and effective instrument for extending the franchise, registering voters, putting forward good candidates for office, influencing the platforms and policies of political parties, and working for the election of public officials who will use their office for the advancement of black people. This presupposes, of course, a constitutional democracy wherein such political action is possible. It also accepts the fact that Christianity has no distinctive counsel to give the citizen in his striving for political power.

In the quest for economic power the same kind of shrewdness, diligence and persistence is required. This may work on two levels. The first is the earliest possible acquisition of financial power through the coalition of persons and institutions which enjoy considerable control. Inevitably this will have to mean the collaboration of many white people with Negroes through banks and commercial enterprises, through the securing of governmental appropriations, and not least through the joint action of churches. The second level, always related to the first, is the task of securing educational opportunities and training in productive skills. In so far as these economic measures pertain not only to well developed nations such as Britain or America but also to the many poor nations in which white people are very small minorities, it is evident that correcting the gross inequities existing between peoples of differing colour will depend upon the success of the vast complex of plans and projects for world development.

Whatever the social or economic system of a country may be, the struggle for power will involve constant competition and conflicting interests. To the extent that Christians and others act unselfishly, recognizing both the moral mandate and the critical urgency of the matter, this redistribution of power will take place sooner. But their persistence in selfishness or callous disregard for the poor and oppressed will only heighten the likelihood of revolutionary action with perhaps concomitant acts of violence.

A genuinely Christian counsel to those seeking racial justice may seem too radical to the conservatives and too bland to the revolutionaries. Yet it can have practicability without being merely expedient; and it can imply the maximum of love and justice without being utopian.

Such counsel affirms that white persons who support and practice discriminatory acts against non-white people must be dislodged from their racist positions. Appeals to reason, morality and religious sensitivity should be directed towards them as vigorously and cogently as possible. But beyond these verbal exhortations there are legitimate means by which they must be jolted, loosened and pried away from their racism. These means are the ones of economic, political and psychological power. Not only individuals need to be changed by pressure, but likewise the institutional embodiments of racism: governmental agencies, police forces, commercial corporations, trade unions, educational institutions, and even churches.

The forms of power should not be such as to bring undue or disproportionate harm or suffering to any persons. Certainly the current revolt against white racism cannot be purchased without such costs. White people for many years and generations have been sowing the winds of racial discrimination; so they must expect to reap some unpleasant whirlwinds. Those who have enjoyed privileges and securities in life which are the consequence of past years of economic injustice and political advantage at the expense of other races should not be astonished to learn that these privileges are inevitably threatened by the economic and political elevation of the unprivileged and insecure. Holdings of property and wealth will be jeopardized. Contributions will be required through taxation, church offerings, and donations to independent organizations in order to make some restitution for past grievances and provide the means for present development of poor people. In many instances the dedication of one's time to constructive programmes and projects will be needed. All these and more such sacrifices will have to be made by countless white people if the minimum demands of justice are soon to be met.

This kind of costliness on the part of white Christians was not requested, but demanded, in the spring of 1969 by adherents of the Black Economic Development Conference in the United States. Churches and synagogues were confronted by strong words and physical presence of many blacks: Give reparations for the sins of the past! No moral appeals, no exhortations for justice, no marches to Washington to favour civil rights have had the equivalent impact upon American churches. Reparations is a much disputed concept. But it was affirmed in principle by the Consultation on Racism, convened at Notting Hill in London by the World Council of Churches in May 1969. It provided leverage to persuade the Central Committee of the World Council to undertake costly actions for the empowerment of Negroes. And in America, even while being bitterly debated, it has prompted many white church leaders to advocate the allocation of funds to black-controlled economic projects, and also to make room in church councils and organizations for Negroes to assume positions of high responsibility. As this kind of movement for the redistribution of power for the sake of human justice gains momentum, it is most appropriate for Christians to counsel one another to be generous and long-suffering.

Moreover, the Christian counsel of non-violence is equally appropriate in all but the most extreme instances. The exception to this rule can be justified only by a situation of such unremitting oppression and tyranny or of dangerous threat to life, that physical damage or injury must be inflicted in order to secure and maintain a minimal level of order and safety. It was in respect to such situations alone, and to none other, that the World Council of Churches' Consultation on Racism, held in London in May 1969, took the position which was widely misinterpreted in the press and hence misunderstood. When *all else fails* to effect the needed changes, the churches should 'support resistance movements, including revolutions, which are aimed at the elimination of political or economic tyranny which makes racism possible'. There come such times in personal and corporate action when it is necessary for the sake of order and justice 'to sin bravely'. Current racial tensions, hostilities and conflicts present such occasions.[1]

VI

This essay may not be permitted to conclude with a panegyric on brotherhood. Fraternity among men is indeed the goal for Christians to seek in human society. But it is evident that the course of history leading towards the widest realization of that objective will be marked by constant struggle for elemental justice for people of all races. Much of this endeavour draws upon motivation and employs methods which are of a strictly secular nature. These affect Christians and non-Christians alike. But Christians believe that there are deeper sources of motivation and stronger resources of power which are to be found in the faith informed by Jesus Christ. In the Christian understanding of humanity itself, in recognition of God's activity through Jesus Christ and the church, and in the conception of love, power and justice as learned from Christ – in these elements especially are the distinctive forces which militate against racism.

NOTE

1. In the autumn of 1970 this policy was implemented by the World Council of Churches in supporting radical movements in South Africa and an intense discussion has resulted.

14

Discrimination against Women

MARGA BÜHRIG

The Church must actively promote the redistribution of power, without discrimination of any kind, so that all men, women and young people may participate in the benefits of development.

It was this statement (par. 23 of the Report of Uppsala Section III) which prompted the observations that follow. One presumes that it was incorporated into the Report as a result of the impression made by the much-criticized composition of the delegations attending the Fourth Assembly of the World Council of Churches at Uppsala in 1968. As is well known, only 9 per cent of the delegates entitled to vote were women, while of all the delegates, both men and women, who were entitled to vote, only 4 per cent were less than thirty-five years old: these are facts which allow one to draw certain *a posteriori* conclusions concerning the power structures of the member churches. Virtually no statistics are available to tell us how many women and how many people under thirty-five occupy decision-making positions in authoritative ecclesiastical bodies. As far as women are concerned, what is absolutely certain is that the number bears no relation to the preponderance of women who attend church services and other religious functions. But apart from these points, it is meaningful to undertake an examination of the problem they raise, namely that of the position of women, because ever since Amsterdam 1948 this has been a key topic in the deliberations and discussions of the World Council of Churches and the Ecumenical Movement.

1 The Theme of 'Women' in the Documents of the World Council of Churches

At Amsterdam in 1948 'The Life and Work of Women in the Church' was discussed as one of the concerns of the World Council of Churches.

An inquiry among the various churches had produced so many answers, both from official church quarters and from various women's organizations and groups, that one thing emerged very clearly: we were faced here with a very real problem. Kathleen Bliss was entrusted with the task of assessing the material which had been gathered, and in his preface to her book, W. A. Visser 't Hooft wrote:

It is not only the opinion of Dr Bliss, but the almost monotonous and impressive leitmotive of the reports from all countries that (in the words of the Amsterdam Assembly) 'the Church as the Body of Christ consists of men and women, created as responsible persons to glorify God and do His will', but that 'this truth, accepted in theory, is too often ignored in practice'.[1]

The second half of this sentence requires no alteration even today, more than twenty years later. The problem of how to reconcile theory and practice or, to put it another way, the translation of theoretical insights into responsible action, is probably the core of the matter, and throughout this study we will find ourselves asking what exactly are the forces which are preventing this translation from taking place and which are thereby perpetuating discrimination against women instead of removing it? But first of all we may perhaps be permitted briefly to cast an eye back over the work of the relevant department of the World Council of Churches.

The 'Commission on the Life and Work of Women in the Church' was founded at Amsterdam in 1948, and at Evanston in 1954 the executive secretary of this Commission, Dr Madeleine Barot, presented a report on its workings. She gave the reasons for changing its title to read 'Department on Co-operation of Men and Women in Church and Society', and the document she presented makes clear the total rejection of all forms of feminism:

The first title, 'The Life and Work of Women in the Church', must now be replaced by a new name that will not give the false conception that this is a Women's Department. The most accurate name we have found is: 'The Department on the Co-operation of Men and Women in Church and Society'. As titles cannot entirely describe the full work of a department, and as questions related to the place of women, of women's work, of women's organizations, must be considered in the light of the co-operation between men and women, this title has been chosen as the best possible one.[2]

Elsewhere in the same document we find a description of the church's task as regards women which may doubtless also be applied to the Department itself:

to help them [i.e. women] find the right balance between their family responsibilities and their professional life; to help them, while changing from dependent, protected beings to responsible members of society, to remain feminine even if they are working in an exclusively masculine environment.[3]

In 1955 this policy was further underlined by the so-called 'Davos Statement', where we read:

If the implications of the co-operation of men and women in all doctrinal and practical issues of the church were generally recognized by the member churches and the departments of the World Council of Churches, there would be no further need for this Department. For the good of the church and the effectiveness of its witness in the world, it is necessary, for the present, to continue to emphasize this special concern. The Department is trying to put the whole discussion on this issue on a new level and, on the basis of theological thinking and sociological observations, to stimulate the churches to rediscover the full meaning of co-operation between men and women in church and society. It serves within a functional area, concerned with methods and procedures for achieving that co-operation, rather than as an agency related to organized constituency groups of men or women in the church.[4]

For the next few years the objectives stated here were to provide the course for action: the Department did not see itself as set up to represent a group 'being discriminated against' and did not see its task to be that of helping to change existing power structures. On the contrary, it saw the way open to the mutual study of basic problems. The themes of its earlier deliberations provide the milestones on this way, and the problems which were the centre of its preoccupations were formulated as early as 1954 by Madeleine Barot in the words:

Lastly, we see on every hand an attempt being made to determine what equality means when it is applied to men and women. All are agreed that equality between men and women does not mean identity, but what *do* we mean? A similar effort for definition is necessary when one speaks of the specific gifts – qualities – functions – of women. Too often, we say that woman must be free to utilize all the gifts that God has entrusted to her and, paradoxically, we are still imprisoned by the definition of womanliness based on a psychology and sociology which are outmoded. The day of aggressive feminism – denying that there are differences between men and women – seems to have passed. Today, women do not desire to be like men, but realize that they can contribute fully as women, not conforming to patterns and methods of life and work which are masculine.[5]

These questions were given a provisional answer in the 'Davos Statement' to which we have already referred. The basic ideas, which occur over and over again, are the following:

The church is a whole, and can only be a whole if all its members make their own contribution.

The gifts of men and women are different. Their 'unity in diversity' is part of God's creation.

This is the reason why the exegesis of the two creation accounts has played a large part in so many discussions. 'The reason we are urging co-operation and partnership is because we believe it is biblical' is what we read in the Report of the Odense Consultation of 1958.[6] Partnership and co-operation were favoured because of the conviction that they are anticipated in the Bible. It follows that there has been intensive study of the relevant biblical passages, such as: Eph. 5.21 ff.; I Cor. 11 and 14; I Tim. 2.15; Gal. 3.28, etc.

It was evident that although these principles are recognized as having biblical foundation, they were far from being realized even in the churches themselves. This is why the Odense Consultation in 1958 wanted to find out what obstacles were standing in the way of the realization of partnership and co-operation. It was equally obvious that the incentive to examine personal attitudes was coming from outside. This is how Madeleine Barot describes this matter in her little book *Co-operation of Men and Women in Church, Family and Society*:

A wide enquiry has shown that the economic and political emancipation of women has already had profound repercussions. A great hope was born: would not a better use of these new feminine capabilities give birth to new forms of witness and service?[7]

One cannot therefore discuss woman's place and service in the church and come to any conclusions without also examining her role and function in contemporary society. It took a relatively short time for it to become generally accepted that the church does not exist simply as an isolated body in antithesis to society but rather that – from a sociological point of view – it is a social group dependent in many different ways on society and therefore naturally enough exerting its influence on society too. This is why the Department included sociological and psychological problems and research data in its work as well as theological ones. The objective was to equip the churches to take up a position in the face of social problems and responsibilities.[8] This they were to do as a 'church for others', relying on their biblically-based insights.

In the course of this preparatory study and as a result of contact with experts from various scientific disciplines, problems of a specifically practical and concrete nature made themselves increasingly felt. As far as the church was concerned, one question to arise was that of the ordination of women; from the social point of view, one of the most frequent problems was that concerning the changing roles of men and women.[9] In the process a fact that was repeatedly encountered was the so-called double burden of both career and family imposed on women, and indeed the changing structures of the family, especially in Africa and Asia, and of marriage, especially in the USA and Western Europe.

Within the scope of this article it is quite impossible to enumerate all the topics which the Department dealt with. But it is certain that its work gave much food for thought to many people and provided a basis for the churches subsequently to take up considered attitudes towards certain problems such as the ordination of women for instance. Here, in the context of the church itself, this resulted in fruitful co-operation with the Faith and Order Department, and led to the question of the ordination of women being placed on the agenda of the World Conference at Montreal and to the publication of a combined pamphlet.[10]

If one examines attentively the names of those taking part in the various consultations organized by the Department, one discovers that, although men were deliberately included not just nominally but in the basic conception of the Department, the preponderant majority of those participating were in fact women. It is true (see above) that any idea that it should in any way represent the interests of 'powerful' women's organizations at the World Council of Churches had been firmly rejected right from the start. The Department had pledged itself to deal thoroughly with essential topics in loyal co-operation with both men and women, and in doing so it had achieved some very real results. Yet now, twenty years later, it would seem that the real balance of power within the churches has changed scarcely at all, if one thinks, for example, of the small number of women delegates at Uppsala. All we can do is accept the fact that the good, thorough and comprehensive work of the Department has as yet failed to bring about a change in the existing set-up, and has not produced a genuine balance or a real partnership between men and women in the church. Thus we in the church find ourselves in about the same position as society itself, if one may be allowed to use so wide-ranging a comparison. Making allowances for a measure of exaggeration, one might almost say that these meticulous theological and psychological inquiries into the 'true nature of woman', her intrinsic gifts, the mission entrusted her by God, and the correct appraisal of the unalterable contrast between man and woman which is part of creation, have perhaps led to an inability or reluctance even to appreciate that 'discrimination' against women exists, even though its existence is borne out by the facts. It may be that lucid theological insights make people blind to the practical conditions which require change. At all events the enormous discrepancy between the splendid theological arguments put forward concerning the divinely willed and ordained co-operation of men and women and the various power structures to be encountered in the majority of churches belonging to the World Council of Churches may lead one to suppositions of this kind. There may indeed be a parallel here to the statements made concerning racial equality and the actual conditions generally prevalent.

Faced with these facts, we ought perhaps to look at the position of women outside the churches and see how it is regulated.

II   *The Declaration of Human Rights and its Consequences*

In June 1946 the Economic and Social Council of the United Nations decided to set up a commission on the status of women in society which was theoretically to meet once annually and to represent the particular concerns of women at the very heart of this world organization. Since the Declaration of Human Rights in December 1948, its work has had a theoretical basis as expressly formulated particularly in Articles 1 and 2:

Article 1: All human beings are born free and equal in dignity and rights. . . .

Article 2: Everyone is entitled to all the rights and freedoms set forth in this Declaration, without distinction of any kind, such as . . . sex. . . .

Of special significance to women are Articles 13 (the right to freedom of movement) and 15 (the right to nationality, of particular relevance to women marrying foreigners), and

Article 16: Men and women of full age, without any limitation due to race, nationality or religion, have the right to marry and to found a family. They are entitled to equal rights as to marriage, during marriage and at its dissolution.

Marriage shall be entered only with the free and full consent of the intending spouses.

Other relevant Articles are 21 (political rights), 23 (the right to work and equal pay), and 26 (the right to education).

In Human Rights Year, 1968, the twentieth anniversary of their declaration, the President of the French League for Women's Rights, Dr Andrée Lehmann, declared: 'It must be recognized that as yet no state has fully endorsed these ideals.'[11] Nevertheless, the mere fact that these principles have been formulated constitutes a very real step forward, for now all those working towards their realization can always refer to this formulation. It is significant that a UN commission is making these questions its constant concern, and equally significant that a department is dealing with them at the World Council of Churches. Perhaps one of the most fundamental differences between their approaches is that the UN commission has worked out conventions on a whole range of practical questions and has brought them to the vote at the General Assembly or other relevant organizations, whereas the Department has opted for the more prolonged method of bringing about a change of conviction from within by establishing and publicizing fundamental insights.

One result of the work of the UN commission was the declaration concerning the elimination of discrimination against women[12] which was accepted by the General Assembly of the UN on 7 November 1967 following the comprehensive report drawn up by the Secretary-General in 1966.[13] This declaration is a working version of the general principles of Human Rights. In formulating what changes are needed in practical terms, it clearly shows up those points which have been the cause of difficulty and draws attention to the areas in which the equality of men and women, though accepted in principle, has not been realized, or at any rate not uniformly or completely realized. Thus it demands that the equality of men and women be incorporated in the constitutions of states, and that various statements of the non-governmental organizations of the UN such as UNESCO and the ILO, be officially ratified by all nations (Article 2). It demands both active and passive electoral rights, and the right for women to assume every public office (Article 4), insists on the right to the free choice of partner, the right to freedom of movement, the right of inheritance, and the equality of the rights and duties of both parents with regard to their children (Article 6), it forbids white slave traffic and prostitution (Article 8), and expatiates on the real meaning of equal rights to education (Article 9).

Of particular relevance to the questions we have been asking are Articles 3 and 10. In Article 10 the 'right to work' defined in the Charter of Human Rights is given an interesting practical interpretation when the demand is made that women, regardless of their legal status, be allowed to train for a profession and practise it, to choose their profession freely, to enjoy equal pay, paid holidays, social security and family allowances subject to the same conditions as their male colleagues. In practical terms this last stipulation implies that a woman may also be the 'head' of the family. A further section (Article 10.2) lays down stipulations with regard to marriage and motherhood:

In order to prevent discrimination against women arising in the event of marriage or motherhood and to safeguard their proper right to work, measures must be taken to prevent the dismissal of women in the event of marriage

L

or motherhood, as well as to ensure paid leave of absence for maternity with the guaranteed freedom to resume their former employment, and to provide the appropriate social services, including child care facilities.

We will return to this Article in due course. It shows us why it is so difficult to translate the postulated equality of men and women into practical terms. To it may be added Article 3:

Every relevant means must be taken to educate public opinion and foster a world-wide desire to eradicate prejudices and to abolish all practices, customs, etc., based on the idea of the inferiority of women.

This makes it very clear that the abolition of discrimination against women is not just a case of and indeed may not primarily be a case of the need to alter existing legislation and constitutional requirements, but rather that it involves a *gradual education of public opinion*, in which an essential factor is the removal of deeply-rooted prejudices; the deepest aspects of human existence are caught up in such a process, for the existence of the sexes and the contrasts between them are of course a fundamental condition of human life.

If we ask how the UN and its associated non-governmental organizations are attempting to attain the objective outlined above, we shall see in the first place that not only have a great number of special statements been worked out and placed before member states for their consideration and ratification, but that working groups have been set up to consider a variety of problems both on a world-wide and on a regional scale, that surveys of women have been undertaken in different countries (USA, Sweden, Federal Germany, etc.) – in short, that a process of collective thinking based on the Declaration of Human Rights has been set in motion. This process of educating opinion has developed with growing impetus from purely formal and rather empty ideals to concrete social and economic stipulations. At the same time the need to develop the so-called underdeveloped countries both economically and socially has done much to contribute to the increasing relevance of the problem of the equality of women. This is an aspect to which we shall have in due course to return. At this point all we need emphasize is that the Declaration of Human Rights has given rise to a new era as far as the position of women is concerned in so far as it propounds an ideal and formulates a fundamental principle which are accepted as binding and which can be invoked in cases of abuse; these in turn have resulted in pacts and conventions which have the force of law or at least should have as soon as they are ratified by a state. But the Declaration of Human Rights is of course also subject to all the problems attending international agreements and to the relative in-effectuality of even the most beautiful ideals. It is precisely here that we must ask ourselves *what the churches can contribute and what are the implications of the gospel which they preach.* There can be little doubt that from the historical point of view the Declaration of Human Rights was in large measure impregnated with Christian elements. Consequently it is all the more urgent that we should ask to what extent the churches today are really committing themselves to interpreting, fulfilling and ultimately also to improving the stipulations that were formulated in it or, in other words, whether they are capable of recognizing the 'humanum' which they too are seeking, when it is being sought and paraphrased by the secular world.

III *Towards a Definition of Discrimination against Women*

I have before me a Swiss newspaper dated 1969, or to be more exact, a supplement which was issued along with a number of Swiss newspapers, the object of which was to encourage a sensible choice of career. On the front there is a photograph of a boy and a girl; they are supposed by the author to be school-leavers, both faced with the choice of a career, and the slogan beneath applies to both of them: 'It is all too easy to choose the wrong career.' But how are these two young people depicted? The boy is several inches taller than the girl and is shown in profile looking keenly ahead into the future which for him is bound to mean a 'career'; he is alive to the opportunities the future has in store. Unlike the girl – she stands slightly turned towards the young man and is leaning her head against his shoulder, her eyes closed; she is dreaming of a future, not choosing one, just letting it emerge. In any other context we would immediately think 'what a charming young couple'. They are facing the future together, and for the girl this future does not mean first and foremost a career – it means marriage. Of course this photograph is advocating a sensible choice of career for both the boy and the girl; yet the implication it in fact conjures up is that the boy is choosing a career with which he can support a family whereas for the girl the whole thing is far less important.

Naturally we do not wish to read too much into one picture chosen more or less at random. But it can serve to remind us how discrimination arises and what its nature is. The discrepancy between conscious intentions and subliminal wishful thinking is an essential part of the problem. Today agreement is often quickly reached on the level of deliberate intentions and principles. Yet these cannot be realized because subconscious attitudes steer a course in a different direction.

But what is really at stake in this whole question? Again and again woman is not seen as an independent human being (cf. the picture described above). Instead she is seen in connection with her husband and family. Simone de Beauvoir has described the situation thus in her lively, outspoken but fundamentally irrefutable book *The Second Sex*:

A man would never set out to write a book on the peculiar situation of the human male. . . . A man never begins by presenting himself as an individual of a certain sex; it goes without saying that he is a man. The terms *masculine* and *feminine* are used symmetrically only as a matter of form, as on legal papers. In actuality the relation of the two sexes is not quite like that of two electrical poles, for man represents both the positive and the neutral, as is indicated by the common use of *man* to designate human beings in general; whereas woman represents only the negative, defined by limiting criteria, without reciprocity. . . . She is simply what man decrees; thus she is called 'the sex', by which is meant that she appears essentially to the male as a sexual being; for him she is sex – absolute sex, no less. She is defined and differentiated with reference to man and not he with reference to her; she is the incidental, the inessential as opposed to the essential. He is the Subject, he is the Absolute – she is the Other.[14]

One does not need to share the author's whole philosophy of life and follow all her trains of thought to recognize the relative accuracy of her description. The phenomenon she is alluding to is unique in one respect, in that this kind of discrimination is not aimed at a minority like, for example, the Jews, or the Negroes in the USA; on the contrary, it concerns one half of the human race, regardless of nationality or colour – that is, if we are really to describe the different position of women as discrimination pure and simple. This is what Simone de Beauvoir does not hesitate to do, basing herself on her conception of humanity. This she shares with Jean-Paul Sartre, seeing the human being as one who chooses his own identity and thereby transcends the limitations of factual reality. Because woman is more tied to biological demands, man has assumed pride of place:

The female, to a greater extent than the male, is the prey of the species; and the human race has always sought to escape its specific destiny. The support of life became for man an activity and a project through the invention of the tool; but in maternity woman remained closely bound to her body, like an animal.[15]

In remarkably similar though more empirical terms the American Betty Friedan speaks of the 'sexual ghetto' in which women are held captive behind a 'silken curtain' unless they are alive to the situation and take precautions against it:

What do we mean by the sexual ghetto? Ideologically speaking it is what I have called the feminine mystique, or, in other words, the contemporary tendency to define the relation of woman to man exclusively in sexual terms, whether as wife, mother, sex-object, or housewife, but never first and foremost in human terms, as a personality or as an individual.

In connection with this view of woman Betty Friedan speaks of a coming revolution:

In my opinion, the sexual ghetto inhibits not only the development of women, but also the freedom of men and their search for happiness, and the development of children. It inhibits sexuality and sexual love, although paradoxically this is concealed under an obsession with sex. And it basically even inhibits the economy, even though it might not appear that the highly-developed industrial affluent society is immutably founded on the perpetuation of the sexual ghetto. Were this really true, it would indeed be a grave miscalculation both from the historical point of view and for the foreseeable future, because the sexual ghetto is very much a house built upon sand and the breeding-ground for a revolution which will have to be faced and to which an end must be put. . . .
I am convinced that this feminine revolution will take place non-violently. What we need are simply innovations, technical innovations, such as any progressive country today is perfectly capable of carrying out. . . . This could be done everywhere as soon as the problem arises.[16]

We have deliberately chosen two extreme views in order to demonstrate what was felt twenty years ago by Simone de Beauvoir and what is felt today by Betty Friedan in two Western countries to be the real nature of discrimination. Alongside them there are countless other women in these same two countries who would regard such views as exaggerated and indeed unjustified, and who would fail to detect any trace of discrimination against women either in the USA or France; the same facts can be given different interpretations based on a different set of values. We shall return presently to their Christian interpretation which is our chief concern here. But first let us submit the facts to a closer scrutiny. Let us try to exclude value judgments and penetrate the jungle of prejudice, attempted emancipation and confused interpretation in as unbiased a manner as we can, and then ask ourselves *what are the sources of discrimination against women*: there can be no doubt that we shall then come up against one or even two basic facts of human nature. The first is the undoubted fact that it is women and not men who bear children and feed them in their infancy, and the second perhaps that the sexuality of women, their needs and experiences, are basically different from those of men because of their different physical make-up. Concerning this second point there is a wide divergence of opinion and it is moreover very difficult to distinguish here between culture and nature, especially as it is now realized that sexual attitudes are very largely dictated by cultural and social factors. It is almost impossible to assess the changes that have already taken place and will continue to do so in this area, as women increasingly find that their sexual experience need not be conditioned by the fear of unwanted pregnancies or the fear of the failure to produce the offspring they themselves want or which are demanded of them by their family or tribe. Many generations of women of every nationality have been influenced or inhibited in this respect by all kinds of false expectations, quite apart from the measures still taken in many tribes to prevent women from enjoying satisfaction and to make them into the passive possessions of men. In talking of 'false expectations' we have of course been guilty of a value judgment. What we meant was that expectations are false if they result neither from the personal feelings of a mature woman nor from the loving partnership of two free individuals.

But because so much of all this is uncertain and in the process of imponderable changes, let us confine ourselves in the following remarks to that ineluctable fact which has been with us since the beginnings of the human race – motherhood. The fact that it is the woman who bears children and that these children are in their infancy totally dependent on human help, which generally means that of their mother, in order to survive, renders the life and position of women fundamentally different from that of men. Demands for equality can do nothing whatever to change this. It is true that much has changed even in this respect. Wherever methods of birth control have become accepted and permitted, the number of births has been substantially reduced, and this has led to decisive changes in the lives of women. Modern medical treatment and methods of painless childbirth have exerted great influence. Social measures, such as the granting of leave of absence to working women during the final weeks of pregnancy and after the birth, and protection against dismissal because of having a baby, have been introduced in an increasing number of countries (cf. the unanimous stipulations in all the international conventions). On the other hand, mothers are subject to all the horrors of modern total warfare, to the threat of starvation owing to the growing discrepancy between rich and poor, and to the levelling tendencies of technological civilization. The contemporary world offers no refuge to any category of human beings, and secularized society has little reverence for mothers and motherhood.

Nevertheless the fact remains that women become mothers and, as Simone de Beauvoir said, are bound to carry more responsibility than men and to be more practically involved in the duties of bringing up children. This is clearly seen, for instance, in the case of women students who, though as gifted as their male counterparts, are unable to follow them as regards career, etc., once they have children; a further consequence of this is that there are few women in senior positions because they are bound by family responsibilities to their homes during the crucial years when their husbands are working on untroubled in pursuance of their scientific, professional or political careers. Can all these facts really be summed up under the heading 'discrimination'? Would it not be much more justifiable to talk of woman's privilege, of God's particular gift to her? The experience of countless women would favour this interpretation. There can be no doubt that discrimination does not reside in this fact itself so much as in its social consequences. According to Professor Dreitzel of Berlin, the process of discrimination consists in

the interpretation from outside of group membership. With the interpretation from outside of group membership an order of preference of certain relevant areas of behaviour is imposed on certain people although it is really not their own; their behaviour is measured according to type-categories which do not arise from mutual interaction and interpretation but from external patterns of behaviour being granted by the group outside.[18]

In the case of women this outside group consists of the wielders of power, i.e. in all societies built on a patriarchal system, these are the men. By interpreting the role and function of women basically in terms of motherhood, they confine women to the sphere of the family and the household. In doing so they establish priorities which are then accepted by a large majority of women but which in modern society are increasingly proving to be discrimination. The traditional division of labour between the domestic and the public sphere is no longer valid in an industrialized society; all areas of society are dependent on the co-operation of women and mothers are very deliberately included in this universal responsibility, as for example when the present Prime Minister of Israel, Golda Meir, described the task of women as follows:

Hard will be the task and difficult the way which lies before us. But we women are not merely a part of the population. We are more than that; we are responsible for the population of today, we are responsible for the population of tomorrow. In our hands lies the future of our nations. The future lies with the babies we bring into the world, the children we bring up. It is on what they are that our future depends.[19]

Even where this is recognized in theory, the consequences which could make possible the complete integration of women are seldom drawn, and this results in a form of discrimination against women.

Well may one ask what the attitude of the movement for the emancipation of women is to these problems. In this movement, or at least in its middle-class manifestations in the Western world, the idea used often to be put forward in the past that a woman's choice lay between marriage and motherhood on the one hand, and career and action in a wider field on the other. This view has certainly not been borne out by subsequent developments. The desire to get married is very widespread in the industrial nations, and in many of the so-called underdeveloped countries it remains quite impossible for a woman to live alone and embark on an independent career. The need to combine the two roles is therefore something universally felt today, and even the example of celibacy in religious communities and orders seems at the moment to lack any great influence. A very large number of modern women all over the world is claiming that women have the right to love, marriage, motherhood, profession and career, and this right is being protected by all the international organizations (see above). But in practical terms the different position of women resulting from motherhood in its broadest sense and also from the different sexual role of women is not being taken really seriously and is not being made an integral part of the structure of society. The effect of this is discrimination. Equal rights simply cannot mean complete equality in this particular case; equal rights can only mean the impartial inclusion of these differences in the society which men and women are building together.

IV   *Instances of Practical Discrimination against Women*

In the limited scope of this article it is quite impossible to provide anything like a truly comprehensive survey, all the more so as such a survey simply does not exist on a world-wide scale. All we can do is select certain exemplary aspects and provide the most accurate data we can with reference to them.

The backward state of women's education

It is beyond question that women's education is lagging behind that of men all over the world. The gap is admittedly decreasing year by year, but it is still a fact to be reckoned with. Sweden is generally regarded as the most advanced country as far as the emancipation of women is concerned. In 1968 Sweden submitted a report to the UN which had government approval and which provides a wealth of figures connected with these problems. It puts forward exceptionally progressive ideas such as, for example, the introduction of domestic science and instruction in housecraft for boys as well as girls. The basic school education for both sexes is a matter of course in all industrial countries and it is equally self-evident that girls have the theoretical right to attend whatever school they wish. Yet in this report we read:

... There are at present about as many male as female pupils in the various institutions to which pupils can go after comprehensive school in Sweden, namely schools of general studies, vocational schools, teacher-training establishments, and so on. There are still fewer women university graduates than men but the number of women enrolling at universities and colleges is increasing rapidly. Out of a total of 22,300 newly enrolled students in the autumn of 1965, 9,300 were women.

Thus the problem of inequality is no longer due to women being heavily under-represented in education. The difficulties now consist rather in the considerable differences between the sexes as regards distribution between different kinds of education. Girls on the whole go on for vocational education on a far smaller scale than boys, and they choose shorter courses of further education. For instance, girls are now just as numerous as boys in the general, non-vocational streams in the high schools, whereas the technical high-school streams offering vocational education are dominated by the boys. In the continuation school, a new type of school offering two years' education after comprehensive school, over 95 per cent of the pupils in the technical stream are men, while 75 per cent of those in the social stream are women. The technical stream is the more vocationally oriented of the two, the social stream providing no more than preparatory instruction concerning vocational education.[20]

It is obvious from the above that even when opportunities are equal, girls do not make the same choice as boys. We can assume that this results from the influence of the patterns generally accepted by society and we may well ask whether this is indeed a case of 'discrimination'. But perhaps we do not as yet know enough about the background to such matters, and a study is actually in the process of being carried out by UNESCO on precisely this subject. Specialists in four countries – India, the UAR, the USA and Romania – are trying to find out why still so few women are going on to vocational training in the scientific and technical stream. Only in India has this inquiry been completed. There it has been established that 'as a result of still prevailing traditional habits' far fewer women are even now choosing this type of career, but that once they have the training they are increasingly being given positions though, in spite of this, few women are to be found in permanent responsible positions. The summary of this report concludes with the words: 'The socio-economic bases of this situation still need to be made the subject of further detailed study.'[21]

An issue of *Convergence*, the international journal for adult education, has also been devoted to the problem of the education of women. This provides a wealth of material as far as the theme of this article is concerned. Let us at least quote two typical examples. One article in the issue is devoted to 'Education for Womanhood in East Africa', in which – as in other contributions to the same issue – reference is made to the special difficulties that arise in rural situations. The emancipation of women is to a very great extent the result of industrialization. Let us quote:

> East African women, particularly those who live in rural areas, are brought up to consider men leaders and themselves of secondary status. Women are brought up to obey their husbands rather than to develop a relationship of companionship in marriage. They learn to do housework, take care of children, and to farm. The biggest events in a woman's life are coming-of-age, marriage, and child-bearing. Her status derives to a great extent from her husband's status. Places in agricultural colleges are offered to women in Uganda and in Kenya but, at this stage, most women lack the necessary entrance qualifications. In Malawi, six women achieved higher results than the men in the entrance examination for the agricultural college. However, the college did not feel that it could admit these candidates because the accommodation was not geared to their needs. Also, it was felt that to appoint women agricultural officers, when there was a high rate of unemployment among men, would be unpopular. This may be so, but it is not logical to accept the fact that women can do all the hard work of the farms and yet should not compete with men for professional posts in this field. Women are quite likely to take scientific agriculture seriously if some of them can see a career in it. As an alternative, it was proposed to run a short course of the non-career type at the Soche College for these able Malawi women. They might, as a result, improve their marketing.[22]

Such examples must suffice, though they could be reinforced by the observation that in countries where tradition is strong and there is little technological development, the basic school education of women is also influenced by similar conditions, namely that where there is a scarcity of teachers and schools, boys as a rule take precedence over girls, while the latter are more dependent than boys on obtaining places in boarding schools. Progress towards equality seems to be taking place most successfully in countries under the influence of Marxism. The facts we have to hand certainly seem to support the thesis we were outlining above, that the practical inequality between the sexes continues to exert a discriminating influence even when equality has been achieved in theory. Only when this practical inequality in the situation of women is taken into account in the drawing up of curricula, the allocation of grants, and indeed in all the aspects of *éducation permanente* shall we be able to speak of equal opportunities for both men and women. This point of view is very well expressed in another article in the journal already alluded to; it is devoted to the situation in France, and in it we read:

> Women who are past the stage of formal schooling or whose studies were interrupted by marriage or child-bearing can avail themselves of several

opportunities: for example, courses which are provided practically free of charge by the National Centre of Education by Correspondence and Television and its regional outlets. Yet since the family responsibilities of women make it difficult for them to profit by such opportunities, some are asking what the term 'continuing education' can and must mean for women and their goals in life.[23]

The economic position of women

Under this heading it is even more difficult to provide a general survey without being guilty of making sweeping and inaccurate generalizations. In the first place it is all too easy simply to accept the Marxist thesis of the universal exploitation of women and of women as the last remaining proletariat or the last colonies not yet granted independence. But the variations between conditions in various parts of the world and in various cultures are very great. It would moreover be unjust to minimize the fact that women, particularly middle-class and upper-class women, have been and still are given a position of security by their husbands' incomes and that if they have children and have a large share in their education they are justified in regarding their husband's income as their own because they contribute their share towards the running of the home and the education of the children. Nevertheless the 'right to work' was in fact one of the objectives of the middle-class movement for the emancipation of women and was incorporated into the Declaration of Human Rights under Article 23.

In a very interesting report from Pakistan[24] (1964) we are told that 91·2 per cent of the female population was not actively earning a living. Of course this figure should be compared with another which informs us that only about one-third of the total population was actively earning a living. In the same article we are told that in 1951 30·7 per cent of the total population was employed and that of this number only 5·8 per cent were women. Let us compare these figures with the corresponding ones of industrial nations: in 1961 34·4 per cent of the total number employed in Great Britain were women. In Austria it was 41·3 per cent and in the USSR in 1965 it was 49 per cent.[25] These figures clearly prove that on the one hand a country's economic and technological development and on the other hand varying conceptions of the roles of men and women are both significant factors in the inclusion of women in the working population.

Does the inclusion of women in the working population mean that discrimination will be overcome? Let us once again turn to the report from Pakistan; there we read:

Women form barely one-half of the 100 million population of Pakistan. They, as in all underdeveloped countries, are more hard pressed. The principle of one man feeding ten mouths has been in vogue until recently, so the women found themselves enslaved because of their economic inactivity. Women in our country are considered to be liabilities rather than assets and they suffer from an inferiority complex. There is no doubt that this is a direct result of our cultural heritage but I believe that one of the most significant and obvious reasons is their overall economic inactivity and dependence on the male. This is also one of the root causes of the low status of women.[26]

What clearly emerges from this passage is that the economic independence of women is regarded as an integral part of their emancipation. On the basis of the considerations we have already outlined, one could of course raise several points of criticism in this connection. If the implication is that the economic activity of women should result in their embarking on a full-time career alongside their traditional domestic duties, this will lead to a duplication of the demands made on them and consequently to seventy or more working hours per week, a total which has been worked out in studies of women in the USA and in many Western European countries. This is why more opportunities for part-time employment are being sought in the so-called capitalist countries.[27] The trades unions are opposing this solution by pointing out that an increase in part-time employment for women leads to new forms of discrimination and that the only solution to the problem resides in an all-round reduction of working hours. In a study carried out by the OECD[28] a plea is made for more flexible working hours and the synchronization of school hours with working hours. What is above all apparent here is that on the one hand the complete economic dependence of women has the effect of discrimination but that, on the other hand, such discrimination cannot be abolished simply by the establishment of theoretical equality.

In this context we can only touch on two further points which are however of considerable importance: the *opportunities for professional promotion* and *equal pay*. The second of these forms part of the Declaration of Human Rights (Article 23, 2) and is also the subject of Convention 100 of the ILO of 1953 which has to date been ratified by fifty-four countries. Of course this does not mean that differences have been entirely swept away as yet. This is a reflection of an earlier situation in which women were able to earn less because they were provided for by their husbands' incomes.

The Swedish report to the UN to which we have referred already contains a plethora of ideas on these topics, going far beyond the principle of equal pay for equal work. Among the reforms it urges we find the adjustment of the taxation laws, the right for either a wife or a husband to remain at home for as long as the children are small without losing, for instance, their claim to a full pension, and equal holidays, etc. As far as opportunities for professional promotion are concerned, it should be pointed out that the great majority of women in all industrial countries are employed in what is termed the tertiary sector and predominantly in subordinate positions. Concerning the situation in Europe we read in a publication of the ILO (1968):

Women's employment, the problems that is raises and the measures that may be taken to facilitate it and to enable women to enjoy equal opportunities in regard to access to training and employment have received much greater attention during the recent period than in the past. This has been the result of many factors. In particular, countries faced by a tight employment market have been concerned to make fuller use of their labour reserves, including married women outside the labour force, and this has brought to the forefront the problems involved for many of these women in reconciling their home and work responsibilities. There has also been a growing awareness that women, who still tend to be concentrated in relatively few fields of employment often at low levels of skill, might be relatively more threatened than men by the repercussions of structural and especially technological change, which . . . tends to raise skill requirement and to reduce the amount of unskilled work to be done. The contrast between the tradition-bound concepts of 'women's work' that still prevail in many places, and the rapid pace of economic evolution, bringing with it profound changes in patterns of employment, has been increasingly felt and greater efforts are being made to bring about a more realistic view of women's occupational future and needs.

This passage reveals the extent to which these matters are at present in a fluid state and how it is likely that developments will tend towards the fuller integration of women in the working process. Probably much the same can be said as far as the role of women in politics is concerned; but in the scope of this article there is no space for examples of this, though doubtless here, too, there are instances of discrimination. But this is an aspect which is very closely connected with women's education and with careers for women, both of which we have looked at in somewhat greater detail. Instead, let us at least mention another quite different area of discrimination which, interestingly enough, has been overlooked in all the documents produced by the UN and its associated organizations.

The commercial exploitation of sex

The fight to end prostitution and improve welfare work amongst prostitutes was once a prime concern of the feminist movement. It was included in the declaration on the abolition of discrimination against women as Article 8. In the affluent society, however, the problem has reappeared in a new form. The female body is being utilized for commercial motives and is thereby being degraded, at least in pictorial form, into becoming an item of consumer goods; there is not a magazine without pictures of women in a state of more or less undress which are supposed to have a particular lure; no advertisement is free from sex. In his book *Die Krise des Mannes* Bednarik writes in this connection:

As a result of the commercialization of sex, human beings are coming more and more to regard sex as a saleable commodity. This is particularly true of women, though men are not exempt. . . . By a long detour our age has succeeded under the slogan of sexual freedom in making sex a greater commercial proposition than ever before and in turning it into an item of consumer goods, admittedly in abstract form, whereby sex is sold not as satisfaction but as stimulation.[30]

Clearly enough, men have played up the use or abuse of the female body, but women have met them half-way. This in turn is influencing the image of woman more than we may care to admit and is producing a renewal of discrimination since it scarcely contributes to fostering respect for women as worthy and equal partners. Whether the other aspect of advertising, that which is aimed at the housewife, does more to make women appear as real partners, is another matter. This type of advertising always depicts women in their 'traditional sphere' as housewives, and it has discovered a clever formula for making this traditional sphere palatable to women. The housewife is presented unrealistically; she is always young, attractive, soignée, she never has dirty hands, and her life is one that men and women dream about – intimate, secure, insulated, made into a dream world or paradise, as it were, by every conceivable labour-saving device.

It could be said that these are the specific problems of just a few countries in the world, those belonging to the so-called affluent society. But owing to the media of mass communication this image of woman is in fact being disseminated universally, and how is it to remain without any impact in places where men and women are leading lives full of suffering and deprivation? Such an image is bound to awaken unattainable desires, and is steering the emancipation of women, already under way, in a completely false direction.

v   *The Contribution of the Churches to the Overcoming of Discrimination*

Many of the texts we have quoted have shown that great strength is required to overcome existing forms of discrimination. Moreover the international conventions themselves make it clear that much still remains to be done in this field. It is an integral part of discrimination that many of the most basic concerns of a group being discriminated against very often fail to penetrate beyond the sphere of those affected. In other words problems concerning women are dealt with by women and this may lead to the formulation of their concerns, but hardly to any real solution. This was one of the weaknesses of the so-called feminist movement; it should not be blamed for this – what other alternatives did it have? Today the imperative question is, how are these concerns to be dealt with in the future; and it is precisely here that we encounter a wide divergence of opinion. There is something of a new wave of the feminist movement at work in the world, that is, action groups of men and women (with women usually in the majority) passionately committed to the solution of these problems. What is certain is that women cannot avoid committing themselves in practical terms. In general, their chances of success are greater if they do so not in isolation but in the context of a comprehensive movement (e.g. Marxism). Can the church's mission be regarded as a movement of this kind, and what could the contribution of the churches be?

When perusing the documents of the 1966 Geneva Conference with regard to the problems discussed here one gains the impression that, in the first place, the recommendations of the international organizations are accepted but that, in the second place, totally different standpoints and attitudes are juxtaposed to them with little point of contact; these latter stem from the Christian tradition of marriage and family guidance, reinforced by certain tendencies in modern psychology. Has the church or the gospel a specific contribution to make to the overcoming of discrimination against women? Undoubtedly there are the rudiments of one in the documents of the World Council of Churches which we quoted to begin with. But these can and must always be given a personal interpretation. I shall here offer the following points for further discussion.

1. In the New Testament the dignity of the individual is recognized and taken seriously – not only that of men but of women too. In the Report of Section IV of the Geneva Conference we read (par. 36): 'Woman's role in contemporary society is to realize her individuality.'[31] The significance of the dignity of the individual is underlined with particular emphasis in the Roman Catholic documents. It was precisely this realization that led so many Christians, in many parts of the world, to found the first schools for girls, thereby opening the way for the emancipation of women; for non-Christians, for example Muslim and Hindu sociologists are unanimous in the view that education was the first step towards emancipation.[32] It would be rewarding to study the motives which led to the foundation of the first schools for girls

in different countries and cultures and to clarify the part that was played by Christian missionary societies and churches. Be that as it may, the appreciation of the individuality of all men and therefore women, too, is part of the indispensable contribution of the gospel. It opens up a way for human relations to be developed on a personal level, for relationships between husbands and wives, parents and children, to be deepened; it also opens up genuine possibilities for the single person to stand alone, something which is by no means everywhere possible for women in contemporary society. The extent to which the theory and practice of celibacy, a single state seen in spiritual terms as a *charisma*, can help in this context is a matter which will have to be realistically aired and debated by men and women in conjunction.

2. The New Testament, like the Old Testament, was of course written in a society based on a patriarchal structure, and this structure is presupposed in its text. But it is no more binding on us than is the conception of the world we encounter in the creation accounts. What is significant and of help to us is the way in which this patriarchal structure is every now and again broken through in the New Testament and made into something relative. Instances of this occur in Christ's encounters with women, encounters which contradict all the codes of behaviour prevalent at the time. We come across further examples of the same kind in the New Testament epistles, especially in the so-called tables of domestic rules (e.g. Eph. 5.21 ff.). Here the patriarchal social order of the period is interpreted with reference to Christ and is thereby exploded from within. The term used here for 'submission' – *hypotassesthai* – is one not often used in the ordinary language of the time. As such it is typical of the New Testament, and is applied to Christ himself, for instance in I Cor. 15.[33] The term is used when wives are told to submit themselves to their husbands, with the added comment that they should do so 'as to the Lord'. In the same way, however, husbands are told that they should love their wives even as Christ loved his church. These separate exhortations to the two partners in a marriage, further underlined in v. 21 by the words 'submitting yourselves one to another in the fear of God', produce between them a *true mutual partnership* which endows the conventional relationship based on submission then accepted by society at large with new impetus from within, or indeed even undermines it.

We come across the same mutual relationship in I Cor. 7 when, in each practical case of marriage or remaining single, one party is never addressed to the exclusion of the other; instead husbands and wives are addressed in different or identical words according to the particular situation. It is hard for us to realize the implications this had at the time, when husbands were regarded as a matter of course as the heads of their families, indeed to such an extend that they always spoke on behalf of their dependants.

Once we have realized how the gospel shattered the accepted order of its day from within and brought about its upheaval, we must proceed to ask ourselves what the corresponding approach ought to be today. For instance, it might imply that we should refuse to be satisfied merely with the equality of men and women. But at this point it is essential to preclude a dangerous misunderstanding. What we have just said must never be allowed to stand in the way of the achievement of equality; indeed it can only begin to have any relevance once equality has been permanently secured. There can be no question of opposing the complete emancipation of women, or indeed of not committing oneself to it, of drawing back because one has realized that it alone is not enough. But what does need to be stressed is that equality does not mean complete identity; what it means is the genuine acceptance by both sides of each other's different situations. Partnership of this kind is by no means confined to the personal sphere of marriage and the small family unit of today – indeed this may well not be its primary context at all; it must apply to the co-existence of men and women in every area of life. As D. S. Bailey so cogently says:

Fifty years ago, in connexion with emancipation, reference used to be made to the 'woman's question'. Neither then nor later was it recognized that there is also a 'man's question' which has never been fully considered, and which many are not disposed to acknowledge or to take seriously. None the less, the two 'questions' are interdependent, and cannot be isolated one from the other. It is futile to discuss woman's social role, and to assume at the same time that man's has been predetermined and must not be disputed. There can be no satisfactory solution to the cultural problem of sexual relation until man himself sees that his own social role is not self-evidently that which tradition has assigned to him. . . . [Man and woman] have simply been called to a life of partnership in all things – and as partners, therefore, they must seek together in love and humility to understand and fulfil their common destiny as Man. For each sex this is bound to prove a hard demand at first. While headship has its powers and privileges, subordination is not without its compensations and its opportunities for exploitation.[34]

This seems to me to be a good line of approach to this mutual problem in the contemporary context. Two points which require particular attention in this connection are the role of the man in marriage and the family and the role of the woman, even if she has children, in her career and public life. This presupposes that both sexes must learn to accept that aspect of their lives which by tradition has hitherto been suppressed so that they can integrate their personalities: men must become more aware of the emotional side, and women must care more about rational thought.

3. In the New Testament the *relationship between man and woman* is never seen in isolation; it is always *viewed in a larger context*. Thus they are never just confronted with each other, but are always drawn into a wider context as members of Christ's body. A classic instance of this view is Gal. 3.28: 'There is neither Jew nor Greek, there is neither slave nor free, there is neither male nor female; for you are all one in Christ Jesus.' Here the relationship between man and woman is seen in the framework of other relationships of superiority and inferiority. An integral part of the new life in Christ is the fact that old polarities are no longer relevant. Those that are enumerated here are ones which at the time clearly denoted traditional gradings and orders of precedence. Nor should we forget that the background to this enumeration is the custom whereby a Jewish man would give thanks in his daily prayers for not being a Gentile, a bond man or a woman. In the Christian community gradings of this kind are done away with: but what did this mean in practical terms? It certainly did not mean simply a levelling off, any more than can easily be seen in the two other groups to which reference is made. Christian Jews and Christian Gentiles together made up the community, though the distinctions between them as regards origin remained valid. Israel will for ever be the root of that tree into which non-Jewish Christians are grafted (cf. Rom. 11). Thus at one and the same time both unity and diversity were preserved, slaves and free men both belonged to the community, but slavery as an institution was not abolished. In the same way men and women were brought together in a new unity 'in the Lord' although the patriarchal system was not done away with.

Today our reading of this text is different because the equality of man and woman is no longer a question of principle. But we should perhaps pause to consider the way in which those to whom this passage is addressed are joined together anew. We are not just told that polarities no longer have any meaning; we are also told that those formerly separated from now on together form the body of Christ. Hence they are both together included in the church's mission in the world. Admittedly the passage has often been interpreted simply as a statement on the kingdom of God to come, and as a result it was regarded as irrelevant to the problems we have been discussing. This is true in so far as in the context only those baptized are in fact being referred to: in other words, it is a statement about the Christian community which represents an anticipation, as it were, of God's kingdom. What is said in the passage therefore certainly cannot be applied to society without qualification. Yet we ought surely to learn to consider things more from the point of view of the future and of the new creation in Christ. In the New Testament the *eschaton* is always projected right into the present. The new world gives direction to the old world, not *vice versa*. Surely this is of significance in a 'dynamic society'?

In the examples we have given of discrimination today we alluded in various ways to the connection between technological or economic development and the emancipation of women. In proportion to the extent to which a country becomes involved in the dynamic of such development and acquires its share, so to speak, in world history, women too become involved in this historical process and are emancipated as a result. In Europe all this began to happen about a century ago, generally without the churches or even in opposition to them. One wonders what will happen today as regards this world-wide process. Will the churches simply give their belated and retrospective blessing to what is taking place without them and what is passing them by? Or will they take as their model the body of Christ, which is a community of heterogeneous and free members and which includes the partnership of men and women, and really be able to provide guide-lines for this process of development? Will they realize that their mission as regards the partnership of men and women is also a break with tradition, or will they just cling to 'sacrosanct traditions' in this particular respect? The strength of such traditions is great, as is the temptation to hold fast to the *stoicheia tou kosmou* ('elements of the world'; cf. Gal. 4.1 ff.). Certainly, they will only retain their credibility in this respect if they cast aside their reservations and alter the power structures within their own ranks so as to bring about a genuine sense of partnership between men and women. Perhaps this way, though it will not be easy at first, will then lead them to a new awareness of the riches of the gospel and make them better able to fulfil their function as the 'city on the hill' and the 'light of the world'.

NOTES

1. Kathleen Bliss, *The Service and Status of Women in the Churches*, SCM Press, London, 1952, pp. 9 f.
2. Madeleine Barot, 'Report to the Assembly on the Commission on the Life and Work of Women in the Church', Second Assembly of the WCC, Document no. 39A, 1954, p. 4.
3. Barot, p. 2.
4. *Men and Women in Church and Society*, The Department on the Co-operation of Men and Women in Church and Society of the World Council of Churches, Geneva, 1956, p. 5.
5. Barot, p. 5.

6. Barot, 'The History and Raison d'être of the Work of the Department', *Odense Consultation*, the Department on the Co-operation of Men and Women in Church and Society, wcc, 1958, p. 3 (duplicated report).

7. Barot, *Co-operation of Men and Women in Church, Family and Society*, wcc, Geneva, 1964, p. 10.

8. Cf. *ibid.*, p. 10.

9. Here it may be relevant to mention some of the topics discussed by the Department concerning which published reports are available: 'Obstacles to the Co-operation of Men and Women' (Odense, 1958); 'The Christian Approach to Women's Questions' (Geneva, 1958); 'Towards responsible Co-operation between Men and Women, our Christian Responsibility' (Uplands, 1960); 'Changing Patterns of Men-Women Relationships in Asia' (Madras, 1961); 'Marriage and Family Life' (Paris, 1962); 'Relationships of Men and Women at Work' (Founex-Geneva, 1964); 'Sexual Ethics' (Founex-Geneva, 1964); 'For the Family' (Family Counselling and Family Education) (St Cergue, 1967).

10. *Concerning the Ordination of Women*, Department on Faith and Order and Department on Co-operation of Men and Women in Church, Family and Society, Geneva, 1964.

11. Dr Andrée Lehmann, *Was die Frauen der allgemeinen Erklärung der Menschenrechte verdanken* ('What women owe to the Declaration of Human Rights'), a publication of the Swiss branch of the International Alliance of Women, 1968, p. 7.

12. *Declaration on the Elimination of Discrimination against Women.* United Nations, opi/297-05287, April 1968. 50 M.

13. *United Nations Assistance for the Advancement of Women*, United Nations, e/cn.6/467.

14. Simone de Beauvoir, *The Second Sex*, Jonathan Cape, London, 1953, pp. 14–16.

15. *Ibid.*, p. 90.

16. Betty Friedan, 'The sexual ghetto', *Hemmende Strukturen in der heutigen Industriegesellschaft* (report of a symposium on 'Inhibiting Structures in Contemporary Industrial Society'), Gottlieb-Duttweiler-Institut, Rüschlikon/Zürich, 1969. Cf. Friedan, *The Feminine Mystique*, Victor Gollancz, London, 1963.

17. Cf. the studies by Margaret Mead, Helmut Schelsky, etc.

18. Taken from a talk on the subject of 'Isolation' broadcast by the author on Swiss Radio in September 1969.

19. *Women's Role in a Developing Society*, Ministry for External Affairs of the State of Israel, 1961.

20. *The Status of Women in Sweden*, Report to the United Nations, 1968, in the series *Sweden Today*, published by the Swedish Institute, Stockholm, pp. 34 f.

21. *Rapport sur les activités de l'UNESCO interessant particulièrement les femmes au cours de l'exercice 1967–68*, published by unesco, Paris.

22. *Convergence*, an International Journal of Adult Education, the Ontario Institute for Studies in Education, 1969, vol. II, no. 2, pp. 32 f.

23. *Ibid.*, pp. 24 f.

24. *Pakistani Women look to the Future*, Triennial Conference of the All Pakistani Women's Association, 1964.

25. Viola Klein, *L'emploi des femmes; Horaires et Responsabilités familiales.*

Une enquête dans 21 pays. Organisation de coopération et de développement économiques, 1965.

26. *Pakistani Women*, p. 18.

27. Cf. the relevant studies of the ILO, especially Reports VI (1 and 2) of the 48th Session, 1964: *Women Workers in a Changing World*.

28. Cf. note 25.

29. *Manpower Aspects of Recent Economic Developments in Europe*, Second European Regional Conference of the ILO, Geneva, December 1968, *Report* II, p. 133.

30. Karl Bednarik, *Die Krise des Mannes*, Verlag Fritz Molden, Vienna–Munich–Zürich, 1968, pp. 90 f.; now published as *The Male in Crisis*, Secker and Warburg, London, 1970.

31. The Geneva Report, p. 163.

32. Cf. for instance R. Arnaldez, 'Le Coran et l'emancipation de la femme' in *La Femme à la recherche d'elle-même*, Semaine de la pensée marxiste de Lyon, La Palatine, Paris–Geneva, 1966; also K. M. Panikkar, *Hindu Society at the Crossroads*, Asia Publishing House, Bombay, 1961.

33. On this aspect in general see Else Kähler, *Die Frau in den paulinischen Briefen*, Gotthelf-Verlag, Zürich/Frankfort, 1960.

34. D. S. Bailey, *The Man-Woman Relation in Christian Thought*, Longmans, London, 1959, pp. 283 f.

15

Food, Population and Man's Environment

ARNOLD S. NASH

A short bicycle ride from my native village in England, on the edge of the Sherwood Forest near the town of Cresswell, there is the oldest known home in the land. After the lapse of 50,000 years there are now no obvious signs to indicate its claim to fame, but its significance is remembered by the contents of a room at the British Museum. We may not know much about its life long ago, but what we do know is that here fathers, mothers, and children lived. Here mothers had suffered in childbirth; here fathers, having failed to catch food for their families, had come back home with the gaunt look of unemployment on their faces. And here children had played in the slowly flowing river which touches the banks of the road which now wends its way between the cliffs on the side of which these homes were to be found.

Anthropologists refer to these people as Cresswellian man. Biologists, however, refer to them as instances of *homo sapiens neanderthalensis*. What exactly happened to Neanderthal man, widely scattered as he was over the earth, is largely a matter of speculation. We do know that his average size brain was larger than that of twentieth century man and that he and his families went their way up and down what we now call Europe and elsewhere in accordance with the movement of the polar ice packs. Whether he faded away because he was unable to adjust his pattern of living quickly enough as the ice inexorably came down or whether he was defeated in battle by Cromagnon man, the ancestors of modern man, again we do not know. We *do* know why Tasmanian man disappeared: it was because of 'the spread of civilization'. We do know why prehistoric monsters like the brontosaurus disappeared: it was because they could not adjust to climatic changes.

As one surveys the sad story of the emergence and disappearance of so many wide and diversified forms of sentient life upon this planet, one question in the trying days in which we now live, as in this volume we try to understand what it is to be 'human', is bound to assert itself. It is whether it is anything more than a kind of mass egocentricity which leads us to believe that Cromagnon man as we know him in ourselves today has a kind of permanent status on the earth such that not even his own foolishness or his own sin can challenge it. Such a question has been asked before. It was first raised by the ancient Sumerians early in the third millennium BC. Later still in the account of Noah the question is raised in biblical literature. For twentieth-century man it is a real question, for we can no longer be sure that man will be able to accept successfully challenges of his own making, as he has accepted countless challenges from nature itself since he spread in Upper Palaeolithic times from his original home south of the frostline to every part of the globe.

Man is now faced with two possibilities for his own self-destruction. The first is that of a nuclear war. All the resources of press and book, of film and theatre, have been used to bring before the world the terrible danger of wholesale nuclear destruction. Every schoolboy knows that the major nuclear powers among them contain sufficient bombs to destroy several times over everyone who lives on the earth. Thus the very widespread awareness of this danger in and out of the churches has meant that Christendom has found it impossible to ignore the dangers from nuclear destruction. Hence the many commissions and committees which have been set up to ask what is the relevance of the Christian faith to this terrible danger. But this has not been so for the second danger of man's self-destruction or at least the destruction of his civilization: I refer to this possibility as the result of the so-called 'population explosion'. It is increasingly imperative that we seek to ascertain why this has been the case. It is not because the issue is seriously in doubt. Government commissions in many countries and spokesmen for all the international bodies tactfully and quietly have raised the issue. The report of the Section on World Economic and Social Development at the Uppsala Assembly of the World Council of Churches refers to the world's unprecedented population explosion.[1] So did the General Secretary in his report to the Assembly.[2]

The problem is that it is so easy, apparently, to speak dispassionately in terms of statistics. Thus whereas the Report of the Committee on Church and Society in its paragraphs on the elimination of racism[3] could talk about the urgent need for 'a crash programme' it could speak of the population problem in too sober language:

At the end of the century, assuming there are no world catastrophes, the world population of 3·5 billions will have doubled; half of the population will be under 25; a great percentage of people will be over 75 years of age; food supplies need to be doubled; twice as many habitations must be built as have been built during man's entire history. This situation must be dealt with by concerted and world-wide action and the fullest and most responsible use of science and technology.[4]

Nuclear war is vivid and real, but population growth is quiet and steady and there has been no political equivalent to the cold war to bring it pointedly and ceaselessly before the world. Moreover, there have been some deep ideological reasons for refusing to face the over-whelming probability and meaning of an expansion of population as dangerous. On the one hand there has been the strong biblical tradition whereby man should multiply, and on the other hand there have been all the pressures of an economic system for which maximizing the number of consumers seems to be the royal way to economic pros-perity. As one drives over the plains of America, for example, the bill boards put up by chambers of commerce gladly tell the traveller when the population of a county or a town has increased since the last census. But there are never any signs to indicate to him how fortunate it has been in those cases where there has been a fall in population.

Another ideological factor which weights down any effort to see the problem is the immediate introduction of such questions as the theological significance of sterilization or the validity of the safe period or its consistency with natural law. Yet the relevant demographic facts are simple and inescapable. At the time of the discovery of America the population of the earth was approximately 500 millions. In short, it took at least 50,000 years to reach that total but little more than a further 300 years for triple that number to be reached. In the lifetime of the older officers of the World Council of Churches the population of the earth has doubled. Indeed the rate of growth itself is increasing so fast that unless there is a radical reversal the population of the earth will double in half a normal lifetime.

There are two quite different dangers. The first originates in the fact that the area of the earth is finite, which means that sooner or later we must aim at a growth rate of zero in the size of the population of the earth, i.e. the rate at which babies are born should equal the rate at which people die. We have been able to ignore this question for so long because natural forces in the shape of early death have served as a brake upon the expansion. But man now has achieved a substantial measure of what one can call 'death control'. To some extent it is the result of public health measures in the fashion in which disease has been conquered. Thus children no longer die in large numbers in infancy because of diphtheria. Even more, the postponement of death all over the world has become possible because the increase in the amount and value of food leads to greater resistance against disease. Such a sequence means that not only do more children live but they live until the time that they themselves become parents. The conclusion is inevitable. To the extent that man achieves 'death control', then in some fashion man must accept 'birth control'. This word, unfortunately, raises, especially in Christian ears, all kinds of connotations which in the present context of discussion are irrelevant. And this word means what it says, no more and no less: the control – in the sense of the limitation – of births. But unfortunately the word has come to be synonymous with the utilization of certain specific methods of birth control, i.e those which depend on the use of certain physical and chemical methods. But we ought to remember that when Mr Gandhi recommended abstinence from sexual intercourse he was recommending a method of birth control. When His Holiness the Pope recommends the use of the safe period he is recommending another method of 'birth control'. In short – to repeat – the word means what it says: the deliberate effort of man so to conduct his life on earth that the population of the earth is not increased by his actions. In that context even the celibate priest is playing his part.

Another way in which ideological considerations irrelevantly confuse counsel is provided by those who look optimistically upon the impressive calculations of agricultural economists like Colin Clark of the University of Oxford. Taking the world resources of agricultural land as approximately 4,000,000,000 acres, it is argued that the world, properly cultivated, could feed 50 billion people at the American standard of living and three times that number at, say, the Japanese standard of living. Arguments like these are based on the so-called green revolution.[5] But without for one moment denigrating the significance of the discovery of new strains of high-yielding varieties of cereals a word of warning is necessary here. We must not necessarily assume that simply because these new strains theoretically will produce larger yields that more food will naturally be produced. On the whole it will. But so will other troubles. It may be that certain elements in the community such as urban workers and the landless poor who work for landlords, and even more the landowners themselves, will profit, but for the rest, for peasants, severe economic distress and political dislocation is likely.[6] These farming members of the community do not have the capital to get the water nor the credit to buy fertilizers, and so they will not be able to compete with the large land owners who have the economic resources to ensure the proper exploitation of the new hybrid seeds, and the capacity to bring down food prices so that peasant farmers will be squeezed out. And even if these warnings are proved to be erroneous and, instead, substantial increases in food supply appear to such an extent that on extrapolation we can predict that our earth can feed fifty thousand million people,[7] what is the relevance of this line of argument to that of the kind of world in which we really want our grandchildren to live? That is the essential question we have to raise. What in qualitative 'human' terms is the optimum size of the population for our planet?

The second – equally important – danger involved is the rate at which a population is increasing. Each child born today in any part of the world is born in an age when it is taken for granted that he or she has a *right* to food and clothing and education. He must therefore be supported, at least in the sense that he ought to be supported until he reaches an age where he himself becomes an economic producer. But there is a problem. As President Nixon rightly points out, many of our present social problems can be related to the fact that the USA has had only half a century in which to accommodate itself to the second hundred million of American citizens. In short, America over the last few decades has had to make an adjustment which previous generations could make over the centuries. So, too, for the developing countries. One African nation has found that to educate growing children at the rate which has been allowed by the planners means that although a greater number of children are taught than before, a smaller proportion of children will be able to read and write in ten years' time than today. It is no solution to say that clearly more schools are needed and so they must be built; for if more schools are needed, more teachers are needed. If more teachers are needed, more colleges for training them would be needed. But where would the money come from to achieve these means towards the larger end? One suggestion made was by economies in the expansion of the transportation system. But this expansion itself was needed, among other things, in order to increase the national income to pay for the schools! So, too, in Latin America. Between 1960 and 1967 the number of children enrolled in primary schools increased by twelve million. But there were still twenty-seven million children not enrolled in school, and that was almost a million more than were without schooling in 1960.[8] The UNESCO prediction for the world as a whole is that the year 1970 will see seventy million more illiterates than in 1969 reach adulthood.[9]

Thus it is now pellucidly clear that we can no longer take it for granted that simply providing more food is the heart of solving the population problem. The initial issue is the *kind* of life that we want to live on this earth as distinct from the *number* of people who are to live this life. Thus the basic question is not whether the world can feed itself with a population ten, twenty, or thirty times what we have today, but rather whether we could stand living on such an overcrowded earth without overwhelming chaos through the entire world in our social life, the economic and political repercussions of which would make the dislocations after World War II look child's play. Have those who see the problem as essentially one of producing sufficient food for a world population double, treble, or tenfold its present size really faced up to the implications of one of their conclusions? Do they recognize what this would mean in the increase in the size and number of our huge cities? Indeed, we can say what it already means. As *The* (London) *Times* editorially pointed out: 'It is in communities where technological change is rapid, and where people are gathered together as rootless individuals in mammoth cities, that the crime rate tends to be highest.'[10] But the increased crime rate in our cities (in the USA 30 per cent of the most serious crimes occur in the 10 per cent of the population who live in those cities with a population of one million and over) is only one painful feature of the life of large cities throughout the world. The city of Calcutta, where more than half a million people eat, sleep, live, and die with no home other than the streets, may well represent the city of the future, for it is to the cities throughout the world that the excess rural populations drift in their search for food and work.

And so we are called upon to see population growth in an incredibly more complex setting than that of food production. Theologians, of all people, one would have thought, should be the first to realize that simply to deal with one factor like food is to ignore the wholeness of things.[11] But that is exactly what Roman Catholic ecclesiastics seem to be doing. Unfortunately, the effort to see theology in synoptic terms has been too easily dismissed also by too much of professional Protestantism on both sides of the Atlantic on the grounds that it is a reversion to metaphysics, scholasticism, and medieval methods of thought.[12] It is thus to those who stand at the frontiers of scientific speculation that we now look for more relevant intellectual patterns. In terms of the notion of ecology, the sciences of physics, chemistry, botany, zoology, and the like are now standing for a sense of the wholeness of things. It is in such a context, therefore, that initially we have to see the population question.

What man has been doing in upsetting so violently the world's natural ecology is simply a prolongation of what he has been doing from the very dawn of his history. He has been trying to change the world of nature. And he has always had to pay a price for this. This price has now risen sharply. The more we increase food production using the sciences of chemistry, botany, zoology, and the like the more we have to use pesticides. The more we deforest land to grow more food the more flood control dams we must build. The more we use nuclear energy to increase our power resources the more we contaminate the recesses of the earth and the depths of the ocean with radioactive waste. The more roads we build to take to the various markets the products of our developed lands the more we have to farm marginal land. The more cars we use the more smog we produce. The larger our cities the greater the crime rate. The more water we utilize in our developed countries the more we have to recycle it.

What is involved, therefore, is nothing short of the deepest recognition of man's finitude and this, as the Genesis stories remind us, man does not want to make. He is now called upon to remember that not only the space on the earth is limited but so is its atmosphere. This, too, is finite and we are poisoning it. At the present rate of contamination the proportion of carbon dioxide in the air will become 50 per cent greater than it is today in little less than thirty years' time. More heat will then be trapped from the sun and we can expect, therefore, by the year AD 2000 a temperature increase of five or six degrees. In short, we shall find that the repercussions of a minor version of a retreating polar ice cap will be upon us, and land well beyond present shore lines will be lost as the ocean level rises from the melting of trillions of tons of ice and snow. There will be an inescapable logic about all this. Caught up in the need to produce more food in shrinking territories we shall turn more and more to intensive agriculture and the increased use of chemical fertilizers. The chemicals of these fertilizers on the one hand will lead to a colossal growth in algae that even now is poisoning much of aquatic life. We shall try to produce more food from bigger herds of cattle and from bigger flocks of chickens. More trees will then be cut down to make more space for more animals to feed man and concrete will displace foliage. What this will do to the process of photosynthesis we do not know, but it will certainly lead to a decreasing proportion of oxygen in the atmosphere and biological results of which we can only say that they will be bad.

All these sad conclusions are not only in the realm of possibility, but at the rate at which we are going they are in the realm of high probability. These cautious predictions are not the ravings of emotional revivalists but of serious scientists. The analysis which I have just given is from my neighbour professor, Professor Paul Kramer of Duke University, a member of the National Academy of Sciences in the USA and a specialist with an international reputation on the relation between plants and water in the soil.

Mineral shortages will soon emerge. Some attention should be given here to this issue since it is so often ignored. It is sometimes argued by those who dislike Dr Colin Clark's picture of more and larger cities, but who are not disconcerted by the total world population which he has in mind, that the evil effects of overcrowding in cities can be eliminated by distributing the human race over desert lands. Thereby, it is maintained, the psychic effects of overcrowding would be lessened and so consequently would be eliminated the human equivalent to what has happened in the well-known experiments with animals subjected to overwhelming overcrowding. Let us assume that – at least theoretically – this is so. But if we do, then there is no reason to believe that we shall not have run out of raw materials before we have practically accomplished these ends. This is the careful conclusion of Charles F. Park, the professor of geology and mineral engineering at Stanford University in his book, *Affluence in Jeopardy: Minerals and the Political Economy*.[13] For the world consumption of iron ore to reach by the year AD 2000 *half* of what America is now consuming per head would require six times the amount of iron ore now being mined. For lead it would involve an eightfold increase. And it is no use to put our faith in reclamation of the most valuable metals such as silver from photographic plates or mercury from thermometers. If we are to build the schools, the hospitals, the roads, and all else necessary for the doubled increase in the world's population by the end of the present millennium such reclamation would be economically prohibitive. The result, however, well before we run out of ores, will be mountains of refuse on a scale which will make the slag heaps of mining villages look like molehills. Aluminium, unlike iron and steel, does not rust away: it accumulates. Plastics if burnt, because unlike wood and paper they do not rot away, simply fill the atmosphere either with unoxidized carbon as smoke or with oxidized carbon as still more carbon dioxide. And it is the height of naïve optimism to believe that increased technology can solve these difficulties on the scale with which increasingly we would have to cope with them.

It ill becomes ecclesiastical leaders to be optimistic about science and its impact upon human life when scientists themselves begin to challenge the very simple optimism which the scientific movement has engendered. It was a scientist, not a priest or minister, who asked the question whether we should not get worried by the fact that the amount of DDT in a mother's milk in the USA is four times that allowed in commercial foodstuffs. As I write, four million pounds of turkey meat are being held from the market before the coming Thanksgiving festival because the amount of heptachlor epoxide is too dangerous for human consumption. This compound, a chlorinated hydrocarbon, like DDT affects the central nervous system of animals. It was used on the range land to kill the chiggers which irritated the skin of the turkeys.

The Canadian government has just endorsed a plan costing four billion dollars to restore the pollution-ridden lakes and rivers on the American border and has called upon the USA to take its part in removing the phosphates from detergents and fertilizers which have already helped to kill all the fish in Lake Erie, a body of fresh water equal in area to that of the country of Belgium. Professor George R. Stewart of the University of California, who in his novels *Storm* and *Earth Abides* shows a deep respect for nature and her ways, tells us in his latest book, *Not So Rich As You Think*, that mankind is already like a family which has lived for many years without a proper clean up. He is speaking of his own land, America, but this is the land which is emulated and admired throughout the world, a land where it costs ten cents to pick up a beer can from our highways where it has been thrown by passengers from a car whose exhaust gas, coming from a modern high-compression engine, is increasing the nitrogen peroxide in the air to a dangerous level and which is burning lead tetraethyl so that, as in my own university, nearly a hundred thousand dollars are being spent this year to find out whether in our large cities we are not in danger of slow lead poisoning. It is therefore no wonder that scientists can refer to the possibility that man's rash attempt to feed an ever-growing population can itself accelerate the very disaster that it is trying to avoid.

The magnitude of the problem with which man is now faced thus becomes clear. It is nothing less than his future and the stewardship of the planet which we must picture as a gigantic space-ship now that, so successfully, he has interfered with its 'natural' evolution. He has come a long way from the days when, about half a million years ago, with his erect posture, his free-moving arms and fingers, his sharp-focusing eyes, his superior brain and his heightened capacity for speech, he first began to struggle successfully with the perils of nature, animate and inanimate. He has been plagued by problems which, so far as we know, do not seem to have perplexed his fellow primates. Some, like 'What shall I do, granted the consciousness of my own inevitable death?' or 'Why is there pain and suffering?' he has had to bear with whatever consolation the teaching of the saints or the speculations of the philosophers could provide for him. Other problems, like his ever-widening quest to control the world of nature, seem to have become so susceptible to his skills and knowledge that he has now worked out a technique for leaving the earth just after, on it, he has triumphantly rivalled the sun in his ability to 'transmute' matter into energy.

His control over the forces of nature now seems to be virtually complete. But in so doing he has put his entire home in peril; and although no one can guarantee his earthly salvation, in the sense of his continued survival as a species, it is the thesis of this chapter that one step towards it is a conscious and calculated limitation in the number of passengers which our space-ship is expected to carry. And this limitation[14] will have to apply to the rich countries as much as to the poor ones, to rich families as well as to poor ones, to the members of the white race as well as to the other races of mankind. Since the earth is finite it is inevitable that *some* day, unless famine, war, and disease again interfere, the space-ship earth will be full. In other words, it will be suicidal for the human race to refuse to work for a zero rate of population increase, for *some* day the number of births will *have* to equal the number of deaths. Some day the logic of sheer fact will bring to an end our present arithmetical sequence of approximately two births for each death whereby there is a net gain in the passenger load of seventy million each year.

There is urgent need for the affluent nations to identify themselves with this world-wide obligation. Fortunately the two nations most often linked with cultural imperialism, the United Kingdom and the USA, are awakening to what is here involved. Americans are now being widely called upon to give up the notion that at least three children is a constituent element in the ideal.[15] In the words of *The Wall Street Journal*,[16] 'American parents want too many children. And the responsibility is being fairly placed.' As one of the speakers at the annual conference of Planned Parenthood – World Population forcibly put the matter:

All the evidence indicates that our population problem in the United States is being caused by well-educated, middle-to-upper-income families, predominantly white, confirmed contraceptive users, having the number of children they want.[17]

Both the two major political parties for the first time, in 1968, dealt with population and family planning. And while it was the Republican Party which used the phrase 'population explosion' it was the Democratic Party which talked of 'population control'. American public opinion has come a long way since a few short years ago when the late President Eisenhower maintained that these matters were not for political discussion but for the bedroom. At the present moment, far-reaching bills before Congress have been sponsored by twenty-four senators and sixty representatives.

Public opinion in Britain is not as articulate as it is in the USA, at the point of legislative proposal. But one Member of Parliament, himself a university teacher of geography, Dr Edwin Brooks, pointedly asks[18] his compatriots if they are fully aware of the significance of adding each year to the population of their country a number equal to that of the size of a city like Bristol. Stating that 'the time has surely come for a wide-ranging public discussion on population growth in Britain', he then goes on to enquire whether it is 'not time[19] to consider the justification for those forms of taxation and social benefit which tend to encourage parents to feel that the State is their children's fairy god-mother'.

His anxieties are fully in place. A few months after his article was printed, Dr Kathleen Ollerenshaw, a statistician who struggles as Chairman of the Association of Municipal Corporation Education Committees with the politics and economics of education, published some disturbing findings.[20] In 1969 Britain's budget for education for the first time in history exceeded its budget for defence. But the country has been obliged to economize everywhere so that whereas over the last two decades spending on education grew at an annual rate of more than 10 per cent, this year the rate of growth will be less than 4 per cent. The distressing results of that economy are obvious when one remembers two significant facts. The first is that the present school population will increase by one-third in the next ten years, and the second is that this year has seen for the first time what can only be called teachers' strikes.

But the most far-reaching analysis of the situation in the United Kingdom is the case for a deliberate attempt to work out a social philosophy which, accepting a *reduction* of the present British total to forty millions, has been made by the Professor of Agriculture at the University of Cambridge, Sir Joseph Hutchinson. In his presidential address[21] to the British Association for the Advancement of Science, Sir Joseph asks his fellow countrymen if they 'really believe that a population twice the present size – as it may well be a century hence – can live and work and enjoy adequate leisure and recreation within the confines of this island? And if we do not, now is the time to set about ensuring that our numbers are stabilized.' He continues:

Surely we can learn to take account of the fact that large families are detrimental to the interests of our children later in their lives, and to accept as normal a family size of one or two, or occasionally three children. For, make no mistake, this country already carries a population as great as the environment can support without degeneration, and it will call for all the knowledge and skill we can command to prevent irreparable damage before we achieve a stable population, even if we set about stabilization without delay.

This is the great remaining challenge of our time. We have mastered the physical world and the world of biology. We ourselves remain untamed. Our greatest need is to master the threat of our own numbers.

It is in this context that Christian leaders of both East and West can rightly be called upon to summon the world to face with courage and understanding the epoch-making significance of the greatest cultural breakthrough in human history since man became literate more than five millennia ago. Man has no need to hold fast to his once necessary obsession with patterns of high fertility, necessary if the human race was not to follow the pattern of the dodo and die out. Indeed the shoe is on the other foot.

From those to whom much has been given, much is expected; and here is the one point at which the Christian 'word' to the world can be spoken to a ready ear: ready in the sense that many leaders want to hear said what they themselves, for all kinds of political reasons, cannot say. This is as true on the national scene as on the international scene. To begin with the former: by suggesting that the world is better off if Ruritanians are brought into it at a slower rate than now occurs, the Prime Minister of Ruritania gives ready ammunition to an opposing political party. To be more specific: ethnic balances in delicate political situations like Ceylon cannot easily be ignored by any responsible politician. The Roman Catholic vote in some places, like the Protestant vote in others, must be considered by any realistic man of affairs. Christian leaders in countries where such political repercussions of any frankness about the population problem are inevitable (and any exceptions among the hundred or so of the nations of the earth are unknown to me) can surely help by clarifying public discussions of these issues among their own nationals.

And on the international scene the struggle, within the various assemblies of United Nations bodies, for recognition of the problem as something to be dealt with rather than one to be demographically described is not yet won. To take one instance: at the recent Twenty-Second Assembly of the World Health Organization the carefully drawn up resolution on 'Health Aspects of Population Dynamics' successfully disguises the problem we are now discussing. The nearest reference is to the desirability of 'family planning'. No one would deny that 'family planning' is involved, but for too long the central issue of 'population limitation' has been veiled by using the two terms as if they are synonomous. Diplomatic niceties may thereby have been served but not the cause of intellectual clarification of what really is involved.

In the simplest terms, therefore, the world must be called by some-one[22] to *control* its population. And while we can sympathize with those for whom the problem is beset by so many political vicissitudes such that all kinds of circumlocution must be used, the prophetic leaders of the Christian church have a different responsibility: it is to 'public truth'. And the term 'family planning' is grossly misleading.

I know a surgeon and his wife who, for the oddest of reasons, are *planning* to have nine children, one every two years. They now have reached six. I know another family who planned to have at least *one* boy and *one* girl. They reached three of the latter before getting two of the former – as twins.

That a simple trust in widespread family planning is not enough can be seen by analysing further what is involved for those who use the phrases 'family planning' and 'population control' interchangeably. There are five separate questions to be answered before a programme for family planning is successful as *family planning*.

1. How can we arrive at methods which are both scientifically adequate and which have no bad side-effects? Here I have in mind problems (just to quote a few) like the adequacy of the pill when apparently it encourages venous thromboembolism, or like the psychic impact of sexual abstinence upon husband and wife, or the inevitable dependence on arithmetic as a guide to the 'spontaneity' of marital love in the use of the safe period.

2. Which method is consistent with the ethical patterns and standards of a culture and the couples in it?

3. What are the appropriate educational techniques for removing ignorance of what methods of family planning are possible and how they should be used?

4. How can the economic problem of paying for supplies, where necessary, be dealt with?

5. How can the administrative requirements of the answers involved in dealing with questions (3) and (4) be achieved?

Now if each of these questions can be answered perfectly and if consequent perfect action by couples and governments can follow, what number of children would *the world have*? The answer is the total number of children that the parents of the world *want*. And on any standards or patterns of behaviour and parental intention that we can now discern, that number is not the number which *the world needs* if a zero rate increase in population is to be successfully achieved.

Thus, a frank recognition of a rate of zero for the population increase as the ideal both for developed and undeveloped countries must be called for. At this point – that of serious thought about the question – all the countries in the world are, alas, 'undeveloped', and all of us are still beginners.

Although, as we have seen earlier in this chapter, the need to take the population explosion seriously is being widely accepted by political leaders all over the world, statesmen – for intelligible reasons – do not wish to work out all the full implications of their spoken conclusions. Thus, one can go with a fine tooth comb through President Nixon's far-reaching utterance of 18 July 1969 without finding a full commitment explicitly stated to limitation in population expansion. And no first-rank statesman has, as yet, produced as full and complete a statement. That the need for limitation in population growth both in his own country and abroad saturates, as an ethos, his statement, I do not think that any serious reader could deny. But it does leave Dr Oscar Harkavy and his fellow opponents of Professors Kingsley Davis and Judith Blake[23] free to affirm that 'there has never been an official policy regarding the virtue or necessity of reducing US population growth, much less achieving population stability'. Literally that is so, but literally there is no place in the constitution of the USSR for the Communist Party! It is only fair to hard-pressed politicians to recognize that they do not receive too much guidance from professional demographers to aid them in the clarification of the position.[24]

There is a similar ambiguity about whether present methods are being genuinely successful. Dr David Wolfers, the Director of the Population Bureau of the Ministry of Overseas Development in the United Kingdom, can say that 'at most we can claim to have hacked out the first one or two foot- and hand-holds at the base of a mountain'.[25] But Professor Dudley Kirk of Stanford University in a recent article can say:

Fortunately, there are grounds for optimism that birth-rates can be brought down in time to avert a rise in death-rates, barring some catastrophe such as nuclear war. The prospect for reductions in the birth-rate in the less industrialized countries has never been more hopeful than it is today.[26]

I fear that Dr Wolfers' caution is the more justified. Professor Kirk can quote only Taiwan, Korea, and Singapore to justify his optimism, and although we know now (1969) that perhaps Pakistan (and the USA) can be added to the list, it looks as if Taiwan must be removed because of the consequences of a rapid increase in the number of early marriages.[27]

But if it is difficult to get explicit agreement about the inevitable social end, that of zero growth rate, then it is doubly so for sufficient agreement about the means to be achieved if they are to be politically effective in achieving this end. The very word 'control' brings up – however illogical it may be so to do – thoughts of totalitarian rigidity, ethnic genocide, cultural imperialism, and the like. But every modern society 'controls' education, 'controls' marriage, 'controls' speeds on the highway, 'controls' the selling of poisons to children. The essential difference here between a democratic society and a totalitarian one is about the forms which controls take and about the methods to be adopted in arriving at public decisions about them.

At one end of the spectrum we have simply programmes which seek – by contact with individual physicians, public health institutions, marriage counsellors, and educators – to disseminate as widely as possible reasons for, and methods of, family planning and fertility control. Also included are proposals for the liberalization of abortion laws – since they share with information proposals the common objective of increasing the possibilities of autonomous individual choice. The one increases access to information, the other makes possible a greater range of choice based upon that information.

A second type consists of all proposals for including population dynamics courses as a regular part of public educational curricula. It could be argued that this is merely a subdivision of the first range of proposals for better dissemination of information, but there is an important difference. The first type merely 'offers' the information to a willing hearer who presumably can 'turn the information off' at will. The second requires 'sitting through'.

A third category of proposals urges governmental inducements to voluntary restrictions upon bearing children. The welter of such proposals may be subdivided into two sorts: (1) positive incentive payments for limiting births, for voluntary sterilization, and for spacing children through periods of non-pregnancy or non-birth; and (2) negative incentives built into the tax structure – for instance, taking away exemptions for exceeding 'N-children' or levying fees on births above the Nth.

Lastly, a fourth category of proposals would legislate involuntary controls: for instance, 'marketable licences to have children', temporary sterilization of all females or males or permanent sterilizations after N-births, required abortion of illegitimate or post-Nth pregnancies, and 'general fertility control agents' added to, say, the public water supply, with counteracting 'agents' distributed to individuals who have demonstrated economic and emotional readiness for parenthood.[28]

Clearly these issues are far-reaching to an extent that is only credible because they are there staring us in the face as soon as we begin to ponder the problem. For the ecumenical movement all the old issues about church, state, and community, from the days of Stockholm 1925 and of Oxford 1937, are still with us. In a sense all the original questions of the social gospel movement raised early in this century by Rauschenbusch in America and by Harnack and Herrmann in Germany and in the previous century by F. D. Maurice and his fellow Christian Socialists in England are also still with us. I think of: 'What kind of life is appropriate here on earth for children of God?' That essentially was a *qualitative* question. And it will always be with us. But we are now raising a question that no previous generation of Christians has had to face. It is the *quantitative* question, for it is about the number of human beings on earth for whom a fully human life is to be sought.

Alternatively, the far-reaching – and, indeed, well nigh terrifying –

significance of this distinction between the qualitative and the quantitative question can be reached along other lines by looking at the evolution of 'foreign missionary' enterprise of the Christian church in the modern era, once the explorations of Columbus, Magellan, and Drake had opened all men's eyes to the reality of a spherical earth. Basically the Christian missionaries in the Age of Discovery said, first of all, 'Let's save souls'. And this was particularly so when the Protestant churches in the nineteenth century caught up with the Roman Catholic initiative of three centuries earlier. Then they said, since education and health are good in themselves and since provision of these services will provide means whereby our message can be communicated, 'Let's teach the mind of the heathen and heal his body'. Then followed the concern with industry and with agriculture in the mission field. What in this chapter we are asking is whether it is not an equally Christian concern to be consciously concerned with the question of *the number of souls here on earth to be saved*. There is no place that I know in the history of Christian theology where this question has been seriously faced in the light of genuine knowledge of the numbers involved. We have no precedents since Christian history began. Our thinking – if that is not too extravagant a term – has for almost two millennia been moulded by thought forms taken from the Old Testament; and this was a literature whose teaching on this question was originally ordered by the military needs of one set of wandering Semitic tribes, the Hebrews, in the second millennium BC as they sought to overcome another one, the Canaanites, who, already there, naturally did not share the invaders' notion that the Creator[29] of the universe had decreed their dispossession. For them all the earth was regarded as an infinite undulating plain intersected by rivers, mountains, and seas. As we have seen, we must now think of it as a huge airship in a sea of space where we have to take oxygen to breathe as well as water to drink. Its passenger list is bound to be limited just because it is finite, and so three basic questions have to be frankly faced:

1. What is the maximum load it can carry at any stage of economic and technical development? This can never be infinite and so population control is finally inevitable.

2. What is the maximum load it can carry if we are to live the kind of qualitative life asked for at a particular time, e.g. AD 2000?

3. What is the rate of increase beyond which it is dangerous to go even when we see the possibility of increasing its load?

The central issue that we are seeking to face in posing these three basic questions is the same for His Holiness the Pope as it is for Shri Dhanvanthi Rama Rau, the President of the International Planned Parenthood Federation, and they, like all of us, must face it. I venture to predict in conclusion that before man has adequately done so, we shall all have been compelled basically to re-examine many of our cherished notions. The Communists will have looked again at the original anti-Malthus, Marx-Engels theory that over-population is simply an expression of under-employment; the liberal humanists will have questioned radically whether, side by side with an espousal of the desirability of a welfare state which is publicly responsible for feeding, clothing, or educating every child who is born they can absolutize, at the same time, the ideas of freedom and individualism which came with the *laissez-faire* view of the state; and Christians will have fundamentally reinterpreted traditional Christian teaching about marriage and the family in such a fashion that this teaching becomes guidance for a world where the act of sexual intercourse has been placed in a universe of discourse for which such an act is seen as far beyond a simple one leading to procreation, as a cocktail party or an anniversary dinner is now regarded as beyond a meal viewed as necessary for man's nutrition.

NOTES

1. The Report of Section III, par. 25.
2. *Uppsala Official Report*, p. 290.
3. *Ibid.*, p. 241.
4. *Ibid.*, p. 244.
5. For a good description see the article 'The Agricultural Revolution in Asia', by Lester R. Brown, in *Foreign Affairs*, July 1968 (New York). For two authoritative treatments of this issue see the text of a statement issued by Dr A. H. Boerma, the Director of the Food and Agriculture Organization, at his press conference, Rome, 20 June 1968, and one by Dr W. M. Myers, Vice-President of the Rockefeller Foundation, presented to the American Association for the Advancement of Science (Section O) at its meeting in Dallas, Texas, 26–31 December 1968. One should also add that the exploitation of these new discoveries is speeding up an increase in world food production already under way. The US Agency for International Development reports that whereas the population of the developing countries increased by 20 per cent between 1961 and 1968 the increase in grain production rose by 24 per cent.
6. Indeed, this has already begun to appear. See the *New York Times* editorial, 8 January 1970, under the heading 'A Green Revolution Turns Red'.
7. My colleague, Professor H. G. Baity, who was for many years Director of the Division of Environmental Sanitation of the World Health Organization, warns me that he doubts that, in any case, such a state of affairs could last very long. We do not see today, any more than did past civilizations, an effective and economic treatment for leaching, below the necessary subterranean water levels, the salts crystallized out over the years during the sun-evaporation of irrigation water.

8. See *New York Times*, 24 March 1969.

9. *Sunday Times* (London), 7 September 1969.

10. 11 January 1969. By bringing out the calamitous effect of the expansion of the large cities in the world, I do not wish to minimize the increasing problems in rural society. For example although, as the recent United Nations survey, *Growth of the World's Urban and Rural Population, 1920–2000* (ST/SOA/Series A/44), points out, the urban population of the undeveloped countries will more than double over the next twenty years (from 410 millions to 930 millions), the absolute increase for rural areas will be larger still (from 1,600 millions to 2,200 millions).

11. Not the least debt that the whole of Christendom owes to Dr Richard Fagley is for his long patience and persistence in continually calling for a full recognition of this fact. See, for example, his paper, 'Population Growth and the Family in Relation to Development', prepared for the Beirut Conference, April 1969.

12. And as I read the writings of the members of a younger generation of theologians I can only join my fellow sociologist, Dr David Martin of the London School of Economics, in his plea for eliminating the concept of secularization (in his chapter with that title reprinted from the *Penguin Survey of the Social Sciences*, 1965, in *The Religious and the Secular*, Routledge, London, 1969). Fortunately the work of demolition (to use Dr Martin's word) is now proceeding on a wide front. One influential voice is that of Paul Abrecht who, in his searching article, 'The Revolution Implicit in Development' (*Christianity and Crisis*, 23 June 1969 (New York), p. 180), suggests that 'perhaps we have been overly influenced by thinkers like Arend Van Leeuwen in regarding the development process as an essentially secularizing process in which the criteria of the human would emerge in some, almost automatic, way'.

13. San Francisco, 1968.

14. I would have liked to deal here with the need to consider another limitation, viz. that of economic development itself. This topic, however, will be dealt with elsewhere in this volume. However, I could mention here the kind of issue raised by Dr E. J. Mishan of the London School of Economics in his book, *The Costs of Economic Growth*, Penguin Books, 1969. See also the article, 'Life and Soul of the Parties', by Rudolf Klein in *The Observer* (London, 14 September 1969).

15. See *The New York Times*, 18 November 1968, for an interesting analysis of the results of a Gallup Poll in ten different countries on ideal family size.

16. 15 September 1969.

17. *The New York Times*, 15 November 1968.

18. In his article, 'Does Britain Need a Population Policy?' in *Advances in Fertility Control* (Excerpta Media Foundation), Amsterdam, The Netherlands, January 1969, p. 56.

19. The City Editor of the *Daily Mail* (18 July 1968), Patrick Sergeant, clearly thinks that it is. He writes as follows: 'The selectivity principle could be applied especially to the hundreds of millions paid a year in subsidies to encourage people to have large families. In a free society, people can have as many children as they want. But in an overcrowded island, with more than enough young people in it, I do not see why we should pay for their pleasure unless they are really in need.'

20. Dispatch from *The* (London) *Times* in *The New York Times*, 17 June 1969.

21. The full text can be found in *The Listener* (London), 1 September 1966.

22. The influential voice of *The Economist* gave an opening here for the Christian church in its comments on Mr Robert McNamara's statement about the population issue when he took over his position at the World Bank: 'We still believe, as at the time Mr McNamara publicized his plans, that the bank has neither the image nor the moral authority to implement them' (5 April 1969).

23. In the latter's contention that the most perfect programme of 'family planning' is no solution to the problem of 'population limitation'. See *Science* (New York), 2 May 1969, for their original argument, and the same journal, 25 July 1969, for the reply by Dr Harkavy *et al.*

24. For an excellent illustration of the present ambiguities about where thought on this question now stands, see 'Should the United States Start a Campaign for Fewer Births?' by Ansley J. Coale in *Population Index* (Princeton, N.J.), October 1968.

25. In an unpublished paper presented at the Ditchley Foundation Conference, Oxford, on Population Growth, 3–6 January 1969.

26. In the article, 'Prospects for Reducing Natality in the Under-developed World', in *The Annals of the American Academy of Political and Social Science* (Philadelphia), January 1967, p. 49.

27. *The New York Times*, 31 March 1969.

28. I am indebted here to A. E. Keir Nash, Assistant Professor of Political Science in the University of California, for this analysis of the possible ranges of individual and governmental action.

29. That is, if we can follow W. F. Albright and his disciples in regarding 'Yahweh' as essentially meaning 'He Causes to be what Comes into Existence' (see, for example, Chapter IV, Section A, par. 3, of *From the Stone Age to Christianity*, Johns Hopkins Press, Baltimore, 1940).

PART SIX

Conditions of World Development and

Social Change

Since the struggle against world poverty and promotion of development involve government policies and changes in economic, social and legal institutions of nations, the creation of political instruments of development becomes important.

The Report of Uppsala, Section III, par. 14

16

Political Conditions of Development and Social Change in Africa

SAMUEL A. ALUKO

The development gap

The 1968 Uppsala Assembly called for radical, drastic and revolutionary changes in institutions and structures at every level and in all countries if the second Development Decade is not to be like the first, a 'decade of disillusionment'.[1] The Development Decade was a disappointment, because while the United Nations sought to reduce the development gap between the rich and the poor nations within the decade, the record bore out that the gap in many cases, particularly in Africa, was in the opposite direction.

Table 1 shows the comparative growth of the annual *per capita* national income in selected countries between 1958 and 1966. Apart from Libya, Zambia and Ghana, where petroleum, copper and gold exports respectively boosted domestic national incomes, the rates of increase of the *per capita* national incomes, during the period, were generally much lower in Africa than in the developed countries of Europe, North America, Japan and Oceania.

The United Nations estimates of comparative global increases in the *per capita* annual national incomes between 1958 and 1966 were 30 per cent in Africa, 42 per cent in the Caribbean and Latin America, 45 per cent in Asia, 45 per cent in the Middle East, 48 per cent in North America, 65 per cent in Oceania and 70 per cent in Europe.[2]

These global ratios even did not reveal the true income relationships. For instance, while the *per capita* national income of Nigeria was about 4·5 per cent of that of the United Kingdom and 2 per cent of that of the United States in 1958, it had fallen to 4·3 per cent of that

Table 1   Growth of *per capita* national income in selected countries
1958–1966 in United States dollars

Country	1958	1963	1965	1966	1966 as % of 1958
		Developed Countries			
1 Australia	1126	1486	1643	1764	158
2 Belgium	936	1186	1428	1502	160
3 Canada	1766	1892	2155	2329	130
4 Denmark	888	1335	1677	1808	204
5 France	1003	1270	1448	1542	154
6 Japan	284	559	694	791	279
7 Netherlands	695	996	1274	1362	195
8 New Zealand	1172	1504	1695	1763	150
9 Switzerland	1195	1677	1929	2056	172
10 United Kingdom	1014	1298	1466	1517	150
11 USA	2361	2857	3240	3504	146
		Developing Countries – Africa			
12 Algeria	237	207	235	248	105
13 Dahomey	63	64	68	72	114
14 Ethiopia	37	45	57	59	160
15 Ghana	140	188	233	267	191
16 Guinea	83	93	100	105	133
17 Ivory Coast	123	172	202	215	170
18 Kenya	69	87	89	99	144
19 Liberia	98	146	151	154	155
20 Libya	110	430	563	682	620
21 Nigeria	46	58	60	65	140
22 Sudan	80	91	88	94	118
23 Tanzania	50	61	64	65	130
24 UAR	111	140	158	170	154
25 Zambia	100	120	182	202	202

SOURCE   *United Nations Yearbook of National Accounts Statistics*, 1967,
Table 7B. United Nations Economic Commission for Africa: *African Economic Indicators*, Addis-Ababa, 1968.

of the United Kingdom and 1·8 per cent of that of the United States
by 1966. While, between 1960 and 1966, the average annual rate of
growth of real gross domestic product was 5·7 per cent in the world
as a whole, and 5·2 per cent in the developed countries, it was 4·4 per
cent in the developing countries.[3] If population growth during the
period was taken into account, the average annual *per capita* rates of
growth of real gross domestic product was 3·8 per cent in the developed

countries and 1·5 per cent in Africa.[4] The rising expectations of the African countries and peoples in the 1950s are not, therefore, being realized in the 1960s. The rich nations are getting comparatively richer while many of the poor countries, particularly in Africa, are getting comparatively poorer.

It is obvious that the distribution of happiness is not the same as the distribution of wealth. There are, for instance, numerous other ways in which human societies can be evaluated and, according to many of these, the differences between the developed countries in Europe and North America and the less developed ones in Africa may disappear and, indeed, in some categories it is the less developed countries that excel; nevertheless, it is obvious that the wealthier states are in reality the more cheerful and hearty while the poor and stationary states are dull and melancholy.

The development gap between the developed countries and those of Africa is not solely economic. There are other gaps in the political maturity of the citizens, in the skills of artisans, in business management, in administrative skill or in distributive justice. The social and economic development gap which is a consequence of these other gaps is directly tied to the spirit and entrepreneurship available in a country and the nature and policies of its government. Indeed, the whole prospect of economic and social development often rests largely on the possibility of political development.

Political conditions for development in Africa

The appallingly low rates of growth in the economy of the African countries and the almost static modernizing trend in their social institutions call for greater political actions to meet the unprecedented need for rapid development in the socio-economic fields. Before the requisite political actions can become effective, certain political preconditions must exist. These can be categorized as the need for national integration and political stability, administrative modernization, political participation, ideology of distributive justice and regional unity and integration.

In many African countries today the central government is unable to assert its authority throughout the country. Often there may be many areas of revolt beyond the reach of the national government, such as Biafra in Nigeria, the Southern Sudan in the Sudan, Buganda in Uganda, large areas in the Chad Republic, disputed territories in Ethiopia and Somalia, and Katanga in the Congo, to mention only a few. Most of the African countries are mosaic states, made up of numerous pieces, each of which has its distinguishing characteristics, and is separated from all the others mainly on the basis of languages and religions: Nigeria, for instance, has about two hundred language groups within its borders.

In addition, differences between the city and the countryside are more marked in Africa than elsewhere. The leaders in the city often understandably look abroad for models of national development and political and economic management, while in the countryside, which is the predominant part, the citizens look to tradition and the ways of the elders. While the man from the urban areas often deals with his fellows on the basis of their skill and competence, the man from the countryside deals with his fellow man on the basis of family connection and inherited position rather than by what he can accomplish. The man from the city often considers the man from the countryside backward, supersititous and primitive, and the latter often suspects the wealthier and more politically active city-dwellers. Where such feelings exist, it is difficult for a sense of national feeling to emerge and with the absence of fellow feeling the basis of common citizenship is absent. In almost all African countries, men and women find their real loyalty not within the nation as a whole but within their particular regional, ethnic, language or religious groups. The bringing together of the disparate parts of each of the various countries in Africa into a more integrated nation is indispensable to social and economic modernization.

Changes in social structure

Social and economic modernization and political integration cannot occur until revolutionary changes take place in the social structure of many African countries. Such changes can best be described by brief references to the changes that took place in many of the present developed countries prior to their economic and social advancement.

Before modern Japan began its phenomenal advance, for instance, it was ruled by an oligarchy that wanted to be worshipped and that lived in abundance while the rest of the Japanese lived in penury and squalor. Japan was divided, before 1867, into two hundred and sixty domains, each ruled by a feudal lord, like many present Obas, Chiefs, Emirs and Sultans in Africa, each jealously guarding its ethnic boundaries and trying to keep others away, as strangers in the same country. Ninety per cent of the Japanese were farmers and they held their land at the pleasure of the feudal lords. Until the régime that gave succour to these two hundred and sixty feuds was overthrown and the people were permitted to think and act for themselves and have modernized attitudes, Japan was backward.

In Russia, economic and industrial growth was discouraged by both the state and the powerful Orthodox Church who saw in rapid development and industrialization a breeding ground for social discontent, popular unrest and non-conformity. The society was based on social hierarchy and serfdom. The serfs who constituted 90 per cent of the population were clothed by their lords and in return farmed the lords' estates. The then prevailing social attitudes in Russia encouraged master-servant relationships, discouraged investment and encouraged pleasure and extravagance. The Bolshevik revolution of 1917 swept away privilege, political corruption and local parochialism and set the Soviet Union on the road to economic and social advance.

German experience is also relevant. Before Germany was unified as a country in the 1870s it was oppressed by a heavy burden of traditional anti-growth values. The traditionalists and parochialists were in power. There was political instability, immobility of labour and capital, and a lack of respect for manual and technical work. Then in 1870 the nation was unified, serfdom was abolished, freedom of persons and capital to move across state and status lines gained, and the barrier between the city and the countryside removed. All these released popular energies for national advance.

The United States never had such backward-looking social and political systems as kept down Europe and Japan. Most of those who believed that Europe was not adjusting fast enough for them migrated to the United States and still do today. In every other country in Europe, be it Italy, the Netherlands, France or the Scandinavian countries, until the inhibiting social and political structures were abandoned there was no rapid development.

It is, therefore, necessary that before economic and social development can take firm root in the African countries there must exist a more influential modern *élite* which is socially and politically committed to economic and social change. There must exist a new group with a value system oriented towards economic and social progress and not prepared to continue to bask in the sun of social approval or respect for outmoded traditions, institutions, and groups.

Education

The structural changes that are essential cannot occur without another external stimulus which will quickly help not only to free men's minds but also to improve their skill in modern techniques. That stimulus is education.

The industrial revolution occurred first in Britain and spread from there to the countries that we have mentioned. At the end of the eighteenth century, on the eve of the industrial revolution, Britain had the highest literacy rate in the world. By 1840, 60 per cent of the males and 40 per cent of the females could read and write (compared with 15 per cent of the males and 8 per cent of the females in Africa in 1966). Scotland, for instance, was of exceptional interest. The superiority of the Scottish educational system to that of the English, from primary to university level, made it possible that many of the innovations of the industrial revolution originated in Scotland, and that between 1750 and 1850 the rate of economic growth in Scotland was the highest in the world. This converted Scotland from a primitive tribal economy into one of the most heavily industrialized countries of the time. A similar relationship between education and economic and social advance was noticeable in Germany, Switzerland, the Netherlands, France and the Scandinavian countries in the nineteenth century.

In Germany, after 1870, the educational system was about the best in the world. Large sums of money were invested in education so that a high literacy rate increased the productivity of the workers. The school system brought out and encouraged hidden talents. The development of technical education was emphasized and was the most efficient in Europe after 1870; and the discipline in the schools was rigorous and good. As a result a large number of highly trained technicians and engineers were produced, able to appreciate and exploit scientific and technological skills. The general admiration for education and for the educated citizens made the technicians occupy pre-eminent positions in German society.

Japan started its rapid industrialization with a widespread and well-developed tradition of formal education. On the eve of the Meiji era, in 1868, literacy was higher in Japan than in any European country at a comparable stage of development, other than the Netherlands and Germany. Japan placed high priority on technical education. On the other hand, in mid-nineteenth century Russia, a high proportion of the population was illiterate, as in Africa today, and education received very low priority. After the overthrow of the Tzarist régime, education received the greatest priority in Russia, and industrial and technological advance became obvious. Today, the two most highly technologically developed countries are the USA and the Soviet Union. It has been estimated that the Soviet Union alone produces annually as many engineers as all the other countries of Europe and America put together.

The lesson for a continent like Africa wanting to modernize is clear. A modern, widespread and variegated educational system, far from being a luxury that cannot be afforded, is a necessary cost which must be incurred if social and economic progress is to come about. It is therefore incumbent on the political leaders and governments in Africa to make the rapid expansion of education a political weapon for social and economic integration.

Internal or external threats

One other very vital integrating factor is the existence of a threat either from abroad or from within. The existence of a common foe is often useful in welding together a disparate group of people for joint action for national survival. The threat of Western European imperialism in Japan contributed immensely to national reform, unification and the great economic upsurge in Japan after 1868. The defeat of the Russian army by the French army and the threat which the French victory posed contributed largely to the political unification of Germany and the rapid growth of German industrialism. The fear of Western invasion of Russia contributed immensely to the success of the Bolsheviks in unifying the disparate peoples of the Soviet Union after 1917 into a dynamic industrial state. The experience of the American Civil War led to the establishment of a more permanent Union of American states while the threat of absorption by the United States drove the Canadian provinces into a closer confederacy in 1867. Examples could be multiplied throughout the developed countries.

While external aggression is today greatly minimized through the activities of the United Nations, and the integrating bond usually forged by the external invader is virtually nil in Africa, the series of internal revolts, military coups, secessions and threats of secession in Africa are gradually performing the integrating role which external foes played in the nineteenth and early twentieth centuries. For instance, most of the internal revolts in African countries today are due to the weaknesses of the central authorities. The very attempts to contain and suppress the revolts and prevent their recurrence are gradually making for stronger central governments in Africa.

In Nigeria, for instance, the over-emphasis on the autonomy of each of the former four regions in the Nigerian federation contributed largely to the political upheavals which began in Western Nigeria in 1962, when the Federal government had to suspend the regional government and assume its direct administration, and continued through the 1966 military *coup d'état* and the attempted secession of Biafra from the federation in 1967. The experiences led to the splitting of the former four regions into twelve smaller states, with the effect that the Federal government will, hopefully, become the political nerve-centre of the country, able to contain the hitherto disturbing centrifugal political tendencies. Similar problems led to the abolition of regional councils in Ghana, the weakening of the provincial powers in the Congo and Uganda, and to constitutional centralism in Tunisia, Guinea, Tanzania and Zambia.

The series of *coups d'état* in Africa in the last five years, when about twenty independent civilian régimes in Africa have been overthrown by the army for various reasons such as corruption and disregard of the general welfare of the population, have become object lessons to political leaders that their secure political future is dependent upon how much they are able to bind city and countryside together; how much they are able to bridge the social and economic gaps; and how much of the social and economic expectations of the governed they are able to satisfy.

The military régimes themselves are kept on their toes by the fears of counter *coups*. So that even though it may appear that the political turbulence in Africa today is inimical to economic and social progress, in the long run, as well as in the short, the net effect is to make governments much more responsive to the needs of the greatest number of the governed and to serve as unifying factors in an essentially heterogeneous continent. Even though political tumults are risky, it was out of the tumults and revolts of the sixteenth- and seventeenth-century Europe that the eighteenth- and nineteenth-century industrial and commercial Europe emerged.

Political leadership and political parties

Another factor in national integration is the existence of effective political leadership. It is out of the general political chaos now rampant throughout Africa that the charismatic political leaders that are so essential, not only to national unity but also to economic advance, will emerge. The political style of leaders can make or mar national integration. Some leaders needlessly intensify the fears of minorities, while others reassure religious and cultural minorities and thus win their energies for national development. Enlightened and dynamic leadership, by personifying the nation itself, often succeeds in obtaining the allegiance of various component tribes, geographic areas and religious groups. It was such leadership that won national independence with the active support of the trade unions, the student organizations, the market women and even the clergy.

Once the symbolic head of state, with his immediate lieutenants, shows genuine interest for the overall welfare of the diverse peoples under him, it is easy for him to become a focus of affection for the majority of the active population and thus enhance the rate of development. As Howard Wriggins rightly said, 'in every community, there will be mediators, men who are much at home in both the modern world of the cities and the traditional world of the countryside. These are the key human assets which any government wishing to integrate its people [into one nation] must nurture.'[5] Nasser in Egypt, Sekou Touré in Guinea, Nkrumah before his fall in Ghana, Nyerere in

Tanzania, Banda in Malawi and Bourguiba in Tunisia are examples of some African political charismatic leaders who have succeeded, to a great extent, in unifying disparate tribes into modernizing nations, through effective political actions combined with what appeared to the common people genuine concern for all citizens irrespective of tribe, clan or religion. Even though mistakes are often made by many of these leaders, elsewhere in Africa where such political leaders have not emerged the ethnic and religious struggles have been enormous and disintegrating.

The existence of national political parties may even be more important than the existence of charismatic leaders. For while a charismatic leader may be a rabble-rouser without a definitive programme, and may succeed temporarily, particularly in a backward community, a political party with a programme and an acceptable ideology can be a unifying force. In many cases the desire to unify a country has led to the establishment of a single political party that attempts to encompass all the main political thoughts. Even where there is more than one political party, the existence of a very powerful and dominant party can be a strong integrating force. Such powerful single or dominant political parties as the Arab Socialist Union in Egypt, the Kenya African National Union, the United National Independence Party in Zambia, the Tanzanian African National Union, the Parti Démocratique de Guinée in Guinea, and the Convention People's Party of Nkrumah's Ghana attempted integrating measures in the same way as the Alliance Party in Malaysia, the Congress Party in India, the Party of Revolutionary Institutions in Mexico or the Communist Party in the Soviet Union.

However, lasting national integration is likely to find its most congenial atmosphere where the political party structure is responsive to the competing claims of the various groups which inhabit the nation and where it is willing and capable of mediation and of making sensible adjustment of the prevalent differences.

Political stability

The existence of the right types of social values, education, the presence of political threats, political leadership and political parties, though essential to national integration may not produce the political stability needed for lasting economic and social advancement. One of the most apparent problems delaying development in Africa is the instability of political institutions and governments compared with the developed countries.

In Nigeria, for instance, since the Six-Year (1962–68) Development Plan was launched in April 1962, there had been a series of disturbing political turmoils. In May 1962 there was a constitutional crisis in

Western Nigeria that engulfed the whole country until January 1963. Later that year there was a series of 'treasonable felony' trials based on an alleged attempted overthrow of the government by the main opposition party in the country. In late 1964 and early 1965 there was a constitutional crisis after the results of the federal elections of December 1964 had been rejected by the opposition parties. In 1965 there were riotings, lootings and killings after the Western Nigeria elections of October 1965 had been rigged by the party in power. The disturbed political situation led to the military *coup d'état* in January 1966, and this mainly led in July 1967 to the outbreak of the civil war of secession. In the face of the political instability since 1962, less than 60 per cent of the planned programme was executed, much of which was spent on internal security and the importation of arms and ammunition. Nigeria is, perhaps, poorer *per capita* today than it was in April 1962. Similar recurrent instabilities have kept down the rate of economic advance in Latin America.

Political stability *per se* does not itself guarantee rapid economic and social advance. On the other hand it may, by preserving the *status quo*, keep down the energies for national advance and sustain the primitive rule of reactionary and tradition-bound régimes. The two hitherto most stable and ancient régimes in Africa, Liberia and Ethiopia, are two of the most backward countries in the continent. It may require revolutionary and constant changes in the domestic balance of power to get the two countries to rise from their torpor.

Therefore unstable political institutions may produce the catalyst for national advance in the same way as much of the modern industrial and technological advancement of the West occurred during the turbulent and uncertain periods of the world wars. Nevertheless, an assured political stability is essential for perspective planning if worthwhile development is to take place in many African countries.

Administrative modernization

While national unity and integration is the most important factor for development, the fundamental changes in the functions of governments, particularly in the African and other low-income countries, and the complicated environments in which the governments function have enhanced the awareness of the need for administrative reform if rapid social and economic advance is to occur. The achievement of a meaningful independence, a growth oriented public service, the need for national economic and social planning, the need to meet the ever-growing demands of the people on their governments for more and better education, health facilities and other social services, require far-reaching changes in the administrative system.[6] There is the need for the building up of an efficient and national administrative system, able and willing to collect taxes, mobilize savings, direct investment to desirable channels, maintain law and order, and guarantee security to the private domestic and foreign entrepreneurs.

The problem of administrative reform is the more complicated where the right political and social environment, which we discussed above, does not exist and where governments are unwilling, or unable, to take the necessary political measures which are prerequisites of administrative reforms. As Kleber Nascimento of Brazil rightly asked, in such immature political societies are administrative reforms to be 'holistic rather than partial, sudden rather than gradual, general rather than specific?'[7] Even though partial, gradual and specific reforms are easier and more pragmatic, and long-run development is a series of short steps, the problems of Africa are holistic, sudden and general rather than partial, gradual and specific, and must be treated as such, if the second Development Decade is not to be more frustrating than the first. Waterston's advocacy of partial administrative reforms in Africa will not touch the heart of the matter.[8]

For instance, the prevalent large-scale corruption and nepotism in the administrative systems have to be wiped out in the same ruthless manner as high-level man-power has to be trained for the public services. If corruption is not wiped out the skilled administrators may not achieve much, because the basis of promotion and remuneration is then not efficiency and talent but bribery and clan or ethnic connections. If corruption is wiped out but expertise is low, the level of national administrative performance will be so low that the resultant inefficiency in the public sector will not only be a drag on the private sector but will also be an invitation to bribery, corruption and nepotism, which are usually the results of too many people struggling for too few facilities.

Furthermore an effective and modernized civil service, by opening opportunities to young men and women of talent from many parts of the country and by assigning them to different parts of the country, can serve as an effective integrating factor. If promotion is based on merit instead of region of origin, language, religion or other inherited criteria, the administrative system begins to develop a corps of individuals who know the whole country, who see their task as a national assignment, and who work on behalf of the nation rather than on behalf of a part.

But an over-hasty bureaucracy may generate bitter regional feelings against the central government. The areas of revolt and insurgence will grow and underprivileged minorities will be resistant and sullen. The administrative authority must, therefore, respond to local differences where necessary, while still promoting a greater sense of national uniformity.[9]

Amidst the welter of compelling needs the administrative system, bent on growth, must be competent to take the most appropriate decisions. The educational adviser presses for greater educational investment; the agricultural adviser for a greater agricultural development programme; the industrial and commercial adviser for greater industrial and commercial modernization; the economist for reform of the budgetary and tax systems and for an elaborate planning programme; the sociologist for a more comprehensive programme of community development and social overheads; the political scientist for the expansion of the local government system; the communication expert for the establishment of a radio or television network as a means of mobilizing the nation behind the government; the technical expert for a national network of roads, railways, electricity and telecommunications; and the legal adviser for the reform of the legal code and the expansion of the magistracy. All these advisers are many today in Africa and they are all right in terms of the needs of the continent. Yet the very African governments that are besieged by these compelling and competing demands are, paradoxically, the very ones that have the lowest capacities for the execution of balanced, comprehensive development programmes. The choice of priorities and the execution of programmes fall on the administrators and the administrative system. This is the more reason why the modernization of the administrative system and the staffing of it by the most capable and nationally conscious citizens in Africa are essential imperatives of rapid development.

Political participation

The more effectively the administrative and the political operators co-operate with the masses of the people, the more rapid will be the rate of change in Africa. To meet the unprecedented need for rapid development, governments are playing an increasing role in the socio-economic fields, a role which adds to their power and in turn creates certain political and social problems. There is, therefore, need for a corresponding increase in popular control of power in a rapidly changing socio-economic scene. This popular participation is not incompatible with the need to maintain strong and unifying central governmental authority for national integration, as many political leaders in Africa today tend to assume. Very few of the independent African countries encourage active popular participation, other than in shouting political slogans which idolize the temporary political leaders.

Among the various multi-year economic and social plans which are very common in almost all African countries today very few of them derive from the active participation of the masses. Rather they are imposed from the headquarters, usually from the government ministries, and mainly on the advice of foreign economic and technical experts. The result is that the aspirations of the leaders and the administrators are hardly ever shared by trade union organizations, school teachers, peasant associations, organizations of university teachers and market women.

Also many of the African countries do not accept opposing political parties but are so intolerant of criticisms that even fair and helpful critics of governmental social and economic policies write cautiously, or not at all, for fear of being imprisoned, detained, expelled or denied social and economic opportunities. The press is often similarly muzzled. Although there are a few exceptions, like Nigeria before the civil war, Sierra Leone, Gambia and Kenya, there is a denial of active political participation to those whose opinions differ from the government of the day.

It is the denial of popular participation that has caused so much political instability in Africa. Since the only means of changing a recalcitrant and tyrannical government is through violent overthrows, secret associations and plots and subversion logically become the tactics of the main opposition parties in Africa. In self-defence the party in power spends much needed energy and resources on internal security and witch-hunting. The result is that the efforts to participate in national development involve only small numbers, with a consequent retardation in the rate of social and economic change.

It is desirable that as the governmental functions expand and affect the lives of more and more sectors of the population, measures should be devised whereby regular consultations will be held with the various political party leaders, the trade union organizations, the voluntary societies and the various ethnic and religious groups, and opportunities given to them to give the best in them to the nation. If men see opportunities open to them beyond the confines of their neighbourhood or their limited traditional groups, they are less concerned with irrelevant anti-state activities, whereas exclusion from economic and political participation sharpens conflicts and intensifies competition and social antagonism and revolts.

The desire to permit maximum and free political participation must not lead the government of the day to surrender to irresponsible political behaviour. Democratic participation must not be confused with indiscipline, abuse and subversion. Nothing is more dangerous to democracy than the lack of discipline. The incapacity of a government to apply the necessary compulsion in order to enforce its decisions and execute its plans is itself one of the greatest impediments to rapid economic advance.

Ideology and distributive justice

Closely related to the problem of political and economic participation is the equally important problem of devising an ideology that is widely acceptable to the majority of the population or that is capable of bringing the greatest good to the largest number. An ideology is a set of related ideas that define objectives for the society and provide some clues as to how the objectives can be achieved. It is also a contrivance for manipulating mass behaviour.[10]

In many African countries the struggle for political independence created mass movements of workers, middle-class intellectuals and professionals who were united by the common ideology of political independence. Since independence, in many cases, the movements have collapsed for lack of any substitute common ideology. They have therefore disintegrated into tribal, linguistic and religious factions, each struggling for the limited objectives of its own group, that is, to share as much as possible out of the national wealth and power which are assumed to have been transferred from the colonial masters to the new rulers.

Realizing the dangers in such a lack of direction, some African leaders have recently been trying to formulate ideologies as banners behind which the masses can be arrayed. The ideologies mostly advocated in Africa are socialism and pan-Africanism. Because of the emotive implications of socialism, particularly to the Western powers, the socialist ideology in Africa has been distinguished from the socialism of the communist countries by designating it 'African socialism'. This is designed to make the concept more acceptable to the United States and Western European countries which are the main sponsors and financiers of the development programmes in Africa, and which still provide the main market for both the imports and the exports of the African countries.

The socialist ideology appears to me to be the best ideology likely to meet the social and economic aspirations of the masses of the African peoples and release their individual and collective energies for co-operative national development. The socialist ideology stresses the idea that, as a matter of right, citizens of a country are entitled to as much of the amenities of human existence as the resources and the productive capacity of the country will allow.

However the demand for distributive justice requires more than a better sharing of the national cake. It requires, in addition, that whether the economy is essentially controlled by private or public enterprise, or jointly by both, the government should devise new and satisfactory ways to meet the increasing and varied appetites of the citizens, regulate the economy so as to maximize the amount of goods and services available to the country as a whole, and allocate resources appropriately between consumption and investment. Socialism is therefore a substitute name for economic and social planning in Africa. The extent of the success of planned development will determine the rate of national political integration and stability in the various countries in particular and in the continent in general.

The classical political ideology of free enterprise appears to me to be unsuitable for rapid economic and social progress in many of the African countries, not only because it is not likely to ensure a fast enough rate of economic growth, but also because it will open the continent more to the exploitation of private and public foreign finance capital and to a new form of economic imperialism. Socialism should be able to enthuse the peoples of Africa to make the necessary sacrifices and to make them accept the measures necessary for development through a programme of distributive justice. The socialist ideology usually involves revolutionary changes in the social structure, particularly where the ruling groups are oppressive or indifferent to the aspirations of the people, and where they are supported by foreign interests to resist the necessary changes by the use of coercion.[11] Even where the transition to socialism is violent, it has to be understood as the price to be paid in the search by the common people of the continent for justice and equality.[12]

Regional unity and integration

Pan-Africanism provides the ideological basis for continental and regional economic and political integration in Africa. Although the ideology has not fired much imagination other than at a purely intellectual and visionary level, the tendency towards integration in the developed and other developing countries – like the European Economic Community, the European Free Trade Area, the Organization of American States, the Central American Common Market, the Latin American Free Trade Association and the Arab Common Market – has given rise to the concern in Africa for economic and political integration, as a means of achieving a more rapid economic, political and social development.

At the political level, the basic motivation for integration and co-operation springs from the belief that many of the African states are too small for individual effective rapid development and genuine political independence. There is need, therefore, for co-operation with other African countries.

The Organization of African Unity (OAU), created in 1963, is designed to harmonize common interests and present a united front in external affairs. The Economic and Social Commission of the OAU decided in Niamey in 1963 to set up a Free Trade Area between member states; to harmonize and co-ordinate national development plans, particularly in transport and communications, by land, sea and air; to study the problems of payments agreements between African countries until the establishment of an African Payments and Clearing Union; to standardize a common external tariff among member states and set up a monetary zone and a central bank. It planned to achieve most of these objectives by co-operating actively with the United Nations Economic Commission for Africa.

At the regional level, within the French speaking African countries, there are co-operating organizations like the West African Customs Union (WACU), founded in 1959 by Dahomey, Ivory Coast, Mauretania, Niger, Senegal, Mali and Upper Volta; the Equatorial Customs Union (UCE) established in 1960 by Congo, Gabon, Chad and the Central African Republic, and the Entente set up in 1965 by Ivory Coast, Upper Volta, Niger, Dahomey and Togo. These economic and political groupings have the economic objectives of creating customs unions, redistributing revenue to support poorer members, and harmonizing development plans. In 1960, Congo Brazzaville, the Cameroons, Gabon, Chad and the Central African Republic created a customs union and a Central Bank. In 1964, proposals were put forward for the establishment of a West African Free Trade Area to include Ivory Coast, Guinea, Liberia and Sierra Leone. The four countries have now set up an Organization for West African Economic Co-operation in Sierra Leone.

In South Africa a customs and currency union has existed between South Africa and the three High Commission Territories of Basutoland, Swaziland and Bechuanaland since 1910, while there has been a Trade Agreement between Rhodesia and Malawi since 1964.[13]

There are other recent proposals for sub-regional co-operation. The Maghreb countries of Morocco, Tunisia, Algeria and Libya have taken measures since 1964 to create a customs union to harmonize trade policy and development plans, co-ordinate tourism, the external marketing of agricultural products, and jointly to establish an iron and steel plant. The United Arab Republic and Sudan are contemplating joining the Maghreb Union. In May 1966, Ethiopia, Kenya, Malawi, Mauritius, Tanzania and Zambia signed articles of association. The articles of Association for a West African Economic Community were considered in Niamey in October 1966 and at Accra in April–May 1967. An African Development Bank had already been set up in Abidjan in 1964.[14]

Although the gains of the various attempts at integration in Africa have been small, they represent the eagerness with which it is becoming increasingly realized that a wider political and economic community is essential for rapid development. Such integration is particularly essential for industrial development in Africa. The small scale nature of most of the national resources and markets renders industrialization in the individual countries an expensive and precarious process, while closer union among contiguous countries facilitates fiscal, monetary and trade integration.

Economic integration cannot, however, succeed to any major extent unless there is also a strong degree of political unity, which implies the surrendering of national sovereignties by many of the independent African countries. It does not appear that there are many African countries which are willing to surrender their political autonomy and independence to a larger union. This general attitude has made even the OAU become mainly a debating forum for the independent African countries. Until there is a greater willingness among African countries to surrender political sovereignty to regional or continental political and economic organizations, the rate of development in Africa will be determined by the ability of the individual countries and governments.

Conclusion

Since the struggle against world poverty and the promotion of development involves government policies and changes in economic, social and legal institutions, the creation of the political instruments of development becomes important. Nowhere is this more important today than in Africa. It is necessary for the states to have goals for the building of new nations in Africa. Among the goals that have been adumbrated in this essay are the creation of broadly based social, political and economic organizations, the creation of broadly based social justice, security for the people and the state, adequate educational and cultural opportunity for all citizens, adequate participation of the people at all levels in decision-making processes and the humanization of the impact of technology and rapid social change.

Whatever may be the roles of government and politics, the most important instrument for change will be found in the attitudes and character of the individual Africans. Since governments are made by men, modern societies grow through the application of new knowledge by men with the capacity to understand the secrets of nature, self-reliance, an orientation towards the development of skills and a spirit of creativity. These are the essential qualities which Africans need to create modern industry, modern society and modern government. In addition the modernizing Africans must be ready to accept new ideas and try new methods; must be more interested in the present and the future than in the past; must have a better sense of punctuality; must have a greater concern for planning, organization and efficiency; must learn to see the world as calculable; must have a faith in science and technology; and must believe in distributive justice.[15]

Both modern men and modern institutions are in such short supply in Africa that the rate of development has been largely dependent on the whims and caprices of foreign peoples and governments. Whatever may be the amount of external assistance, if there are no ready internal co-operating factors of production, the net effect will be minimal. It is imperative that the African countries have to build their own political and economic structures through their own sweat and tears.

Even if the much canvassed 1 per cent of the national incomes of the developed countries is granted as aid to the African countries alone, it will hardly make a dent on the development needs of the continent. But when less than 1 per cent of such incomes has to be scrambled for by Asian, Arab, Latin American and African countries, the degree of self-reliance necessary for rapid development in Africa can be imagined. Political and economic self-reliance is therefore essential to the development of Africa. Self-reliance can better be fostered through arrangements that make maximum co-operation possible among African countries and peoples.

This is not a plea for non-co-operation with the non-African world. To quote the Uppsala Report again, it is necessary that we must move from a welfare state to a welfare world and that the technological abilities in the developed nations should be made available to meet the socio-political and economic needs in the developing countries.[16] But much as external links are necessary, internal African links are more important. The reduction of external economic dependence is a necessary condition not only for the kind of economic diversification being aimed at in Africa today but also for the attainment of political and economic autonomy.

NOTES

1. The Report of Uppsala, Section III, par. 6. The United Nations Development Decade was launched in 1960. The second Development Decade was launched in 1970.

2. *United Nations Yearbook of National Accounts Statistics*, 1957, Table 6B.

3. *Ibid.*, Table 4B. Between 1960 and 1966 total average annual rates of growth of real gross domestic product at factor cost were 9 per cent in Japan, 8·2 per cent in the Middle East, 7 per cent in USSR and Eastern Europe, 5·2 per cent in North America, 4·9 per cent in the Caribbean and Latin America, 4·4 per cent in Europe, 4 per cent in Africa, excluding South Africa, and 4 per cent in East and South-East Asia, excluding Japan.

4. *Ibid.* Figures for geographic areas were 5·9 per cent in the Middle East, 5·8 per cent in USSR and Eastern Europe, 5·2 per cent in Japan, 3·5 per cent in North America, 3·4 per cent in Europe, 1·8 per cent in the Caribbean and Latin America, 1·5 per cent in Africa, and 1·4 per cent in East and South-East Asia, excluding Japan.

5. Howard Wriggins, 'National Integration' in *Modernization: The Dynamics of Growth*, edited by Myron Weiner (Voice of America Forum lectures), Basic Books, New York, 1966, ch. 13, p. 187.

6. Report by the Secretariat. Meeting of Experts on the UN Programme in Public Administration, 16–24 January 1967. ST/SG/AG.6/L3, pp. 36 f.

7. Kleber Nascimento: *Public Administration in Brazil*, 1966, cited by Albert Waterston, 'Public Administration for What? A Pragmatic View', in *Administration*, the quarterly review of the Institute of Administration, University of Ife, Nigeria, vol. II, no. 1, October 1967, p. 5.

8. Albert Waterston, 'Public Administration for What? A Pragmatic View', *op. cit.*, pp. 7–10.

9. Cf. Ralph Braibanti: 'Administrative Modernization' in *Modernization: The Dynamics of Growth*, ch. 12, pp. 166–80.

10. Leonard Binder, 'Ideology and Political Development' in *Modernization: The Dynamics of Growth*, ch. 14, pp. 192–204.

11. The Report of Uppsala, Section III, par. 15.

12. Cf. *Social Change in Developing Areas*, ed. H. R. Barringer, George I. Blanksten and R. W. Meek, Schenkman Publishing Company, Cambridge, Mass., 1965, Part I, pp. 19–26.

13. Peter Robson, *op. cit.*, p. 6.

14. *Ibid.*

15. Myron Weiner, *Modernization: The Dynamics of Growth*, ch. 1 ('Introduction'), p. 4.

16. *Uppsala Speaks*, pp. 39–41.

17

The Structural Ambivalence of
Latin America

CANDIDO A. MENDES DE ALMEIDA

1 *The Social Process of Latin America during the Development Decades*
The years since 1950 have been labelled 'development decades' for the
nations of the 'third world'. 1970 provides the first good standpoint
from which we can assess the validity of this phrase and the extent
to which the idea of change can justifiably be identified with the
present-day social process of Latin America. The last twenty years
show a long, sustained drive towards a cumulative growth, that is
'development' as it is understood and fostered by our 'intelligentsia'.
The ultimate significance of this kind of change must be related to
qualitative modifications in the social structures, since new forms of
capital formation and the redistribution of income imply a change in the
patterns of power and the interplay of structures. Thus emerged the
concept of development as involving all aspects of society and revealing
the limitations of strictly economic development on the one hand, or
of social or political development on the other. This 'global approach'
to development gave rise to strategical forms of tackling the problem
and an effort to discover the dynamic factors in the interaction between
its economic, political, and social components.

Development has come to be understood not only as a *total social
fact*, but also as a *historical experience*, as an opportunity for nation
building and as the hallmark of countries capable of directing their own
social processes. Thus the last ten years have seen development linked
with nationalism as an emancipatory process, and indeed the only one
leading to a viable programme for changing present structures.

The colonial structure

Two consequences arose from this new understanding of the term. The first was that the sociological background from which development started was recognized as a highly coherent régime of social relations which could be called the colonial structure. It could be characterized as a situation of social atrophy, in which economic and political behaviour (e.g. capital formation and the diffusion of power) did not develop. The interplay of atrophies, the regressive interaction between the upper and lower social structure, the many reciprocal relations between the two with an inverse dynamism, show how the situation could turn into a recognizable pattern which could clearly be identified as a régime, without being a real *system* of social relations. It could produce an amazing and elaborate resistance to change, to what was perhaps too quickly called the 'modernization process'. Through an elaborate pattern of subtle relationships between political and economic collective behaviour, underdevelopment has come to be labelled an 'equilibrium of scarcities'.

Transition and social change

The second consequence was the recognition that the situation necessitated an entirely new form of historical change that would be the opposite of evolutionary change. This modification of the social setting would not occur by the mere addition of new variables which would create gradual change simply by interaction and combination; rather it presupposes the simultaneous presence of two different sets of social forces, progressing by tension and (assuming the ultimate supremacy of the most dynamic), by the 'abduction' of elements of the old structure by the new, and the revitalizing of those elements which had been crippled and thwarted under the colonial régime. This is the fundamental premiss for understanding the ambiguity or structural ambivalence of Latin-American society. Its most important consequence is to raise the question of revolution in that society.

Transition and revolution

It is impossible to achieve qualitative change in a structure of this kind simply by the modification of the patterns of power, essentially by a vast confiscatory policy, for this is to understand the malfunctioning of the old society solely in terms of the structure of property and the control of institutions within that society. For example, the nationalization of the Bolivian tin-mines in 1952, although it gave the state full control over the export sector of its economy, did not make it less subject to the persistently colonial-like behaviour of the international market. If there is to be a genuine qualitative change in the social process of Latin America there must be a simultaneous interaction between the economic and political levels of transition.

The present perspective of social change

Unfortunately effective development is much more the exception than the rule today in Latin America. Perhaps only one country – Mexico – has succeeded in reaching the take-off point, and in matching the growing industrialization and re-orientation of its economy with both political stability and significant popular participation in this process. At the other end of the scale, countries like Ecuador or Paraguay are still struggling to assemble the basic factors which would give them strength to break the vicious circle of a colonial economy and to enter upon a viable development effort. In between are many countries in which economic growth is not necessarily associated with structural changes led by industrialization but consists rather in a succession of extractive or primary activities. Some of these countries, such as Venezuela, have a *per capita* income comparable to that of many developed countries, yet may still suffer from a polarization of the new wealth, acute regional imbalances, absence of general social mobility and over-dependence on external economic dynamisms. On the political side, the maturing of a national consciousness, a tradition of political stability and a general participation in the political process, or the strengthening of an authentic trade union movement, may sometimes lead to an emphasis on the modification of super-structures which may displace the real priorities for effective change. This may be happening today in Chile where general backing of President Frei has been linked to the 'Chileanization' of the copper-mines, but this has largely been postponed on the grounds of the alleged need for a coherent progression of change. The toll this is taking upon the popularity of his government shows how risky is the task of synchronizing political and economic emancipation. The other extreme of this imbalance between economic performance, genuine political participation and diffusion of power is dramatically illustrated by the two biggest countries of South America, Brazil and Argentina. Both have lost the chance to reach the take-off point by means of spontaneous development, although they have by far the best natural endowment. Both embarked upon a process of quick and decisive change during the '50s, through industrialization and the disruption of oligarchic patterns of power effected by 'varguismo' in Brazil and 'peronism' in Argentina. Their growth was finally slowed down by a severe slump in exports or by rampant inflation.

From thorough to rationalized change

Argentina and Brazil have now re-launched development policies following the classic neo-capitalist model with a classic curbing of inflation and a maximum degree of integration with the international economy of investments and foreign aid. These economic policies have been matched by the appearance of power-*élite* groups, generally based on an alliance between the military and a limited group of civilian planners, for example the Aramburu–Alzogaray joint venture in Argentina, and the intimate collaboration between the Brazilian President Castelo Branco and his Minister of Planning, Roberto Campos. This latter régime aims to create a completely new political model – a technocracy – to match the present rationalized version of development. In this model, a power-*élite* group, extremely homogeneous in ideology, would enforce a definite policy of rational approach to planning and social change. It would underline the significance of popular backing in its system, either by seeking legitimacy through extended popular suffrage, or by broadening the need for immediate participation in the political process. Such régimes try to perform these tasks 'from the top', based on further acceptance by the people of the modifications now entailed by a process of development with limited 'participation'.

Emergent asynchronisms and latent structural tensions

What role has the ambivalence of the social structure played in the present slow-down in growth and the frustration of the hopes raised at the dawn of the 'development decade'? The fact that some of the countries which appeared most prepared to seize the opportunity to bring about this change have missed it, shows that the key problem in achieving development lies in this ambivalence and especially in its side-effects. New bottle-necks may develop owing to the inadequacy of new economic forces. The elaborate new mechanism of resistance set up by the colonial order, and distortions in the growth of a national consciousness, may lead to curious traits in the emerging new classes and their enslavement to the classical articulations of the old régime.

The extension and meaning of ambivalence or ambiguity

The transition process in which the whole of Latin America is involved is based on the coexistence of two social structures which are absolutely incapable of being integrated or related to the same social framework. This theme of duality is basic to an understanding of the present tensions of Latin America, and the pattern in which two sets of social forces may develop an extended interplay without ever inte-grating. It explains why growth does not result naturally from the

N

simple quantitative increase of the many factors responsible for change, but rather from the permanent confrontation of the régimes, and by the 'abduction' of elements of the old by the new. This, to succeed, presupposes the 'maximization' of efforts in certain privileged periods, in which full advantage would be taken of a special constellation of elements, both internal and external, which could provide a definitive imposing of development upon the colonial structure.

The time effect of this coexistence on the overall process of growth creates unexpected set-backs or blockages in the continuum of change. The clash of development with the colonial structure can be attributed to the protracted effect of mechanisms such as:

(*a*) the planting of an embryonic middle class into the superstructure of the society, through the permanent over-expansion of its bureaucracy;

(*b*) the over-expansion of subsidies and state controls, essentially in the export sector and through public investment and the exchange and devaluation policies, permanently 'capitalizing the gains and socializing the losses', which make useless any true economic behaviour;

(*c*) the permanent interplay between the market economy and the maintaining of a subsistence level whereby the colonial régime can count on a huge labour surplus which it can absorb or reject without fear of political consequences.

All these mechanisms impinge deeply upon the continuity of change, either by harnessing new social forces to old social patterns, by protracted disruption, by creating new bottle-necks between the super- and infra-structure in countries which are well advanced in their economic development, or by slipping old unintegrated elements into the new dominant structure.

From structural ambivalence to ambiguity in the universe of thought

A certain ambiguity is significantly apparent between the 'third world' and the Western nations, for there is a fundamental 'semantic gap' in the confrontation of the 'haves' and the 'have-nots'. The presupposition that all social dynamisms fit within the classical evolutionary patterns of change is dominant. The specific new changes of Latin America are measured and understood in Western categories of historical time. Transitional change is forced into categories of evolutionary change. Some typical antinomies have made a veritable 'tower of Babel' of the polemics of development.

1. Development versus progress

Latin America's growth cannot be encompassed within the classical linear and cumulative idea of progress. Asynchrony, and a change 'by jumps', is much more descriptive of the effective qualitative change presupposed by development. Latin America cannot count on the continuity of change, and she may be misled by the conventional idea of the inevitability of progress. On the contrary, there is a specific moment for this change, and this whole continent may let it pass by. Moreover, the chances to seize it are unequally distributed in time, and one generation may have a historical mandate to accomplish it.

2. *Modernization versus cultural authenticity*

According to the dominant stereotype, Latin American societies are traditional, not colonial, régimes. The modernization process is seen as a gradual rhythmic evolution from old to new forms of social life, involving a general cultural basis for the dialogue between the centre and the fringes of the Western world. This view fails to take into account the fact that the old society is a very elaborate complex of relationships based upon classical international capitalism. We forget the essential dualism and the non-integrated character of these societies. We forget that this dichotomy penetrates to the very heart of these complexes of relationships which, as long as they are under a colonial structure, cannot be called nations. They are not the historical subjects created by the West but only its external proletariat. The civilization process is world-wide today. But what about the social process, the cultural process, to follow Alfred Weber's famous distinction?

Modernization deals only with the civilization process; it is irrelevant to the true cultural process, which can grow only from within, challenged in this case by development, and maturing into a certain conception of the world and a definitive style of life. As the historical external proletariat of the West, Latin America was diverted from a true cultural process, and has been unable to create a community with its own identity.

3. *Nationalism versus collective egoism or xenophobia*

Nationalism in Latin America today may be defined as the political consciousness of development and the effort through a collective decision to exploit all the energies of society towards a successful nation-building experiment. It is a movement of promotion, not of resentment or xenophobia, based on the conviction that those who live on the fringes of these collectivities have to count massively on their own effort to overthrow the colonial régime and use the nation as the most effective instrument for maximizing the exploitation of their potentialities.

4. *Formal democracy versus popular participation*

In the 'third world' and especially in Latin America, the formal legitimacy of political régimes bears little relation to the inner values of democracy, and to effective popular participation in this process. This antinomy challenges traditional Western ways of thinking, whenever the new dynamics of instant and increased participation prevails over formal democracy, or when formally constituted régimes, which are in reality tiny power *élites*, lack the capacities for effective nation-building.

II   *The Impact of Ambivalence on Social Change*

Revolution – the luxury of wealthy countries

Perhaps the most striking result of the ambivalence of Latin American social structures is the failure of the labour sector to be socially articulated; the huge reserve of manpower is shrewdly used as a permanent cushion to nullify both its bargaining position and any sustained patterns of dynamism, and this sometimes leads to violence. The workers are permanently caught between the economic market and the subsistence level, simply merging into the latter when they are ejected from the former. They 'fade away', but do not ultimately starve. In Latin America, in contrast to the developed societies, massive unemployment has not on the whole produced revolution in the classic sense. For revolution as the climax of social tension presupposes previous forms of effective social bargaining, the creation of a social conscience and, above all, the incorporation of the whole population into an effective system of social relations. That is why revolution is a luxury of a certain stage of development and why it never appears in colonial structures built on the interplay between two unrelated levels of social life, since it obviously has no scope there for destroying class alignments or other homogeneous social groupings by linking them with other classes or by fomenting divisions within them. For example, in Brazil this situation is destroying the proletariat as a social force, owing to the following factors:

(*a*) The urban workers tend to behave like the middle classes and are deprived of all contact with the rural areas or with other groups of workers.

(*b*) The rural workers employed in the plantation system are generally at the mercy of fluctuations in the foreign markets; they operate within an economic enclave, surrounded by the labour reserve, at the subsistence level.

(*c*) The rural workers who produce agricultural commodities for the new urban areas are entirely dependent on the financial support of the mercantile *bourgeoisie*.

(*d*) The proletariat, trapped at the subsistence level and used as a reserve labour supply for the other three layers, thereby contributes to depressing their wages.

The pseudo-capitalist sector

Since economic conditions in the colonial régime have not encouraged private investment, productivity or the rationalization of markets, the state has become the main economic agent. Through manipulation of the rate of exchange it insures the transfer to the whole collectivity of any losses suffered by the wealthy. Any accumulated surplus immediately assumes the form of waste, or is used for ostentatious living, or hoarded. With the advent of development, the ambiguous position of the group supposed to direct industrialization in the national interest immediately became obvious. The national *bourgeoisie* kept to the tradition that state support is not merely a contingency of an early period of development, but part of the economic structure which has grown up in the ensuing years.

Generally speaking they were ideological captives of the old order, one of the strongholds of conservatism, often opposing fundamental development policies. When inflation produced an abnormal and sterile form of redistribution of income, the industrial bourgeoisie became more predatory, refused to reinvest its capital, and counted entirely on government loans and subsidies. When attempts are made to re-launch development, this private national sector is seen to emerge as a very marginal one, socially eroded by inflation. It becomes a minor partner of one of the remaining sources of capital formation; namely foreign investment or the state. Nevertheless, the latter, instead of emulating some kind of a semi-socialist model, devotes its whole potential to a nominal capitalist economy.

The intellectual versus the university

The role of the university in social change in Latin America also reflects the ambivalence of its social structures. Instead of a commitment to study and consider the mandatory tasks of transition, we generally find official culture propagandizing for the 'establishment' and showing utter insensibility to the needs of the emerging Latin American countries. This forces the intelligentsia to break with the universities (which have become a key feature of the 'establishment') in order to perform its functions as a creative minority, especially in the early phase of this process of change. Their task is a tough one: they must not only build ideological links between the fundamental forces of change, but must develop a critical national consciousness willing to recognize the utter alienation produced by the colonial structure. They must assess and denounce the many trends by which the drive towards development can be distorted and even thwarted. That is why the 'intelligentsia' carries out its function outside the universities, sometimes in Institutes of Advanced Studies, with the double task of applying traditional social thinking to the problem facing the country and of serving as a permanent critic of the government's development policies. Brazil has created an Institute of Superior Studies (ISEB) with the specific task of formulating an ideology for development. This divorce between the intellectual and the university is a clear demonstration of how impervious the colonial structure is to any authentic change in the cultural process from within.

The compromise of the church with the status quo

In the colonial régime the attitudes of the secular and the religious orders towards the *status quo* are much more mutually dependent than in Europe or the United States. In some Latin American countries Roman Catholicism is still the state religion. When the old régimes collapsed, the church either had to go along with the establishment or support the new social order in which it could no longer benefit from a privileged position. But the problem was never clearly formulated. On the one hand, the church never openly supported the hardening of the old order, on the other it advocated gradual change by what was understood by many as 'reformism', i.e. some redistribution of income and the divesting of old privileges to reduce scandalous disparities. Here the prospect of evolution prevailed over the needs of transition. Many catholics, in an average or even distorted understanding of the church's social doctrine, opted for the old order by stressing only voluntary change and a philanthropic or indeed romantic conception of charity.

The effort to interpret the social doctrine of Catholicism within the perspective of evolution and organic change in this case prevented the church from giving full support to the political forces struggling for development and thus helped to defend the *status quo*.

The more evidently circumstances prevent a spontaneous change the clearer becomes the church's dilemma and the risks a developmental policy creates for it. In fact at one of the extremes, and mainly because of a reduction of the conventional democratic systems, the voices of both Roman Catholic and Protestant clergy become a vicarious expression of social dissatisfaction, whenever tough policies to re-launch development involve great social sacrifices and undertakings. At the same time, at the other extreme, authoritarian voices, identified with policies to overtake the economic development effort of recent years, tend to emphasize the importance of social order symbols and, consequently, the consolidation of the church's traditional role within those structures. It means that the church has had imposed on it the risk and the temptation of an easy shift of attitude, even within an effective policy of reforms in the context of the pursuit of temporal power; the new attitude merely aims to refine the old perspective of privilege, and to confine the true notion of social order within a perspective of a strict legitimation of social inertia in the societies undergoing change.

The abduction of power by the technocrat

Transitional change is absolutely dependent on the emergence of a new social order based on planning and on social behaviour derived from logical correlations and rational models.

This places tremendous power in the hands of a new priesthood: the economists, sociologists, and political scientists who are concerned with the manipulation of the fundamental equations of social change and the working out of policies to assure it. This group, which behaves like a 'clan', seeks to rid itself of all sociological conditioning and to remain absolutely neutral concerning 'class' or 'status' interests. Evidence of the emergence of this super-structure is increasingly apparent in the underdeveloped countries, especially in situations in which spontaneous growth has failed and had to be re-launched artificially. In rare cases this technocracy has arisen within the civil service (as in Tunisia, for example). In others it has required the direct backing of a military machine although keeping separate from it (predominantly in Latin America, as for example in Brazil and Argentina). As a third way the power *élite* has emerged from the structural transformation of the military into technocrats (as in Egypt). It is possible in Latin America today to establish a correlation between the awakening of a development policy and the acquiring of a new store of techniques and skills which have been developed by professions dedicated to the improvement and acceleration of the various factors connected with the expansion of the national income.

Although this attitude is positive, it brings with it the danger of an excess of 'technicism' which weakens or even annuls sensitivity to the historical or meta-economic conditions of the social structure. It leads to the cult of rationality and to the idolatry of the lucid approach both of which are often incompatible with the rational procedures which characterize the developing country. The final crystallization of this perspective consecrates an international formula for development through a neutral technocratic *élite* capable of repeating endlessly with slight adjustments the same diagnosis and the same therapies. In other words, the technocrat, seeking the mountain peaks of social progress, may die in this rarefied atmosphere in which he has lost contact with the historical and concrete elements required to make viable his stern rational approach towards development. Lacking this setting, a conflict between his uncompromising attitudes and the response from within the community would seem inevitable, although the technocrat may compensate for it by developing what may amount to a lust for unpopularity. Thus the reign of the 'philosopher kings', now at its dawn, may be short, for it is in danger of rejection by the popular classes. What is really at stake in this drama is the difficulty of ideological role-playing in the process of transition between total social structures.

The emergence of popular culture

Immediately related is the fact that the transition process gives full prominence to a genuine new form of culture, different from the typical product of creative minorities. For instance, the maturing developments in Latin America tend to be characterized by such distinct phenomena as the emergence of national consciousness, and of a popular culture. These are the direct effect of the speed of the collapse of the old structure, the increase in social mobility, and the significant role generally given to the collective. Popular culture is thus a result of the historical challenge posed by development: it derives from the direct call to the entire community for significant action against the colonial situation and results in the quick obsolescence of that situation. 'Conscientization'[1] becomes its fundamental element, accompanied by the immediate awakening of associative feelings expressed in many forms of 'syndicalization', or by the increased disciplinary behaviour that leads either to the more generalized use of labour surplus (in changing the ratios of production), or to new attitudes towards consumption, capable of increasing the propensity to save in the economy. Essentially what emerges from this effort is the shaping of a 'social memory', that is to say the whole community is itself the ultimate and complete agent of the change. This means that the people themselves and not an *élite* group are the protagonists in the nation-building experiment of these countries. That is why in this experiment the inner meaning is to be found beyond the horizon of the technocracies, that is to say in an irrational dimension akin to the feeling of exploitation, the sense of being on the fringe and of being alienated, which characterize the population of the underdeveloped countries.

We see then that the authenticity of the nation-building effort must be determined by the degree of permanent popular participation in it.

Only then will the ultimate result of development cease to be the paltry success of the technocrats, and become instead the deep, historical, experience of an amorphous mass which has become a unified people.

NOTE

1. This term refers to the process by which hitherto unprivileged groups on the margins of society come to think and take decisions for themselves. (Editor)

18

Status Quo, Evolution or Revolution?

CHARLES C. WEST

What are the political conditions of world development and social change? The most striking thing about this question is that it would hardly have been posed this way in any previous age. The fact of social change has always been present, of course, and its meaning has always been a problem for political philosophers. One civilization after another has arisen in war and by conquest, establishing its rule *de facto* before any rationalization of its authority in law or morality took place. History is full of the savage laments of defeated or enslaved people who survive by hoping and planning for the destruction of their oppressors. But time is also a soother. One by one the conquerors have learned the lesson a Confucian philosopher is reported to have taught the unifier of China, Ch'in Shih Hwang Ti: that one can conquer an empire on horseback but one cannot rule it from there. And ever again the losers in the social struggle have tended to accept the security of even a lowly place in a new social order once that place was assured. If conquest – or rebellion for the redress of grievances – was one pole of traditional history, the search for lasting principles of order which depend not only on power was the other. Where these principles were secured in the ultimate ground of being by either religion or philosophy, and where the wielders of power themselves became subject to the law they recognized and enforced, there trade, the arts, culture, prosperity, and civilization began to flourish. Where this order oppressed and exploited some for the benefit of others, and where the ruling *élite* dissolved the discipline of its loyalty to God and the law in self-indulgence and corruption, conflict arose and the society weakened or broke down, perhaps torn apart by internal conflict, perhaps conquered from without by barbarians to whom its gods and its civilized structures had no meaning. Stability has been a precious thing in political history, as the soil in which the fragile flowers of economic and cultural development might grow. Only to the internal and the external proletariat of a civilization – those deprived of their own history by conquest and enslavement or those outside the structure altogether – did it appear expendable.

It would seem at first that the modern world is totally different. Rampant, massive change in technological development, in science and in social conditions, and not eternal order is the premise of all participants in modern civilization, even the most conservative. No longer is this change the episode of a conquest or a rebellion disrupting the social peace; rather the agents of change are the leaders of commerce, industry and science themselves, sometimes with governmental help. These are the forces out to modernize ancient cultures in Asia and Africa, to transform large parts of the Western world into a vast urban complex, to develop and exploit nuclear power whether for war or for peace, to remould the mass human culture through mass communications and perhaps even human nature by biochemical inventions. It is the conservatives, the powers of the *status quo*, who on the whole are doing these things. Those who raise questions about these changes, who seek to subject them to some rational plan, to choose among them or to resist some of them in the name of some human ideal are the radicals, the socialists, even the communists. But even they do not deny the dynamic premise of the age. They only seek that it be carried out by different agents from those who now hold power and for different goals from those that these agents have in mind. The assumptions behind the question with which we began are common to us all but are new in our time. The question is not whether the endless dynamic of development of social change shall continue, but only how.

All of this is true but also deceiving. Conservatism has changed its form in a technological society but it has not disappeared. Radicals may draw their principles of protest from great humanist systems of the past, but they are no less fundamentally in revolt against the powers that be. It is the thesis of this article that we still witness today the ongoing struggle between two basic philosophies of social change, each humanistic in its way, each rooted in ancient Western history, each claiming to understand and incorporate Christianity into its system, and neither adequate to the realities of social change or its political conditions in theological perspective. Let us consider them in turn.

1 *The Search for Ultimate Order*

'The order of history emerges from the history of order', writes

Eric Voegelin.[1] Thus begins one of the most comprehensive expositions of an ontological philosophy of politics in this century, a philosophy to which another modern writer has given the name 'theocentric humanism'.[2] Ultimate reality, Voegelin believes, is a structure, a constitution of being which is beyond human understanding but is the transcendental ground of all that exists. Philosophy 'is the love of being through the love of divine being as the source of its order'.[3] Political philosophy is the effort to discern this divine structure within the conditions of human social existence, to construct a paradigm of what society would be like if it were attuned to ultimate order.

Voegelin recognizes that this relation between the ultimate order and historical activity is not a smooth one.

History creates mankind as the community of men who through the ages approach the order of being that has its origin in God; but at the same time, mankind creates this history through its real approach to existence under God.[4]

The earliest examples of this dialectical tension are in the cosmological mythologies which sanctified and gave structure to political powers in ancient Egypt and Babylon and until much more recent times in China and India. A. T. van Leeuwen calls them 'ontocracies': governments, supported and given ultimate sanction by a structure of being in mythological form.[5] These cosmic mythologies break down, of course, with the societies they celebrate, or indeed when the conquest of foreign peoples forces them to reckon with the humanity and culture of their subjects. In Voegelin's view, however, decisive progress came with the discovery of a macro-anthropological symbol for ultimate reality among the ancient Greeks to replace the cosmological ones. With Plato and Aristotle man discovers that his own nature properly understood is the analogy of the divine order. The structure of the psyche as found in the truly rational man of wisdom, and not the structure of nature as such, expresses eternal being in the conditions of temporal existence.

Given this standard, history still remains a creative struggle for human self-interpretation in which man becomes acutely aware of the fact that his knowledge and his structures are not the ultimate but only a more or less adequate symbol thereof. For Voegelin the history of Israel is a classic illustration of this tension between 'the divinely willed versus the humanly realized order of history'.[6] Christ comes to Israel as a moment of redemption in the midst of this struggle, reconciling human history to the unchanging divine order in spite of that history's continuing relativity. There will be no transformation, no *metastasis*, of human society in time. To expect one is, Voegelin maintains, a form of Gnosticism which is not content to live by faith and analogical reasoning but seeks an experience of the ultimate and absolute within this world. What is possible is *metanoia*, a change of mind, so that reason may order existence in this world while being attuned to the eternal order of being beyond it.

This is one great tradition in political philosophy, one answer to the question of the political conditions for development and social change. Voegelin is important not because of the accuracy of his interpretation of the historical world views of the ancient world, or the profundity of his Christology, but rather because he has expressed in comprehensive terms an approach to history and society which is basic and almost instinctive to millions of people even in today's world, giving form to their values, their fears and their hopes. An order of being is the first premise of reality; historical change is the second. The eternal and unchanging is fundamental; the movements of human society reflect it inadequately within the conditions of the temporal and the relative. This is conservatism in its basic form. It can be expressed with more or with less sense of distance and tension between the eternal and the relative. It can take different forms, such as the cosmic mythological or the rational humanistic. Less important than these differences, however, is the view of life they all hold in common. It is a view shared in modern society by the most diverse and surprising groups. Let me illustrate with three examples.

(*a*) One finds it most urgently expressed in the efforts of races and cultures which are threatened by the power of a largely white-dominated Western technology to discover their self-identity usually in terms of continuity with their past. The day when this could be done in terms of the cosmic mythologies, which gave meaning and substance to the great religious civilizations of eastern Asia, or in a less developed way to the tribal society of Africa, for millennia, is now long passed. The order of these societies has been broken to pieces by the brutal attacks and the human attractions of Western civilization during the past century. But this brokenness only makes the task of reconstruction in the eyes of many conservatives more important and forces it to proceed along what Voegelin would call macro-anthropological lines. Whether one turns to the search for Black self-identity in the United States or in Africa, or to the efforts of a great culture like India to discover that form of continuity with its past which will come to grips with the power of the future, the problem is the same. It is to find that form of Blackness, or Indianness, or of any other cultural or ethnic group, which reflects in the conditions of this world the true being or ultimate order of things. The Black American theologian Nathan Wright suggests, I think rightly, that one root of the concept of Black power is Aristotle's teleological concept of self-fulfilling human nature.[7]

Modern Hindu and Buddhist apologists have emphasized more the roots in their own tradition of the human values which have been presented to them in a Christian context, and of the historical power which Western invaders have demonstrated, in the name of the universal character of the inclusive religious culture they represent. Nor is this search limited to the threatened or exploited cultures of coloured peoples. The small town Protestant ethos of the United States of America faces a similar crisis. So does the Catholic society of southern Europe, the Orthodox Christian civilization of Greece and the Middle East, the national self-identities of eastern European nations under Marxist control. In all of them the issue is the same. Deep emotional involvement in the traditional structures of life cannot be saved by defending the particularism of these traditions against all change or raising them to absolutes against the world. This way lies fascism and ultimate catastrophe. They can only be rediscovered in a new context, and one way to attempt this is to rediscover these particular values as contributors towards a universal order of human society.

(*b*) A second and more intellectual expression of this conservative theme is the effort of many philosophers and theologians to reinterpret and re-establish, especially in the Western world, the tradition of natural law. The spiritual drive of this effort was eloquently expressed by Jacques Maritain several years ago in his interpretation of St Thomas Aquinas:

What strikes us in the contemporary world, dominated as it is by anti-theological and anti-metaphysical civilization, is this unfortunate product called modern man, this being cut off from all his ontological roots and from all his transcendent objects, who, for having sought his centre in himself, is no longer, as Herman Hesse put it, anything but a wolf howling in despair towards eternity.

On the other hand, if we look at the dynamics of this world 'what we perceive, on the contrary, is a profound, and immense need of metaphysics, a great *élan* towards metaphysics, towards the restoration of ontological values'.[8] Maritain then proceeded to expand the conviction that there is indeed such an ultimate ontology expressed in the eternal law of God and perceivable by all men through their rational nature which is analogous to the being of God. This perceivable structure of being is for Maritain the natural law, 'an order or a disposition which human reason can discover and according to which the human will must act in order to attune itself to the necessary ends of human being'.[9] From this premise Maritain and his fellow Neo-Thomists developed a whole political philosophy of a pluralist commonwealth in which various social groupings from the family to the largest voluntary association will be joined in an organic unity while enjoying positive liberties to make their contributions to the common good.

Not all advocates of natural law are as sure as these Catholic reformers of the 1930s that they know the alternative to capitalism and socialism, to totalitarianism and libertarian democracy, as the political form within which social development and change can take place and the temporal ends of human life can be ordered in their proper hierarchical subordination to the eternal end. Charles Curran has recently demonstrated how varied and imprecise is the content of natural law in the history of the church.[10] *The Pastoral Constitution on the Church in the Modern World* does refer in one place to the 'permanent, binding force of universal natural law and its all-embracing principles' (par. 79), in the context of opposing criminal acts in war. But this is the only place this phrase is used so unequivocally in a document which in its oscillation between a structural ontology of human nature (pars. 14–18) and the family (par. 48) on the one side and a dynamic missionary Christology (pars. 22, 38, 39) with a vigorous dialectical analysis of the promise and ambiguities in modern society on the other, reflects the creative ferment in the Roman Catholic Church today. Natural law, although the word is still used, has undergone a thousand qualifications so that in many circles its very meaning is problematic. But the continued use of the term indicates a habit of thought among ethicists in both Protestant and Catholic circles and even among such secular philosophers as Walter Lippman[11] and such abstract political activists as the World Federalists, which cannot break with an essentially static vision of ultimate moral order. The Protestant version of this perspective was expressed in the World Conferences of Stockholm, 1925, and Oxford, 1937, whose reports spoke of Christian teaching which 'should deal with ends, in the sense of long range goals, standards and principles in the light of which every concrete situation and every proposal for improving it must be tested'.[12] We find it today in the continuing tendency of many liberal theologians to think of the Sermon on the Mount and the ministry of Christ as a transcendent law to be for ever approximated in human behaviour,[13] and in a conservative biblicism which finds the biblical commandments themselves to be a positive law of absolute validity.[14] It is, however, no less widespread in the tendency of ethicists, both Protestant and Catholic, to imagine that their task is to clarify and refine in a thousand life situations the meaning of various timeless and theoretical moral concepts or values.[15]

(*c*) My third example may seem at first incongruous. It is the structure of modern liberal pragmatism which underlies the planning and the policies of many of the wielders of technological power today. Most of them would hardly recognize themselves in the company of the above two groups. Their conscious philosophy is rooted in a revolt against the metaphysical and moral authorities of a religious past. They are themselves the principal agents of the destruction of traditional customs and values in the name of a functional utilitarian technology. Dante Germino calls them 'anthropological humanists' as distinct from the theocentric or metaphysical humanism of the classical tradition.[16] They are on the whole secular men with a pragmatic turn of mind. They are not concerned to discern or enforce an ultimate structure of custom and law. But they have their ultimates nevertheless, even if they are in the realm of social dynamics. They believe, no less than the classical humanist, in the rationality of human nature and the friendliness of the natural environment to man, even though they would find the *locus* of this rationality in the planning and control of the physical and social and psychological world rather than in the discovery of its ultimate structure. For example:

First, these liberal humanists believe in the inherent beneficence of the explosion of scientific knowledge and technological power which has taken place in recent years despite the immense potential for destruction which it has created. This belief is implicit rather than explicit. Projections of the state of the world in the year 2000 come in the form of predictive extrapolations from current scientific developments rather than as moral judgments on their value to man.[17] But in these predictions one finds very little reference to the probable effects of human conflict on technological development, or the even more probable misuse of technology by private interest or national security for injustice or exploitation. Often indeed moral exhortations to the responsible use of new technological power are made. But these exhortations are extraneous to the inherent rationality of science-based technology itself and to the forces which determine the shape of its development. The inner logic of this development itself is a transcendent absolute.

Second, our modern liberal humanists believe in the inherent beneficent rationality of economic development on a world scale. This is not to say that they think the economic policies of the nations or even of private industries are always rational. But there is, in their view, a logic which self-interest dictates and which on the whole prevails over the emotional forces of nationalism, tradition and the arbitrary will to power of special groups. According to this logic, development is an inherently evolutionary process which, to quote one expositor, 'requires a people to choose a new set of philosophical values that are compatible with modernization and industrialization, along with associated changes in social and economic policies'.[18] Social conflicts and dislocations, exploitation, and inbalance of power between the poor and the rich – the human costs of development in short – are submerged in a quantitative measurement of the total improvement in the economic condition of a nation. By the same logic, it is assumed that the long run self-interest of technologically advanced societies will lead them to give intelligent aid and trade preferences to help the development of the less advanced. Economic development is for these believers a science with its own immutable methodological laws.

Third, our liberal humanist believes in the inherent rationality and success of democratic methods of balancing and controlling power within a society as well as in the slow development of structures of international political agreement and co-operation which will mitigate the world conflict of interests. At this point he is more of a realist about irrational factors than in the field of technology or economics. From long experience in domestic class-conflicts he realizes that any effective order is to some degree a balance of power in which the various forces of society have influence. He seeks to establish or to maintain this balance in world politics and to prevent its being upset by violent and totalitarian forces. This makes him then the opponent of violent changes in the *status quo* everywhere, even though he may be an advocate of radical, peaceful change. His assumption must be that the basic forces of the people in every country are on the side of this kind of rational politics and that the future belongs to it.

W. S. Gilbert in the late nineteenth century put into the mouth of his Private Willis in *Iolanthe* that

> every boy and every gal that's born into this world alive
> is either a little Liberal or else a little Conservative.

The comment today is as dated as the operetta. Liberalism *is* the conservative philosophy of the late twentieth century. It has been a bold and often creative effort to contain the forces of social change within the bounds of a certain method after they had overturned every traditional structure of ultimate being. It was at the same time an attempt to believe that the ultimate harmonies which could no longer be found in the eternal orders which earthly structures reflected were present in human nature and society itself. Liberals have become today the embattled guarantors of this methodology and this faith in an increasingly unfriendly world.

With this we have described in broad outlines, with deliberate economy of criticism, in order that its own inner logic might be more clear, one answer to the question which the first sentence of this essay posed. We turn now to the opposing answer in order that they may confront each other.

II   *The Drive Toward Utopia*

'Utopianism', says Ernst Bloch in his massive Marxist interpretation of history *Das Prinzip Hoffnung*, is 'dreaming forwards, anticipation as such'. Being is not an eternal order but an 'ontology of the not yet' which is to be realized by human action continually projecting itself forward towards new possibilities, transcending those which are objectively given to the human consciousness at a particular time.

Objectively possible is everything that is to be expected or at least cannot be excluded on the basis of a partial *perception* of its existing condition. *Really* possible is everything, the conditions of which are not yet fully gathered in the sphere of the *object itself*, whether because they must yet mature, or because new conditions – mediated by the present ones of course – must grow out of a new reality.[19]

Reality then for Bloch is not a structure but a movement of human history corresponding to the movement in material existence itself. It is pressing and striving beyond the limits of the given. It is rebellion against all structures which claim to be eternal, exodus from them and projection of new possibilities, the content of which will only be discovered as they are worked out in practice.

The not yet known, as a whole, is the psychic representation of what has not yet developed in a time and its world, on the frontier of that world. To make conscious what is not yet known, to give form to what is not yet developed is concrete anticipation where the Vulcan of productivity stands and throws his fire.[20]

And this 'Vulcan of productivity' is a symbol of conflict as well as development. The utopias of self-realizing mankind are not simply improvement projects which a bourgeois research scientist would present to his employer for approval. They are campaign strategies to overthrow the powers that be which are exploiting and dehumanizing mankind in order that new and more creative relationships between human beings and between man and nature may emerge. The law of historical development is the law of human self-fulfilment through such conflict, in the light of utopian visions which change and develop as man realizes them.

This for Bloch is the pattern of world history. To illustrate it he selects not the official mythologies of past cultures, but illustrations of the hidden and ambiguous drive of man towards self-emancipation: Prometheus in Greek tragedy, *The Republic* of Plato (Voegelin gave more attention to the *Laws*) and other utopias from the ancient world and later. But there is no doubt that for Bloch the standard illustration is the formation of the Hebrew people by its exodus from Egypt and the pursuit of the kingdom of God which drove this people and later the Christian church forward with hope towards the future.

By the efforts of Moses the content of salvation which had always been a settled external goal in pagan religions, especially in those with a cosmic mythology, was changed. In place of this settled goal a promised goal now appears which must be achieved; in place of the visible god of nature an invisible God appears, of justice and the kingdom of justice.[21]

This God of justice, to be sure, was for Bloch the projection forward of human possibilities, the symbolizing of the human future in a way which would stimulate human action. The movement of history is towards the emergence of the *homo absconditus* who is the real meaning in the biblical symbols, not the *deus absconditus* of traditional theology. The being of God is the being of the future promise, the being of mankind itself when the kingdom comes. Bloch therefore has the deepest admiration for Jesus as the symbol of this hope for the poorest and most oppressed of mankind as he shared their life and their suffering, but *not* as the mediator of forgiveness and the life of grace alone. Bloch traces this developing consciousness of messianic humanism, gradually shedding the concept of a Divine Other altogether, down through Christian history in such figures as Joachim of Flora, Thomas More, Thomas Müntzer, Robert Owen, Charles Fourier and Karl Marx. It is, in his view, however, a still to be achieved humanity.

The heritage of religion becomes the conscience of the final Utopian function *in toto*: human self-surpassing, the act of transcending in alliance with the dialectical transcending tendency of the history which human beings make, transcending without any heavenly transcendence and yet with an understanding of what that heavenly image meant – a hypostatized preview of human self-sufficiency.

'God,' he concludes, 'appears thus as the hypostatized ideal of a human essence which has not yet been realized.'[22]

Thus the alternative view of the political conditions of development and social change. We have chosen Ernst Bloch to present it rather than Karl Marx because, like Voegelin, he puts a philosophy of history in general terms of which Karl Marx is one of the recent concrete examples. The contrast between him and the conservative could hardly be more complete. History is not order but rebellion against order. Eternal transcendent being is not expressed analogously in the relativities of human politics, but human politics in the name of an emergent humanity explodes and destroys all that presents itself in terms of fixed transcendent being. Voegelin regarded ideology as a kind of poison of the mind. Bloch sees it as the symbolic form in which a man projects his emancipation against the future and guides his action in realizing it. This view of history also is held by surprisingly different groups in society today. Let us once again take three examples, somewhat, though not exactly, parallel to the ones in the previous section.

(*a*) The deepest conflict which is shaking many nations of Asia and Africa today is between a conservative and a revolutionary concept of self-identity. 'We must not be content with delving into the past of a people in order to find coherent elements which will counteract colonialism's attempts to falsify and harm,' writes Frantz Fanon towards the end of a long article on National Culture. 'It is around the peoples' struggles that African-Negro culture takes on substance and not around songs, poems or folklore.'[23] The most thoroughgoing illustration of his thesis is the communism of the People's Republic of China. Nowhere on earth has the philosophy which Bloch set forth been taken more seriously than there. The first and fundamental movement of the followers of Mao Tse Tung was to discredit and uproot all continuity with China's past, whether the concepts of Confucian morality or the structure of the family system in society. But if we are to believe the reports, this cancellation of over two thousand years of history was still insufficient. The bureaucratic structures and the intellectual reinterpretations which the revolution itself had thrown up were attacked and overthrown again in the 'cultural revolution' of 1966–68. In the twenty years of China's communist history, first the structures and the concepts which had defined her as a civilization were abolished in favour of a purely Western system of thought and politics, adapted by shrewd practitioners to the Chinese scene. This became the vehicle of a new humanity, a new sense of destiny and a new social pride and self-confidence. But this structure also could not be allowed to become an ontocracy. Rather than have them undermine the spirit of self-giving in the search for a finer future, Mao chose to risk the economic achievements of the new society, to re-establish its spirit. This restless search for the form of a future humanity which will really negate the restrictions and illegitimate pretensions of past structures, this ruthless iconoclasm towards all that exalts itself as complete and satisfying remains a continual challenge, not only to the dissatisfied cultures of the third world, but to the poor and the spiritually alienated of the industrialized West as well.

(*b*) It is one of the striking ironies of history that Bloch's messianic humanism represents a revival and reinterpretation of Marxism in eastern and western Europe, which is almost a mirror image of the efforts to revive Christendom by reinterpreting natural law. The roles are, of course, reversed. It is the Marx–Leninist orthodoxy of the communist parties of eastern Europe under the leadership of the Soviet Union which has become a kind of ontological conservatism with elements of all three types mentioned above. A dash of traditional cultural nationalism combines with complete confidence in the efficacy and righteousness of the methods and policies of a developing system of planned technological economy. The whole is held together by the transcendent absolute of the ultimate stage of communism to which existing socialist societies claim to be a continual approximation.

Against all this the neo-Marxist *avant-garde* has rediscovered the revolutionary humanism of the early Marx and indeed, with Bloch, of a long tradition in Christian and pagan society. This humanism faces every society, socialist or not, not only with the question of a collective ideal such as that in which Mao Tse Tung believes, but with the question: what in fact serves the liberation of man, and where are the forces which continue to exploit him and fit him into the mould of their own systems? All would agree that the achievement of the socialist system of political economy is a solid gain for justice and freedom over against capitalism, and that one of the political conditions of world development should be the establishment of socialism in some form. But with this the question of human nature is far from solved, not to speak of the problem of effective production and just distribution. Man continues to be alienated from his fellow man, even in a socialist society. Selfishness, greed and exploitation continue in various forms. How then is the struggle for human self-realization to continue and against what enemies is it to be directed? To what degree is the enemy in man himself? Where are the resources not only to transform external reality, but for the *metanoia* which would transform the self? It is questions like these which bring these Marxists into a conversation with others such as Christians and existentialists, whose faith and philosophy are quite different from their own.

(*c*) The messianic humanists of Bloch's persuasion do not reject the exploding scientific-technological revolution of this generation. In fact one significant group of them sees it as creating the conditions under which man can at last become 'free transforming activity' as Marx once described his essence.[24] For these believers, however, as for their counterparts in Latin America and elsewhere, a prior condition is that technology shall not proceed according to self-determined lines, but under the control of a deciding and planning centre responsible to the people whose welfare is affected by it. They do not believe in the inherent beneficence of economic development as such. Indeed, most Latin American analysts of this persuasion would regard the present effects of technological change as dehumanizing and exploitative on that continent. A prior condition to any effective development then is that the people be politically liberated so that they may take power in their own hands through political agencies of their choosing. Social conflict, revolution even in violent form, must therefore precede development. The efforts by industrially advanced countries to restrict and control this revolutionary process and to seek economic arrangements on the basis of mutual self-interest only reflect the oppressive dominance of a conservative structure of power. The proletariat of the world must oppose it by what Bloch would call utopian thought and action to destroy the old structure and establish a new one.

Once again we have described a point of view, with a minimum of criticism. These are the alternatives which present themselves as answers to our question today. To a certain extent they effectively criticize each other. But between them stands the Christian with his own sources of insight and perspective to which the documents of the Vatican and the World Council of Churches on development issues among many others have tried to give expression. To this Christian contribution, and to the critique of both conservatism and revolution, in the light of it, we now turn.

III   *The Relation of Hope: A Christian Comment*

It is no accident that behind the clashing political perspectives which we have so far described lies a fundamental conflict about the nature of ultimate controlling reality operating in the lives of men, in other words about the character of God. This is in fact where the political question begins. Even when it receives an atheistic answer, this atheism is a species of political theology. Although Zeus is a more traditional prototype of divinity, Prometheus becomes no less divine when his rebellion in the name of human power and ambition is exalted to the ultimate dynamic principle of things. Indeed, surprising as it may be to many Christians, the image of Prometheus lies closer to the character of the biblical Yahweh, the Father of Jesus Christ, than that of Zeus.

Yahweh is, as K. H. Miskotte has pointed out, 'far from being a variant of the general concept of god'.[25] Indeed it is evident in the story of his encounter with Moses (Ex. 3) that in the latter's eyes he did not at first seem to have the characteristics of divinity at all, especially the central characteristic of definable being related to the orderly structure of the cosmos and human society. Yahweh is not Zeus. The biblical Yahweh is one who breaks into this cosmos and this society to call men out of it towards a future, the form of which they will only know when they explore the relation which he establishes with them, the relation known biblically as covenant. Yahweh is first of all act, not being. He is known as the believing people commits itself to respond to him, obey him and define themselves in relation to his gift and promise. Yahweh is power, but not in the sense of some abstract omnipotence. He is the power to accomplish his purposes, to call men into being and into new being through his election and to conquer the forces of evil which oppose him. He is the power demonstrated in the life, death and resurrection of Jesus Christ.

On the other hand, Yahweh is not Prometheus. Ernst Bloch in his interpretation of the biblical God as a symbol of man's own ultimate power and purpose forgets an essential element, not only in the biblical but also in the universally human picture: man is defined by, and realizes himself in, the relations with others which surround him as he moves towards his future. He is not only an actor, he is also a responder and that to which he responds is not an ultimate structure of being but the others who are with him and without whom he would not be who he is. The biblical Yahweh, precisely as he stands among us in Jesus Christ, is the totally other, in relation to whom we learn to respect, love, and seek freedom and justice for the other human beings who share our world. The ultimate reality which governs world politics is not an eternal structure, neither is it an unfettered superman, whether individual or collective, but a covenantal relation in which man is continually limited, changed and thereby liberated to explore the promise given him.

This leads to a second question, on the importance of which all antagonists agree: the meaningfulness of history and therefore of change and development within it. In accepting this, however, all sides, even the most conservative, are children of Israel. If Israel had not lived there would have been no history, says Voegelin flatly, for history is the creative effort of man to make his future and to build his world into something more complete, more prosperous and more filled with the fruits of the spirit than the present. It was the contribution of biblical faith to have understood this dynamic as a divine calling.

If we take this fact seriously, then the formulation of the question with which this essay began is justified. 'There is no divinely ordained social order – there are only relative secular structures subject to constant revision in the light of new human needs,' says the Report of the World Conference on Church and Society.[26] The maintenance of a *status quo* is therefore not an option for a Christian. Indeed, something of idolatry clings to every effort to preserve a political or social structure when its time of creativity is past. But this does not mean that change as such is best. 'There is in history a dynamic of evil as well as a dynamic of good,' the Geneva Report continues. Let us illustrate the problem this raises in three areas.

(*a*) Both the Geneva Conference Report and the Pastoral Constitution on the Church in the Modern World of Vatican II give praise to the scientific and technological development of modern society as a legitimate expression of man's historical calling.

Far from thinking that works produced by man's own talent and energy are in opposition to God's power, and that the rational creature exists as a kind of rival to the Creator, Christians are convinced that the triumphs of the human race are a sign of God's greatness and the following of His own mysterious design.[27]

Christians believe God expects man to exercise dominion over the earth, to name the creatures and to cultivate the garden of the world. It is thus

not accidental that modern science flowered first in a culture informed by the Bible's emphasis on the world as the field of man's responsibility. Although churches have often met technological innovation with anxiety and distrust, Christians may trust the universe that God has created and delight in exploring its composition and unlocking its possibilities.[28]

Both documents then go on to recognize that this explosion of human knowledge accelerates and intensifies the crisis of human society. They join with responsible secular liberals in pleading for a deepened sense of responsibility in using these new powers for the common good. They suggest that technology must not be allowed to have a dynamic of its own, but must be guided by moral purposes and goals. But both documents fall short of Christian prophecy in relation to this problem. Neither speaks convincingly from the perspective of those who are the victims of the immense new power delivered into the hands of technocratic planners. The tone of both, as is the case with so many other ecumenical documents, remains on the level of moral exhortation and a plea for the broad use of reason rather than an analysis of the ways of God's judgment and redemption.

In point of fact there is a dynamic of evil as well as a dynamic of good operating in modern technology. It cannot be identified as a conspiracy of evil men. It is rather the resultant of the fearful and self-interested decisions of many holders of some power, none of whom are forced to take public responsibility for the whole implications of their acts which pollute our air and waters, accelerate the arms race, degenerate culture in the mass media, and allow our cities to decay. In a sense these petty decisions are acts of self-protection seeking to inhibit or distort the public purposes which technology was intended by God to serve. Research not only in the nuclear field, but in hundreds of other areas is primarily financed with funds appropriated for national defence in every country that can afford to do so. Large industries maintain research departments in order to protect their investments by foreseeing and controlling inevitable changes. The situation differs from that of Israel in Jeremiah's time only in the scale and the danger of the habits of self-centred idolatry by which the people live. The principalities and powers with which the Apostle Paul wrestled have reappeared in full force, rooted in human nature and decisions but transcending and dominating man as well.

(*b*) The same problem can be seen with regard to world economic development. There probably is no issue in the post-war world which has called forth more downright hypocrisy than this one. Moral responsibility for closing the gap between the rich and the poor and raising disadvantaged peoples to a condition of equal opportunity has been proclaimed by the churches and accepted by humanists of every variety. Yet in point of fact the gap between rich and poor is growing wider. With a few exceptions, the rate of development of the poorer two-thirds of the world at those critical places such as food production, housing and sanitation which affect the masses, has been negligible. In response to this and in the face of every moral obligation the redistribution of resources from the rich countries to the poorer ones by aid or trade concessions has decreased in recent years. In fact the case can be made that in many parts of the world the wealthier nations, with the help of a small wealthy class in poorer lands, are exploiting those lands for their own profit.

Here also a historical crisis is developing which requires detailed prophetic analysis from Christians rather than exhortation to good works. It is the influence of the Christian gospel which set Western civilization on its historical direction which has brought forth so many new possibilities for human life and such power for good and evil in human hands. It is in the economy of God's grace that peoples who for centuries lived in stable limited economies have been forced into the insecurity and the vast new opportunities of a technologically and economically unified world. The question now is what God's power is doing with human power – industrial, political or revolutionary.

(*c*) Natural law theologians to the contrary notwithstanding, the Christian churches have had to learn in recent years anew the lesson which the biblical covenant history in both Old and New Testaments made clear: that to grasp the promise of God for the common life and express it there is the real meaning of *torah* or law, and that this requires concrete analysis and prediction in terms which reckon with the judgment and the mercy of the Lord.

The discernment by Christians of what is just and unjust, human and inhuman in the complexities of political and economic change is a discipline exercised in continual dialogue with biblical resources, the mind of the church through history and today, and the best insights of social scientific analysis. But it remains a discipline which aims not at a theoretical system of truth but at action in human society. Its object is not simply to understand the world, but to respond to the power of God which is recreating it. . . . Christian theology is prophetic only in so far as it dares, in full reflection, to declare how, at a particular place and time, God is at work, and thus to show the church where and when to participate in his work.[29]

With this calling we are in the midst of the modern problem of ideology formation. The problem is not itself new. Augustine's *City of God*, the ethics of Thomas Aquinas, and the political ideas of Luther and Calvin were as ideological as any political theory today, though the common assumptions of medieval Christendom tended to obscure the fact. But awareness of the problem, thanks to the growing clash of many world views each claiming universality, to the shrewd Marxist critique of the religious and the bourgeois consciousness, and to new reflection on the response of faith to the biblical message, is a special modern problem and achievement. To think ideologically means two things:

(*a*) To believe in the truth of one's analyses and predictions as reflecting the implications of ultimate reality for action now, much as the Old Testament prophets believed, as Augustine believed when he defended the Christian church against the pagan charge that it had weakened the Empire, as Luther or Thomas Müntzer believed when they defended their particular forms of reformation, or as Ignatius Loyola believed with his disciplined service of counter-reformation.

(*b*) It is a picture of reality and its ethical demands to which one commits oneself as a basis for action and hope, although one knows this commitment is a risk. In both cases the problem is the relativity of the ideology to the standpoint and interests of the person or group which rules it, and yet the necessity of acting on it as if it were the truth. No theory which leads to practice avoids this difficulty, whether it be concerned with scientific technological change, social revolution, or Christian action.

Today the confrontation of various ideologies is more acute than ever in history. There is no space into which they can escape from one another. The achievement of our age is that we recognize this fact and are prepared on the whole to live with the pluralism it involves. The problem and danger is that by living in our own world we may fail to understand each other and respond to each others' legitimate interests and aspirations, with the danger of ideological war lurking in the background. To this problem three things need to be said from a Christian perspective. First, the Christian understands that truth is not an abstract proposition, but a relation with the reality which claims his allegiance. There is therefore no universal language of politics and society; there is only a common humanity. Believers in different gods can communicate with each other best by each witnessing to his faith in the common human context. Second, the Christian recognizes that there is no abstract truth, but only transforming truth which makes the world anew. Therefore it is his responsibility, with others, to project possible structures of the future which a worthy human life would make imperative and to work for the realization of these structures. He cannot content himself with the 'futurology' of the scientists or with moral generalities. He does this recognizing the ideological risk he is taking, confident of God's correction and justification. Third, for the Christian, witness to his faith in these concrete terms is an invitation to dialogue with those who believe differently from him. This dialogue is certain to be painful because of the basic commitments on both sides. It will take place, to a certain degree, in an atmosphere of power conflict since each will be acting on his conviction while he is talking about it. But this kind of dialogue is precisely what the Christian first experiences in his encounter with God. As the Geneva Report put it once again:

Christians like all human beings are affected by ideological perspectives. But their witness is the way in which they show themselves to be constantly corrected in their encounter with God and their neighbours while acting on their faith.[30]

This sets the pattern for the discovery and realization of justice and peace in and through the social change whose author and finisher is finally the triune God. The process can be well illustrated with reference to that much misused word 'justice'. It is, in the biblical context, not a legal structure or a moral proportion giving each man his due. Rather it is a word which refers first of all to a power – the ability to prevail, to fulfil one's nature in action, to be a respected, successful person and to be innocent of distortions of the inner character or outer fortune. It was this which the psalmist had in mind when he would proclaim himself to be righteous and in the next breath ask the Lord to justify him. His inner certainty of relation with a righteous God was already a power which must work towards his outward social justification. There is a tension between present and future, between reality and realization in the Bible, but there is no dualism.

Secondly, justice was a relational word. It referred to faithfulness in the covenant and contribution to upholding it. Justice was the whole mutual affirmation of one another in all their prosperity and peace which the partners to a covenant made. This relationship might be defined in a given time and place by laws, but written laws could never exhaust it and indeed might be a hindrance to it if the relation was reduced to what is legal. Black man and white man in the United States, for instance, have never really made a covenant in the biblical sense with one another, and therefore the black man does not receive his justice in a white society and the justice of God is defied no matter how many civil rights laws are passed. Despite the United Nations there is no covenant between aid-giving and aid-receiving nations today, and therefore even at best a relationship of paternalism and resentment builds up instead of justice, no matter how much is given and received.

This leads to a third characteristic. Justice in the biblical context is outspoken partiality in favour of the poor and the weak. The source of this meaning is Yahweh's choice of the Hebrew people to be his covenant partner. On this point the Bible is unequivocally clear. For the wealthy and the powerful to do justice means to seek out the poor and the helpless, to take up their cause against their oppressors, to vindicate them and to establish them in their freedom as persons in the covenant relation. Nothing is said here about the rights of contract, and property rights are relative to this justifying purpose. More radically yet, in the biblical understanding justice is justification: the deliverance of those who cannot help themselves, whether because of their sins or because of their poverty. It is the establishment of a new relation, first by God with men and then by men with one another.

The establishment of this relation is never a smooth transition. 'Development is the new word for peace,' said Pope Paul VI in his encyclical *Populorum Progressio*. To this the Indian Dr S. L. Parmar in his introduction to the Report on Development at the World Council of Churches' Uppsala Assembly replied:

> But development is disorder; it is revolution. Can we attempt to understand this apparently paradoxical situation which implies that disorder and revolution are the new name for peace? If we believe in progress and development let us not flinch at disorder and instability. Order so often provides a camouflage for injustice that the very quest for justice generates disorder. But we must live with the dilemma. Our task is to imbue the revolutionary movements of our time with creativity and divest them of their anarchic content. The same is the case with development.[31]

It is, in other words, the task of the wealthy and the powerful to seek the justice and freedom of the less advantaged. They cannot do so, however, by operating only with their own concepts of what justice is. Their justice and their order is inevitably tainted with concern for their own security and their own interest. It is they who are the unrighteous before God and who need the inner justification which will make possible an effective covenant relation with their poorer neighbours. This cannot be done except at the cost of disorder and instability. Repentance – *metanoia* – is not, as Eric Voegelin imagined, to be moved from one's waywardness to reconciliation with an eternal order, but to recognize, in and through the often unreasonable and sometimes violent opposition of the disadvantaged, the judgment of God curbing one's self-justifying power and showing the way to a new and deeper justice. For example:

(*a*) There is no objective ideology-free science of economic development. There are highly sophisticated insights which have been worked out largely by economists from the industrially developed nations. But the question what constitutes development can only be answered with reference to cultural and human values which cannot be quantified or easily communicated. Development itself can only be carried out as persons who are native to the country concerned take charge of it and believe in it. What constitutes development then must emerge from a dialogue in which no participant's sense of what is right and good emerges unchanged and no group's interests are unscathed.

(*b*) Behind this dialogue lies a struggle for power. The basic hindrance to effective justice in the modern world is the outrageous inbalance of power that now prevails. It remains true, as it has been from the day of Christ's resurrection, that the poor and the powerless in this world bear witness to the powers that be of God's purposes for human life. In their condition, if not always in their methods, they have a relative righteousness, a claim on the powers above them in human society. Since the powers that be of this world have not changed their character this will lead to conflict and there will be no resolution of this conflict on the purely secular level short of sacrifices by the powerful of what they have. Most especially it will mean sacrifice of control over the process of change itself. This confrontation cannot be domesticated within the provisions of one political system, however democratic, or one economic system, however flexible. There is no way by which those who have power can be brought to see the interests and the welfare of those who do not with sufficient clarity and force to plan for the development of the have-nots intelligently, unless the powerless themselves bring the force of their opposition to bear. It is for the powerful to learn the ambiguities of their rational plans and their benevolent impulses and the grace of compromise with what they fancy to be their principles in order that a new relation of equality may be established and institutionalized.

(*c*) The questions of violence versus non-violence and of revolution versus reform are an aspect of this dialogue in the midst of our struggle. The issue has been beclouded by ideological illusions from all sides:

the illusion, for example, that a non-violent action is a less fundamental and therefore a more acceptable challenge to the *status quo*, or that violence is a more effective last resort when non-violence seems not to accomplish fast enough results. Revolution, too, is a cloudy word, often used more to symbolize an emotional attitude than to designate a particular programme. The underlying question which all this vagueness conceals is how to realize among men that effective and continual change, that everlasting dynamic of justification which is the work of God. The vain hope of the established powerful tends to be that small changes and piecemeal reforms can strengthen the basic structures of the society from which they gain security and profit. The foreign policy of the United States of America is a classic example of this at the moment. But the vain hope of the revolutionary is that one basic upheaval will liberate mankind and solve the problem of social justice. Between them the Christian stands with his confidence that the revolution which justification brings about is more fundamental, more continuous, and more in tune with reality than any which self-justifying revolutionaries can conceive. Therefore he is prepared to ask of each particular step towards change whether and how it reflects a real *metanoia* and gives promise of a creative new relation out of which new changes will come.

All of this comes to focus for the church and eventually for the world in the paradox of the suffering servant who will bring forth justice to the nations (Isa. 42.1 ff.). Here is the ultimate clarification of the meaning and function of earthly power. It is the power of intercession for the transgressor, the power of witness to God's saving purpose for him. It is the power to make men new, to transform and to reconcile them and therefore to subordinate the superhuman powers and principalities which are rooted in human nature to their proper humanizing functions. All human power, political, economic, technological, psychological, is shown its proper place by the life, death and resurrection of Jesus Christ. Its inner secret is the repentant rediscovery of that promising relation by which God will bring his future to pass, overruling human efforts to set up other absolutes and other hopes in its way.

This means that the form of Christian witness to the world is proexistence. It is the fundamental renunciation of self-centred rights and powers, even when one must exercise the power given one for a time as God's steward to serve others. There is no change for the better in this world that does not involve repentance by the powerful for the power they must exercise, a repentance which seeks to establish new relations with the enemy and the resister. To incorporate the renunciation of power into the exercise of it and thereby to be a witness that the real transforming power in this world is justifying grace is on the one hand a witness which only the church can bear, but its consequences make good practical politics as well. Let me close with the mention of three brief examples.

(*a*) It is clear that any nuclear disarmament or indeed any renunciation of an escalated arms race will involve a risk to national security. The nemesis of total destruction which awaits the world at the end of this competition is clear. It would be good politics of survival to take the risk of re-evaluating national security in the light of the hope which might come from reassessing the intentions of the potential enemy in the light of what the God whom we know in Jesus Christ may be doing with him.

(*b*) We have stressed often enough that two-thirds of the world is not developing economically and that the conflict between rich and poor nations and classes is intensifying. The judgment of God expressed in this conflict needs no underlining. It is still true that no human power can put a camel through the eye of a needle. It would be practical economics, perhaps a means of survival, to find a way of bringing the poorer nations into effective decision-making responsibility over the international economic power which the wealthy nations now hold.

(*c*) It can be argued that, confronted with violent resistance and revolutionary action, the powers which can do so must maintain or re-establish by force the conditions of peaceful development. But we are confronted to an increasing degree with classes, races and nations for whom established structures of law and order themselves represent a violently repressive situation. If we are to avoid an endless global civil war it would be good practical politics for the custodians of law and order to seek in dialogue with their enemies how the action of God's justification might be transforming them both and creating the conditions for a society in which they could live without doing violence to each other.

In each of these cases an art is involved – the art of effective discernment of the operation of God's power in human relations, so that in the use or the renunciation of human power Christians may bear effective witness to God's work. The political conditions for development and social change are an on-going process whereby man becomes truly political through learning how to use his power as a witness and a servant.

NOTES

1. *Order and History*, Louisiana State University Press, 1956, p. ix.
2. Dante Germino, *Beyond Ideology*, Harper and Row, New York, 1967.
3. *Op. cit.*, p. xiv.

4. *Ibid.*, p. 128.

5. *Christianity in World History*, Scribners, New York, and Edinburgh House Press, London, 1964. See especially chs. 1 and 4.

6. *Ibid.*, p. 461.

7. 'The Ethics of Power and Black Revolution', a paper delivered to the American Society of Christian Ethics, January 1969.

8. *St Thomas Aquinas*, Sheed and Ward, 1931, pp. 62 f.

9. *The Rights of Man and Natural Law*, p. 60.

10. 'Absolute Norms in Moral Theology' in *Norm and Context in Christian Ethics*, ed. G. H. Outka and Paul Ramsey, Scribners, New York, 1968, SCM Press, London, 1969, ch. 5.

11. *The Public Philosophy*, Mentor, 1955.

12. *The Churches Survey their Task*, ed. J. H. Oldham (the Official Report of the Conference on Church, Community and State, Oxford, 1937), Allen and Unwin, London, 1937, p. 90.

13. A sophisticated version of this which has operated with great influence in World Council of Churches circles is the concept of universal principles from which 'middle axioms' are derived appropriate to a particular society at a particular time. The term was originally suggested by J. H. Oldham, and has been developed most fully by John C. Bennett. See especially his most recent statement of it in 'Principles and the Context' in *Storm Over Ethics*, United Church Press, USA, 1967, ch. 1.

14. For example Carl F. H. Henry: 'The content of love must be defined by divine revelation. The biblical revelation places the only reliable rule of practice before the community of faith.' *Christian Personal Ethics*, Eerdmans, Grand Rapids, Mich., 1957, p. 255.

15. As an illustration, Richard McCormick (a Catholic) quotes with approval Paul Ramsey (a Protestant) criticizing John A. T. Robinson's comment that all Christians would admit that lying, stealing and killing could in some circumstances be right. 'Never,' says Ramsey, 'have Christians – at least not those Christians whose vocation it is to reflect as ethicists upon the nature of the Christian life – admitted any such thing. Instead they have asked: what is the meaning of the forbidden theft, what is the meaning of truth-telling, what is the forbidden murder? They have explored or deepened or restricted the moral meaning of these categories or rules of conduct' (Ramsey, *Deeds and Rules in Christian Ethics*, Scribners, New York, 1967, p. 37; McCormick, 'Human Significance and Christian Significance' in Outka and Ramsey, *op. cit.*, p. 246). This is, in the medieval sense, a realist position. The concepts, rules and categories have an absolute being in themselves. It is the human situation in historical time whose reality is ambiguous.

16. *Beyond Ideology*, pp. 27 ff.

17. Herman Kahn and Anthony Wiener, *The Year 2000*, Macmillan, New York, 1968.

18. Neil H. Jacoby, *The Progress of Peoples*, Center for the Study of Democratic Institutions, 1969.

19. *Das Prinzip Hoffnung*, Suhrkamp Verlag, Frankfurt/Main, 1959, pp. 225 f.

20. *Ibid.*, p. 143.

21. *Ibid.*, p. 1454.

22. *Ibid.*, pp. 1522 f.

23. *The Wretched of the Earth*, Penguin Books, 1967, p. 189.

24. Radovan Richta, *The Scientific and Technological Revolution and the Alternatives for Modern Civilization*, published by the Philosophical Institute of the Czechoslovak Academy of Sciences, Prague, 1968, pp. 21, 23.

25. *When the Gods Are Silent*, Harper and Row, New York, 1968, p. 118.

26. Geneva Report, p. 200.

27. *Gaudium et Spes*, par. 34.

28. Geneva Report, p. 188.

29. Geneva Report, p. 201.

30. *Op. cit.*, p. 202.

31. *Uppsala Speaks*, pp. 42 f.

O

19

Theology and Society: Ten Hypotheses

DEMOSTHENES SAVRAMIS

I

The general trend in 'modern' theology is to use fashionable terms like revolution, social change, development, etc. It was therefore to be expected that such terms would come to the fore during the Assembly of the World Council of Churches held at Uppsala from 4 to 20 July 1968. And indeed it is quite obvious that this international conference met under the influence of a theology of revolution and development, a fact borne out by the content and significance of the final Report of Section III on World Economic and Social Development. The impartial observer of events at Uppsala must therefore be allowed to ask a leading question highly justifiable in the circumstances. Does the concern shown by the assembled representatives of the churches for phenomena such as revolution and the 'third world' really mean anything? Are they not simply playing the part which is expected of those who perform the role of reformers and renewers in society and who therefore *must* display a certain amount of sympathy both towards the so-called revolutionary forces at work in this world and towards the underdeveloped countries?

An easy or definite answer to this question cannot be provided on the basis of the Report. On the one hand it is easy to appreciate the honest endeavours of the theologians concerned with Section III to discover a way that can lead to social justice throughout the whole world. It is equally obvious that all those who took part in drawing up the Report are well aware of their responsibilities in bringing about a renewal of the world and of society, and that they have recognized and openly acknowledged the importance of Christ and of his teaching and help for this renewal. As the Report says:

The great majority of men and also of Christians are aware of their responsibility for members of their own national societies who are in need. But few have discovered that we now live in a world in which people in need in all parts of the world are our neighbours for whom we bear responsibility. Christians, who know from their Scriptures that all men are created by God in his image and that Christ died for all, should be in the forefront of the battle to overcome a provincial, narrow sense of solidarity and to create a sense of participation in a world-wide responsible society with justice for all. Our hope is in him who makes all things new (par. 3).

On the other hand the Report is full of those empty formulas and standard clichés which appeal to all human beings in the least concerned with the fate of their fellow men. They arouse no controversy and fit equally well in the framework of modern theological thinking and in the attitudes of those Christians who openly agree with general statements and with declarations not binding on them, provided that these declarations and statements overlook various unpalatable facts and bitter problems. What this means is that much trouble was taken at Uppsala to reach compromises with all possible attitudes at the expense of an objective discussion of concrete facts. Those who doubt this have only to read the report of Section IV which was supposed to make concrete statements on the theme 'Towards Justice and Peace in International Affairs'.

What was quite overlooked at Uppsala is that justice and peace cannot be secured by drawing attention to the so-called poor countries as victims, while at the same time calling the 'rich' countries and their forms of society diabolical: the latter's complex and many-sided problems cannot hope to be grasped by theologians drawing their 'sociological' knowledge from superficial studies of culture and society. Justice and peace will only prevail where subjective reactions are replaced by rational actions clearly intent on furthering the humanization of man which Christ made and continues to make possible through his life, death and resurrection, and through his message. But rationally conditioned actions presuppose criticism of all systems and institutions – including the churches – which stand or threaten to stand in the way of man's humanization. Moreover, rationally conditioned actions are the outcome of thorough, systematic and objective preparation in which there is no place for any kind of dilettantism.

The Assembly of the World Council of Churches at Uppsala, and especially those responsible for the studies and reports of Section III and IV, forgot two extremely important statements which we owe to the Study Conference organized at Zagorsk from 17–23 March 1968 by the Commission on Faith and Order and by the Commission on Church and Society of the World Council of Churches. There two things were established. First, the churches must learn more seriously than hitherto to understand their existence and structure as social institutions from a historical point of view: the inclusion of anthropological and ethical questions might be of use here. Secondly, the churches must avoid more seriously than hitherto any dilettante engagement in social problems: the tasks that could once be accomplished in this field are now too complex, and sociological knowledge is too advanced, for such dilettantism to be indulged in any longer. Far from being illusory, the hope of Christianity – as the cross tells us – is highly realistic.

In the light of these two weighty statements from Zagorsk it here seems to me to be right not to develop a series of general and standard observations on the theme of world development and social change, observations which would be in no way binding, but to examine instead two concrete problems, the solution of which can be of decisive importance if theology and the churches are to deal objectively, usefully and effectively with the developments which concern us in the world and the society in which we live. Thus I will first draw attention to the danger which I detect in the neo-conformity of the churches, and which finds expression for instance in the fact that they and their representatives uncritically and without reflection assent to judgments and prejudices now regarded as 'modern'. What they overlook is that when speaking of the spirit of the times one must be able to distinguish between its essential elements – they may be of relevance to the future – and its peripheral manifestations which are no more than ephemeral. The mistaking or indeed identification of the essential elements of our age with these peripheral manifestations often makes people take the latter as a criterion, with the result that they judge our age wrongly and in disregard of the facts. Having defined this danger to which contemporary theology and the church are so susceptible, I will turn secondly to what I regard as the main purpose of this study. This is to outline the function of Christian theology in society, from its origins as New Testament theology to the present day, in the form of ten hypotheses, in the hope that the positive function of ecumenical theology within the context of constantly changing social conditions may in this way emerge more clearly, as may also the theological dangers which such a function must necessarily bring with it.

II

The tendency of the church to conform to the spirit of an age is nothing new. Latent conformity first appeared when Constantine the Great raised the bishops of the church to the 'nobility', and the tendency continued in the form of open conformity between church and state (in the Byzantine Empire, Russia, Greece), between the church and forces of various kinds (the Crusades, the Inquisition, St Bartholomew's Eve, etc.), between the church and fascism (in Mussolini's Italy) or between the church and national socialism (in Germany). Such conformity brought about a considerable abandonment of institutionalized Christianity, and this was necessary if Christianity was to realize its essential characteristics, since these latter presuppose a society capable of change and renewal.

Contemporary society is of this type, since its existence and evolution depend not on institutionalized Christianity but on the personal charisma and faith of individual Christians and on various functional equivalents of Christian convictions, that is, convictions which are not regarded as specifically Christian but which contain sociologically significant characteristics which are Christian in essence. Seen in this light, one of the most basic characteristics of our age is its gradual abandonment of a pyramid-shaped paternalistic order based on the inequality of those above and those below and on compulsion, ignorance and lack of freedom. But this process is taking place in such a way that it is producing a variety of secondary manifestations which give the impression that what we now have to deal with is a world which no longer knows what it wants and which is hastening towards its own destruction. This impression is further strengthened by the fact that the growing popularity of sociology and its terminology has produced a number of fashionable words such as 'social', 'establishment', 'manipulation', 'repression', 'consumer society', 'affluent society', etc. Coming from the mouths of semi-literate demagogues, such jargon appears to express great truths to all those contemporaries of ours whose sociological education is derived from the television and from magazines. The term 'revolution' in particular is being more and more emptied of meaning because, next to the word 'sex', it has become the most frequently used and most fashionable term of our age.

The churches, and more specifically the Protestant churches, are doing much to give this situation a certain justification, because this neo-conformity between the church and the spirit of the age meets with their approval, expressed as it most typically is in the jargon favoured by the many theologians who are turning to popularized sociology. The result is a kind of *pop-theology* in imitation of the *pop-politics* and *pop-sociology* which are such characteristic ingredients of the sub-culture of contemporary youth protest. The solidarity of pop-theology with this sub-culture is scarcely to be wondered at. This clearly shows what devastating results can be expected by both theology and the church if they try to come to terms with the peripheral manifestations of the present day without pausing to consider the consequences. But theology and the church are all too often prevented from thinking and acting in a post-modern way by their lack of the courage it needs to be un-modern and by the existential fear that nowadays one cannot hope to get anywhere without modern means and attitudes. The ways in which Protestant theologians set about dealing with the 'revolutionary spirit' of the sub-culture of contemporary youth protest, and their attitude towards revolution in general, are obvious illustrations of the neo-conformity of the churches today.

The revolutionary spirit of Christianity or indeed the Christian revolution has nothing in common with the revolution that has become such a fashionable phenomenon in our day. For in the first place revolution means for the Christian the complete and lasting alteration of the principles on which this world is founded, with as its sole objective the victory of good over evil – evil which is to be found everywhere, not excluding the churches. The Christian and the revolution he is entrusted to carry out can never identify themselves with a specific ideology, because every ideology regards as good only what suits its purpose, rejecting everything else as hostile and evil. Whereas the revolutionary attitude of an ideology really only questions and modifies such values as stand in its way, the revolutionary attitude of the Christian modifies and indeed rejects everything which might hinder the humanization of man. Ideologies only strive to do away with men's domination of their fellows in order to make room for a new type of dominion; the Christian on the other hand strives to do away with all types of human domination. Finally, moreover, the Christian knows that communities 'cannot be any better than the men who create and preserve them', and he therefore strives to bring about a revolution in himself so as to change himself completely and permanently before setting out to alter and improve the world. Whereas modern 'revolutionaries' and their theologian sympathizers feel a need to be heard by one and all and talk about everything without adequate knowledge, the Christian, in order to avoid jeopardizing his cause or making it appear ridiculous, confines himself to a matter-of-factness of the strictest kind, achieved by meticulous self-discipline, self-control and self-criticism.

The revolutionary spirit of Christianity is capable of creating that ideal type of man whom I have elsewhere termed the *homo religiosocio-logicus*.[1] This ideal man can, whatever the circumstances, hold fast to the maxim 'do not rule, do not be ruled' because, acting empirically as a social being, he is always able to act according to his social convictions: 'The Lord is on my side; I will not fear: what can man do unto me?' (Ps. 118.6). Revolution in the sense of a violent upheaval of the existing order so as to create a new one is in his eyes only legitimate if the existing order prevents him or his fellow human beings from living out the maxim 'do not rule, do not be ruled'. For the Christian any revolution involving violence is, like the chaos it brings with it, a matter of the gravest concern. But modern revolutionaries regard revolution and violence as a kind of game played to dispel the boredom of wealthy young people who no longer know what to do either with themselves or with their surroundings. Nevertheless there are amongst these modern revolutionaries a great number of young people who are motivated by a longing to see a better and more humane society than the one with which their parents are satisfied. The dreams and aspirations of these young men and women bear out Christ's words 'Man shall not live by bread alone' (Matt. 4.4). Meanwhile those theologians who adopt the jargon of the modern revolutionaries are placing themselves in the hopeless situation of a prodigal son who would gladly have fed on the pods that the pigs were eating (Luke 15.11 ff.).

Anyone who, like the author himself, has personally experienced poverty, hunger and misery of all kinds cannot ever, as long as he lays claim to the name of man, just stand by and with an easy conscience watch the way in which chaos and its attendant sequels, poverty and misery, are being deliberately provoked here in our society by semi-literate revolutionaries. What greater hypocrisy than that of those modern theologians who inveigh against the war in Vietnam under the shadow of portraits of Mao Tse Tung, Ho Chi Minh or Ernesto (Che) Guevara while at the same time declaring their solidarity with students whose call is for 'more Vietnams'! Any human being who genuinely condemns the war in Vietnam and all its horrors cannot ever possibly wish to see a similar war break out elsewhere.

According to Chairman Mao the central task and highest form of revolution is 'armed seizure of power', because he sees war as the solution to all problems. 'This revolutionary principle of Marxism–Leninism is universally valid, both in China and abroad.' Those modern theologians whose enthusiasm leads them – to quote Kurt Tucholsky – 'to run with hypocritical tongue after the latest slogan of the age' are participating in the Mao-cult despite the fact that a victory of the revolutionary spirit Mao represents would mean the final abolition of every kind of freedom. It takes considerable *naïveté* to believe that in a uniform society shaped on Maoist lines there would remain any opportunity for accomplishing man's most important task, which is to make himself more human and to respect the human being in his fellow men. For, quite apart from the fact that the realization of the Maoists' revolutionary dreams presupposes war and therefore the de-humanization of human beings, the respecting of the human in one's fellow men and the perfecting of one's own humanity both take for granted the fact that human beings have a fundamental claim to freedom.

But freedom is guaranteed only by those forms of society whose pluralism affords every individual the opportunity to develop his own personality in accordance with his own personal beliefs, i.e. in accordance with the degree to which he is motivated by what he has most immediately at heart. Yet this pluralism is precisely what is most threatened by the professional revolutionaries. Destroy it they cannot, it is true; they do not possess either the physical or the intellectual strength to do so. But they provide an alibi for the growth and ultimate victory of those forces of the left or the right which have in common the fact that they refuse to tolerate either pluralism or freedom. Thus modern theologians are collaborating in the suppression of precisely those greatest of values for which Christ himself died on the cross.

This is the case when, for instance, modern theologians fail to distinguish between the professional revolutionaries at work in Western Europe and the revolution taking place for example in South America. For it is quite clear that the purpose of the revolution in South America is to do away with the poverty, starvation and distress prevalent there, whereas the intention of Western Europe's professional revolutionaries is to create the very conditions prevailing in South America – i.e. poverty and distress – in a part of the world which has just recovered from the ravages of the second world war. Whereas many South American Christians would praise God day and night if but a fraction of Western Europe's social justice, freedom and prosperity could be realized there, Europe's modern theologians declare their solidarity with revolutionary forces intent on destroying what many gave even their lives to bring about. Finally these modern theologians should note that it is no mere coincidence that it is the adventurer Ernesto (Che) Guevara who has been raised to the pantheon of the professional revolutionaries' sub-culture, and not the priest Camillo Torres, who laid down his life for Christ's cause. The immense financial success which the 'capitalist' world has made out of Guevara's diary and indeed out of a whole Guevara cult could be mentioned as further proof that what we are dealing with in the case of Western Europe's so-called 'revolutionary spirit' is a fashionable phenomenon and that the theologians who approve of it are guilty of bringing about a neo-conformity of theology and the church.

Alongside the attempts of some theologians to proclaim their 'solidarity' with the 'revolutionary spirit of our age', serious attempts are being made which would like to be more than the whims of passing fashion. To these belongs the attempt to draw up a 'theology of revolution'. Despite the academic character and the seriousness of the enterprise, this 'theology of revolution' is really nothing more than an imitation of modern revolutionary phenomena, as is revealed for instance by the obvious influence of Herbert Marcuse and of the mentality of the professional revolutionary sub-culture on the ideas and vocabulary of Richard Shaull who was the first to make the theme of revolution the centre of theological discussion. But the discussions which have since centred on the 'theology of revolution' do show that some theologians wish it to be more than a passing fashion. For example we have Eduard Tödt, who concludes his remarks on the 'theology of revolution' with the following words:

Revolutionary action coupled with violence is an *ultima ratio*; for by tending to destroy everything to do with the justice and law that makes life livable, such action incurs the risk of destroying what it would like to free for its own future. But the primary injustice is rigid action intended to preserve what exists, for this provokes precisely those revolutionary actions which it regards as a threat to existing ways of life.[2]

In contrast to this 'theology of revolution' which arose in imitation of contemporary phenomena, we have the attempts at a dialogue between Marxism and Christianity, and in particular the dialogues being conducted under the auspices of the 'Paulus-Gesellschaft' and in the pages of the *Journal for International Dialogue*. These may be regarded as activities which are fully aware of the essentials of our age and realize that they may be of significance for the future.

The essentials of our age, such as the emancipation of the world, humanity's coming of age, secularization, rationalism, etc., all have a remedial effect on the church in so far as all contribute towards purifying Christianity. I will mention just a few examples. The ecumenical movement, the Second Vatican Council, the interest shown by the churches in sociology, and their systematic inclusion of it in their pastoral policies – all these show that the spirit of the age is forcing the churches to make decisions which could lead to a genuine renewal. Running parallel to mere conformity – or in other words the passive assimilation of the church into the 'modern' world – we therefore also find the church adapting itself in the sense that it is reforming itself so as to be able to confront society as a genuine religious community.

The experience gained from being confronted by social change and contemporary world developments is forcing the ecumenical movement and, more precisely, the World Council of Churches to adapt its theological thinking and its programmes of action to what is commonly called the 'modern' world or contemporary society. Both Uppsala in general and the preparatory studies for and final report of Section III on World Economic and Social Development in particular, bear the unmistakable hallmarks of this process of adaptation. But in order to evaluate them both correctly, we should see them as phenomena standing at the end of a process which started when theology and society began to interact upon each other in the age of Constantine the Great, and which has gone on right up to the formation of the World Council of Churches and the convening of the Second Vatican Council.

III

Hypothesis 1 When the sociologist thinks of the theology of the New Testament he is principally interested in those utterances which could be of practical sociological value. And when he is primarily concerned with the interaction of theology and society he must first and foremost concentrate on those New Testament sayings which on the one hand form the basis of all Christian theology and which on the other hand were at one time, or still are, relevant to society. An important example seems to me to be the utterance 'the old has passed way; behold, the new has come' (II Cor. 5.17). These words are not only important in the context of the theme here under discussion because the word 'new' makes us think of social change. In addition to this, the radicalism of these words forces us to seek the answers to two questions. Firstly, did Christ draw up a new programme of social renewal? And secondly, what is actually meant by the word 'new', and in what way is the 'new' to be distinguished from the 'old' that is passed away?

Perhaps I can provide the answers to both these questions by means of the following hypothesis. Christ did not draw up a practical programme for the renewal of society. In the first place, his struggle against the social abuses prevalent in his day was conceived in religious terms. In the second place, Christ was no utopian who simply failed to see that contemporary society was not to be altered as the direct result of his teaching. Thirdly, the proposal of a scheme for a practical social and economic system would contradict the basic truth that where the spirit of Christ is, 'there is freedom' (II Cor. 3.17). For, as we may learn from the history of theology and the church, each time when Christianity has claimed to be a practical programme of a social, economic or political kind, it has always degenerated into an instrument whereby some men have dominated others.

New Testament theology thus offers no practical programme which can be used to renew society. But it does provide basic presuppositions for the removal of social abuses and for the creation of a new society. Of these the first and most important is the concept of the *new man*, a man whose faith can enable him to free himself from all constraints so that he can devote himself entirely to the renewal of the world in a truly Christian sense.

In contrast to the pre-Christian world, the world Christ wanted appears ideally as one in which each individual, regardless of his social or other origins, is by far the most valuable element. All other material and abstract values are there only to help the individual to make a real human being of himself. In this context the term 'love' acquired a special significance which it had not had in the pre-Christian world. Love in the Christian sense removes all the barriers that separate men, and in so doing it also makes possible the removal of every kind of egoism, including the collective egoism of the state.

The cross is the symbol of the price Christ had to pay to the powers of this world in order to free his fellow men from the constraints imposed upon them, while the resurrection symbolizes a victory over the powers of this world in favour of the subjective and objective natures of man. New Testament theology therefore consists of the glad tidings that through the death and resurrection of Christ man can completely revolutionize and change both himself and the world in which he lives.

From this New Testament theology it therefore follows that the church is conceivable only as the community of all who believe in Christ. Consequently the New Testament recognizes only one function for the church: that of service. Its assumed function as authoritarian ruler, and whatever else later theologies and ecclesiastical traditions have brought about at the expense of the constructive and joyous character of New Testament theology, must therefore be regarded in the main as the results of the interaction between theology and society that is to be observed throughout the church's history.

Hypothesis 2 One of the greatest dangers concealed in Christ's teaching is the misunderstanding that can arise from the fact that for those who wish to live according to it one thing alone is important: to be ready for the great day by making the soul inwardly free, and by freeing it from everything which might impair this readiness. A radical negation of the 'world', its problems and one's concern for them, would be the direct consequence of this, were it not that the theology of the New Testament is not only Christocentric but anthropocentric too. Its concern for people implies a concern for society.

The social order prevalent at the time drove true Christians into isolation, giving rise to a way of life which not only favoured the rejection of the world but actually elevated it into a theologically sanctioned spiritual and practical attitude. This incidentally corresponded to the oriental mentality which prefers a passive attitude rather than an active struggle against a given economic and social order, and which results in resignation, a sense of doom, and a submissive attitude.

In the East there therefore arose a theology based on the renunciation of the world, one which sanctioned otherworldly asceticism as the highest form the Christian life could take. The outcome of this was that in the sphere of the Eastern Church – i.e. those countries whose social structures evolved under the influence of the theology of the Eastern Church – the dynamic elements in New Testament theology were lost. The theology of the Eastern Church could have played a constructive part in society, but allowed itself instead to be made into a servant of the state, thus forcing men who had been freed from all constraints by Christ's sacrifice to accept the state as a power equal to God, to which they had to submit themselves.

When one tries to explain this situation in terms of the sociology of religion, one becomes aware of some of the principal characteristics of the Orthodox Church, characteristics which can only be understood as part of a process which began with a decision closely linked to the Orthodox doctrine of man (anthropology). This doctrine teaches that sin has not entirely corrupted man; in other words the Eastern Church adheres to the optimistic opinion that man is capable of renewing, transfiguring and perfecting himself. The teaching of the Eastern Church is based on a firm belief in God's love and in the kinship between man's nature and the divine. If he follows his church's teaching, the Orthodox believer should see himself as chosen to collaborate with God in the shaping of the world. The conception of duty we find in the more worldly asceticism of the West, in its Protestant forms, for instance, therefore has more in common with Orthodox attitudes than with those of Calvinism, whose markedly pessimistic conception of God and man can easily lead to fatalism. Since the divine attributes of reason, freedom and love have, in the eyes of the Orthodox believer, been rendered weak but not powerless by sin, he should be in a better position to develop these attributes than the adherent of an anthropology which regards man as totally corrupted by sin.

This raises a pertinent question. Why did the Orthodox Church's optimistic view of man fail to make it the vehicle of economic, cultural and political development in those countries where it predominates? The answer lies in the fact that the Orthodox doctrine of man leaves open two possibilities. The first of these is man's participation in the salvation of himself and of society according to God's will, i.e. an active, socially conscious form of Christianity. The second is the self-centred, one-sided attempt to achieve the perfection of the self alone in isolation, an undertaking which can of course lead to a passive, a-social and indeed antisocial form of Christianity. In the latter case, the optimistic view that man is capable of renewing, transfiguring and perfecting himself and indeed of making himself divine is turned into a negative attitude towards the world. A decisive part in this process may well have been played by the doctrine of *theosis* held by the Eastern Church, which has come down to us in the classic formulation of Athanasius: 'God became man in order that we might become gods.' *Theosis* means the elevation of man to the sphere of the divine and his spiritual union with God. Here we can already detect the germs of otherworldly asceticism and rejection of the world. But complete rejection of the world only became accepted when the world began to be excluded from the sphere of the divine, as part of the attempt to achieve the main requirements of *theosis* by overcoming the material world and spiritualizing life in the solitude, for instance, of a monastery rather than in and for the world.

In saying that the Orthodox Church can only be understood as part of a process which began with a decision, what I mean is that faced by two alternatives which its doctrine of man left open to it, it chose the second, with the result that in its sphere of influence a one-sided type of spirituality arose at the expense of a possible renewal of the world. To put it another way, the Orthodox Christian's typical answer to the question 'How can I make sure of my own salvation?' is 'By a spiritual attitude, by mysticism, contemplation, etc., and at the same time by rejecting the world and the values associated with it.'

But from the moment the Orthodox Church began to regard and describe the world as evil, it also sanctioned the rejection of the world as a way of overcoming the evil predicament of man: a set of values resulted which therefore stems from a tradition that ignores the world.

The implications of the social elements in the Orthodox doctrine of man fell into the background. In the West, the pessimistic aspects of a Christian conception of man, such as the doctrine of predestination, were to lead to a this-worldly asceticism, and thus to the deployment of the energies of more favoured individuals and to social, economic and cultural progress. In the East, on the other hand, an other-worldly type of asceticism came to prevail, despite the optimistic character of the Orthodox doctrine of man which might well have led to asceticism of a more practical kind. The a-social character of its asceticism made the Orthodox Church not only ignore the claims of the world but even oppose them.

Hypothesis 3　We have already established the fact that the theology of the New Testament provides the basic presuppositions for the removal of social abuses and for the creation of a new society. In this connection we drew particular attention to the new man whose faith can enable him to free himself from all constraints, to the fact that the world Christ wanted can only be a world in which the individual is the most valuable thing, whatever his social and other origins, and also to the fact that Christian love removes all the barriers that separate men.

In a world which takes the theology of the New Testament seriously there can be no room for man's dominion over man. The only political theology that the theology of the cross and of the resurrection can possibly entertain is one which refuses to give its blessing to assertions of political mastery by calling them holy and willed by God; on the contrary, it will unmask all attempts to deify political power by declaring them to be blasphemy against both God and man.

The rapid social changes which took place during the first few centuries of Christianity's development were, however, also to bring about a change in theological thinking and in the church. This change in turn produced another transformation of society, though hardly one which had anything in common with expectations raised by the theological implications of the cross and the resurrection.

A political theology arose which declared the power of the state to be sacred and, in doing so, gave a metaphysical justification to the dominion of some men over others. Under Greek influence the simple acknowledgment of the early Christians 'Jesus is Lord' (Rom. 10.9; I Cor. 12.3) was made the basis for complicated doctrines and rules which soon made the evolution of the new man impossible. The political theology of the church gave its blessing to a theological conception centring on Constantine the Great in his dual role as Emperor and Victor and, as a result, the formula 'Jesus is Lord' was expanded into the formula '*Jesus and the Emperor are the Lords*'. Many Christians saw a great danger in the facts that Constantine had raised the leaders of the church to the 'nobility' and that theology and the church had come to an understanding with earthly powers in such a way. But they decided on a type of protest against the established church which was bound to bear no fruit. They literally went into the wilderness, leaving theology and the church in the hands of the Byzantine 'establishment'. Such a development left open only two alternatives: either the subjugation of theology and the church to the will of the state, or the assumption of temporal power by the church. Whereas the Eastern half of Christendom was forced for political and social reasons to choose the first of these alternatives, the Western half was able to choose the second.

Hypothesis 4   In the East, theology and the church subjected themselves to the will of the state, thus giving rise to the 'imperial church'.

In the West, on the other hand, there evolved the 'papal church' or, in other words, the absolute authority of the Pope, justified theologically by his primacy. Thus in the West we experience the distortion of another cardinal truth of New Testament theology. In the New Testament we read that the apostles may not call each other rabbi, master or father 'for you have one teacher: and you are all brethren' (Matt. 23.8). In the medieval church there thus arose a hierarchy which was in complete contradiction to the injunctions of the New Testament. It was in effect an accurate copy of the pyramid-shaped paternalistic order of medieval society which was based on inequality from the apex downwards, and on compulsion, ignorance, and lack of freedom, yet which was subsequently endowed with a sacred character by theology and the church. In the West these thus gave their blessing to the absolute rule of men over men. One has only to think of features like the following to appreciate the wide-ranging effects which this was to have: clericalism, the degradation of women and their equation with the devil, witch-hunting, and the effect on people's private lives of a code of sexual morality fundamentally opposed to the body.

The extent to which theology and the church distanced themselves from New Testament theology during the Middle Ages is shown by the fact that they gave their sanction to, and indeed fostered, an order founded on, Judgment and Retribution. Yet in the New Testament we read 'Judge not, that you be not judged' (Matt. 7.1); 'For God sent the Son into the world, not to condemn the world; but that the world might be saved through him' (John 3.17); 'When you judge another, . . . you condemn yourself' (Rom. 2.1); 'Who are you that you judge your neighbour?' (James 4.12). Christ had a lesson for the Pharisees of every age, not only for those of his own day, when he said: 'You judge according to the flesh; I judge no man' (John 8.15).

Hypothesis 5 When defining the essence of medieval society, two of its most basic characteristics must be borne in mind, namely its vertical structure and the political and social immaturity of the majority of its members, compelled as they were in the context of the feudal system to behave and think as their 'masters' at the apex of the hierarchical pyramid thought fit. The attitude of theology and the church to the ecclesiastical structure of the Middle Ages was one which cannot be described simply as conservative in the sense of wanting to delay and preserve. Theology provided the church with the necessary ideological framework within which the vertical structure of medieval society could henceforth be regarded as a divinely-sanctioned order manifesting itself in the name of Christ and the gospel in both the spiritual and the temporal sphere. Yet both the vertical structure of feudal society and the church, and the immaturity of its members, in fact contradict a truth fundamental to New Testament theology, namely that where Christ's spirit is 'there is freedom' (II Cor. 3.17). The secularization of the Christian faith reached its zenith in the Middle Ages when theology and the church attained complete conformity with the prevailing social order. The world had not become Christian, contrary to what many theologians believe; instead Christianity had become equated with the world.

The liberation of Christianity from its worldly fetters could only be achieved by someone who by the sheer force of his own personal charisma could, in the name of Christ and the fundamental truths of New Testament theology, unmask both the political theology of the Church and the hierarchical system it sanctioned and reveal them to be utterly unchristian. The contribution of Martin Luther and the Reformation he started was decisive in this process.

The term Reformation – from the Latin *reformatio* – means reshaping and renewal. The reshaping and renewal undertaken by the Reformation was founded on Luther's conviction that God cannot and does not make anyone ruler over the souls of individual men. The religious human being is his own arbiter because as a Christian he is responsible for himself. Individualism thus received theological justification in the West and was given the blessing of religion, and this opened up new opportunities for each individual to seek his salvation independently of the community by means of independent thought and action. Man is allowed to think for himself, and thus to discover that his unredeemed state is identical with his 'self-inflicted' spiritual minority. From now on his hope will be to put an end to this state by declaring his freedom from tutelage of every kind to be the supreme value. Since where the spirit of Christ is there is freedom, we are surely justified in maintaining that by the removal of this tutelage humanity has come closer to what New Testament theology originally required of mankind for the sake of mankind. Seen in this light, the form of society in which we exist here today is nothing other than the final product of the rediscovery of some of the fundamental truths of New Testament theology. Of course we cannot call our society Christian, but it acts as a catalyst for theology and the church by compelling them to renew themselves according to Christ's teaching; the result is that a christianization of denominations is now under way and is replacing the splitting-up of Christianity into denominations. Such a process cannot fail to have social repercussions.

Hypothesis 6 It is quite true that Martin Luther made a decisive contribution to the liberation of men from their spiritual minority;

but he subordinated both himself and his theology to the vertical structure of the society in which he lived. Above all he failed to free the individual from the state. Rather the reverse, for Luther took over terms like 'authority', 'command', 'obedience', 'rule', 'subservience', etc., and gave them his theological sanction, thus contributing to the fact that right up to the eighteenth century the domination of men by men was interpreted as being divinely ordained.

Yet because Luther and the Reformation did help men to recognize their intrinsic right to freedom, they may be said to have made the way easier for man to think and act freely. When men began to think for themselves they not only discovered the value of their own freedom, they also learnt to appreciate other values which we owe to Christ and his gospel. Above all, the values of equality and fraternity were recognized – alongside liberty – to be essential prerequisites for the humanization of mankind. The French Revolution, socialism, secularization and other similar phenomena all contributed to the recognition of the supreme values liberty, equality and fraternity as the basis of that new social order we call democratic.

This order in turn encouraged new approaches in theology, which cleared the way for a new type of Christianity which comes closer to New Testament theology than did the 'political theology' that preceded it, because for one thing it has proved able to free itself from the world and from the influence of temporal powers and to concentrate on serving Christ and all mankind. Thus the gradual humanization of man has begun to take place within the framework of theology and the churches; it is a process which contains much of that revolutionary spirit we find in the gospel, and which manifests itself only when each individual, regardless of his social and other origins, does in fact represent the highest of all values.

Hypothesis 7 The social order which arose in the wake of the rediscovery of the revolutionary spirit of the gospel and which we call democratic exerted and is still exerting a great variety of influences on theology and the churches. For instance it has made them re-examine their relationship to the state, submit their social past to close critical scrutiny and, above all, set about healing the divisions and rivalries between various churches and denominations. Out of this process arose one of the most important phenomena of our century, namely the ecumenical movement and the ecumenical spirit which underlies it.

For those who are aware of the beginnings and history of the ecumenical movement there can be no doubt that it was prompted in the first place by political, economic and social factors rather than by theology. The same was of course true of the divisions in the church which had preceded it, the non-theological causes of which are often overlooked in favour of biased theological and dogmatic interpretations. The aim of the ecumenical movement is to achieve on the religious level that world community which other institutions are trying with varying success to bring about on the political and social levels. But its political and social engagement is so strong that in its political and social thinking it belongs as much to the field of sociology as to that of theology.

Within the ecumenical movement we can observe that same interest in sociology operating on an international and interdenominational level which was at one time confined to certain minority theological groups in specific areas. In those days responsible theologians saw that sociology offered a practical opportunity to correct the fatal mistakes made by their fellows who were laying all the emphasis on spiritual considerations and failing to realize that what matters is the whole man – a psychosomatic being whose problems arise from having to live in the world along with his fellow human beings.

But as the ecumenical movement became more and more institution-alized a situation arose which compels us to draw a dividing line between *spiritual ecumenism* and *pragmatic ecumenism*. The institutionalization of the movement in the framework of the World Council of Churches amounts in fact to a new form of theological and ecclesiastical con-formity, the main characteristic of which is the retention of old-fashioned conformity alongside the adoption of new or fashionable theological approaches which appear at least to suggest that theology and the church really do have something new to offer. When the term 'state' was popular, it was fashionable to speak in the World Council of Churches of the church and the state; when everybody started talking about 'society', Geneva started talking about the church and society too; and today when every schoolboy thinks in terms of 'revolution', ecumenical circles of course have discussions on the church and revolu-tion as well. Surely this suggests a pitiful lack of imagination, an inability to look forward to a better world closer in spirit to the gospel. All too many of the movement's active members lack the courage to think and act for themselves; instead they conform, using 'theological fashions' as an alibi. And this is why they are incapable of being ahead of their time.

Yet all the same the ecumenical movement does remain one of the greatest theological events since the Reformation. The spiritual ecu-menism which it has brought about does not need the trappings of its pragmatical counterpart in order to achieve victory. We can see it triumph everywhere where there are Christians who value the fact that they are Christians above all denominational allegiances. Unencumbered by the straitjacket of old-fashioned or contemporary conformity, Christians such as these are propagating the real ecumenical spirit of our day. It may refer little to God or Christ, but it comes much nearer to what we have defined as the theology of the New Testament.

Hypothesis 8 Roman Catholic theology too has not remained untouched by social change. Indeed this has brought about the best and most sincere attempt the Roman Church has made this century to renew itself: this was the Second Vatican Council initiated by John XXIII, who placed Christ and his gospel above all other values. There can be no doubt that Pope John's wish was that the church should adapt itself to the world without merely imitating it or harmonizing blandly with it. But what was most significant and should on no account be underestimated is that he was the first Pope to realize and openly admit that freedom is an essential spiritual force.

When we consider the effect on social development of the recognition of man's intrinsic right to freedom by Luther and the Reformation, it is easy to appreciate the significance in practical sociological terms which the Second Vatican Council is bound to have as the disseminator of Pope John's spirit. The ecumenical overtures of the Roman Catholic Church and the dialogue they have made possible would for instance have been quite unthinkable had it not been for Pope John's determination to start the Roman Catholic Church off on a process capable of liberating not only theology and the church but laymen too from a structure and attitudes reminiscent of the vertical structure of medieval society and its assumption that, socially and politically speaking, man has yet to reach maturity.

The ecumenical overtures of the Roman Catholic Church deserve this description in a double sense. In the first place the Roman Catholic Church has shown its genuine readiness to enter on a dialogue with all men of good will: here the word *oikumene* appears in its original geographical sense, meaning the whole of the inhabited world. In the second place the Council tried to appeal to all Christians. By doing so it was addressing an *oikumene*, which, according to Origen,[3] consists of all those who have been redeemed from sin by Christ and who believe in the Father, the Son, and the Holy Ghost.

When we turn to the more practical aspects of the Roman Church's ecumenical overtures, reference should be made to the Decree on Ecumenism, because in our opinion it is here that the most valuable bases are to be found for an ecumenical approach on the part of the Roman Catholic Church. Moreover it reveals very clearly indeed that the Roman Catholic Church genuinely wishes to co-operate with Christians all over the world in propagating and carrying out God's will on earth.

However, not everyone is going to understand this document in its deepest sense. Those theologians who look at it from the point of view of their own denominations will not be able to rid themselves of their 'Pope complexes' and will therefore interpret it in a biased way. But those who read it with their own eyes and not through tinted spectacles will discover that the Pope and the Roman Catholic Church are not represented in it as the focus of ecumenism, but rather that 'conversion of heart and sanctity of life together with private and public prayer for Christian unity must be regarded as the very soul of the ecumenical movement' (par. 8). What we are in fact presented with here is a 'spiritual ecumenism' which may be taken as a guarantee that Roman Catholic ecumenism is not going to degenerate into a one-sided attempt to draw all the other churches into Rome's orbit. It seems to us that the Decree on Ecumenism lays greater stress on 'spiritual ecumenism' than on its pragmatical counterpart; and such spiritual ecumenism is of particular importance today, because it alone can overcome the great danger that the ecumenical movement may turn into a movement intent on attaining unity artificially and superficially by concentrating solely on social, political and economic considerations.

'Spiritual ecumenism' is still the main guarantee we have that the unity we are aiming at will grow out of a consistently Christian way of life. Unity of this kind can never be centred on Athens, Constantinople, Rome or Geneva. It can and must centre on Christ alone. Christo-centric ecumenism alone can inspire all those who long for unity with real optimism. For the future belongs to Christ only. And since he wants only the best for his people, he will show us the best way to attain the unity of all who believe in him: towards this goal he will guide his elect, who are hardly likely to be identical with the staff running the ecumenical movement! Sooner or later a purely pragmatical form of ecumenism is bound to lead to new conflicts because, looking back, the points that provoked controversy in the past were nearly always on the practical rather than the theological level, and this is something likely to be increasingly true of the future.

Of course, in the Decree on Ecumenism the Roman Catholic Church does appear as the one and only church which 'possesses the full richness of divinely revealed truth and the means of Grace'. But a statement like this can surely only surprise people who actually hope that the Roman Catholic Church may deny that it is the *Una Sancta*. It can only disappoint those idealistic dreamers who cannot understand that ecumenism is not the same as the abandonment of one's own convictions for the sake of synthetic unity.

Christians capable of realistic thought and of understanding problems in a genuinely ecumenical spirit can surely appreciate the fact that the

Roman Catholic Church cannot and indeed ought not to disown itself. This is why they welcome the fact that the Second Vatican Council was able to draw up a Decree on Ecumenism which deserves to be called an ideal one for three reasons. Firstly, because it outlines its themes succinctly, objectively and unmistakably, yet without hurting those of other persuasions. Secondly, because it recognizes that the renewal of the church is of 'particular ecumenical significance', and in this context concentrates primarily on self-criticism. Thirdly, because from start to finish the document itself is borne on the conviction that unity cannot be the work of men but that all our hopes must be centred '*entirely* on Christ's prayer for the Church, on the Father's love for us, and on the power of the Holy Spirit' (par. 24).

These three factors, which in our opinion give the Decree on Ecumenism its ideal quality, may also be adopted as guide-lines for practical ecumenical work. Thus all the churches must realize that the meaning of ecumenism must not be equated with a false kind of eirenicalism. Ecumenism does not mean that the polemics which in the past turned theology into religious bigotry and theologians into fanatics should be replaced by a peace more like the quiet of the grave. For all churches must consist of people for whom in the last resort there is only one choice, namely Christ or nothing. But since every human being who tries to live his faith in his daily life forms his own personal and living contact with God, any levelling out at the expense of variety cannot help or advance the church or indeed Christianity as a whole. This is why thought and action in a truly ecumenical spirit does not mean the same as thinking and acting like everyone else. Ecumenical theology cannot in our opinion be either polemical or eirenical. It must be an understanding theology. By this I mean quite simply that we must be able to forget our individual standpoints without renouncing them. We will then be able to put ourselves in the position of our opposite numbers, unencumbered by prejudice and ready to experience other forms of belief. If our opposite numbers respond in the same way a genuine dialogue can ensue and not just an empty exchange of words. People who do not listen 'understandingly' to what others are saying are guilty of listening with only half an ear, their inadequate excuse being that they already know what they are being told. This is what Dietrich Bonhoeffer described as 'impatient, inattentive listening that despises the brother and is only waiting for a chance to speak and so get rid of the other person'.[4] This is no way to fulfil our mission; we should be careful to remember that our attitude towards our fellow speaker is just another reflection of our relationship to God.

The Roman Catholic Church's new approach to the ecumenical question since the Second Vatican Council has opened the way not

only to a dialogue with all Christians but also to one with all men of
good will. This in turn is giving Roman Catholic theology the opportunity of renewing itself by becoming alive to values the influence of
which had previously only been felt outside the church. The Roman
Catholic Church and its theology will thus be able to gain back some of
the Christian values which the world once received from it, but which
it later came to forget or even to fight against in its attempts to
gain control over mankind. Our so-called secularized world will thus
have something to contribute to a desecularization of theology and the
church, which will become evident when the latter cease to concern
themselves with the creation of a permanent 'Christian world order'.
For to this there is indeed an alternative: a theology and a church free
from all the constraints of this world and therefore able to demonstrate
to all men that they are both the instruments of the will and the power
of that invisible Lord to whom Christianity owes its name.

Hypothesis 9   Post-conciliar Roman Catholicism shows us that the
greatest weakness of Roman Catholic theology today is what was once
its strength. By helping Roman Catholicism to assert itself as a Christian
institution which believed itself capable of creating and preserving
a Christian world order, its theology contributed to the establishment
of a tradition which stands in the way of the free development of the
individual Roman Catholic and indeed of its own renewal. This
tradition is based on a social order which has however lost much of its
power and importance in the context of the so-called Christian Western
world. But because this social order was sanctioned and sanctified by
theology and the church as something divinely ordained, the theological
and ecclesiastical tradition which it nourishes has acquired an absolute
value: in other words it has become traditionalism. When the world
then rid itself of all the ballast of inhuman social structures, inspired
by the ideals of liberty, equality and fraternity, the church remained
hopelessly caught up in them. In order to shore up its credibility and
prevent its theology from being questioned, it felt it had to declare
permanent and sacrosanct its secularized forms and values.

Only a great Pope possessing a remarkable degree of personal
charisma and a whole-hearted faith in Christ and his gospel could
liberate Roman Catholicism from its bonds: for of these the most
important was the absolute power of the Pope himself, theologically
sanctioned as it is and firmly anchored in dogma. This Pope was the
product of our allegedly secularized twentieth century: his name was
John. But his actions put all Roman Catholicism and especially its
traditionalist-minded hierarchy in a state of fear; one is reminded of

Sören Kierkegaard's definition of fear as the 'vertigo of freedom'. In earlier days theology and the church exploited men's fears to force them into obedience: today they themselves are scared. They are scared at the prospects freedom opens up.

Only in this way can one satisfactorily account for certain features of post-conciliar Roman Catholicism such as the encyclical *Humanae Vitae* or the attitude of the hierarchy to important questions like that of celibacy. Yet fear at the prospects freedom opens up can also have positive results. It may preserve Roman Catholicism from that neo-conformity which often drives Protestant theologians to ridiculous lengths. If it is not just the fear of losing authority and power, but a really sincere fear as to the fate of Christian truth and of the human beings it concerns, it can be really constructive and will at the decisive moment be removed by the sure knowledge that the fate of Christianity is decided not by Christ's vicar on earth but by God himself.

Hypothesis 10 Our examination and inquiry into the effects of theology and society upon each other has helped us to draw up nine hypotheses, the usefulness of which is twofold. In the first place, they help us to bring the problems caused by the alleged 'secularization' of the world nearer to a solution. Secondly, they show us what the theologian's function in society is in as objective and as unprejudiced a light as possible, by indicating how inextricably theology has always been linked to structures and social systems, and how dependent it has always been on non-Christian and non-theological factors.

All nine provide justification for advancing our principal hypothesis, which is that this so-called 'secularization' is nothing but a theological fiction. The inquiries I have undertaken to verify these hypotheses, and all the historical and other material I have examined in connection with them, have only strengthened my conviction that the theses that have been advanced on the subject of secularization do not stand up to the sociological facts: they are in fact items in a theological creed. This creed is either an attempt to objectify the subjective lack of faith of its adherents, or the product of an a-historical mode of thought which imagines it can provide figures to prove the presence or absence of God in this world of ours by having recourse to a type of religious sociology which has fallen prey to empiricism. It is easy to prove that though there has never been a 'secularization of the world' and never can be; the secularization of the Christian faith (i.e. its approximation to this world) began as early as that great turning point, the reign of Constantine, and reached its climax with the complete identification of theology and the churches with the prevailing social orders. With the disappearance of these orders, a discrepancy has arisen between church and world: the churches are trying to remove this discrepancy by going into the world in a new way, a process which can be called a new form of secularization and which is taking the shape of a neo-conformity on the part of the churches and theology. In this a part is being played by the secularization of theology and by its frequent attempts to assume the role of sociology in order to make itself felt. If one wants to see this process not as a secularization of Christianity but rather as a secularization of the world, as its 'dechristianization', one must first be able to prove that the world really was Christian once and that it can really *be* Christian.

But the conclusions we have come to as regards the function of theology in society have shown without any shadow of doubt that theology has always used existent ideologies, systems and structures as its guides, and that as a result it has never been in a position to purvey to the world that Christianity which the theology of the New Testament has handed down to us. The world discovered this Christianity when it won its independence from theology and the church or, to put it another way, when that phenomenon occurred which theologians like to interpret as the 'secularization of the world'. Whereas theology and the churches continued to depend on the structures they had sanctioned, the world won that freedom which is necessary for the realization of what is the alpha and the omega of New Testament theology, namely the new man, whose faith enables him to free himself from all constraints so that he can devote himself entirely to the renewal of the world and of society.

This new man today represents the greatest hope yet also the greatest danger for theology and the church. He is helping to bring about the renewal of theology and the church by forcing them to desecularize themselves, that is, to rid themselves of the secular ballast of many centuries. But in so far as he may be seen in the context of time as something final rather than provisional, this new man is capable of endangering theology and the church by making them dependent on him. For in that case they would be dependent not on God the eternal but, once again, on temporal man, not man in general but a definite type of man, the man of today who, though closer to the new man in the Christian sense, is still far removed from the ideal type of the new man, and therefore still very far away from that state which in the past men and societies thought they had achieved in their generations, namely a Christianity in accordance with New Testament theology.

Theology and the churches will be able to give new life to New Testament theology provided they do not try to correct old mistakes by making new ones. One of their old mistakes was their one-sided theocentricity at the expense of man and his problems here and now.

Another was their deliberate or unwitting disdain of the basic truth that in the light of the life, teaching and death of Christ no economic, political or social order in this world may be sanctioned and accepted as divinely ordained. Amongst the newer mistakes they are already making we have, for instance, their anthropocentricity, their placing of man as the centre of all their theological concerns. There is also their tendency to give their blessing to disorder, nor order, and to call it divinely ordained.

Yet all the same the critical observer of the interactions of theology and society can justifiably entertain the hope that theology and the church are genuinely trying to understand contemporary man and to help him. For his part he, by his healthy restlessness and above all by his longing for something new, is helping them constantly to bear in mind that one of the most important utterances in the New Testament is this: 'The old has passed away; behold, the new has come' (II Cor. 5.17). New is the fact that theology and the church cannot control modern man or the world in which he lives. And that is all to the good. For by not even wanting to be the masters where they realize they cannot be, they are being forced to accept that the one and only ruler is the one on whom they call, the one and only Lord whom a Christian may recognize: Jesus.

NOTES

1. *Religionssoziologie. Eine Einführung*, Nymphenburger Verlagshandlung, Munich, 1968.
2. E. H. Tödt, 'Theologie der Revolution', *Ökumenische Rundschau* 17, 1968, pp. 20 f.
3. Homily 8.1 on Jeremiah (Migne, Patrologia Graeca 13, 336).
4. *Life Together*, rev. ed., SCM Press, London, 1965, p. 76.

PART SEVEN

The Role of the Christian and the Churches

*The Church is called to work for a world-wide responsible
society and to summon men and nations to repentance.*

The Report of Uppsala, Section III, par. 29.

20

Towards an Ecumenical Consensus

HANS-HEINRICH WOLF

At the Geneva World Conference on Church and Society in 1966 a working party was set up to observe the progress of the conference as a whole with special reference to the theological issues raised, so as to be able to outline the underlying theological ideas in more concentrated form in conjunction with the work of the various sections. This was carried out by three working groups (A, B, and C), and there may be more in their reports than the authors themselves at first imagined. In group discussions, and discussions involving the entire conference, an attempt at least was made to reach something amounting to an ecumenical consensus of opinion in which expression is given to guiding principles which must underlie the consideration of social and ethical problems today. If this volume is intended to be a symposium on the World Council's thinking on economics and society, it is fitting that the theological questions arising out of the Geneva discussions should be clarified. Of course one could try to make some coherent pattern out of a whole multitude of random but specifically theological statements – or, to put it more modestly, comments – all expressing Christian responsibility in particular and all gleaned from the minutes of the conference. But I doubt if this would prove very satisfactory, since comments of this kind are so often casual and have little or no connection with the problems actually under discussion; very often they do not bear witness to the fact that the topic in question prompted an exchange of theological ideas between people approaching it from different angles, disciplines and backgrounds.

On the whole this is a lesson which we in the ecumenical movement have yet to learn; we shall only do so if in the future we submit ourselves to the severe and remorseless discipline of inter-faculty dialogue.

This does not mean relinquishing that which is proper to theology, but it does mean that we should allow it to be questioned critically just as we in our own theological thinking direct our critical questions to those talking from a different standpoint. But even from the theological point of view the ecumenical dialogue at the Geneva Conference was not entirely fruitless. It did not simply become a good specialized discussion amongst experts, forgetting theological perspectives; of course a good specialized discussion could be prompted by a theological perspective in so far as it is theology's concern to see that all factual subjects are free to be treated in pertinent terms. But it was more than that. One may indeed say that in the findings of the respective working groups of which I have spoken, we have before us a crystallization of the Geneva Conference's theological thinking and decision-making which was of importance for the Uppsala Assembly in 1968 too.

In the 'context of faith' four facts emerge which must be taken into account when considering the role of the Christian and the churches in the world of technology and social development.[1]

I

There is no structure of society, no system of human power and security, that is perfectly just. There is no divinely-ordained social order, but there is the judgment of God under which every system falls, to be transformed into one that is more just. There can be no self-protecting *status quo* in the light of the judgment, that is the crucifixion, of Christ: it is indeed continuously challenged by the church which is in essence the pilgrim people of God and which can therefore never harden into a *status quo*.

This must lead to corresponding thought and action with the aim of bringing about an effective social change whereby the poor and oppressed will receive their share of justice. If it comes to revolution, the Christian owes the revolutionary 'freedom from hatred, freedom to build a new world in which also the enemy will find a just place, and freedom from self-righteousness – freedom to accept the give and take which must modify even revolutionary plans and power. For revolutions are also under the judgment when they make their cause absolute and promise final salvation.'

Uppsala took up this idea of a social order perpetually correcting and transforming itself in the theme of the Conference, 'Behold, I make all things new'. This brought into play the concept of 'the new' which stems from God's action in history, and applied it to the transformation of social conditions. However, it was expressly underlined that not every new phenomenon in society comes directly from God, and that the newness of modernity requires renewal from God.[2]

The 'new' may announce itself in the form of violent revolutions; this was clearly pointed out in one of the lectures at Geneva. The American theologian Richard Shaull, long active in Latin America, suggested that, if not all-out revolution, then perhaps the violent measures of guerilla units, clearly aware of new social patterns, could be the responsibility of the Christian in situations where change can really only be brought about by the threat or use of violence, and where the underprivileged masses can only thus be saved from annihilation. Uppsala very cautiously repeated this idea, which has since given rise to a whole debate and numerous publications, as we can see in this passage from one of the sections:

Where other means have failed some have chosen to protest against social injustice by economic boycott or by selective destruction of property. In extreme situations some groups of Christians have borne the risk and guilt of shedding blood (examples: the resistance against Hitler, the Cuban revolution against the Batista regime). Those who condemn them should not forget the bloodshed that was inherent in those regimes and the constant destruction of lives carelessly caused by some structures of contemporary society, such as inhuman working conditions.[3]

At other points too in the Uppsala Conference there was mention of the development of a strategy of revolution to lead, though without violence, to social upheaval, and which could be drawn up by the churches.[4] 'Revolution is not to be equated with violence,' we read here, although it is taken into account that revolutionary upheavals may take on violent forms. Or let us recall that passage in the report on the Geneva Conference which runs:

It cannot be said that the only possible position for the Christian is one of absolute non-violence. There are situations where Christians may become involved in violence. Whenever it is used, however, it must be seen as an 'ultimate course' which is justified only in extreme situations. The use of violence requires a rigorous definition of the ends for which it is used, and a clear recognition of the evils which are inherent in it, and it should always be tempered by mercy. . . .[5]

If we look at the pronouncements of the Second Vatican Council in its 'Pastoral Constitution on the Church in the Modern World', they will be found to be considerably more restrained.

Where public authority oversteps its competence and oppresses the people, those people should nevertheless obey to the extent that the objective common good demands. Still, it is lawful for them to defend their own rights and those of their fellow citizens against any abuse of this authority, provided that in doing so they observe the limits imposed by natural law and the gospel.[6]

These limits are not defined, however, so that one gains the impression that the possibility in principle of violent revolution is then removed in practice. In *Populorum Progressio* it is said that every revolutionary rising begets new injustices, produces new disturbances of equilibrium and provokes new conflicts – 'except in the case of an obvious and prolonged tyranny assailing the fundamental rights of individuals and the common weal of the state'.

Here more definitely than in many parts of the Geneva documents we find a vindication of violence in certain circumstances, even if it is its negative consequences that are stressed. I would not go so far as to suggest that revolution under certain conditions is here declared to be a legitimate means of socio-economic development; but the possibility of the use of violence is countenanced, and maybe we can really talk of an important shift in Roman Catholicism's views on the subject which could be of great significance for its involvement in the under-developed countries.[7]

II

'The Christian lives in the world by the hope of the final victory of Christ over the powers of this age.' This hope refers to a fulfilment in which all nations, all human social forces and all human life 'will be transformed in a way beyond the imagination, symbolised in the Bible by the expression "a new heaven and a new earth" '.[8]

This total and ultimate transformation should be distinguished from the other kind of transformation which is realized through the irruption of God's rule which occurs in history with the coming of Jesus Christ and which palpably manifests itself in the struggle for justice and true humanity. This, too, can be described as transformation, though not in the sense of a planned development of the world towards the kingdom of God; human plans and aspirations are subject to judgment which may mean destruction just as much as progress and development. But the resurrection of Christ is the basis and guarantee for the fact that partial transformations can indeed occur in human society and can bring about a more humane world even though they may not be permanent or complete. There is therefore hope that human society can be positively built up on all levels. In this context very concrete measures are envisaged which could represent a provisional trans-formation of the world in this sense, for example the equal distribution of power, the creation and establishment of areas of mutual interest

insured against self-interest by impartial institutions. Thus the great
and all-embracing transformation at the end of time towards which
Christian hopes are equally directed will not simply juxtapose the
perfect and the imperfect, the whole and the part, the eternal and the
ephemeral. Perfection is also something entirely different in the sense
that everything new which comes from God is the continuation of the
old yet also a break with it.

What must be emphasized is that the hope of which Christians are
speaking is not derived from an optimistic view of the course of history
but is drawn expressly from God's act of salvation in Jesus Christ,
which signifies the continuous struggle of Jesus Christ with the powers
of destruction both in the individual and in human society, and in which
Christians participate by taking concrete measures to change both.

It is significant that what we have said here about social and universal
responsibility refers on the one hand quite explicitly to the Christ-event
in history and the beginning of transformation of this world which may
follow from it, and on the other hand refers to a future and transcendental event which is nevertheless to be perceived in anticipation in
the here and now, though without merging with it and thereby removing
our expectation of the *new* in its other sense.

This theological framework was actually first conceived at Evanston
in 1954 at the plenary session on the theme 'Christ the Hope of the
World', though at the time it did not lead to unanimity amongst the
people taking part.

The objection could be raised that the concept of transformation is
being taken here in too definitely and exclusively a social a sense and
not at all in the sense of the transformation or conversion of the individual. In an essay published in the preparatory volumes for the
Geneva Conference under the title 'Conversion and Social Transformation',[9] the South American theologian E. Castro pointed out that
the separation between the conversion of individuals and social change
was both false and unbiblical. The human heart – the object of conversion – does not exist beyond and separate from the relationships
characteristic of the human being. A change of heart entails changes
in all the relationships in which the individual participates. The
inclusion of the converted person in the fellowship of the disciples,
which according to the New Testament was part of the process of
conversion, has obvious consequences for his social action. John the
Baptist and Jesus himself are proof of these consequences. Where a
new relationship with Christ is created by an individual's conversion,
this at the same time includes a new relationship with his neighbour
in the form of duties and responsibilities. Castro denies that there
are two phases in conversion, the first being concerned with conversion

P

to Christ, the second with conversion in one's attitude to the world. Conversion is one *single* event, in which the individual is linked with the Christ of that unique yet continuous act of salvation revealed in the history of mankind, in which he too is now called to participate. Not only does this bring about changes in the interpersonal relationships of men, but also in social institutions, in forms of production, in the distribution of power between social groups, and so on. Sin cannot be understood without taking its social dimension into account, and the distortion inherent in social institutions which exercise influence over people; in the same way the effects of salvation in the form of conversion and rebirth are not to be understood without their social implications.

III

The discernment of Christians of what is just and unjust, human and inhuman in the complexities of political and economic change, is a discipline exercised in continual dialogue with biblical resources, the mind of the church through history and today, and the best insights of social scientific analysis. But it remains a discipline which aims not at a theoretical system of truth but at action in human society.[10]

This poses the problem of the criteria of judgment and action. In addition to this the ecumenical dialogue of the churches has already provided us with a certain tradition of controversy which is still relevant in so far as this dialogue is by no means over yet.

Long before the founding of the World Council of Churches in 1948, the Life and Work Movement, which was one of the currents flowing into the World Council, had already given consideration to the criteria according to which the Christian should act. At the first major conference, at Stockholm in 1925, discussion centred on the Christian 'principles' of love, brotherhood and justice as part of an eternal order, and on how they should be applied to particular social situations in order to promote the restoration of social order. As to how they were to be applied, no one definite system emerged; in each new situation they would have to be applied in the appropriate way. The task of the churches was seen to reside in making human consciences more sharply aware of these situations and in appealing to men's will to improve conditions and provide existing programmes of reform 'with life-giving spirit'. The church ought, they felt, to be a 'central spiritual community' which should be intent on asserting these principles, all derived from the gospel, in every sphere of human experience. The aim of all Christian action was apparently conceived, believed and hoped to be the imbuing of all human intercourse with a truly Christian spirit.

In striving to achieve this goal especial emphasis was laid on the education of men in a Christian spirit to embrace not only the individual personality but also and in particular its social dimensions. Yet this solution proved inadequate.

Further thought was given to the principles of Christian action at a later conference held in Oxford in 1937; the result was the establishment of the so-called 'middle axioms'. These are less comprehensive than is the command of love in its fullest realization, yet they too are an expression of love, and appeal at the same time to the 'intuition of the individual conscience'.

Such 'middle axioms' are intermediate between the ultimate basis of Christian action in community, 'thou shalt love thy neighbour as thyself', and the unguided intuition of the individual conscience. They are at best provisional and they are never unchallengeable or valid without exception for all time; for it is in a changing world that God's will has to be fulfilled. Yet as interim principles they are indispensable for any kind of common policy.[11]

Love as the criterion of Christian action must be translated in practice into justice even where it cannot be realized in its full dimensions. Justice, in the sense of the 'ideal of a harmonious relationship between men', must be helped to assert itself in all social settlements and arrangements, in economic planning and in political systems. It ought to provide the individual with his appropriate place in society in the face of favouritism and exploitation, discrimination and victimization; however, it ought also to draw attention to the responsibility of the individual towards others and demand sacrifices of him in so far as they may be required for the sake of the 'harmony' of society as a whole. In order to attain these objectives, justice needs discipline to prevent man from asserting his own destructive inclinations. Disciplinary measures are 'dykes against sin'. They may themselves become the source of new evils and must therefore be under constant control. They are the lowest rung in the ladder of social order into which philanthropy must be translated. They are the framework within which love in the widest sense may be applied to the creation of social relationships and institutions.

No system of law, government or economics is either so bad or so good (in our provisionally enforced order) that it may remove the individual's responsibility to go beyond what this order demands of him by performing acts of Christian love. . . . Institutional requirements necessarily prescribe only the minimum.[12]

But Christian love of the most comprehensive kind actually possible in practice does not make superfluous those institutional requirements which manifest themselves in the form of legislation and of political and social systems and economic and cultural institutions. Charitable action which imagines it can dispense with institutional requirements might easily become a cloak for injustice. It can of course help an individual or a group for a time, but it cannot help society as a whole, and society after all is responsible for each individual and for the socially underprivileged in particular. Brotherly love takes account of the reality of institutional and social requirements because it is well aware of the destructive inclinations of human beings. But it constantly seeks to reach beyond these requirements in order to attain a system of justice more complete than social institutions can ever hope to provide. But whatever new and better social orders may evolve with time, they can never be equated with the fulfilment of God's will or the realization of the kingdom of God. They may be regarded as partial fulfilments of his will, or as provisional anticipations of his Kingdom in history, but never as their full realization. For this transcends history and defies prediction.

Thus far Oxford. The plenary sessions at Amsterdam (1948) and Evanston (1954) became specially famous because they introduced the concept of 'responsible society' into the social and ethical thinking of the ecumenical movement. A criterion and standard was thus provided by which choices could be made within existing orders and programmes which approximated as closely as possible to that freedom which Christ won for all. There was no deliberate intention to draw up a specific political, social and economic programme when this concept was put forward; the intention was to proceed pragmatically from facts and work towards a 'responsible society', the concrete form of which could not be established in detail beforehand because it would have to emerge from a given situation. But what is certain is that amongst the factors which anticipate it, the concept of partnership is bound to assume a central role, coming to the fore whenever such topics as participation, control of power, co-operation of different groups within families, democratic structures and racially varied societies are the subject for debate. The concept has in fact retained a dominating position in ecumenical discussion until now, though at Geneva in 1966 the question was raised as to whether it was adequate in the context of the world situation today. Dr W. A. Visser 't Hooft in his address to the Geneva Conference argued the case for giving the concept two new dimensions: 'The first is that of a responsible *world* society in which each nation feels responsible for the welfare of all other nations.' The second dimension of a responsible society which should, he thought, be more clearly defined, concerns 'the place of man in the new highly organized society'.[13] But what exactly is man's sphere of responsibility? Man today seems to be placed in a position precisely and conclusively determined by science and technology, and the term 'responsibility' is in danger of becoming an illusion. The answer can only be: 'Responsible men participate responsibly in a world society in which all accept responsibility for the common welfare.'[14] In the light of this it is easy to understand why the World Council in Uppsala decided to set in motion a comprehensive study of human problems: its aim would be to ascertain what exactly goes to make up man's intrinsic humanity in the contemporary world, and this would be done by a very comprehensive survey of theology's relationship to all other subjects, including technology and social practice.

At this point we come back to the quotation from the Geneva Conference cited at the beginning of the third section of this essay. It spoke of a 'discipline exercised in continual dialogue' conditioned on the one hand by attention to scripture and its interpretation through the ages by the church, and on the other by acceptance of the 'best insights of social scientific analysis'. In other words this means that the contemporary opinions and attitudes of Christians and churches on social and economic problems cannot be made hard and fast beforehand and then imposed on a given situation, but must be thought out and discovered anew on each occasion. Of course, the Christian is aware of what are usually termed 'criteria'; for instance, he has heard of the ten commandments and the injunctions laid down in the Sermon on the Mount; he is aware of the so-called catalogues of virtues and vices in the Pauline epistles. But these too should not be understood as indications of a 'theoretical system of truth', but rather as indications for 'action in human society'. It is well known that the ten commandments are connected with the covenant which God made with his people journeying from captivity to the promised land, and represent for all humanity how men ought to conduct their lives when they have assented to obey God and to fulfill his commands. In concrete terms this means that in the application of the commandments relatively wide scope was allowed for the solution of problems arising both from military conflicts, peaceful daily life, and the achievement of personal salvation. The Sermon on the Mount may be regarded as a blueprint for the internal life of the community. But the community is caught up in human society and is transparently open to it, as it is to God, on every side; what happens within it should radiate far into every sphere of human society. The same is of course true of the catalogues of virtues and vices, if only because the terms named there cannot be reduced to any single individual religious meaning but have to be understood in their totality, i.e. with reference to society as well.

From a biblical and theological point of view one is here perhaps reminded first of a cardinal passage in the epistle to the Romans which in a sense sums up many other biblical passages. I am referring to Romans 12.1 ff. This deals with 'Worship and Everyday Life'.[15] It is a question of Christian existence as such, for which 'service' through God's mercy as explained in Romans 1–11 is *the* decisive feature in this world. The act of worship in which the Christian community gathers is itself nothing other than a crystallization of those features which characterize its life in the world. Reference is made at this point to *logike latreia*. The Revised Standard Version reads 'spiritual worship', but one could equally well say 'service in accordance with the *logos*' (the translation 'rational service' seems to me questionable); such service is conditioned by the *logos*, the divine 'deed-word' which signifies both gift and task. The decisive factor in service as thus understood consists of and occurs in the dedication of our bodies, i.e. the dedication of our entire human existence, an existence not conforming to the world but constantly being transformed by the *logos* and proving itself in 'an unrelenting critical distinction between the divine will and every earthly will'. This certainly does not mean mere 'inner life and ethical sentiment'; what it means is 'that God has begun to reclaim for himself the world which belongs to him'. This dedication of our bodies

is not a matter exclusively and primarily of the personality of man but, at least in the passages of greatest theological significance, of his capacity for communication and the reality of his incorporation in a world which limits him. God lays claim to our corporeality because he is no longer leaving the world to itself, and our bodily obedience expresses the fact that, in and with us, he has recalled to his service the world of which we are a part.[16]

At this point the other half of v. 2 becomes relevant. The process of transformation and renewal takes place and is completed in *dokimazein* – in proving, or rather in discerning the will of God, which is 'good, acceptable and perfect'.

The ethical decision which this *dokimazein* or *discerning* entails is one of discovery – the discovery of the unknown, even though we know much. This is what Rom. 1–11, the chapters which lead up to our quotation, are really about. But the fundamental quality of God's will, which is the subject of the church's faith and the *known* as elaborated in Romans 1–11, is also the *unknown*, and is indeed always bound to be unknown as far as God's actual will in any given situation is concerned. It has to be discovered and accomplished anew each time: only then can any criteria emerge, and even then they will not form a rigid system which can be imposed on situations. Another way of putting the problem is this: the accepted criteria, like our knowledge of what can basically be said about man in God's eyes and of what makes man human, are something that can never be simply expressed in ordinary categories of being; yet they must be made part of this process of transformation in which the divine will of obedient action is to be discerned.

Of course an important part in this process of discerning is played by our knowledge of given situations such as is provided today by science, technology and social practice. They too did not arise without God's will, however much his will may appear foreign to such areas of life. The will of God, who is omnipresent in heaven and on earth and at work in history, must be discerned with reference to the realities in which Christians and non-Christians alike are placed: it must emerge from discussion with competent representatives of all these areas.

Another integral part of this discipline is the certain belief that it is God's concern that life in this world should be truly fit for humanness and should depend on love and hope. But what do love and hope mean in a practical situation? Love must be expressed within the framework and structures of justice, as was said at the Geneva Conference. Hope should be placed in the attainable concepts of universal peace. But how is this to be achieved? This can only emerge from our assessment of a practical situation and the decision prompted by it. Only then can we discern God's will in its practical reality. But we should not overlook the fact that this will can only be surveyed by him who ultimately transcends all the practicalities of this world in his perfection and who is the focus of all our hope. In ecumenical discussions concerning criteria everything has become more fluid and more dynamic; problems are looked at in their practical contemporary context and in the context of that divine action which it is our endeavour to discern.

One further point. The quotation which opens the third section of this essay is concerned with 'action in human society', but it is also concerned with the action of one particular human society – that of all Christians, and not just of the individual Christian. Uppsala stated: 'The problem of rules and of personal responsibility in each situation can only be solved within the framework of community'.[17] The individual and the community are inseparable; the community is not a collective into which the individual merges. In the creation the foundations were laid, and God's acts of salvation renew the possibility for man to play his full part as a human being in the community, and for his decisions not to be merely the joy or burden of the individual but of that whole community which is established in the corporateness of the church. This is something which is once again being increasingly realized as the result of the contemporary trend of human beings to come together in communities of very diversified character.

Up to this point we have been discussing the presuppositions conditioning the action of Christians and churches in the context of the scientific and technological world and its social evolution, and considering the ways in which solutions can be found to problems which have been examined individually by the other contributors to this symposium. Turning now to the fourth topic which was dealt with by the Geneva Conference, we come to what is surely the crucial point: it seems to me that it is one which can clarify the relationship between the church and the world or between the church and humanity, and thereby provide us with the essential starting-point for action in the world.

IV

The Church is called, in the world, to be that part of the world which responds to God's love for all men, and to become therefore the community in which God's relation to man is known and realized. The Church is in one sense the centre and fulfilment of the world. In another it is the servant of the world and the witness to it of the hope of its future. It is called to be the community in which the world can discover itself as it may become in the future. When it does not fulfil this mission and reflects the prejudices of the world, as is often the case, it is not faithful to its calling.[18]

Perhaps these words make too extravagant a claim, because the reality of the church as we see it is very far from being conscious even of realizing a fraction of this mission and, bearing in mind the unfortunate development of the church's history through the centuries, one should perhaps refrain entirely from referring to the church as the 'centre and fulfilment of the world'. This could all too easily be misunderstood as a vainglorious boast. Yet the vocation of the church always exceeds what it has actually achieved in precise historical situations, though for all that the reality of what it has failed to achieve is in no way impaired. A distinction must also be made between that pre-existent unity which God has already bestowed upon the church, and its visible manifestation which has still to materialize and which it is our task to bring about. For this task the unity originally bestowed is of the very greatest importance. To call the church the 'centre and fulfilment of the world' is not to give one's blessing to an institution in which the action of divine salvation has found and continues to find expression, and to deprive it in so doing of its openness to all men and to a God whose concern is for all men. The term 'centre' may indeed raise a false claim, while the concept 'fulfilment of the world' might signify a complete confusion of terms, since 'world' according to the generally-accepted usage of the New Testament means mankind in rebellion against God. This indeed is what it means, apart from the universal reconciliation which mankind has already been granted in Christ. And reconciliation is the aim which it is God's will to fulfil for *mankind*. We should now turn to what was said also about the church, namely that it is the 'servant' of the world and the witness to it (the world) of the hope of its future. This presupposes that the church has its own means of gaining power and influence over men, however open to misconstruction this may be. Its means is service, sacrifice and suffering. In the contemporary world situation, as we saw at the beginning, we have become uncertain whether this really is the ultimate means in all situations. Whatever conclusions we may come to in this matter, the concept of 'service' remains unalterable; in the last resort what it means is to lose one's life in order to gain it.

Thus humanity, divided up as it is into a multiplicity of diversely structured human societies with at the centre a church as we have described it – 'existing' in order to 'become' – might be said to have in its midst a community with which it has to co-exist in constant and constructive mutual criticism; this 'church' provides scope for humanity to discern its potential character and its God-given objectives, even if only from a distance and without any unjustified collusion with it.

The idea of a theologically justified correspondence between humanity and the church which was so clearly expressed at the Geneva Conference is in a certain sense connected with discussions at previous ecumenical conferences. Thus the Oxford Conference of 1937, which debated the theme 'Church, Community and State', exhorted the world not to become what the church is, because the church was too much like what the world is, namely reluctant to repent, divided, self-centred, crazed with power, etc. 'We do not call the world to be like ourselves, for we are already too like the world. Only as we ourselves repent, both as individuals and as corporate bodies, can the Church call men to repentance. The call to ourselves and to the world is to Christ.'[19] The church must become what, contrary to all appearances, it actually is through the free intervention of Christ's grace and of his spirit, namely a 'universal brotherhood', the 'true community' of men seeking community. The state should recognize this objective on which the church is intent, and accord it complete liberty to organize itself. But 'the Church can claim such liberty for itself only as it is also concerned for the rights and liberties of others'.[20] Here we therefore encounter the correspondence between what the church is from the point of view of its divine mission and what it can contribute to a multi-racial and multi-national world. This involves problems arising from the struggle against racial discrimination as much as those arising from education, international co-existence, etc. The community of men with God as represented by the church has its analogy in the 'divinely created brotherhood of men' for which the church must strive in every sphere of human life and for which it should provide the pattern. I quote an example of such thinking from one of the reports of the Oxford Conference, in which it is said that the church is ecumenical in character, i.e. it should represent a unity in diversity recognizable both inwardly and outwardly. It is therefore in a position to provide the nations of the world with a realization which the usual political sources cannot provide.

To those who are struggling to realize human brotherhood in a world where disruptive nationalism and aggressive imperialism make such brotherhood seem unreal, the Church offers not an ideal but a fact, man united not by his aspiration, but by the love of God.[21]

The plenary session of the World Council of Churches at Evanston in 1954 touched on the problem of the correspondence between the church and society and between the church and the world in quite unequivocal terms. It described the Christian community as the 'visible centre of the social community' and thus the foundation of social responsibility in the local sphere.[22] Elsewhere it went on to declare:

Their [the churches'] first duty is to fulfil their calling to manifest the Kingdom of God among men. Their fellowship must be a bond of union among all, a bond both more patient and more resistant than any other. The Church must seek to be the kind of community which God wishes the world to become. By virtue of its calling it must act as a redemptive suffering fellowship in the form and manner of its Lord Jesus Christ. . . . Its members must rise above the limitations of nationalism to a truly ecumenical outlook. It must carry into the turmoil of international relations the real possibility of reconciliation of all races, nationalities and classes in the love of Christ. It must witness to the creative power of forgiveness and spiritual renewal. All these things the churches must do as an essential part of their evangelistic task.[23]

The similarity between this and the passages from the Geneva Conference which we quoted at the beginning of our fourth section is obvious. Yet this passage does have its own peculiarities. The church as the manifestation of the kingdom of God (doubtful as it is to talk like that) and as the kind of community which God wishes the world to become is seen as a kind of net thrown over all sections of society and giving the latter something it has hitherto lacked yet which is as essential to it, as it is to the church itself, if it is to fulfil its divinely appointed task. One must be careful to distinguish the *tertium comparationis* in this metaphor, since otherwise it is liable to lend itself to a mistakenly 'imperialistic' interpretation. There is in it no intention of suggesting that people and communities outside the church are to be caught as in a net against their will. The members of the church, scattered throughout the world and forming part of groupings of the most multifarious kind and performing all manner of social roles, nevertheless remain members of a very special community, the hallmark of which affects all aspects of their life in society. But it does not do so in terms of outward violence (so 1954!), but rather, as is very often the case, in terms of suffering patiently borne. For it is as a 'redemptive suffering fellowship' that the church is the 'centre of the social community and the base for social responsibility in the local sphere'.

These points of view, aired as they have been in protracted ecumenical debates, have since acquired new topicality at the Geneva Conference and then at Uppsala, and they are likely to continue to preoccupy us.

Uppsala debated the church in connection with its catholicity. In the Report of Section I we read:

The Church is bold in speaking of itself as a sign of the coming unity of mankind. However well founded the claim, the world hears it sceptically, and points to 'secular catholicities' of its own. For secular society has produced instruments of conciliation and unification which often seem more effective than the Church itself.[24]

Here the term 'sign' deserves closer examination because it is very likely that the various Christian traditions will interpret it in very different ways. The following passage certainly makes it evident that we should not understand 'sign' to mean that the church merely signalizes something which in itself it is not. In defining the catholicity of the church, the Uppsala Report speaks of the church as a 'new community of new creatures', and goes on to say that

The catholicity of the Church means this given reality of grace in which the purpose of creation is restored and sinful men are reconciled in the one divine sonship of which Christ is both author and finisher.[25]

Thus the new world is partially fulfilled in the church in the sense that man – man in community – is made new, which has always been the aim of the gospel. And when one is speaking of the church one is always thinking too of its realization in the local community, for it is there that according to the New Testament the church is to attain its full realization. Its much talked-of openness to the world may now perhaps be seen from a rather different angle. We have long been accustomed to think of the church first and foremost as a gathering of those called out of the world and then sent back into it; but now the relationship between gospel and world (i.e. mankind) has emerged into the foreground in a different way. If the church is produced by and indeed exists by reason of the dynamic interaction of these two quantities (gospel – world), it must bear the characteristic *per se* of being a partial embodiment and anticipation of the universal, and of affecting every sphere of human society in such a way that certain marks of salvation, e.g., contributions to the comprehensive establishment of world peace, will at least in their early stages become visible without the prerequisite of faith. The contrast between the church and the world, a dominant feature at least in some Western church traditions, will find itself superseded by the awareness that they belong together and that they exist in a state of continuous correlation, an awareness which is itself grounded in the universality of the gospel. This does not rule out the fact that mankind too will repeatedly fall short of its original destiny and will need to be called back to it. But this is equally true of the church at least in so far as it is seen from the point of view of its members.

In the light of all this we may then see the celebration of the Eucharist as the decisive focus for that potential human unity which is prefigured by the church.[26] 'In its deepest sense liturgy is the hallowing of all we are for the sake of all that is, that God may be all in all.'[27] Even where the church has been forced out of the openness of society and is compelled to lead its life in strictest seclusion, even where it has been condemned to what may appear to amount to impotence in public life, the Christian community may well be still alive in its acceptance of suffering; if so, the correlation between the church and the world is still present and with it the prefiguration in the community of universal salvation. The church can therefore never give up its search for new structures which would enable it to fulfil the mission for which it exists even more fully.

With regard to the relationship between the church and mankind, perhaps the clearest programme for the practical action of Christians and the churches is to be found in Section IV of the Uppsala Report. There we read that the church is nowadays being confronted with insights from the Word of God which are beginning to be realized in contemporary secular human society or which are being advocated strenuously although they are not realized to be specifically Christian. This is a challenge to Christians and puts them to shame, for in human society now we see taking place, albeit fragmentarily, something which Christians have failed to achieve for themselves and to which they should have devoted all their energies. Christians are summoned first by the Word of

God, but also by what they can see taking place in the world and which seems to be the fulfilment of that Word, to act in complete obedience to the Word and to provide an example in their own mutual relations of what should ultimately come about in human society as a whole.

The Word of God testifies to the unity of creation, and to the unity of all men in Christ. We Christians, who have often denied this unity, observe how through science and technology the world is being tied together in interdependence. The nations are thereby both threatened and made dependent on one another. This calls us to action oriented to the brotherhood of all men.[28]

It is in the light of this correspondence between the Word of God and the world or between the church and mankind that we should read the remarks that follow concerning war and peace, the protection of individuals and groups in the political world, economic justice and world order, and international structures. It is the aim of the Word of God or of Christ to guide all humanity towards a life in which the great problems and conflicts besetting it will find their solution. The church could and ought to set an example to the whole human community by its approach to the solution of its own corporate problems; but at the moment the reverse seems rather to be the case. In their own relations to one another Christians and their church should demonstrate what is really meant by respect for human dignity, for equality, and for the free expression of opinion in both speech and writing. The same could be said regarding racial discrimination, to the abolition of which on a world-wide scale the church can contribute with little credibility until it has abolished it entirely within its own community. Or to take yet another example; the pressing need today for all nations to come together in a wider world community must be paralleled by the regional co-operation of the churches, since such co-operation should be the demonstration of their own intrinsic unity. Only then will the church be able to exert a really effective influence on international relations.

It is through this correlation between the church and mankind that worship acquires its real meaning for, as we have already suggested, worship is really nothing more nor less than the concentrated fulfilment of the life of the Christian community in the world, whatever the special conditions may be. In worship God's people, whoever they may happen to be, appear before him as parts for the whole or, to put it another way, this often small and unassuming section of mankind, of God's people, gathered together to offer themselves up and to receive, is really a concentration of the universal, of all mankind. Therefore that event which lies at the very heart of worship must be seen from the start in conjunction with all that is taking place in the world. The Eucharist in its role as the focus of the community can therefore only be participated in provided there is no trace of racial or class discrimination not only in the religious service itself but in men's lives outside the church too. As we gather together to partake of that food which in the Eucharist is Christ himself 'Our communion with Christ must show that we share our bread with his hungry brothers in the world.'[29]

We have been attempting to extract basic ideas for an ecumenical dialogue from what was said at the Geneva Conference and the Assembly at Uppsala, with some reference too to earlier pronouncements. Inevitably this contribution has laid particular emphasis *vis-à-vis* themes which have already been treated elsewhere and which belong in this general context. I have referred to the pronouncements of official conferences; but of course this does not imply that one can simply assume the existence of an ecumenical consensus of opinion. In the first place the reports drawn up at the big official conferences are normally just handed on to member churches 'for further study and comment'; it is entirely their responsibility whether such reports are accepted as binding or not. Nevertheless the churches which are members of the World Council of Churches are a 'communion of churches', and, if we bear in mind the biblical concept of *koinonia*, communion does in fact mean 'participation' – participation in Jesus Christ and the reconciliation brought about by him, and consequently the participation of all those willing to let themselves be affected by it. This fact must on no account be overlooked when reading and assessing the conclusions reached at these conferences; though one may be well aware that they are often of fortuitous origin, it is impossible to deny them a certain solemn character. Nor should one forget the very careful preparation that preceded them and which is recorded in detail in special volumes, for example the four preparatory volumes for the Geneva Conference 1966.

V

Taking what has hitherto been said here as an attempt to outline a communal social and ethical outlook, it remains for us to see what traces it contains of the thinking characteristic of the various main Christian traditions. After all the attempt to establish an ecumenical consensus does not imply the careless abandonment of our various traditions, but rather that we should submit them to critical examination and be prepared to revise them as we embark on a dialogue leading to new and mutually-shared standpoints. Perhaps we may venture a few suggestions in this context, even though other contributors to this volume have approached the question from different angles.

It is easy to detect the imprint of Orthodox thinking in those passages from the Uppsala Report we alluded to last concerning the importance of worship in the life of a church conscious of its responsibilities towards mankind. Without in any way suggesting that any one person is qualified to speak on behalf of Orthodoxy as a whole, we would like at this point to refer to the views of an experienced member of the Ecumenical Centre in Geneva who is a member of the Syrian Orthodox Church and at present the Director of one of its theological seminaries. Paul Verghese has expressed the opinion 'that both the basis and the direction for a truly Christian social thought can come only from a eucharistic theology'.[30] In his eyes this apparently means that each time the Eucharist is celebrated, those of the world repeatedly allowed to gather in worship become the Body of Christ which is at the same time being offered up to God in the act of worship as a sacrifice of the part for the whole – the whole here being all mankind – as a result of which the whole world is sanctified. In the light of this, three points can be made concerning the place of the church in society: 'The Church serves the society in which it is placed in a threefold sense: first, as the temple of God in the midst of time-space existence.' This means that the church exists inside secular society as something which cannot be equated with it. Secondly, it must serve 'as the royal priesthood within that temple'. This means that the Christian community too is part of the royal priesthood; just as Christ as priest is eternally sacrificing himself to God for all creation, it too is carrying out the continuous service of self-sacrifice and mediation, so that the worship and prayer of the church in the midst of the secular community preserves, transforms and sanctifies it, often without the community realizing this, and sometimes even against its will. And lastly, the church serves 'as a model and pattern for the human commonwealth'. It exerts its influence in the world not so as to dominate it but so as to be able to identify itself with it as its mediator and advocate, and not be relegated to the passive role of a listener giving nothing but merely accepting. And this is achieved by the three principles of love (inseparable from justice), liberty and wisdom, whose source is truth. Thus in the midst of the 'pluralistic human community' the church can find its due place if it is open to God and to the world.[31] We may therefore say that here the inmost core of what constitutes the church, namely the sacrament of the Eucharist, affects the whole of divine creation in such a way that in its personal and social structures it can fulfil the mission set it by God which is prefigured in the church.

It is impossible to define the Catholic point of view in a short paragraph. But some points can be made with reference to the Second Vatican Council and especially the 'Pastoral Constitution on the Church in the Modern World'. Throughout what is said there, the church is conceived as a structure of a unique kind which is none the less aware of its links with all mankind and its history, not in the role of ruler but in the role of servant. It was the Council's view that 'the world of man, the whole human family', is connected with 'the sum of those realities in the midst of which that family exists'.[32] However one should perhaps observe that Roman Catholic social and ethical thinking is still largely conditioned by the idea of a synthesis between 'eternal values' and the *new*, which results from a dynamic order of things and emphasizes their evolution. This does not signify conformity, but it does suggest a perhaps insufficiently radical critical approach, and it appears that ideas associated with natural law will continue to play a large part in Catholic thinking, even though this is at present a matter of lively debate within Catholic theology itself.

For Lutherans, if not for Calvinists, a danger can still result from the distinction they make between law and gospel, however justifiable such a distinction may often be. They are tempted to see the world in terms of an order which is accountable to an absolute law divorced from the gospel itself, while the latter, confined to the sphere of private and personal salvation, is not seen in the context of the universal rule of Jesus Christ throughout the course of history. The same is to a certain extent true of the Free Churches which represent the fourth major group in the diversity of ecclesiastical traditions.[33] In their case introverted and strictly personal piety tends to be an obstacle in the way of their commitment to the world, though here too one should be careful not to impute attitudes to them which they are in the process of overcoming. But they all have voices in the ecumenical dialogue, and they will all have to bear responsibility for the views which we have been outlining here and which, in so far as they imply criticism of traditional standpoints may, let us hope, lead to new and mutually-shared positions.

NOTES

1. In connection with the following, cf. the Geneva Report, pp. 200 ff.
2. Report of Section VI, par. 4, *Uppsala Speaks*, p, 88.
3. *Ibid.*, par. 17, p. 92.
4. Report of Section III, par. 15.
5. Geneva Report, p. 116, par. 85.
6. *Gaudium et Spes*, par. 74.

7. Cf. J. Bopp, *Populorum Progressio – Aufbruch der Kirche?*, Kohlhammer, Stuttgart, 1968, pp. 72 ff.

8. Geneva Report, p. 201, par. 21.

9. E. Castro, 'Conversion and Social Transformation', in *Christian Social Ethics in a Changing World*, ed. J. C. Bennett, Association Press and SCM Press, 1966, pp. 348 ff.

10. Geneva Report, p. 201, par. 23.

11. *The Churches Survey their Task*, ed. J. H. Oldham, the Report of the Oxford Conference on Church, Community and State, Allen and Unwin, 1937, p. 236.

12. *Ibid.*, p. 94.

13. 'World Conference on Church and Society', *The Ecumenical Review*, vol. XVIII, no. 4, 1966, pp. 421 ff.

14. *Ibid.*, p. 423.

15. Cf. E. Käsemann's article, 'Worship and Everyday Life', in his *New Testament Questions of Today*, SCM Press, 1969, pp. 188 ff.

16. For all these quotations see Käsemann, *op. cit.*, p. 191.

17. Report of Section VI, par. 27, *Uppsala Speaks*, p. 94.

18. Geneva Report, p. 202, par. 26.

19. *The Churches Survey their Task*, p. 57.

20. *Ibid.*, p. 60.

21. *Ibid.*, p. 196.

22. *The Evanston Report*, ed. W. A. Visser 't Hooft, SCM Press, 1955, p. 114.

23. *Ibid.*, pp. 142 ff.

24. Report of Section I, par. 20, *Uppsala Speaks*, p. 17.

25. *Ibid.*, par. 21, p. 18.

26. Cf. *ibid.*, par. 23, p. 18.

27. *Loc. cit.*

28. Report of Section IV, pars, 4–10, *Uppsala Speaks*, pp. 61 f.

29. Report of Section V, par. 38, *Uppsala Speaks*, p. 83.

30. 'Two Theological Issues for Church and Society Reflections', *Bulletin*, Division of Studies, World Council of Churches, vol. 10, no. 1, 1964, p. 14.

31. P. Verghese, 'Secular Society or Pluralistic Community?', in *Man in Community*, ed. E. de Vries, Association Press and SCM Press, 1966, p. 359.

32. *Gaudium et Spes*, par. 2.

33. Professor Wolf writes here against a German background (Editor).

21

An Orthodox View

GEORGES KHODRE

The divided world today seeks justice in the setting of a society which either is, or is becoming, technologically developed. How are the demands of justice to be interpreted at the level either of the national community or of humanity as a whole, if it is true that technology is the necessary means, or at all events a necessary evil, for our development? Confronted with this problem, Christians who have been drawn into this common human quest start from the action in which men are engaged and seek the truth of God which must illuminate this common action and give it validity and direction. The permanent Christian vocation to holiness will then really take on the cosmic dimensions which are assigned to it in God's plan.

We are living out the universality of this task in what has been called a 'responsible' society. Responsibility is an ethical attitude which is a translation of the theological truth of the solidarity of man. For the principle of solidarity is already inscribed in the order of creation. Holy scripture affirms this unity of the human species (Acts 17.20 and 27), an order of things (the times assigned to the nations, the boundaries of their habitations) designed to lead on to the knowledge of God. This unity reflects the divine unity, for as Saint Gregory of Nyssa says, the image of God in man is inscribed in the totality of the whole of humanity. 'God created man in his own image, in the image of God he created him, male and female he created them' (Gen, 1.27)

Man here means man and woman together in their final communion. It is the whole of humanity that is assumed eschatologically by Christ. It is the Christ-humanity which is in the image of God. Now the Saviour has made this image operative in the gift of himself to the church (Eph. 5.25). And man regains this lost resemblance to God when, after Christ's example, he follows the way of love. The unity of the human species is given dynamic power by Jesus' sacrifice and by his victory over death. The church is the present sign of this unity. It is torn apart by sin, by Promethean pride, as is the unity of the church. But the disease of our nature and all the temptations to which we are prone take nothing away from the reality of this affirmation of faith that human nature is ontologically one.

This unity is inaugurated on the soteriological plane by the vision of the mystical Body. A tradition which the church has not rejected and which is represented by Fathers as eminent as Gregory of Nyssa, Isaac the Syrian and Maximus the Confessor, allows belief in universal salvation. This doctrine of apocatastasis has not been revealed biblically lest man should abuse God's mercy. But if, as Leo Zander loved to emphasize, this teaching is not an article of faith, it remains an article of hope. Whatever the number of the elect may be, however, it remains true that the mystical Body of the Lord is much vaster than the body of the baptized and that Christian eschatology brings us the final vision of the unity of the human race.

This unity is universally affirmed as being founded upon 'natural law engraved on our hearts'. We are not here concerned with a nature as opposed to supernature, a nature which does not know grace. The East knows nothing of this dichotomy. But we are well and truly concerned with this divine *kenosis* (self-emptying) which from the beginning of creation made us participants in the divine energies. This common origin and destiny, the fact that we are all objects of the same divine solicitude, this sharing in the nature of God, this historical and meta-historical companionship, constitute the theological foundation of an ethic of participation and service in a society which is mutually responsible on a world scale.

It goes without saying that the unity of men, on the level of God's natural gifts, is not an abstract idea. We live our lives concretely in a unity with one and all which makes us spontaneously discover a brother of the same human race in every man. Our total communion is expressed in living with the man thrown down upon all the highways of the world and wounded by every act of brigandage in history, in the unique outpouring of the blood of the Poor One. And in this there is not only the vision of a fundamental dignity inscribed in the nature of every man, and not only the recognition of liberty, of immortality, of justice, of an exact resemblance to the beauty of the divine archetype, as Gregory of Nyssa puts it, but in Origen as in Maximus there is also the affirmation of the holiness of men who 'could practise all the virtues even if they had not a perfect understanding of the mystery of redemption'.[1]

This line of thought continues into the fourteenth century with Gregory Palamas for whom the whole race of mankind attains, through knowledge of created things, to the knowledge of the Creator. This great teacher of the East teaches that 'almost the whole of the inhabited world, all those parts which do not obey the mandates of the Gospels [here he is chiefly thinking of Muslims], now possess, by that means alone, a God who is none other than the Creator of this universe'.[2]

Now, for anyone who is familiar with the profoundly experimental conception of Eastern theology, it is not a question here of non-Christians having knowledge about God but of sharing in the very life of God.

This vision of the unity of the world is salutary as a revelation to us of the real nature of the unity of the church. This is no longer mono-lithic, closed. The church is not defined in ontological opposition to the world, or to history, but dynamically in dialogue with a world which is remaking and constructing itself. The church is becoming a minority in the sense that in a more and more secularized society she is not necessarily seen as the most important value. She is but rarely a decisive reality in the tale of historic events. And she is becoming increasingly conscious of a certain vulnerability which drives her to revise her institutions, to have doubts about the prestige of her past, to reflect that often she must make a new start on the basis of new presuppositions, in a vessel which derives its only claim to seaworthiness from its Lord. That is why history drives her to a search for the unity which can only be constructed by the simultaneous pursuit of the unity of the world in the humility of dialogue and the charisma of a completely renewed service.

The unity of the church is not set over against the unity of the world because the church is not in a relationship of opposition to the created world. She is the ikon of what humanity will become. The church is in this respect the meaning of the world, its intelligibility, or in the very significant expression of Origen, the 'cosmos of the cosmos'. The church is still the heart of the world even if the world ignores its heart. For this reason her life is symbolic in the strongest sense of the term. She recognizes the unity of the world by her own unity revealed through the Spirit until the parousia, when the world and the church will be the one spouse of the Lord of glory.

Certainly the world and the church can best be seen in an identical destiny of involvement, in a historic will to build up the earth. But the church through the mysterious bond which ties her to Christ, through the Spirit who reveals his plans to her and who judges history, lives in a permanent tension with the world. She herself is the tension of the world. For this reason, she is always a thorn in the flesh of history.

She proclaims a light which is to come, a kingdom which is not of this world. She proclaims the hope of a salvation which is given to her, which she awaits in prayer, which she tastes in the sacrament, and which is not purely and simply identified with the energy of men building their own city. The church is plunged in a bath of eternity which no common work of humanity could fully manifest. Her relation with the end is not a simple, ascending linear history. There is in her a catastrophic dimension, for in the world of nature a split has appeared which only the peace of the kingdom will heal.

Hence the quest of the Christian is not ultimately identifiable with any other quest. The Christian is a disturbing element who questions every settled order, who is more at home in the movement than in the 'establishment'. He demands a constant acceleration of achievement and is for this reason regarded as a corrosive element. That is why he is never accepted by his own people, by those who have transformed struggle into a left-wing or right-wing legalistic system. At the very heart of this theology of communion between the church and the world there exists an ethic of rupture or at least an ethic of distance. The Christian has done well to leave the temple to live out the mediation of Christ in work, art, and politics. To him a presence of Christ is revealed in the world of men, and it is through this cosmic priesthood with which the Christian is endued that all human aspirations to justice and beauty ascend towards the heavenly temple. He knows that by taking the body of the Lord he bears within himself the whole body of humanity. He pledges an infinite compassion to this humanity. And he is ready to lose his soul so that this humanity may recover its freedom. In this gesture he shakes off from the body of the church the dust of the synagogue, its ritualistic lethargy, but he is simultaneously crucified by the companions of his earthly loyalty on the cross of an irremediable solitude.

In a dialectic of communion and rupture the Christian is present wherever man seeks to attain to a complete humanization. In spite of the ambiguity of what is given in creation and what is developed by man, the attitude of the believer remains positive and vigilant. Olivier Clément has written:

Our Christian life should be open to all the research, all the joy of inventing and discovering, all the effort of creation and of beauty in human culture. All reality, from the atom to the nebulae, all beauty, from the prehistoric caves to the anguished strivings of abstract art, every struggle for justice and liberty, every new way of possessing the earth . . . we must pass it all through the screen of our love, and whatever love allows us to experience to adopt and garner in the ark of the Church which alone can pass through the final catastrophe. . . . There are no infallible methods of acting in Christian politics, in Christian economics, in Christian art, but there may, there must, be a personal presence of Christians in politics, in economics, in art . . . an open, transfiguring presence.[3]

From the standpoint which we have adopted we can affirm first that the whole human race is the bearer and instigator of its own development. If 'man is unique in all men', as Gregory of Nyssa said, it is the whole of humanity that constitutes this responsible society. The church as the Christian people cannot substitute herself for humanity. She cannot think for humanity. That would be equivalent to declaring that humanity is 'not of age'. She tended to take only too much advantage of the superiority of 'Christian civilization'. In the historical perspective which awaits us, the church will in fact be the little flock because of the greater demographic progress of non-Christian nations. Literally lost in a human mass, called to become aware of the solidarity of the nations, the little flock will fear nothing if, in its sacrificial vocation, it can become the world's living conscience. In so far as the church passes through the fire of the Spirit men will discover in her that God's Christ is the inspiration of the world in its advance towards justice.

Through the voices of the prophets and the fathers of the fourth and fifth centuries on the subject of justice, Christianity finds not only a messianic accent that is extraordinarily fruitful, but also a doctrine of property which a world society can make the very foundation of its responsibility. Biblical revelation from Amos to James is of sufficient eloquence to suggest a universally valid attitude in face of the misery of the world. It is enough here to quote as an example these words of Job's on the subject of the indigent:

> They go about naked, without clothing;
>   hungry, while they carry the sheaves.
> They lie all night naked, without clothing,
>   and have no covering against the cold.
> They . . . cling to the rock for want of shelter.
>
>   (Job 24.10, 7 f.)

This is just the accent for which the world is waiting. Modern man is sensitive to the face of the Christ who lived among us eating and drinking but who was 'Holy, holy to God' without untruthfulness, without any compromising relationships, humble and gentle towards sinners, violent towards the powerful. But there are Christian 'magnates', notorious exploiters, who are members of our assemblies. The eucharistic community which tolerates them lives in untruthfulness, in a kind of religious verbalism which is a scandal to the whole of humanity. And we can talk for ever about the 'prophetic role' of the churches[4] and 'the constant evaluation of structures' while tolerating in our membership those whose 'crimes are many and their sins enormous' (Amos 5.12). Our witness on behalf of the establishment of a responsible society throughout the world will consist first in reasserting the virulence of the prophetic teaching against the oppressors who dominate a country or a continent. These could easily tolerate a general lecture on social justice as long as the sermon does not convict them and as long as they continue to take part in the Eucharist. The ancient church excommunicated for lesser faults than this.

Prophesying which is to be practised effectively in the local church must be undergirded by a theology of earthly possessions which is a true expression of eucharistic theology. St John Chrysostom had this extension of the eucharistic act outside the sanctuary in mind when he spoke of the poor man as a bigger temple than the other. 'This altar [the poor man] you can see elevated everywhere in the streets, and you can sacrifice upon it at all times.'[5]

There is no need here to enlarge upon the social thought of the fathers, the most eminent of whom in this field, Basil of Caesarea, created a social constitution which was regarded as a 'new city'. The doctrine of the ancient church in the East, as in the West, maintains that 'the rich withhold the wealth of the poor, even if this wealth is honestly acquired or legally inherited' (Chrysostom). Clearly the fathers think that nothing short of a new order will do, wherein property is declared to be the common possession of all men. St John Chrysostom envisaged for Antioch an equitable sharing of goods and the elimination of poverty. When St Augustine said 'You give bread to whoever is hungry; but it would be better if nobody was hungry and you gave to nobody' he was thinking of the possible end of the régime of charity in the church.

This aspiration would imply, at the present time, a change of structure in society. None could remain indifferent to a change of structure which would at least tend to remove poverty as the first stage of a development which aims at being global and human.

Is this to say that the churches should themselves propose new structures? 'The churches', says the Report of Section III (par. 31), 'have the task of teaching people how to be politically effective.' It assigns a political task to the churches. The churches should 'help to ensure that all political parties make development a priority in their programmes' (par. 38.1), and should openly take part in movements for 'revolutionary change' (par. 39.3).

We could justifiably ask whether the whole conception underlying this common undertaking of political responsibility by the church does not contradict the notion of a politically responsible society. If the

subject of political action is society, the church as such has no autonomous political role. The political action of its members is deployed
within the national or international community in concert with the
other citizens. The Roumanian theologian T. Popescu was right when
he said:

The Church does not need to create another science, another art, another
technology, nor other political, social or even economic structures. She cannot
annihilate what exists nor does she claim to create out of nothing a new and
ideal world, her own world which has no connection with the existing
world.[6]

*The word 'churches', however, as used in the Report of Section III can
only mean historic Christendom.* That implies a definition of the church
as a society sufficient unto itself, a perfect society 'exerting influence'
(par. 38.2) and accordingly no stranger to political power.

This conception, moreover, reflects the position of countries where
the church is dominant, where she knows herself to be sufficiently
powerful to influence the course of events. It is not sociologically true
in countries where the church is in the minority nor in those where
she has been forced back into silence. The political task of the churches
is only possible in the northern hemisphere. For the Eastern churches
which either belong to the communistic bloc or to the increasingly
socialistic Middle East, the churches are not co-extensive with society.
They could not even if they wished undertake so powerful an ecclesial
praxis. The historical weakness of some of them, the fact that they
share the national destiny and identify themselves with the aspirations
of their people, make them more sensitive to the reality of the national
community which would as a whole be the instrument of social action
and the promoter of technological progress. The church remains for
the Eastern Christian the transfiguring presence of the Eucharist,
the organism which grows and acts through love. The church knows
nothing of economic and social sciences. Even if she had research
centres or institutes of technology she would not, as a church, be
competent to judge of things which by their very nature belong to the
field of independent knowledge. The church undertakes theological
and moral reflection on the data of the human condition, on the structures which are laid before her in the world of production or of labour.
And when she ventures into what is properly the field of scientific
data, she produces results which have the character of false wisdom or
'gnosis' in trying to imitate timidly and tardily organizations which are
really qualified in the field. The latter, while remaining aware of their
own technical capabilities, may listen for a spiritually inspired voice
pointing out a vocation and an objective to humanity.

'Let the church be the church.' Guided by the Spirit, she will be able to say whether all this development is a scandal[7] or whether within the limits of our earthly vision there is some 'omega point' at which it must aim. It is above all important for her not to elaborate a theology which simply sanctifies the economic philosophy of developed countries. The temptation of Christians in the West is the sacralization of the world, the dream of a Christian empire even in a secularized form (scratch a Westerner and you will find a crusader). The ideal of the traditionalist Christian in the East, on the other hand, is a liturgical 'self-complacency', where the world is simply seen in its eschatological significance, where a wasting away of the intellect goes hand in hand with a deceptive apocalyptic catastrophism. A certain monastic detachment often hides a real indifference to the destiny of the world. On the other hand the Western Christian may come to believe in his own effectiveness because he translates the Christian life into a so-called Christian culture of humanism. Certainly 'culture is the path to virtue',[8] but it is only one of the paths. In the general advance of humanity it is a necessary path. That is why, in face of the temptation to escape from the world, Orthodox thought has tried to set culture on a religious foundation. At the present time that means a spiritual attitude which adopts the technology and the socio-political structures which are inescapably interwoven with it. It is within these forms that Christians will try to inspire more humane relationships, to give a meaning to leisure in consumer societies, and to keep hope and the will to fight alive in developing countries. It is a matter of getting involved in technology and not of sacralizing it, of fighting against a scientist morality and a technicist mystique in a necessarily pluralistic society. Theoretically it is not impossible that humanity, seized with panic at the sight of its handiwork, should adopt another orientation than that of prosperity and cultivate the inner life, but that does not seem possible until the benefits of technology are shared by the whole of humanity in dignity, before the bread is broken on the universal table of a just distribution. The man trained in the most modern technological disciplines seems still to be eternally sensitive to the mystical poetry, to the grandiose and 'other-worldly' character of a spritually rich liturgy, to the evangelical simplicity of a loving face.

The essential task of the church in a society whose rapid change is disturbing the whole world consists first of all in knowing the direction of our evolution. In a report submitted to the French government entitled 'Reflections for 1985', one of the concerns of the group to whom this task was assigned was 'Values for the man of 1985'. The values noted were the uniqueness of man, respect for life, quality (quality of silence, quality of rhythm of life, for example), the dignity of man and woman, solidarity amongst individuals and solidarity in relation to the next generation. This group was aware that 'the values of our society may be freely chosen, on condition that we are vigilant and that we do not let our civilization be invaded by parasitic developments which one day we might be unable to control' (p. 11).

Thus 'development becomes essentially a problem of civilization . . . a problem of recognizing the value of man in a generalized régime of humane economy and of harmonized integral development'.[9] That is not at all possible without a final aim which is defined as being 'not only the human betterment of all social strata, but the greatest good, the plus-value, the utmost good'.[10]

If the church recapitulates all that is human, then her role comes into play at the moment of the realization of this aim. The illumination of the Word and the outpouring of the Spirit then bring to fulfilment an anthropological process on a community scale. The church will continue to present to humanity the supreme value of universal communion. What, indeed, is an integral development which does not issue in love? That will mean, on a concrete plane, that the church will direct her efforts towards establishing some coherence between men for the benefit of the poor. The project which awaits us will be that of rethinking economics so that it reflects co-operation between men. An individualistic or collectivist philosophy, a materialistic philosophy in short, underlays economic science. Nevertheless, man needs an economy that does not alienate him from his spiritual vocation. In contact with spiritual men the sights of the economists will necessarily be adjusted: they will not concentrate solely upon the possibilities of production. Another point of view is that of the needs to be met. The range of these needs must include the spiritual. Humanity will have to seek out forgotten values for itself. It can no longer neglect the quality of human relationships nor continue to build structures wherein bureaucracy, speed, anonymity and legalism leave man no possibility of showing himself as a unique and indomitable being. It is impossible that the imagination of men tortured by the reign of the impersonal should be unable to find more adaptable structures, more open to the manifestation of the person.

The church's role will be, on the community level, to be sensitive to man's anxieties and to inspire a common search in the service of man. We shall thus avoid two errors; activism at the top by the church leaders, and activism at the bottom, that is, purely individual action.

Activism at the top is apt to produce official pronouncements which are marred by a certain dogmatism and congeal thought, if only for a time, in a matter as fluid as human development. The sacred nature of the church tends to canonize the texts which it produces. These are generally the fruit of 'consultations' between scholars and theologians and are endorsed by the established authority. This is simply a consecration of the work of more or less extensive Commissions. Things did not happen thus with the proclamation of a dogma. Dogma was lived in martyrdom, in the experience of the saints, and was the true expression of the most profound consciousness of the church.

Moreover it is not seemly that the apostles 'should give up preaching the word of God to serve tables' (Acts 6.2). That is why Eastern Canon Law forbids the clergy to engage in active politics.

Activism at the bottom is equally inadequate. The Christian is already so much driven into the desert of the modern world that to abandon him to his own quest would be to increase his disarray and the sense of his inadequacy. There must be a certain coherence between Christians, a common witness which is all the more necessary when we are talking about community development. A group of Christians of all professions talking about a joint activity may present the real face of the church. In our day men need to know that even the individual witness of a Christian is shared by some of his brothers, that the individual witness reflects in some sense the suffering of the community. The church is truly present in groups which work in co-ordination and freedom, which do not necessarily reach the same conclusions, and which show real men bearing in their flesh the care of the world.

It still remains true that this Christian effort may at the present time take on a certain institutional form where the churches continue to concern themselves with cultural establishments and social services. The reality of justice must be manifested above all in pluralist societies. Preparation of man for the technological era is a fundamental aspect of our *diakonia*. A Christian university or a university where Christians can be influential must orientate its programmes towards research related to the development of its own country, or concern itself with the problems of another country in process of development. Christians who are working in the same institution or complex of institutions must study together ways of transforming them. This is a social reformism which some would conscientiously adopt. But in very highly developed countries a much more radical attitude might be adopted. The important thing is to be guided by the Spirit and to accept each other in 'the unity of the Spirit and the bond of peace' (Eph. 4.3).

Tension between those who support social reform and those who support 'revolutionary change' can become very serious. Here the task of the minister of the gospel is to hold this tension within the eucharistic community.

But whatever political position the various groups of Christians adopt, the church must 'make the cause of the disinherited their own' everywhere (and not only in developing countries, as the Report says in par. 39.2). It is an absolutely prophetic requirement that the whole church should identify herself with the Poor Man, that she should be his interpreter. The church entirely transcends every political situation in espousing the cause of those whom any establishment, whether bourgeois or revolutionary, humiliates. The church often lives in a revolutionary situation. Orthodox priests two centuries ago led a peasant revolution in Roumania. They supported Greek patriots in their war of liberation against the Turks in the last century, and the struggles in Cyprus and Palestine, because they were on the side of men's suffering. There was no question for them of establishing a theology of a just war or a theology of revolution. The Orthodox spiritual tradition is so far removed from the consecration of violence that it does not even admit legitimate self-defence. But the church should never permit one to cry peace, peace, when there is no peace. When the blood of the Poor Man cries out for vengeance, and when the scandal of a monstrous hypocrisy breaks out in a disintegrating world, it may be that the Lord looks on revolution as his servant. The church will then be with the justice and against the injustice of revolution, for the sake of the development which it will in fact bring to those whom it persecutes. She will unmask the pseudo-religious, 'pseudo-ecumenical' character of the revolution, to use Berdyaev's expression. But 'she will minister to a revolutionary people' seduced by revolutionary messianism as she 'ministered' to the Christians who were foolishly seduced by bourgeois civilization. In a rich country one may expand at great length on the dangers of revolution. One may discourse at length on its atheism, on the fact that it consumes itself and always ends by becoming abject. People who eat their fill will not miss the fine points of the analysis. It still remains that man does not always choose a revolutionary situation, and that, on the assumption that man has some freedom of choice according to conscience, there is at least as great a spiritual risk in the preservation of the established order as in the total upheaval of a historic order. The essential is that the church should remain watchful that the beauty of the kingdom is seen through the adversities from which men suffer.

In this great struggle for a more humane world it is of the highest importance on the ecumenical plane that we return to the sources of Christian anthropology (the Report, par. 48). Different churches understand differently the articulation of the human and the divine in the nature of man. The relation between nature and grace and the deification of the Christian are themes closely related to this anthropological problem. But to speak of anthropology is to speak also of cosmology and of ecclesiology. The theological imperative (pars. 44–48) is there in the undivided church. Unity of spiritual experience is expressed in the God-man synthesis on the lines of a theology which is liberating, concrete and more contemporary than ever in confrontation with the present evolution of the world. The Western Christian should help the Eastern Church to find a language to describe the patristic anthropology on which orthodoxy lives in its spiritual tradition. The Christian life as it is defined in par. 43 will bring Christians together in a common witness. And it is in action, as the Byzantine hymn says, that they can set foot upon the ladder of contemplation. There is, in the definition of this individual task understood in the 'group' perspective which we have outlined in this study, a sensitization to the universal such that the Christian who commits himself in this way to human development may attain to the truth of God about man.

Naturally, it would be ideal to be able to include all men in a common effort towards development, and one is guided here by various economic and philosophical concepts. Values are not the same for Marxists and non-Marxists. Neither are they the same in the northern hemisphere as in the 'third world'. The Christian in a developing country has not the same analysis of realities as a Christian in a developed country. It is not within the scope of this study to insist further upon this point, but the reality is so cruel and provocative that many men, whatever their religious convictions, are first induced to meet on this terrain. We feel increasingly that our destiny is common to us all. And the man who rejects the oppression of technology shows through the very eccentricities in which he expresses this rejection of contemporary society that he is not seeking only earthly happiness. Amongst young people today there is a yearning for a less stifling world, against which free love is a protest. But that is a sign that what really matters is the encounter with the other in authenticity. Here, I think, we have a phenomenon of immediacy which is perhaps a reaction against exaggerated intellectualism void of all human content. At the present time simple encounter between men is more important than ideas. It is man in his simplicity and not the idea which draws the world. It is encounter and not dialogue which is decisive. For this reason atheists and believers, if the atheism is not militant and if the believer can see the divine in the unbeliever, could live out the human adventure together. Man is always more profound than his thought. What happens to us in practice is that we know God without naming him.

Those who name him, especially those who belong to the same Abrahamic family, are called ideally not only to the existential encounter but also to share certain elements of faith in the One and Only which would enable them to find a way more or less in common. One thinks immediately of the Jews whose prophets were unsurpassed witnesses to righteousness. Furthermore, Judaism agrees that a universal law, the law of Noah, applies to all men inasmuch as it is rational law, corresponding more obviously than Mosaic law to the intelligible aspect of things. It is not for us here to go into the complex problem of the universal or the particular in the religion of Israel. Hebraic thought, represented by various religious thinkers, does not ignore natural, rational religion.

It is of man in general that scripture speaks to us every time that it is concerned with conduct, and that not only in the prophetic books or the hagiographers such as the author of Proverbs, but even in the Pentateuch. There too we see that moral life is declared to be indispensable to the dignity of all men without distinction.[11]

There is also a moral law which governs all humanity, 'general truths, seeds of future progress, essential rules of public law'.[12] Should we see in this law of Noah elements of religious belief which enable us to start a dialogue with the Jews on national development?

The issue, of course, is no longer a live one at the present time since the Jewish community, apart from a few heroic witnesses, put an end to the Jewish-Christian dialogue by linking it after 5 June 1967 with quite unconditional support for the State of Israel. This state was conceived in iniquity and is perpetuated in injustice. Not only does all that remains of the Palestinian race in the Holy Land suffer from systematic panic, from unwilling exile and from cultural strangulation, but the fact that the immense majority of this people was driven into the desert to live in tents, is aimed at stripping them of their identity. The slow suppression of a people is also a form of genocide. The only difference is the rhythm of destruction.

Zionism, a colonial enterprise if ever there was one,[13] is maintained against the interests of Middle East development, which rejects it because it sees in it an obstacle to its own progress in freedom and self-identity. The Middle East has found here and there a pluralist form of society and aspires towards secular structures. The Palestinian revolution has declared its secular aims in favour of a multi-religious Palestinian state. Whereas the Arabs tend towards the universal in their social quest, Israel is reserved for a single race, a single religion, and Christians are offered a Zionist reading of the word of God. Contrary to the elementary rules of Christian exegesis it makes the Bible say that God is the founder of its state. Scripture is made to serve a national exclusiveness. There is a regrettable confusion not only between the Israel of the flesh and the Israel of God, but a theological search for a foundation for the Hebrew state, a sacralization which is denied incidentally to any other state.

It is not the standpoint of this study to deny any legitimacy to this state on the simple basis of rabbinic theology, although certain Jewish thinkers have already done this.[14] It is with those who believe in the sovereignty of God alone over the Jewish people that a dialogue is possible, with those whose lives express an ethic of the poor. Jews, Christians and Muslims who reject colonial domination and expansion can work together in a religious dialogue which can finalize a development scheme and define its content. Then the Abrahamic relationship will have some meaning. The sharing of the same bread of the Bible only has meaning if the monotheistic peoples look towards God together in justice and peace and if, refusing to harness God to their service, they give themselves to his, and so prepare to become a messianic people together.

The Abrahamic family has been dislocated by Zionism and will only be restored if Jerusalem, the city of Jews and Gentiles according to the best rabbinic tradition, again becomes the meeting-place of all the monotheistic faiths. It is unfortunate that a policy of Judaization and Israelization should be systematically practised in the Holy Land and that the city of peace should have become the very symbol of division. The day when the other sons of Abraham, Christians and Palestinian Muslims, rise out of the ethnical and cultural extinction to which they have been subjected, the dialogue for the restoration of a united humanity will begin again on this privileged scene of the revelation of the unique One.

What concept could undergird co-operation between Muslims and Christians on the plane of development? There is a similar reaction to technology on both sides in the desire to save the spiritual man. The Muslim world is also going through the crisis of modernity. In a sense this crisis is more acute because the Muslim is governed socially and politically by a divine law. The structure of society is, in large measure, defined by the Koranic revelation and its canonical development. Islam presents itself to us as a religion which embraces the whole reality of heaven and earth. And because this quantitatively embracing vision shocks modern man and might limit his social evolution, certain modernists have tried to liberate the things of this world from the empire of divine law. Yet one of the most enlightened Muslim thinkers, Seyyed Hossein Nasr, writes:

All of these activities emanate from a particular attitude of spiritual weakness vis-à-vis the world and a surrender to the world. Those who are conquered by such a mentality want to make the Shari'ah conform to 'the times' which means to the whims and fancies of men and the ever-changing human nature which has made 'the times'. They don't realize that it is the Shari'ah according to which society should be modelled and not vice versa.[15]

Theoretically the difficulty inherent in co-operation between Muslims and Christians is due to the absence of the notion of a secular city in Islam, to the fact that Muslim society has received an ideal form and ready-made structures from the Koranic Canon. Development is not open to the infinite.

But the society where Islam is in the majority or even totally dominant knows many compromises and enters into the rhythm of the modern world to the point of trying to espouse totally the technological civilization of the West. This adaptability is part of its genius, and there is a certain kinship with the materialism of the world so that it is not greatly embarrassed by the adoption of foreign cultures. That was part of its most glorious past. Islam is also becoming aware that it is also part of the present in which it is called to live.

If Islam offers its own line of development it is no less true that it possesses an anthropology which can enrich its progress. The Musulman is naturally attracted to learning and research. The Koran insists much upon reason. It is true that what is meant here is a primary nature (*fitrah*) disposed towards the knowledge of God. But the Koran insists so strongly on the 'signs' of God (*ayat*) in the created world that the mind is also orientated towards the knowledge of human nature and the cosmos.

Ultimate knowledge is in the heart. Islam is a civilization of wisdom and of piety, and unless it becomes, in its modern societies, totally exteriorized and secular, it can by returning to its sources again contribute to the creation of a more humane social life.

Historic Islam has always meditated most systematically on the condition of man in the various periods of its intellectual history. At the dawn of the modern era when Islam made its great contribution with Ibn Khaldoun, the originality of medieval thought in Islamic lands was that it made valuable contributions even in the actual matter of development.

Al-Ghazali, a philosopher and mystic of the eleventh and twelfth centuries, in a work of a dozen pages entitled 'The reality of the World (Dunya) and the worldly occupations which have engaged the ambitions of men and made them forget themselves, their Creator, their beginning and their final end' envisages society as having to meet men's needs, and treats of objectives and of things created in the very process of change. He deplores that the end which society attains can turn men aside from the search for God. But we associate ourselves with Al-Ghazali at the very heart of the quest in his view of the needs to be satisfied and the purposes of development.

I think that a primary contribution by the great religions would be to offer mankind their historic ideals, for the economic and social sciences have not created the actual ideal of development. In other terms we have to ask what were the concerns of the religious thinkers who were not strangers to the social dimension. And is the profoundly religious ideal which will not let itself be transformed into a mere civilization of religious inspiration and which is essentially bound up with love, with the life of prayer, with the discipline of the inner life, an ideal which is always listening to the Word—is this compatible with technological civilization? A dialogue between the spiritual leaders of the great religions and the men engaged in the actual construction of the modern world is indispensable if we wish to avoid vandalism in the believer who feels himself stifled, or a total lapse of the modern world into the inhuman.

The world expects greater vigilance from us. It will not have the church repeat the world's slogans and intellectual fashions. It seeks from us not things, not ideas, not a concept of structures, but values. A spirit of timidity has taken possession of the churches and other religious circles. Man needs to hear a word of life and not a benediction of what he is doing. He respects the 'little flock' which stands out for what it believes. The world longs for the church to listen to it and speak to it in a dialogue that is both humble and intelligent. It expects her to be herself or to disappear. The world has respect only for martyrs and for this cloud of witnesses to God who is the transcendant judge, but whose compassion is so great that he allows us to meet together in him even now, on the earth that the meek will inherit, while awaiting the glorious redemption of the whole body of humanity.

NOTES

1. Maximus the Confessor, quoted by Hans Urs von Balthasar, in *Liturgie Cosmique* (translation of *Kosmische Liturgie*), Editions Montaigne, Paris, 1947, p. 236.

2. Quoted by Jean Meyendorff, *A Study of Gregory Palamas*, Faith Press, London, 1964, p. 119.

3. Olivier Clément, 'L'homme dans le monde (Aperçus d'anthropologie orthodoxe)', *Verbum Caro* 45, 1958, p. 455.

4. Report of Uppsala, Section III, par. 35.

5. Homily 20.3 on II Corinthians (Migne, Patrologia Graeca 61, 540).

6. *Minutes of the First Congress of Orthodox Theology*, Athens, 1939, p. 354.

7. See Jacques Austruy, *Le scandale du développement*, Marcel Rivière et Cie, Paris, 1965.

8. Origen, *Against Celsus* III, 49 (Migne, Patrologia Graeca 11, 985).

9. L. S. Lebret, *Dynamique concret du développement* (Economie et humanisme), Les Editions Ouvrières, Paris, 1963, pp. 43 f.

10. *Op. cit.*, p. 75.

11. Elie Benamozegh, *Israel et l'humanité*, new edition, Albin Michel, Paris, 1961, p. 322.

12. *Ibid.*

13. Maxime Rodinson, 'Israël, fait colonial?' in *Le conflit Israëlo-arabe* (Temps Modernes, No. 253 bis), pp. 17–88.

14. E.g. Emmanuel Levyne.

15. Seyyed Hossein Nasr, *Ideals and Realities of Islam*, Allen and Unwin, London, 1966, p. 117.

SELECT INDEX OF SUBJECTS

There are so many references to the Geneva Conference of 1966 and to the Uppsala Assembly of 1968 that they have not been indexed; neither have references to Technology or Social Justice, the theme of the whole book.

INDEX OF PERSONS

INDEX OF BIBLICAL REFERENCES

OLD TESTAMENT

NEW TESTAMENT

Date Due

APR 1 '75			
AUG 22 '78			
NOV 13 '79			